JUST ONE MORE GOAL

THE AUTOBIOGRAPHY OF
DAVID PLEAT

WITH TIM RICH

FOREWORDS BY ALAN SUGAR AND HOWARD WILKINSON OBE

Biteback Publishing

First published in Great Britain in 2024 by
Biteback Publishing Ltd, London
Copyright © David Pleat 2024

ISBN 978-1-78590-906-1

10 9 8 7 6 5 4 3 2

A CIP catalogue record for this book is available from the British Library.

Set in Minion Pro

Printed and bound in Great Britain by
CPI Group (UK) Ltd, Croydon CR0 4YY

FSC
www.fsc.org
MIX
Paper | Supporting
responsible forestry
FSC® C171272

It's always the same thought: 'Just one more goal.'
I'd like it written on my gravestone.
JOE MERIMOVICH (1924–2011), TWICE MANAGER OF ISRAEL

To my wife, Maureen; the wind beneath my wings.

*50 per cent of all royalties from this book will
go towards charities researching MND.*

CONTENTS

FOREWORD BY ALAN SUGAR

In this book, David tells the story of his life as a player, coach, manager, director of football and TV pundit. Born at the end of the Second World War, it charts his journey from playing for England Schoolboys and making his debut for his home town club, Nottingham Forest, to giving his expert views in the ITV commentary box. He talks frankly about the low points of his life as well as the highlights, including leading Spurs out at Wembley in the 1987 FA Cup final. David's broad knowledge, experience and understanding of the game rightly gives him the title 'Mr Football'.

Alan Sugar
2024

FOREWORD BY HOWARD WILKINSON

I first became aware of David in the early 1960s, when he was a young, emerging star at Nottingham Forest. However, it was only in the 1990s that I really got to know, appreciate and understand him as a friend and colleague via the board of the League Managers' Association.

His knowledge of the game, the clubs, the players, the coaches and the managers goes beyond encyclopaedic. His love affair with football is still obsessive and when he speaks it is with an authority based on experiences at all levels of the game.

His book is interesting, informative and very difficult to put down. It offers some surprising insights and answers every question bar one about his life: 'Did he ever go to bed?'

My colleagues and my family will confirm that one of my favourites sayings is: 'If you are not afraid to think it, you should not be afraid to say it.' In this book, David has said it and more. He has opinions and he has the capacity to discuss them. This book demonstrates his global knowledge, his insight, empathy and, above all, his burning desire to create a better game.

Enjoy!

Howard Wilkinson OBE
2024

INTRODUCTION

Monday 19 April 2021 was quite a day for football. The news broke that a dozen clubs, including Tottenham Hotspur, the club that employed me, had joined a breakaway European Super League. Later that day, Tottenham announced they had sacked José Mourinho, one of the most celebrated managers of the modern era. The plans for a Super League, with no relegation, just games that could be financially exploited, would dissolve within days of their announcement, but the message was clear: football, more than ever, was about big business.

The football world that I entered in 1956, when I first played for Nottingham under-11s, was utterly different. I did not know it then, but when I began my journey, I was entering what would become a wonderful new world. The game that had existed more or less unchanged from the end of the First World War was about to undergo convulsions that would leave it utterly transformed.

In 1956, crowds were high. Division One was the pinnacle and was, roughly speaking, a level playing field. The main thing that determined the wealth of a club was its attendances. The two lower divisions were split into north and south and competed on a regional basis. Third Division North attracted average gates of more than 10,000 and 800,000 people watched league football on a typical Saturday afternoon.

Players were numbered one to eleven and there were no substitutes. The senior team consisted of a manager, a trainer and a physio. There was no sponsorship. Shirt advertising was more than two decades away. The season would climax with the FA Cup final, screened in black and white.

Players were tied to contracts and a maximum wage. Even the talents of Billy Wright, Tom Finney and Stanley Matthews were paid no more than £20 a week – about £500 in today's terms. There were no safety standards and the FA was all powerful. Football was affordable. Fathers took their sons to games. Saturday was football day to which they brought rattles, rosettes and scarves. Hooliganism was unknown and supporters mingled. The games they watched were played on patchy pitches, often heavy with mud. There were no agents and nobody thought football was a place to entertain business clients.

The clubs themselves were controlled by local businessmen made good. They allowed no transparency into their activities and the Football League was a closed shop. There were no academies, but schoolboy football was well organised with internationals that attracted huge crowds.

The ground, however, was beginning to move. As champions, Chelsea had been invited to join a new competition: the European Cup, where teams that had won their league would compete in a continental knockout competition. The FA, which had just come to terms with two thrashings handed out to the national team by a wonderfully talented Hungary, advised Chelsea to withdraw. The following season, Manchester United accepted the invitation. The World Cup, which the FA had ignored before the war, was now becoming the great showpiece for the global game. Two years before, in 1954, Switzerland had staged the first World Cup whose format would be recognisable today; a group stage followed by a knockout. In the final, the brilliant Hungarians were beaten dramatically by West Germany. What became known in Germany as the Miracle of Bern turned football into a source of pride for a nation that was emerging from the ruins of war and the shame of Nazism.

Four years later, the Brazil of Pelé and Garrincha would dazzle their way to the trophy. In that same year, 1958, Everton became the first club to install undersoil heating. Jimmy Hill, the chief executive of the PFA, successfully campaigned to have the maximum wage abolished. Johnny Haynes would become the first £100-a-week footballer.

Two years later, in 1963, George Eastham took Newcastle United to court to have the retain-and-transfer system, by which clubs could hold on to a player's registration even when his contract had expired, declared illegal. Manchester United would start opening corporate boxes in 1965.

On 30 July 1966, England became world champions. Interest in the game reached new heights. Football's elite became glamorous targets for sponsors and advertisers. George Best was referred to as 'the Fifth Beatle'.

In 1968, he would spearhead Manchester United's drive to become the first English club to win the European Cup. The sense of triumph a decade after a brilliant young United team had been wiped out in the Munich air disaster was intense.

There was a slide. The '80s proved to be English football's dark decade. The sport was scarred by hooliganism. It was a time of Heysel, Hillsborough and the Bradford Fire. By 1985/86, some 374,000 people went to watch league football on a Saturday afternoon. Back in 1949/50, it had been more than a million.

There were some consequences, nearly all of which benefited the bigger clubs. Pitches and safety standards improved. Home teams no longer had to share their gates with the visiting clubs. In 1991, five leading clubs formulated plans for a breakaway Premier League that would not share its income with the rest of the football family. Its launch a year later was embraced by the television companies who had previously underpaid for the rights to screen football. Gordon Taylor, a winger with Bolton and Birmingham and now the chief executive of the Professional Footballers' Association, negotiated strongly for his members' rights to a share of the bonanza provided by specialised football channels.

Football became the in-game. The middle classes, who had been turned away by hooliganism and dreadful facilities, returned. Ticket prices soared. A little-known Belgian footballer, Jean-Marc Bosman, won a court case that gave players across Europe the freedom to move at the end of their contracts without a transfer fee. The Premier League was brilliantly marketed and triggered a wave of stadium building not seen since before the First World War. One by one, the great arenas – Highbury, Maine Road, the Baseball Ground, Roker Park – were abandoned.

Middle Eastern airlines began to pay huge sums for the naming rights to the stadiums that replaced them. Of the Big Five that set up the Premier League, only one, Tottenham, is now in English owner-ship. In 1991, they were all owned and administered by people who claimed to be fans of the clubs they ran.

Has football lost its charm? I think so, but it still remains a beau-tiful game, a ballet of skill, speed and athletic movement. The job of a league manager is still precious. It is something that consumes your life. To be able to control a team and affect its results is a job that attracts addicts, of which I was always one. I have been privi-leged to challenge some of the game's most brilliant minds, includ-ing Clough, Wilkinson, Atkinson, Kendall, Ferguson and Wenger. Every manager has a story.

This is mine.

CHAPTER 1

'A FIRE ON THEM'

It was a moment I will never forget. We were watching the 1954 World Cup final on a grainy, black-and-white screen.

Hungary, the overwhelming favourites, were two up inside the first ten minutes. West Germany came back remorselessly and in the eighty-fourth minute, Helmut Rahn hit the winner for the Germans.

As the ball struck the net, my dear mum sprang from her chair and squealed: 'A fire on them.' Her outburst was followed by some words in Yiddish.

I was stunned. Mum knew nothing about football, but I learned to understand that her partisanship was born out of hate for a country that had slaughtered and tortured millions of the Jewish faith. A slaughter that had ended only nine years previously. A slaughter that had caught up distant relatives and family contacts. A slaughter they never spoke about.

I was only nine. I had been born on 15 January 1945, arriving in a wicked winter of heavy snow, a week before the liberation of Auschwitz. It was the first occasion I had seen Mum make such an emotional outburst. I had seen her only as someone who worked day after day, consciously caring to ensure we had enough pennies, clothes and food.

It was then I realised I was slightly different to my other friends at school. They had joined the Life Boys – the junior section of the

Boys Brigade, underpinned by Christian values. They had gone on church visits and recited the Lord's Prayer at assembly.

Dad explained I would have to concede certain activities that had a Christian connection. I did not quite understand, but he gently explained that Jewish people might accept there was a Jesus, but they did not believe he was the son of God.

At grammar school, I waited outside assembly with five other Jewish boys while the hymns were sung and the prayers were recited by 700 others. Then, we would come in to hear the headmaster read out the morning notices. Despite this, I never felt I did not belong. I felt different but not apart.

A few months earlier, Dad had promised that on Christmas Day, he would take me to watch a football match. I had enjoyed kicking a balloon around our narrow hallway and scuffing my shoes as we thrashed a Frido ball around the street with my pals.

This, however, was the real thing. Christmas morning dawned bright as we began our four-mile walk to the City Ground, Nottingham. There were no buses but many walkers, because few people in 1953 owned a car.

Nottingham Forest were playing Leeds United in the Second Division. My excitement was intense; I was smitten by the crowd, the smells, the colour, the players… Leeds in their blue-and-yellow quarters, Forest in their Garibaldi red.

The visitors had a colossus of a centre-forward who became my hero as the years moved on. John Charles was to be known as the Gentle Giant. He scored two that day, but Forest, who were to become my team, hit five!

Not only did they win and inspire my love for, and then my addiction to, the game of football, but they went to Elland Road the next day and won again, 2–0.

I have searched vainly for that Christmas programme among the thousands I have collected. However, some names still ring in my memory. O'Brien, Kerfoot, Overfield for Leeds. Capel, Colindridge, Ardron, Gager, and Walker for Forest, but John Charles was special.

Was it that day that I decided I would be a professional footballer if I were good enough? Who knows. I certainly never thought that nine years on in February 1962, I would be making my debut in the First Division at the City Ground in a 2–1 win over Cardiff City, becoming, at seventeen years and thirty-three days, Nottingham Forest's youngest debutant. I certainly never imagined, never dreamed I would become the youngest player to score on his debut in the history of the Football League.

Although my parents impressed upon me the importance of education, my thoughts would inevitably turn to football. I kept a scrapbook on the Forest games I watched. I knew the players. My pals and I would arrive one and a half hours before kick-off to feel the anticipation and to make sure we were one of the first through the gates at 1.30 p.m., to be certain of getting to the front of the terrace.

The City Ground had a pen by the corner flag where the kids could watch. Right in the front of the pen, there would be a tall guy, wearing a bus-conductor's uniform, who acted as a cheerleader, constantly whirring his rattle. We also watched Notts County at Meadow Lane, just after the days when Jackie Sewell and Tommy Lawton led their attack.

My teachers at Brooksby Lane Primary School saw me play at under-11 level and recommended me for a trial with Nottingham Boys. I did enough to be selected and made my first foray into representative football. We would play on a sloping pitch cordoned off by a perimeter rope, where supporters from the Bulwell area of Nottingham would be standing two and three deep on those Saturday mornings. Reports of schoolboy games received plenty of column inches. Nottingham had two Saturday-night sports papers, the *Evening Post* and the *Evening News Football Pink*. We would buy both to compare the reports of our games and, of course, see all the senior league results around the country. I was scoring goals as a centre-forward.

Two of my lifelong friends were also in that Nottingham Boys team. Alan Birchenall would join Sheffield United and score both goals in the Sheffield derby at Hillsborough in only his second game for the club. Alan would play for Chelsea and Leicester and in 1979 I would sign him for Luton. Micky Somers, an outside left, small and clever, would go to Chelsea and then Torquay but would be barred from top-level football by a lack of pace.

Alan's father, who had taken the family to Nottingham from the East End of London, was a bus driver and his mother always came to the games, but my dad would be away working. Every Saturday morning, he would be lugging a case full of hosiery seconds, bought from a friend at the Nottingham Lace Market, to Loughborough Market by bus.

Sundays could not have been more different. Dad took me into town by bus from where we walked to a school where they staged Hebrew classes. There, I learned the words and the history of the Jewish race in preparation for my bar mitzvah. On my thirteenth birthday, I would celebrate becoming a man by reading a portion of the law from the Jewish bible, the Torah, in the synagogue.

Dad would then go to the market square in front of Nottingham's town hall, the Council House, and enjoy the debating and speeches from the political, the religious, the outrageous and the eccentric who congregated in the centre of Nottingham to form something akin to a mini-Hyde Park Corner. Three hours later, he would collect me and hope I had learned something. I never admitted I enjoyed the fifteen-minute morning break, in which we crashed a tennis ball around the playground, more than the lessons.

It was important to Dad that we retained a connection to our roots. Both my parents' families had arrived as immigrants, forced out by the pogroms in Poland and Latvia, which were both then part of the Russian Empire. Dad's family was from Riga, Mum's from Warsaw. Dad was born in England in 1910, Mum in October 1911.

My father, Joe, grew up in London among a large family, loved the theatre and sport and learned the art of tailoring. During the early part of the Second World War, he doubled as a firefighter and worked in the St John Ambulance. He had a trial for Clapton Orient, as Leyton Orient were then called, and learned boxing skills at the Oxford and St George's Boys Club, situated off the Commercial Road.

In October 1999, I was Tottenham's director of football and decided to skip the first leg of their UEFA Cup tie against Kaiserslautern. The Oxford and St George's was holding a reunion. My father had never driven and by now was a little shaky on his feet so I decided to take him to the club. His joy at seeing his old Jewish friends from his youth is hard to describe. Since leaving the East End for Nottingham during the war, he had not seen any of his mates with whom he used to box, play football and act in theatrical productions. My father was revered by all his old friends and I was treated to plenty of stories about his youth, especially the stories about the left-footed striker he had been.

In the hall-of-fame display of his life, Joe Plotz was shown to be a regular winner of boxing competitions as well as a young man with a passion for drama. Joe Plotz came alive that evening. It had been antisemitism and the need to be accepted that had caused Dad to change his name. Perhaps he chose the name 'Pleat' from his tailoring background. Dad spoke that evening. He still possessed a strong voice and a clear diction. He had always reminded my sister and I of the need to speak 'the Queen's English' correctly.

Mum's father came to England alone, leaving his wife and four children behind in Warsaw. They joined him three years later, but his wife died soon after the birth of my mother. Growing up, Mum was a voracious reader and I once saw a certificate from her school that said simply: 'You have won first place.' However, she had to leave school early but learned German, shorthand and typing and worked as a legal secretary near Gray's Inn. She enjoyed rambling, the theatre and left-leaning politics, although she was never a Zionist. She had no time for the ultra-religious fanatics on the fringes of Israeli politics. She had a sharp mind but fell ill with tuberculosis in her early twenties and survived with just one healthy lung. TB claimed her father, too. It was not easy.

Mum and Dad had mutual interests, met and married. Dad worked for Simpsons of Piccadilly as a foreman and tailor's cutter, but, during the war, Simpsons relocated to Nottingham. My parents moved with the work and to a city where they had distant relatives. They settled into a tiny flat and had two children: Susan, born in 1943, and me, born eighteen months later.

Like many Jewish people, they had been aware of the tide of anti-semitism before the war, highlighted by the rise of Oswald Mosley. Dad had demonstrated against the Blackshirts in Cable Street as they tried to march through the Jewish East End in October 1936. Nottingham was quieter, but occasionally, I picked up stories of conflicts on the factory floor.

One evening, soon after we had watched Nottingham Forest play Leeds, Dad returned from work with my first pair of football boots from Loughborough Market. They were Arthur Rowe One-Piece boots, with proper wooden studs, hard toe caps and a strip of leather across the front. The fact they did not fit perfectly did not matter. I was thrilled and they even covered the tops of my ankles. They were the boots of my under-11 years.

Very soon, I had progressed to the more lightweight boots the German company, Adidas, was aggressively marketing around the world. Passing my 11-plus took me to Mundella Grammar School and continued selection for Nottingham Boys under-13s and under-14s. I was playing a year younger than my age group. Indeed, I got a place in the school under-15s as a thirteen-year-old scholar. I did my best not to let the football interfere with my studies but eventually finished my education with just four O-levels. 'Could do better' was the constant theme of my school reports.

Susan, my sister, was the academic one, gaining a scholarship to Nottingham Girls High School and then a place at Oxford before embarking on a long career as a television scriptwriter. Between 1966 and 1974, Susan would write regularly for *Coronation Street*. She would go on to write scripts for *A Family at War*, *Within These Walls*, *Juliet Bravo* and *Brookside* – as well as the children's TV series, *Pipkins* and *Monty & Co*. Her daughter, Becky Prestwich, has followed her mother into scriptwriting and has worked on *Holby City* and written plays for Radio 4.

During my school days, Mum was a rock, always trying to adjust the meals and her work to suit my football commitments. We were living on the new Clifton Estate, one of the biggest post-war housing projects in Europe that produced Viv Anderson, Jayne Torvill and Jermaine Jenas.

Each weekday, Mum would do the morning housework before rushing to catch the bus into town, whose stop was directly opposite our house – 13 Farnborough Road. Her arrival at the stop almost invariably coincided with the bus's. She worked as a typist at an insurance firm, Lloyds and Scottish, where she was highly thought of and often brought work home with her. Supper had been prepared in the morning and was always on the table.

While living in Clifton, Mum and Dad had a third child, Marion, who grew up to be a kind person with a great sense of social responsibility and had a long career teaching under-privileged kids. She gave all her time to caring for my parents in their last years.

Things became hard for the family around my fourteenth year. Dad had to leave the factory floor with a case of TB that was bad enough for him to be put into hospital, where he was cured with streptomycin. We visited him occasionally, with the help of a lift from a schoolmaster or a neighbour. Dad recovered, but he would no longer work at Simpsons. He therefore retrained as an education welfare officer. Unfortunately, just before he left hospital, he had an altercation with a patient who had made snide remarks about 'Yids'. Dad exploded and was blamed for the incident. We were glad to see him back home, but he had to miss my schoolboy games and the journeys to the markets at Loughborough were long gone.

Not long after taking me to see Leeds on Christmas Day, my father had treated me and four of my friends to go on a coach to watch Nottingham Forest play at Leicester. I would have been about ten. The five of us sat on the back seat and were joking along. One of the lads said he would be going to church tomorrow. He said: 'I am Christian and we have two Roman candles and a ju-ju.' Two of my friends were Catholic. Two men who were sitting in front of us turned round to look.

I felt a tinge of embarrassment. It was as though I had a secret shame that being Jewish made me different. It was only later, when I discovered the immense contribution the Jewish community had made to this country, that I found the subconscious racism easier to deal with.

When Nottingham Forest were drawn away to West Bromwich Albion in the FA Cup, I could not go with my friends to The Hawthorns and when I told them why, they did not quite understand. Saturday 25 January 1958 was also the day of my bar mitzvah, the day I would recite the Torah in the synagogue. In the Jewish faith, it would be considered the most important day of my life.

God, however, smiled on me. West Brom and Nottingham Forest drew 3–3. There would be a replay on the Tuesday afternoon. Mundella Grammar was only ten minutes across Trent Bridge from the City Ground and I left at lunchtime with some of my schoolmates to join a full house of 46,477. Forest were beaten 5–1 in a magnificent game by a fabulous West Brom team that would lose in the quarter-finals to a Manchester United side scraped together from the survivors of the Munich disaster that had destroyed the club less than a month before.

Playing as the youngest member of the City Boys under-15s and the County side, my star was rising. Ray Chaplin managed the Nottingham City side and was adept at giving half-time team talks as good as any professional I met. He would employ Shakespearean quotes to cajole his team into action.

In regional trials across the country, I was seeing off competition to gain a coveted place in the England Schoolboys team. The manager of England Schoolboys was Bill Roberts, a broad hunk of a man in his late fifties who hailed from Ellesmere Port, where he was a teacher and an English Schools coach and councillor. He was an austere, obese man, whom it would be hard to imagine as a football coach, though he told us both Stan Cullis and Joe Mercer had been his pupils. However, he was possessed of a magnetic personality and told us that he could watch a boy walk across a playground and tell, without him ever kicking a ball, whether he was right- or left-footed.

When news of my selection came through, all the players received a typed letter stating what was expected of each position. Mine was outside right. The letter told me to 'try to get into the space behind the full-back and cross the ball quickly. Practise your shooting and sprinting. Look forward to seeing you at York for the first game against Ireland.'

England did not lose any of our five games that season. In April 1960, we overcame West Germany, 1–0, at Maine Road. Ten days later, England would be playing Scotland at Wembley.

It was with a mixture of panic and excitement, nerves, and pride that I received my letter of selection for the Scotland game. Apart from the victory over West Germany in Manchester, my father had seen all my England Schoolboy games and now I was agitated, worried that Dad would be unable to see me play at Wembley. Who will get him tickets? How will he travel to London? Where will he stay? I had been told the game was on television, so Mum would be able to watch it. She would never see me play in a live game.

Mr Chaplin, the Nottingham Schools manager, told Dad he would travel down to London with him and the secretary of the Nottingham Schools FA, another larger-than-life personality in the days when all schoolmasters seemed to be characters. I was happy with the arrangement, since both my father and Mr Chaplin shared a love of the theatre and could quote Shakespeare like a second language.

Our captain was Ron Harris, who would become a legendary player for Chelsea, and my immediate opponent at left-back was Bobby Moncur, who nine years later would captain Newcastle to the Fairs Cup. George Graham was Scotland's No. 10. My partner was Barry Fry, a cocky Bedford boy destined for a long career in football. Then, his only thought was of collecting his signing-on fee from Manchester United.

Ernest Marples, then Minister for Transport in Harold Macmillan's government, was the special guest, introduced to the two teams in front of 95,000 young spectators who had come by coach from every corner of England on their annual pilgrimage to Wembley.

The game is a haze now. I scored and made a couple. It was the day the great Tom Finney played his last game for Preston and in one headline the press proclaimed they had seen his successor. Even my golden moment is a vague memory. A run, in possession from the right, escaping three defenders and seeing my shot slide in off the far post. All a blur, so nerve-tingling and emotional that it was gone in a flash. The score was 5–3 to England.

Back at school, they presented me with a small plaque at an

assembly in front of 600 pupils who clapped as, embarrassed, I accepted the gesture. The Nottingham papers were propelling me towards a future professional career, surmising which club I might sign for.

Three of that England Schoolboys side went to Manchester United. Ray Bloomfield went to Arsenal, although he played most of his career in the United States. Two north-east boys, Billy Atkinson and Denis Thwaites, signed for Birmingham City. In June 2015, Denis and his wife, Elaine, were shot dead in a terrorist attack on the beaches of Sousse in Tunisia.

I knew I would stay and join my boyhood team, despite a temptation to sign for Tottenham. A friend of my father who wrote reports for the *Sunday People* was a big Tottenham fan and was friendly with the club's hierarchy. He implored Bill Nicholson to sign me.

Mum and Dad were bemused by the array of scouts who came knocking at our council-house door. I recall a Mr Chitty from Chelsea and gentlemen from Wolverhampton Wanderers and Manchester City. A car was mentioned, although neither Mum nor Dad ever drove. The only bribe from a scout that was gratefully accepted was a tray of two-dozen fresh eggs, which were brought twice to our home.

Frank Hill, the Notts County manager, came to Clifton and knocked on our back door. I felt embarrassed speaking to him for twenty minutes without once asking him in for a cup of tea or giving him the impression I would sign, even though had I done so I would almost be guaranteed first-team football, within a couple of seasons. But I had decided. I would sign for Nottingham Forest and stay at home with my family and my mum's cooking.

CHAPTER 2

'BRICKS AND MORTAR'

It was a two-mile walk and Mum had told me to dress smartly. The winding Farnborough Road led on to a village called Ruddington where you walked over a hump-backed bridge. The first house on the left, an imposing off-white building, belonged to Mr Walker.

Billy Walker was the manager of Nottingham Forest, a position he had held since before the Second World War. In later years, players would recall his parsimony with the club's money and his selfish traits. His team would not allow him to manage the players' pool for the 1959 FA Cup final for fear he would take a cut of it. He was clearly a wealthy man.

Walker was a formidable presence in English football. He was and remains Aston Villa's greatest goalscorer, who as an inside forward had played more than 500 games for the club. As a player, Walker had won the FA Cup in 1920. Fifteen years later, as manager of Sheffield Wednesday, he won the trophy again.

He had come to the City Ground in 1939, a year Nottingham Forest escaped relegation to the Third Division South on goal average. By the time we met, Forest were a First Division club. He was a tall, hawkish gentleman.

He sat me down and told me that he had not seen much of me – I was only fourteen – but had heard some very good reports. In the conversation one thing stood out. 'Son, if you do well, bricks and mortar.' To tell a fourteen-year-old boy you had not met before to invest in property was a strange conversational gambit.

Not long afterwards, Billy Walker would lead Nottingham Forest out in the FA Cup final against Luton Town. It was a dramatic occasion. Having scored twice in the opening quarter of an hour, Nottingham Forest clung on for a 2–1 victory. A dozen minutes before half-time, Roy Dwight, Elton John's cousin, who had scored Forest's opening goal, was carried off with a broken leg. There were no substitutes in 1959, but Forest, who were reduced to nine men when the right-back, Bill Whare, collapsed with cramp, held out magnificently against a strong Luton side.

I would remain at school, take my O-levels and play representative football for Nottinghamshire under-18s and the England youth team first as an amateur and then as a professional. The England team was managed by Billy Wright, who had just retired as captain of Wolverhampton Wanderers, where he had led them to three league titles. For England, he had won 105 caps and in the summer of 1958, shortly after captaining them in the World Cup in Sweden, he married Joy Beverley, a member of the pop group The Beverley Sisters. On the field and off it, Billy was a star.

He was a lovely man with a warm personality, but even then, I thought he was unlikely to be a top manager, a theory he proved in a short spell in charge of Arsenal.

There is no logical reason why someone who is supremely gifted as a footballer should automatically make a good manager. Glenn Hoddle, who was wonderful with the ball at his feet, found it difficult to build up personal relationships with the men he coached – players who were often in awe of him. Chris Waddle, his teammate at Tottenham, disliked club politics and dealing with the boardroom at Burnley.

Billy Wright was far too nice, far too kind for management. On one trip with England to Flensburg in West Germany, I got drunk with two others and fell down the stairs in the hotel foyer. Instead of threatening us or bawling us out, he said: 'Come on, get yourselves to bed.'

Not only was Wright the manager; he also carried the sponge. He was also carrying a bit of a paunch and when in a game against Scotland in Elgin, he walked off after giving one of his players some treatment, a wag in the crowd shouted: 'Guinness is good for you.' The Scottish crowd roared.

In 1964, shortly after I joined Luton, Billy came to present me with a new car. I had won a competition, run by the Ford Motor Company, to select the best post-war team from Britain and Ireland. I can still recall my half-back line: Blanchflower (Ireland), Charles (Wales) and Mackay (Scotland). The prize was a new Ford Cortina, which I had to hand back because I could not then drive. Ford gave me £500 for it, which had been more than my signing-on fee for Luton.

There would also be games for the school, for Nottingham Forest's B-team and then the A-team, which played in the Midland Intermediate League. In one game, in the Derbyshire town of Clay Cross, I came across a very good goalkeeper called Bob Wilson. He was four years older than me. Bob would go to Loughborough College and find fame as part of Arsenal's Double-winning team of 1971. In my early days as manager of Luton, he worked with me as a goalkeeping coach and I would not come across anyone better in that position. Bob had the ability to coach both potential and senior goalkeepers in a manner that was clear and understandable. Unlike many fine players, Bob knew how to teach.

I was being paid £8 a week as a groundstaff boy with seven other 'potentials' amid all the excitement and anticipation that went with teenaged boys joining a First Division football club. I became great friends with Ian Storey-Moore, who had been discovered playing junior football in Scunthorpe and would be part of the Nottingham Forest side that in 1967 finished second in the league and reached the semi-finals of the FA Cup.

When I invited Ian home for tea, I realised he was someone with whom I could have a good conversation. A civilised boy. On Friday after training, we would go to a coffee bar called El Toreador to talk football. Later in the day, we would go the newly built People's College to take a beginner's course in journalism. Ian's father had insisted on it should he not succeed in football.

Ian was slightly different to the others. He was intelligent, had a dry wit and an interest in world affairs when the conversations of most players at Nottingham Forest did not stretch much beyond horse racing and women. Ian was certainly interested in horse racing – he became a bookmaker after a brilliant career was curtailed by injury at Manchester United. However, he also managed Burton Albion and was appointed Aston Villa's chief scout under Martin O'Neill, who had once cleaned Ian's boots at Nottingham Forest.

By way of refreshments, Forest offered their players nothing more than a cup of tea. If we wanted food after training, we had to make our own arrangements and would go a cafe on Pavilion Road at the top of Trent Bridge, where on a Friday, after the team sheets had been pinned up in the dressing room for the following day, we would get together and do the football pools while discussing tactics.

It was also a gossip group that would discuss other members of the club and praise or criticise them accordingly. It was there that I realised how cliques could form. In subsequent years, I realised how important it was to break these groups up. At Tottenham, who had a far more cosmopolitan array of players than Forest, the same players would always eat together. Others would gather in a different area of the dining room. This would particularly be true of the foreign players. Over time, the club took steps to ensure the whole squad was integrated on a single long table at lunch.

After winning the FA Cup, Forest did not start the season well and avoided relegation by a point. After twenty-one years as manager, Billy Walker was replaced by Andy Beattie in the summer of 1960.

As my reputation grew, I was contacted to ask if I would take part in trials for the Maccabiah Games. The Maccabiah Games were popularly known as 'The Jewish Olympics' and had first taken place in 1932, when what is now Israel was the British Mandate of Palestine. They were open to all Jewish athletes and by 1961 to all citizens of Israel regardless of faith. They would be centred around the Ramat Gan Stadium in Tel Aviv.

The trials were held at Hall Lane in Hendon. I was sixteen and would be going to Israel with a team of Jewish amateur footballers. There was no question I had the ability to be selected for the Great Britain team; my father was keen for me to go and the opportunity to see Israel was fascinating. The year before I had been on my first foreign holiday to Spain's Costa Brava.

After the trials, Andy Beattie came over to me and said, rather sneeringly: 'Your people have been on the phone again.' I did not at first realise the significance of the remark, but I soon realised who he was talking about.

When the *Nottingham Evening Post* ran the headline 'Pleat Selected for Maccabiah', it understandably led to bemusement in the dressing room. I was asked: 'Do you have to be Jewish to go?' or 'Are you Jewish?' I was even asked: 'What do you have to do to become a Jew?'

The tournament itself was intriguing and helped me mature. I was mixing with men who were invariably older than I was, good footballers who had gone into business or the professions. When I was growing up, this was the kind of vision my parents had for me: an amateur footballer who would become an accountant or a doctor. Quite a few of my teammates at the Maccabiah could have played football professionally, but that would have been viewed as no job for a nice Jewish boy.

I remember a guy called Barry Carr, a strong wing-half who was in the furniture business in Manchester. We were captained by Saville Shela, a handsome, tanned, London taxi driver and amateur boxer in his mid-twenties who had an eye for the women. In the final against Israel, in Haifa, he scored both goals in the 2–1 win that would give Britain its only football gold medal at a Maccabiah Games.

There were a thousand competitors from twenty-seven countries and I was impressed by the football teams from Brazil and South Africa and by Rafer Johnson in particular. Johnson was black, had been part of a Jewish fraternity at university and had won gold for the United States in the decathlon in the Rome Olympics. In 1968, in Los Angeles, he would apprehend Sirhan Sirhan, the man who had just assassinated Robert Kennedy. He did not compete in Tel Aviv but gave demonstrations of his sport and appeared at the opening ceremony.

We stayed in Netanya, north of the Israeli capital. We visited a kibbutz and a factory and sat in a cafe in Tel Aviv's main drag, Dizengoff Street, and watched the girls go by. The '60s had not properly begun; there was still a post-war drabness about much of England. Thirteen years after its creation in 1948, Israel seemed relaxed and at ease with itself. One thing that struck me was how much colour there was in the way people dressed, how much they talked and how opinionated their conversation was. From the Maccabiah, I brought back an LP with the Israeli national anthem 'Hatikvah', a song about hope that has always resonated with me.

I was never much good at bringing presents home. When my mother learned I was going to the Netherlands with the England youth team, she asked me to bring her some Edam. As I brought this big round cheese back, Ron Harris, tougher, more working-class, said rather sarcastically: 'What have you got there, Pleaty? You know you can buy cheese in England?' I felt slightly embarrassed. Ron was more than aware of my background; he had grown up near Stamford Hill, one of London's poorer Jewish communities.

Andy Beattie was a severe, austere man from the north-east of Scotland. He was deeply religious and had been involved in the Moral Rearmament Movement, which believed Christian values could solve social problems. He had managed Scotland in the 1954 World Cup and was close to Bill Shankly, who had played alongside him at Preston and been Beattie's assistant manager at Huddersfield. Beattie's most celebrated achievement was bringing Denis Law to Leeds Road, but he had resigned after Huddersfield's relegation and spent eighteen months as a sub-postmaster. For him, Nottingham Forest represented a return to frontline management.

On 17 February 1962, he gave me my debut. At seventeen years and thirty-three days, I would become the youngest footballer to play for Nottingham Forest. As a Nottingham boy, there was plenty of pride accompanied by telegrams from the Nottingham Schools FA and my school, Mundella Grammar.

The club was in the relegation zone, third from bottom, two points behind our opponents, Cardiff City. The 2–1 win lifted us two places in the table. Cardiff would be relegated, alongside Fulham and Chelsea.

I scored the second goal, though it was meant as a cross rather than a shot. It curled past the bemused Dilwyn John in the Cardiff goal, who was only six months older than me. The Nottingham Forest centre-forward, Len Julians, who was closest to the ball as it struck the net, graciously told everyone, including the officials, that he had not got a touch.

The local press heaped praise on me and Dick Le Flem, from Guernsey, nicknamed 'Flip', who had played wide-left against Cardiff. The local paper stated: 'The Forest wing positions should be reserved for years.' By 1964, both of us had left the City Ground. Had

Flip been in love with the game, he could have had a stellar career. After giving Jimmy Armfield the runaround in one game against Blackpool, Armfield said: 'Flip looked like he was playing on skates.' I liked Flip a lot; he was swapped for Alan Hinton from Wolves, a fine winger and a great crosser of the ball. Flip's time at Molineux was hampered by illness and he retired at the age of twenty-five.

Amid dressing-room unrest, Beattie left in the summer of 1963 to take charge of Plymouth. His replacement, Johnny Carey, could not have been more different. He was a Dubliner who had captained Manchester United to the FA Cup in 1948 and to the league title four years later. He was a tall, balding, genial man, seldom without his pipe. His half-time team-talk invariably consisted of just a few words as he sucked on his pipe: 'Fizz it about.' It was a phrase the players would repeat whenever Johnny Carey's name cropped up. 'Fizz it about.'

Some of Forest's senior players were very kind to me, especially Johnny Quigley, a Glaswegian midfielder whom I had seen score the winner at Hillsborough in the FA Cup semi-final against Aston Villa. Others treated a newcomer to the dressing room with a certain disdain. Bob McKinlay was a rather aloof centre-half who had joined Nottingham Forest in 1949 and would play more than 600 games for the club before becoming a prison officer.

On the surface, Bob was pleasant enough, but he had a marked reluctance to encourage young footballers. He was very critical of young talent. I was a young player trying to make his way in a struggling team, which is always harder than coming into a winning side. The older professionals would fear for their future and their judgements would be self-protective. Bob McKinlay might have felt that Forest needed experience rather than young, unproven talent. I thought he did not want me to succeed, that he disliked me. Or perhaps I imagined it. McKinlay was something of a loner in the dressing room. He may have been like that to everyone.

After a season in which they had finished thirteenth, Nottingham Forest took me on a post-season tour to West Germany, where I played against Hertha Berlin. In a hotel room, Ian and I watched grainy pictures from Wembley as West Ham overcame Preston in the 1964 FA Cup final.

It did not really hit me that I was a Jewish teenager staying in what nineteen years previously had been the capital of the Third Reich. I was too obsessed by football and the Holocaust was a subject that, after the initial shock of what had happened in the concentration camps, had been largely and perhaps deliberately forgotten. Certainly, my parents never spoke about it. The documentaries, the books and the eyewitness testimonies would only really start coming out in the 1970s, perhaps because some in the Jewish community felt that memories of the momentous crime were being allowed to fade away.

I was full of anticipation for the start of the new season. However, the previous year, in the Midland Intermediate League, I had played for Nottingham Forest's under-21s against Wolves. They had a half-back line of Goodwin, Woodfield and Knighton, which to me sounded like a firm of solicitors. All would have good careers in the game and Ken Knighton would manage Sunderland. I had got to the byline and, as I pulled the ball back, I felt a whack in my coccyx area. It was an injury that put me back a full two months. That injury might have cost me a shade of pace, which was one of my qualities, though I still had the ability to cut in from the right and shoot with my left foot. From that day on, I would always suffer from back trouble and this particular injury would force me to end my playing career at the age of twenty-eight.

All my career I have been fascinated by what a professional footballer requires to succeed. I possessed a good temperament. I did not become carried away by the headlines sparked by my debut goal against Cardiff, but I lacked the confidence and possibly the drive to make a mark. On its own, pure ability is never enough. You must have self-belief and a strong mentality to fall back on when things do not go well. Having a mentor, someone at a club who believes in you, can also be vitally important.

In a practice match, before I made my debut, I went past Forest's Scottish defender, Joe McDonald, on the outside. McDonald, who was nearly twice my age, shouted: 'If you do that again, son, I'll break your fucking leg.' Perhaps I should have had more courage in league games. I soon realised that old pros can be ruthless when it comes to protecting their status at a club and cannot stand to be humiliated or belittled – however inadvertently – by a younger footballer. It exposed their vulnerability.

The full-backs I came across were tough men like Graham Williams at West Bromwich Albion, Alex Elder at Burnley and Colin Green at Birmingham. Williams was a hard, barrel-chested Welsh full-back who attempted to scare me to death. They were all experienced and ferociously competitive. If I did not go past them early on in a game, or if the defender matched me for pace, I would start to lose belief and be less likely to express myself or want the ball.

Underpinning everything is desire. When, in my more reflective moments, I look back over my playing career, I ask myself whether I had the desire to overcome dropping down the leagues and the injury. Was I a 'self-doubter'? Self-doubt is a condition that is common in football. Nottingham Forest had a young reserve-team player called Billy Younger, who was terrific in practice matches but could not cope with the pressure to reproduce that form in front of a crowd.

Later in my career, watching the Tottenham under-18 team, I saw Dean Marney, a young winger, look across to the bench for approval every time he crossed the ball. Marney would have a very good career with Hull and Burnley, where his character would eventually shine through. However, at Tottenham, he was constantly looking for approval from his coaches whenever he made a contribution. I termed him a 'self-doubter'. I often use Dean as an example when talking to coaches. Self-belief and a 'stick-your-chest-out attitude' is key.

In that summer of 1964, Johnny Carey bought Chris Crowe from Wolves and Mike Kear from Newport. Both could play wide on the right. To me this seemed an indication that Carey did not see me as a first-team regular, and it knocked my confidence. Ian, a footballer with no self-doubt and who scored twice on his debut, was also emerging as a force at Forest on the wing.

If I had no mentor within the club, I had one outside the City Ground. Peter Taylor was born in Nottingham and although he had signed for Forest as a sixteen-year-old in 1944, his goalkeeping career had taken him to Coventry and Middlesbrough, where he had met Brian Clough. The first time I had laid eyes on Taylor was in November 1956 when Middlesbrough had come to the City Ground and won 4–0. Clough scored all four.

By 1962, Peter Taylor was back in Nottingham and managing Burton Albion. He lived with his wife, Lillian, at 3 Vernon Avenue in Wilford, which was a two-mile walk along the Trent from Nottingham's two main football grounds. Peter would come to watch us play in what was known as the Thursday League, where a young Forest side would face teams such as the Police, the Fire Brigade and the 6th Battalion Royal Army Ordinance Corps, whose team contained three Sheffield United players doing their National Service. One was Ken Mallender, who was to spend seven years at Bramall Lane, another was Jack Nibloe, who was to die in a car crash at the age of twenty-five.

This was a tough grounding, pitching Forest's under-18s, bright, young, elusive talents, against the 'old sweats', some of whom were still playing non-league football to a high standard. Because

Thursday was half-day closing in Nottingham – the shops did not open in the afternoon – there was always a decent crowd to watch Forest's future. After one of these games, I found myself talking to Peter Taylor and we got on very well. His talk was football laced with socialism, and it began a relationship that would last until his death in 1990.

I was never one for pubs, but sometimes I would walk a mile and a half to the Ferry Inn in Wilford, where on Sunday lunchtimes Peter would be holding court with three other football obsessives who would later become his scouts: Colin Revell, Bob Rayner and George Pyecroft.

One day, Johnny Carey called me into his office and, very pleasantly, said I could go to Luton Town if I wished. He had agreed a transfer fee. 'You can stay and fight for your place,' he said, 'but I have to tell you that your opportunities will be limited.'

I had been signed by Billy Walker and backed by Andy Beattie, but now I was being cast aside by Johnny Carey. Youngsters in such a situation had little ammunition with which to fight their corner. I sat opposite him and listened.

As with all transfers, I was told I had to make an early decision and informed that if I did not join Luton, they would probably sign someone else. I tried to phone my parents, who were on holiday in Bognor, but could not get through to them at the bed and breakfast where they were staying. I rang Peter Taylor, who, without knowing any of the circumstances, told me I should go. He impressed on me the importance of playing first-team football in front of a crowd. Peter had always admired my ability but told me it was being wasted in the reserves.

I was nineteen. At that age, impetuosity strikes. It is hard to be patient when your career needs to be sustained by hope, and at Nottingham Forest, the opportunities were closing. It's not a pleasant feeling to be not wanted, to see the dream deflated. How many times in the future would I be on the other side of the desk and have to deliver similar phrases to those uttered now by Johnny Carey?

Travelling down to Luton, I met their manager, Bill Harvey, whose conversation was backed by a fund of jokes. Every paragraph he spoke was interwoven with the phrase: 'Listen to this one.' Luton had been relegated from Division Two in Harvey's first season as manager and had just finished eighteenth in Division Three. Their gates were a third of Nottingham Forest's, but Harvey told me that Luton 'could become a great club'.

They also told me Luton would be building a new stadium at Stockwood Park. More than half a century later, the dream put to me by the Luton secretary Bob Readhead has still not been realised. The club has still not moved from Kenilworth Road, its home since 1905.

My feet were sufficiently planted on the ground to dismiss that kind of talk, but what clinched it for me was that two of my friends from England's youth teams, Ray Whittaker and John O'Rourke, were at Luton, having been released by Arsenal and Chelsea. We talked things through on the pitch-and-putt course at Wardown Park, where they persuaded me the potential was there.

When I finally got hold of my parents, they gave me their usual advice: they would support me in whatever I did. Luton paid Nottingham Forest £8,000 for me and I was given a signing-on fee of £400, which took a while to be paid and arrived in my wage packet, taxed.

The Forest players had urged me to take advantage of the move and improve my salary. Your negotiating position is always at its strongest when you sign your first contract. The maximum wage of £20 a week had been abolished in 1961. I had been so highly thought of at Nottingham Forest that I had been put on £20 a week before

I had made my debut. By 1964, my wages had gone up by a quarter and Luton offered me the same money – £25 a week – that I was on at the City Ground.

There were all sorts of questions I should have asked Bill Harvey but did not. The one question I did ask was whether Luton could improve my salary. Harvey called my bluff. He said to me: 'Look, son, the contracts are in that drawer. I can take them out and show you any one of them and you'll find you are being paid the best rate. Twenty-five is the top wage.' Bill Harvey knew I would not have the courage to ask him to open the drawer and hand me the first-team contracts. I would not call his bluff. Had I done so, it would have led to a difficult relationship.

The Luton team was full of old sweats. Footballers who could see the end of their careers and who were playing out time. Men like Dave Pacey, who had scored against Nottingham Forest in the FA Cup final five years before, Bob Morton, who had joined Luton in the last days of the Second World War, and Gordon Turner, a goalscorer who spent more time in his sports shop than he did on the training ground. The goalkeeper, Ron Baynham, good enough to have played three times for England in 1955, was another of those who gathered around the stove for a cup of tea and a smoke before training.

Ted Phillips, a striker with a cannonball shot who had joined us on loan, was an older player with whom I got on. He was revered at Ipswich for leading an attack that, under Alf Ramsey, had taken a newly promoted side to the league championship.

I could not believe the lack of professionalism at Luton Town compared to what I had left behind at Nottingham Forest, where Billy Walker, a man I never saw in a tracksuit, had brought in an outstanding coach called Joe Mallett. Joe did not believe players should have cars and walked four miles to training every day from his home in Carlton. 'Cars', he would tell us, 'will be the ruination of you youngsters.' At the end of the day, he would walk four miles back.

He was the man who first gave me a real appreciation of tactics and of working in triangles from a wide-right position. All the youngsters loved him. It was through Joe Mallett that I first had the inkling that I might enjoy coaching.

At the age of eighteen, I had taken and passed my preliminary coaching certificate. Some senior players at Nottingham Forest would have found it presumptuous that a teenager who had barely made his first-team debut should be looking to become a qualified coach. Joe had persuaded me I had nothing to lose by listening and learning at a coaching course and then taking the examination.

He left Nottingham Forest in 1964 to manage Birmingham. He would coach in Greece and the United States, where he would work with Pelé, Johan Cruyff and Franz Beckenbauer at New York Cosmos. Much later, I would put Joe on the scouting staff at Tottenham. He still did not own a car and on a Saturday would take the train from Eastbourne and watch the London clubs on our behalf. He would take the train back from Victoria and get home late in the evening. Joe's dedication was absolute.

It extended to the players he coached. At Forest, we would often come back after lunch to do further training, whereas at Luton, nobody would expect to see you after twelve o'clock. However, after training, I would take the bus back to my digs in Waller Avenue, have lunch and then Ray Whittaker, John O'Rourke and I would go back to Kenilworth Road and play head tennis in what was called 'The Bear Pit' – a small, claustrophobic squash court at the back of one of the stands.

I made my debut on a Wednesday night in August at home to Colchester. Luton won, 3–1, and would beat Bristol Rovers at Kenilworth Road on the Saturday. I was named man of the match. Suddenly, I was on a high. It was not to last.

For a start, there were plenty of suggestions Luton would make a quick buck by selling me to Norwich. After training on the Friday, we would go to a cafe, the Spanish Doll, where we would sometimes be joined by Sam Bartram, the great Charlton keeper, who had managed Luton a few years previously and had settled in Harpenden.

Bartram now had a newspaper column that dealt in transfer gossip and over a coffee and a sandwich he would ask the Luton players if they knew which footballers were unhappy or who they thought might hand in a transfer request or when the manager might get the sack. The players would sometimes feed him misinformation, linking themselves with other clubs just to strengthen their bargaining positions with Luton. The results of that conversation would appear in his column.

Luton was a town that would change my life. Not as a footballer but as a manager and, more importantly, as a man. Luton was where I met Maureen Brown, who was to share my life for more than half a century.

When I first met Maureen, I knew there might be barriers. Before coming to Luton, I had taken out one or two girls to the cinema but there had been nothing serious. I felt subconsciously that when I did want to start a serious relationship, the religious divide would prevent me. These thoughts were in my mind when, in my early days as a Luton player, one of my teammates, a wing-half called Mark Lowndes, introduced me to this lovely girl and we started talking.

I told her I was a professional footballer who had just signed for Luton. Saying that gave me confidence, but it made no impression on her. Maureen had her small hairdressing shop, her little blue Mini and her black poodle, Cindy. She was fully occupied. She was four years older than me and already had a boyfriend who had a decent job as a planning engineer at the Vauxhall car factory. Luckily for me, he accepted an appointment in Swansea and Maureen had no wish to move to Wales.

I approached the religious question early and head on. I told her I was Jewish. 'So what?' she said. 'Some of my lovely customers are Jewish. I'm C of E. So what?' There was no hint of prejudice. It made me so happy. It transpired that her grandfather on her mother's side was Jewish. In subsequent years, her expressions and mannerisms led some to believe she was more Jewish than I was.

I spent a spell living in digs with a Jewish couple and they did their best, in a very nice way, to persuade me that a relationship with a Gentile may not survive. I was not deterred, although I felt, initially, her family were lukewarm and not just because of my religion. Maureen's father felt that footballers were an unreliable breed in an uncertain profession. When, two years later, we discussed marriage, they were less nervous about two religions mixing.

My parents took immediately to Maureen, who became an expert in making chicken soup, chopped liver and meatballs. They embraced her because they saw only good in her and Maureen treated them with respect and kindness. In their later years, she looked after them at every possible moment. Maureen did not worry on my behalf about winning and losing games of football. Indeed, at that stage, she seemed completely oblivious to the sport.

The results of those games were changing and not for the better. Luton began sliding down the table and I broke my leg in a practice game. I was kicked after I had delivered a cross and suffered what was known as a Pott's fracture. This is where you receive a blow to the outside of the ankle that twists it and causes a fracture where it meets the tibia.

It would cost me three months out of football and, more importantly, it would cost me the pace that was so vital to my game. I would be coerced into making a comeback too soon. Marked at right-back by the Watford player-manager Ken Furphy in a Boxing Day fixture, I struggled. Luton lost 4–2. I knew Ken Furphy from my increasing interest in coaching. I had qualified as a preliminary coach and was taking my full badge at Lilleshall in the summer. After the game, he took me aside. He said: 'You're jeopardising your career. You shouldn't play when you're not fully fit. Get yourself 100 per cent right.'

Luton's medical facilities were almost non-existent. They were best described as a trainer with a sponge, a heat lamp and the ever-present bucket of ice. Resting in plaster, I had gone back home to stay with my parents. Peter Taylor took me to watch Burton, who had a very good team that had won the Southern League Cup. Shortly afterwards, Peter accepted Brian Clough's offer to join him at Hartlepools United. When Clough made the offer, it was the first time the two men had spoken in four years.

During my recovery, Luton sacked Bill Harvey in the wake of a 7–1 defeat at Queens Park Rangers. In April 1965, Luton's relegation to the bottom tier of league football was confirmed with an 8–1 defeat at Scunthorpe. Their centre-forward, Barrie Thomas, scored five.

The defeat cost the Luton players not just their place in the Third Division but their prawn cocktails. On the way back from the Old Showground at Scunthorpe, we stopped for dinner in Lincoln in a pretty desolate state. Usually, if we had a long away trip, the team would be given a meal in a hotel on the return journey. We usually had the options of two courses. However, the wife of Luton's vice-chairman, Len Hawkins, who was travelling on the bus with the players, decided we did not deserve a starter.

CHAPTER 3

'YOU'LL PLAY. I'VE ONLY GOT TWELVE PLAYERS'

In the space of a year, I had exchanged the First for the Fourth Division and was being coached by a man standing in the centre circle dressed in a brown Crombie overcoat and a matching trilby hat.

George Martin had taken over as Luton's manager in November 1964 but had been unable to prevent the club's relegation. As a player, Martin had won the league with Everton in 1928. He had managed Newcastle, where he had astonished supporters by selling Len Shackleton to Sunderland.

He invariably came dressed to Luton's training sessions at Stockingstone Road in the Crombie and the trilby. His sidekick, a ruddy-faced former Everton player called Stan Bentham, took the training, but Martin always had the whistle.

I have two great memories of these sessions. One was a fantastic goal by the seventeen-year-old Bruce Rioch, which saw him play three one-twos before finishing with a rasping drive. It was a talent that would see Aston Villa pay £100,000 for him in the summer of 1969 – a record transfer fee for a Second Division club. Six years later, he would win the league title with Derby. His tackling bordered on the dangerous; he was fearless and possessed a ferocious temper.

The other training ground memory is of an incident involving Graham French. While I was recuperating, Luton had bought

French from Wellington, which is now part of Telford new town. He played in my position and was massively talented.

With George Martin officiating from the centre circle in his trilby, French beat three men, reached the byline but failed to squeeze the ball in at the near post. From the centre circle, Martin shrieked: 'Cut it back, boy!' To which the nineteen-year-old retorted at the top of his voice: 'Fuck off, you silly cunt!' Martin was apoplectic: 'What did he say? WHAT DID HE SAY?' But the players kept shtum. Martin may have been the manager, he may have acted like a sergeant major, but he lacked the respect of the players.

I had been in the same England squad as French in the 1963 European Youth Tournament, an under-18 competition staged in England that was dubbed 'the Mini-World Cup'. England won the trophy without conceding a goal in any of their five matches. Our defence included Len Badger, Ron Harris and Tommy Smith, who between them would play 1,500 league games for Sheffield United, Chelsea and Liverpool.

I had played in the first two group games, where we beat the Netherlands 5–0 and Romania 3–0 and I had expected to play in the final at Wembley, against Northern Ireland. When the manager, Pat Welton, announced the team, saying Graham French would take my place, it was a massive blow to my pride. I was so upset. Pat Jennings, then of Newry Town, was in goal for Northern Ireland, but they lost their right-back, Tom Corbett, to a broken leg after half an hour. England won 4–0.

As a reward, we were given a trip to the Canary Islands, where French had been very rude to Denis Follows, the secretary of the FA, who had questioned why Graham was late for the bus that had been booked to take us to a reception. Follows was given a mouthful of abuse.

While we were there, Tommy Docherty, who was manager of Chelsea, arranged to meet French at London Airport to sign him.

However, Ron Harris spoke to Docherty ahead of our return and told him not to touch him. Even as a teenager, Ron was a man with enormous qualities of leadership, which Docherty already trusted. French was signed by Swindon for £13,000 but played only five times before being transferred to Watford and then returning to Wellington.

Graham French's problems, in my view, were those of attitude rather than skill. I felt that he mixed with the wrong company. While at Luton, he owned and ran greyhounds at the track at Bletchley. He had problems at home and went back to Wellington for three weeks. I was still injured and Allan Brown, who had replaced George Martin as manager, thought French indispensable and desperately wanted him back. He said to me: 'You're big pals with Frenchie; do a favour for me and drive to Wellington and try to persuade him to come back.'

I managed to coax him back to Luton. He had not trained for three weeks. French had a training session on the Friday and played on the Saturday. He performed brilliantly. However, Graham was a gambler and a boozer and was particularly attracted by the opening of Luton's version of Caesar's Palace, which contained a nightclub and a casino and attracted the likes of Bob Monkhouse, Tommy Cooper and Matt Monro. It was the place to go on Saturday evenings. Maureen and I would treat ourselves to a meal and the cabaret while Graham would disappear into the casino.

In 1970 he went to a pub called The Unicorn and shot and wounded a man, allegedly over gambling debts. The judge who jailed him for three years called French: 'An unsavoury man with synthetic glamour.'

He returned to Luton after his sentence and scored for the reserves against Millwall on his first game back in front of a big crowd, nearly all of whom had gathered to welcome him back. However, prison had taken too much out of him and Graham was a shadow of what he had been. A few years later, he turned up at Southport, where Allan Brown was now managing, and played two games under the assumed name of Graham Lafite. The FA discovered the ruse and banned him.

Allan Brown had taken over from George Martin in November 1966 when Luton were twenty-first in the Fourth Division. Brown was a tough, serious Scot. He had played in the same Blackpool teams as Stanley Matthews and appeared for Luton in the 1959 FA Cup final against Nottingham Forest.

He spent three years as Luton manager, where he was backed by the club's new owners, Reggie Burr and Tony Hunt, who ran the Vehicle and General insurance company. Luton won promotion to the Third Division in 1968 as champions, but Brown was sacked after he challenged the directors and told them he wanted to be interviewed for the Leicester job. His employers used this as an excuse to dismiss him. Three years later, Vehicle and General would collapse, leaving 800,000 motorists uninsured.

In Bruce Rioch and Alan Slough, who went on to play for Fulham in the 1975 FA Cup final, Luton had good young players. Brown also signed a loan deal for Derek Kevan, who had scored 173 goals for West Bromwich Albion but who was in his thirties when he came to Kenilworth Road. Kevan still lived in the Midlands and was always anxious to make a prompt getaway from training. However, the sessions used to end with several skill drills, one of which was to sprint thirty yards, keep the ball up a set number of times and then dribble back with the ball through some cones to pass to the next man. It was supposed to be fun and improve ball control. For a man who had played for England in the 1958 World Cup, Derek Kevan's ball skills were questionable. His style of play was best summed up by supporters at The Hawthorns who nicknamed him 'The Tank'. Often, Derek did not get away quite as quickly as he would have liked.

Shropshire did not appear a likely destination on the day in 1967 I received a curt, registered letter from Luton Town, thanking me for my services, wishing me well in the future but giving me a free transfer. I was at the crossroads. Shrewsbury, an agricultural market town with no great football tradition, beckoned when I turned down slightly more money being offered by non-league Chelmsford City.

There was an offer to go to Australia and play for Maccabi Hakoah, a club founded by Sydney's Jewish community. There were tentative phone calls from other clubs. My pride was hurt and injury had knocked my confidence, but I was determined to stay in the Football League.

Shrewsbury had finished sixth in the Third Division, but the club was most famous for employing a man in a coracle to fish out the footballs that had been kicked out of Gay Meadow and into the River Severn. It would also mean leaving Luton, where Maureen owned a hairdressers. The dilemma was whether our relationship would survive if I moved away and stayed in digs for another year. There were many heartfelt discussions before we agreed I should go.

I was going to play for a most uninspiring man. Arthur Rowley had broad shoulders and a heavy frame. He had been a great goalscorer for Leicester City with a sledgehammer left foot and an amazing appearances-to-goals record. In the 1956/57 season, which had seen Leicester promoted to the top flight with Nottingham Forest, Rowley had scored forty-four league goals.

He had come to Shrewsbury the following year as a player-manager exchanging the First for the Fourth Division, scoring 160 goals in his first five seasons at Gay Meadow. He had retired in 1965.

When I met him, Rowley seemed casually indifferent about me signing for him. He said: 'If you don't agree to sign within forty-eight hours, I have already spoken to Bernie Lewis at Cardiff who would love to come.' Talking to him, I felt uncertain. I should have been braver with my conversation, because from the very start

Arthur Rowley did not seem a manager I would be comfortable with. I was torn. I was putting my relationship with Maureen at risk, but Shrewsbury had a decent side and I was desperate to resurrect my career. My desire to keep playing overrode my initial suspicion of the man.

Arthur Rowley's dreary Black Country dirge was counteracted by the enthusiasm of the coach, Gordon Lee, who had been a right-back for Aston Villa. It was no surprise to me and to the rest of the players when at the end of a very good season, which had seen Shrewsbury miss out on promotion to Division Two by a point, Gordon succeeded Stanley Matthews as manager of Port Vale. Gordon was a workaholic who must have been stretched to breaking point by the diplomacy required to be Rowley's assistant.

Rowley rarely smiled. The training sessions at Shrewsbury would end with a small-sided game that would not finish until Rowley had scored with this thunderbolt left foot. His great passion was horse racing. He owned a horse called Tern Eran, and before one home game he stayed in his office to watch the TV race. He came down to the trainers' box when the game was already fifteen minutes in. I cannot recall whether Tern Eran won, but if it had, Arthur Rowley would never betray that knowledge with a smile.

His captain, Ted Hemsley, was a fine all-round sportsman who would win cricket's County Championship with Worcestershire. He was Arthur's 'favourite son'. Whenever his horse had a chance of a win, Rowley would inform Ted, who would never tell the other players.

Our centre-forward was Frank Clarke, one of the famous Clarke footballing family. He was the eldest of five brothers, all of whom played league football. The youngest, Wayne, won the championship with Everton in 1987 and scored the decisive goal in the Charity Shield against Coventry. Allan, the second and most famous brother, was a confident, almost arrogant goalscorer for Leeds and

England. I considered Frank's ability as a front man to be top class. He was not quick, but he could keep the ball, was always available and his positioning, when you had the ball, always gave you an alternative. His talents were rewarded with a move to play First Division football with Queens Park Rangers.

I felt my form and fitness were improving at Shrewsbury, but I wanted more regular games. I was also restless. I decided to move to lovely, sleepy, sunny Exeter.

The manager of Exeter City, Frank Broome, a happy-go-lucky man who had been a fine striker for Aston Villa before the war, came to my rescue. The players enjoyed his company and my previous two moves had taught me to ask more delicate questions. The most important point I wanted to put to Broome was: 'I do not want to be a squad member. I need to play.'

He replied: 'Don't worry. You'll play. You've got to play. I've only got twelve players!' Broome was a friendly, family man. A bit of a joker.

Exeter was even further away from Luton than Shrewsbury. It would mean more time apart from Maureen, although we agreed that she would wind down the hairdressing business and she would join me in Devon at the end of the season. That summer, we promised ourselves we would get married.

Almost immediately, Exeter had a run in the League Cup. The first round produced a Devon derby against Plymouth that was won on the second replay. Sheffield Wednesday, a First Division club, were beaten 3–1 at St James's Park. I gave Don Megson, regarded as perhaps Sheffield Wednesday's finest left-back, a hard time. The next game was the big one. We were drawn at Tottenham Hotspur. Little Exeter and thousands of Devonians would travel to the great theatre of White Hart Lane.

The drama was intense. When Pat Jennings fumbled my shot, John Mitten scored to put Exeter 2–1 up in front of a crowd of

25,000. It was then that the genius of Jimmy Greaves intervened. His hat-trick included racing from the halfway line and ghosting past three statuesque defenders to score. Tottenham won 6–3. They would reach the semi-finals, only to lose to Arsenal.

I was enjoying my football in Devon. I had seldom felt fitter, partly due to the excellent training, some of which was done under the direction of Exeter University's fitness specialist, Dr Peter Travers. It was at Exeter that I experienced weight training for the first time. I felt stronger and quicker – as I had to be on the mud-bound St James's Park pitch.

Maureen and I were married on 3 June 1969 at Luton Register Office. I approached the wedding with some trepidation. Maureen was not Jewish and my father had, deep down, always wanted me to remain within the fold. We discussed the dilemma many times and Maureen was wonderful about it, but her parents and family I felt were slightly less approving. Ours was not a religious marriage but a union of two liberal, free-thinking people, who were horrified by prejudice.

Most importantly, we settled in Exeter and Maureen became pregnant with our son, Jonathon. On days off and spare weekends, we would travel to Dawlish, Teignmouth and Budleigh Salterton. In a small way we were living the dream. I even revived my enthusiasm for Sunday games of cricket. At school, I had played for Notting-hamshire at under-16 level as a wicketkeeper.

The FA Cup provided two brushes with glamour. In January 1969, we played at home to Manchester United, the reigning European champions. Westward Television, which ran the ITV franchise for the south-west, dispatched its television cameras to interview us. The whole of Devon appeared captivated by the tie and the chance to see George Best. The game was watched by a crowd of 18,500.

I was named substitute, though I did come on during the game and fifteen minutes before kick-off our full-back Mike Balson, in his full kit, went down the narrow corridor that linked the dressing room at St James's Park to the secretary's office to drop off some complementary tickets. There, standing in a corridor in a suit, was George Best, chatting away. Balson rushed back to the dressing room to announce: 'Great news, chaps: George Best isn't playing.' When we ran out on to the pitch, Best was standing there in his No. 7 shirt. Ian Storey-Moore, who played with Best during his last years at Old Trafford, told me this was typical of the man. He would do no warm-ups, go into the dressing room, put on his shirt and play, forever the street footballer.

Facing Exeter City in front of the BBC television cameras, Matt Busby employed a front line of Best, Bobby Charlton and Denis Law – the trio whose statue now stands guard outside Old Trafford. None of them scored and, a minute before half-time, Exeter were leading 1–0 through a goal from their Liverpudlian striker, Alan Banks. Just before the interval, John Fitzpatrick equalised and an own goal from John Newman and another from Brian Kidd settled the fixture.

In November, we beat Fulham 2–0 in the first round of the following season's FA Cup. It was only later that it sank in that I had played against Johnny Haynes, the first £100-a-week footballer and perhaps the most glamorous player of his generation, just as George Best was of his. Frank Broome had gone by then, sacked in February after a defeat at Newport left Exeter second-bottom of the Football League. John Newman began a seven-year spell as Exeter's manager, initially combining the role with playing centre-half.

Although I had a good relationship with him, it made me think more about the future and of getting back into football's mainstream. However lovely Exeter was, it was also isolated. To watch first-class football meant a near 150-mile round trip to see Bristol City. Maureen had retained her interest in the hairdressing business in Luton, but she realised that those running it were taking too much of an advantage of her absence and could not be trusted. A heart to heart with John Newman led me to my third free transfer. What a record!

Jim Iley, whom I had known at Nottingham Forest, was now at Peterborough and persuaded me to come to a club that was in commutable distance of Maureen's parents, where we lived while she was pregnant with Jonathon. Eventually, we would buy the flat above Maureen's hairdressing business, a stone's throw from Kenilworth Road.

Iley was an often-dour Yorkshireman who had moved from Newcastle to become Peterborough's player-manager. Jim needed to dominate the game. He wanted to take every throw-in, corner kick and free-kick himself. The joke in the dressing room was that he would have liked to have headed in his own corners. My greatest gripe with Jim's coaching was that whatever the result Monday morning would always involve long, hard, repetitive running. I hated it.

Two-thirds into my one season at Peterborough, I received a call from Peter Taylor, who was now at Derby with Brian Clough. He told me Nuneaton Borough in the Southern League had a vacancy for a player-manager.

'Why are you ringing me?' I asked him.

'You could do that job.'

'I think I'm too young, Peter.'

'If you're good enough, you're old enough. Make no mistake, a load of the managers out there are crap. You won't even need an interview. I'll make sure you get the job.'

I thought there would be interviews and I was invited to talk to the club, as were others. Maurice Setters, the tough wing-half who had played for West Bromwich Albion and Manchester United, was rumoured to be interested. So, too, was Davie Gibson, a very talented inside-forward, who had won the League Cup in successive seasons at Leicester.

In subsequent years, I told people, half-jokingly, that I got the job by accepting less money than Nuneaton offered. I knew it would be a way of getting that first opportunity in management. I was twenty-six.

There would be more travelling, more staying in digs. However, it meant I would be able to use the coaching certificates I had worked for. There was something else. I had not been impressed by some of the managers I had played under. I thought I could do better.

Later, Peter Taylor would explain how he was so certain I would get the Nuneaton job. Six years before, he had moved to the north-east to join Brian Clough at Hartlepools. The managing director of the removal firm was a man called Sam Downes. I am pretty sure that Peter would not have paid him but would have promised to do him a favour in the future. By 1971, Sam Downes was a director at Nuneaton and I was the favour.

There was an alternative. I spoke to the pinstriped figure of Stanley Reed, the erudite, articulate chairman of a Southern League club that was going places – Wimbledon. I went to Plough Lane to be interviewed for the job, as was Howard Wilkinson, who was then managing Boston United. Neither of us was appointed – the position went to Mike Everitt, who had been an aggressive full-back at Northampton and managed in a similar style. Stanley Reed would see Wimbledon become a Premier League club. Poignantly, his funeral in May 2002 came seven days before the club was given permission to move to Milton Keynes.

Nuneaton had finished sixteenth in the Southern League Premier Division, where the big clubs were Yeovil, Hereford, Chelmsford and Wimbledon. I began the new season as player-manager, but I was increasingly afflicted by problems with my back.

In my final game, which was on Yeovil's famous sloping pitch at Huish Park, I suffered excruciating spasms in my back, which completely locked. After the match, I had to be put into traction at the

Coventry and Warwickshire Hospital, where I was treated by the surgeon, Tom Sergeant, who was a director at Coventry City. He advised me not to have an operation and, as always, I trusted the surgeon. I knew my time as a player was up.

My chairman at Nuneaton was a man called Alf Scattergood, who ran Century Oils, a firm based in Stoke that produced industrial lubricants. He was a short, portly, pipe-smoking man who was a well-known local figure.

Early on in my time as his manager, he told me: 'Any fool can spend someone else's money.' By money, he meant his and by fool, he meant me. I understood his message and ran, as I always did, a tight ship.

The club employed a secretary, Vera Robinson, for three days a week, but she had to take time off, and for several months, I did the job. The directors could tell themselves they were getting more for their money from me. However, it made me aware of the intricacies of the accounts, player registrations and how much money was coming in and going out. The experience would stand me in good stead for the future.

The club allowed me a second-hand Ford Cortina, supplied by one of the board members, a tall, ex-public schoolboy who ran a car dealership. He had a loud voice and, as I stood by the boardroom door waiting to be invited into a meeting, I heard him say: 'Shall we call Goldberg in now?' It may have been his idea of a joke, but I never found prejudice at Nuneaton. It was a tight-knit mining community and they had probably never encountered a Jew before.

My first experience of the FA Cup as a manager saw me take Nuneaton to the first round proper. It was a big deal for the club. Nuneaton had a reputation in the competition, and in 1967, 22,000 had packed into their ground, Manor Park, for a third-round tie against Rotherham.

On a dreadful, wet afternoon in November 1971, we played

Torquay in front of 5,000. We had won five preliminary games to get this far. Some 2,000 had travelled down to Devon from Nuneaton. We could not cancel out an early Torquay goal and in the final minute we saw what everyone at Plainmoor thought a legitimate equaliser disallowed. It was my first crushing experience of football management.

One day Peter Taylor, who was transforming Derby into league champions, rang me and said: 'Do you need anything?' I replied that we lacked pace and could do with someone on the right. He said: 'I'll have a word with Brian and see what I can do.'

The next day, Brian Clough rang me. 'I'm told you want a winger,' he said. 'I've got just the player for you. A boy called Hutchinson. A Geordie. He'll be good enough for you.'

I went to watch him at an A-team fixture at Birmingham's training ground at Elmdon. He did very little. A few days later, Clough rang me and said: 'What about Hutchinson?'

'Brian, with the best will in the world, I can't take him. He seems to have no appetite for the game.'

'Exactly. You'll help him regain his appetite.' That was what conversations with Clough were like. He always had an answer. We did not take the player.

Nuneaton rose two places to fourteenth in my first season, which saw Hereford elected to the Football League, and finished ninth in 1973. However, the end came when I started my third season poorly and lost 4–0 at Kettering, a wealthy club, managed by the 34-year-old Ron Atkinson.

They were backed by John Nash, who had made a lot of money playing the Japanese stock markets and was the chairman of a company called Caravans International. He had signed Roy Clayton from Oxford United and Eddie Dillsworth from Chelmsford City for a combined fee of £42,000 which was an absolute fortune for non-league football in the 1970s.

Sitting on the bus after the game, a disconsolate Alf Scattergood told me to see him at Manor Park the following day, Sunday. I knew the writing was on the wall and later he phoned me at home. 'We won't need that meeting, David,' said Scattergood. 'The directors have met and we've decided the time has come.'

Not long before and realising my position with the board was becoming fragile, I had phoned Peter Taylor, who himself was walking on eggshells with the directors of Derby. 'You would not believe what's happening here,' he told me. 'Don't worry. I will always give you a job.' In October 1973, some eighteen months after taking Derby to the league title, Clough and Taylor walked out of the Baseball Ground.

I also heard that the Luton manager, Harry Haslam, whom I had met a couple of times, had spoken well of me. The sacking did not overly perturb me. I knew there was something out there.

CHAPTER 4

'ALWAYS TELL THE CHAIRMAN'S WIFE HOW LOVELY SHE LOOKS'

There is often irony in opportunity. Harry Haslam promised me a coaching job, but I would have to start on the ground floor. My first job at Luton involved taking lottery tickets and spot-the-ball coupons to schools and factories.

There was no vacancy when Harry Haslam invited me to join Luton, but he was confident there would be one. He was certain that Jimmy Andrews, the newly appointed manager of Cardiff City, would take his reserve-team coach, Ken Whitfield, to Ninian Park, thus creating an opportunity for me. In the meantime, I would have to muck in.

In the summer of 1974, the summer Luton were preparing for a return to the top flight after an absence of fourteen years, this is what happened. Harry gave me the job without discussing my coaching methods. He was a Yorkshireman, a heavy smoker, a smiler who was rarely publicly affected by the twin impostors of defeat or victory.

I had passed my coaching qualifications early and I thought somebody must have recommended me, but when I asked him: 'Why did you appoint me, Harry?' he calmly replied: 'Because I like you.' Harry's office was not far from our flat above Maureen's hairdressers, tucked away in the bedroom in one of the three shabby terraced houses at the top of Kenilworth Road, from where the club was run. Luton would be replacing a relegated Manchester United in the First Division. Their offices were very different.

One house contained the manager, the club secretary and two personal assistants occupying the converted bedrooms upstairs. The commercial and the pools offices were downstairs, connected by the narrowest staircase I have ever seen. There were no banisters.

Next door lived Sheila and Bob Kent. He was the irritable, loud-mouthed groundsman who protected his grass as if it were spun from gold. Sheila was the cleaner. Luton's maintenance man lived in the third house and he could always be seen walking around with his tool bag looking busy. His wife, Mary, an attractive woman in her forties, worked in the commercial office. It was a big, happy family.

I worked closely with Danny Bergara, who ran the youth team. Danny was born in Uruguay but had moved to Spain as a teenager and played for Real Mallorca and Sevilla. He had married an English girl, Jan, who was a travel guide, and moved to St Albans. He still loved to show off his skills on the training ground. He could balance a coin on his foot, flick it up and catch it in his top pocket. With a football at his command, he possessed a tremendous volley.

I learned a massive amount from Danny. He was highly strung, highly talented and possessed a confidence that could border on arrogance. I often strove to control that strong ego. We would talk football incessantly and often trained the reserves and youth groups together. After a day's training, we would go up to Harry's office, where he would ply us with tea and tell us interminable jokes. There were so many that, after we had left, we could not remember a single one.

He was an old-fashioned manager who thought he should stay in his office until five o'clock. We thought his fear was that if the chairman rang and he was not there, he would be accused of taking afternoons off. Harry had come to Luton after scouting for Fulham, working with Bobby Robson and the first-team coach, Roy Mc-Crohan. In 1968, Robson found out he had been sacked as Fulham manager by reading an *Evening Standard* billboard. The three of them went out along the Fulham Road and had a few drinks too many.

Haslam went to Luton to work for Alec Stock, a grand, upstanding figure who would manage in four different decades. Like nearly all managers, Alec suffered from nerves before games, which was made worse by his asthma. Prior to kick-off, the Luton doctor would have to give him injections to calm him down. When Alec left to manage Fulham, who he would take to the 1975 FA Cup final, Harry replaced him.

One of Haslam's favourite sayings on a Friday as he contemplated team selection was: 'The Lord moves in mysterious ways.' It was though he were praying someone would go down with flu or some other ailment and make his choice easier. After the match, he knew instinctively how to deflect attention from a defeat. If he was questioned about a loss or a poor performance, he would direct the answer towards another issue.

He felt the need to represent the club at every available local function he was invited to. Rotary, Round Table, Boy Scouts, Masonic Lodges – he found it difficult to refuse any invite. He wanted to be popular and felt it important to burnish the image of the club. One morning, we asked him if he had seen the previous night's football on television. He replied: 'I couldn't, because I had to attend three different functions to hand out prizes. I was thoroughly pissed off because they started at different times – I missed the food at all three!'

He had three principles of longevity for a manager. The first: 'Walls have ears.' The second: 'Always count to ten – slowly.' And his third pearl of wisdom: 'Always tell the chairman's wife how lovely she looks in the boardroom, particularly after a defeat.'

Harry, who was already in his fifties, let us coach. He showed trust in his staff. Our characters and coaching skills were different. Roy McCrohan was a serious man, a disciplinarian. He was a pair of safe hands, steady, predictable but popular with the senior players, which was important. He was also a buffer for Harry, who spent most of the day in his office. Danny was excitable, knowledgeable and demonstrative in his coaching. I was the middleman, though I thought I was the creative one. I prepared my work carefully and looked for different angles.

Luton's scouting network was virtually non-existent. It was all done through contacts, most of which were Harry's. In 1976, he felt Luton needed a striker and phoned one of his Scottish contacts, who recommended the Celtic striker Dixie Deans. Harry looked at Deans's record of appearances and goals – eighty-nine in 126 league games for Celtic – and without ever seeing him play live paid £20,000 for him. He effectively signed him from his statistics in the *Rothmans Football Yearbook*.

The transfer did not work. Deans had separated from his wife and frequently drove back to Glasgow to see his three children. He was drinking too much and life in a hotel did not suit him. He was loaned out first to Carlisle, then Partick Thistle before going to Australia to play for Adelaide City.

After watching the 1974 World Cup in West Germany on television, Haslam decided he liked Australia's centre-forward Adrian Alston, who had emigrated after a spell on Preston's books. He sent the club secretary halfway round the world to Adelaide to sign Alston, who had been offered terms by three German clubs. Alston signed for Luton, a decision he described as 'the worst of my life'. Despite the fact Luton were in the First Division, they were unable to pay Alston's wages and he was sold to Cardiff, who agreed to pay the money he was owed.

One of Harry's qualities was that he trusted his coaches and their judgement. He never hesitated when I sang the praises of the young Brian Stein after watching him play at Borehamwood for Edgeware Town. When I watched an English Schools Trophy game at Hitchin, I saw Ricky Hill, a strong, skilful black player from the John Kelly Technology College in Neasden. He shone and we signed him. Ricky made his debut as a seventeen-year-old in a 3–1 defeat to Bristol Rovers in April 1976.

Ricky would have a sterling career that would feature international caps with England and I would employ him as a coach at both Sheffield Wednesday and Tottenham. He returned to Luton as a manager but was dismissed within a year. He moved to Florida and on his return would campaign against the lack of coaching opportunities for black players in England.

Harry's achievement of taking Luton to the top flight in 1974 ahead of clubs such as Aston Villa and Sunderland, who could boast double the gates at Kenilworth Road, was a considerable one. However, Luton lasted only one season in the First Division and it was a slog. They won just one of their opening twenty-one fixtures – and that at home to Carlisle, who had been promoted with them. By the time they faced Derby, on 21 December, Luton were six points adrift at the foot of the table.

It was then that Haslam played his ace. He had signed Ron Futcher and his twin brother Paul from Chester in the summer and now he played them and also introduced Steve Buckley, whom he had signed on my recommendation from Burton.

In three games over Christmas, they beat Derby, who would win the title, Ipswich, who would finish third, and also overcame Wolverhampton Wanderers 3–2. In the last game, Ron Futcher, who had scored the winner at Portman Road, hit a hat-trick. Those players had been in my reserve side for half a season, along with the outstanding Andy King, who in one reserve game at Swindon scored three goals from midfield to overturn a two-goal deficit.

The three victories over Christmas breathed fresh life into our club. Luton completed their season with three wins and a draw to take us one place above the relegation line. However, Spurs still had one fixture left to play, at home to Leeds on the Monday night. They needed a draw to relegate us on goal average. Tottenham won 4–2 at White Hart Lane and Luton were relegated alongside Carlisle and Chelsea. Relegation increased the constant financial pressure on Luton. In December 1975, Harry Haslam was forced to sell Peter Anderson to Royal Antwerp to stave off bankruptcy. A year later, when the spectre of administration had returned to Kenilworth Road, Andy King was sold to Everton for a knockdown £35,000. Andy was just nineteen, a local lad from Luton, who was then consumed by shyness. As the reserve-team manager, I knew him better than the rest of the backroom staff. He met me in the car park and asked if I could go down to the boot room and collect his boots. He did not want the embarrassment of having to say goodbye to the team. His midfield skills would make him a crowd favourite at Goodison Park.

Luton's reserve games kicked off simultaneously with the seniors. If the first team were away, Luton Reserves would play at Kenilworth Road in the Football Combination, where we drew crowds of over a thousand. One of the attractions of watching the reserves was that the club would relay the first-team score every fifteen minutes. It was a great learning curve to be in charge of my reserves travelling to places like Arsenal and Tottenham. Years before, as a teenager, I had played on these grounds. I recalled being marked at White Hart Lane by the left-back Mel Hopkins in a side brimming with outstanding players who could not get into Spurs' Double-winning side.

Hopkins had played for Wales in the 1958 World Cup. Tony Marchi played in the 1963 Cup-Winners' Cup final victory over Atlético Madrid. Frank Saul won the FA Cup in 1967. Eddie Clayton made a hundred appearances for Spurs at their peak and John

Hollowbread was the goalkeeping understudy to the great Bill Brown. Then, reserve-team football provided an enormous fund of experience, and it was this kind of experience I was determined to give my players at Luton.

One of our directors had persuaded Eric Morecambe, who lived nearby in Harpenden, to join the board. Harry Haslam got on with him wonderfully well. There was a smile in the boardroom and every visiting director wanted to meet him. Later, it would be the same at Chelsea when Roman Abramovich took charge. However, the Tottenham directors never came close to being allowed into his private box at Stamford Bridge. The only time I met him was in a hotel foyer in Spain after Chelsea had played Barcelona.

Eric Morecambe, however, was very approachable. He was a warm, friendly man with no airs or graces. He would pop down to the dressing room to crack his jokes and pull his daft faces. We enjoyed his company and his attachment to the team. Morecambe did not travel with the team to away games because he would invariably have a weekend theatre commitment. Instead, he was made director in charge of hospitality at reserve-team games at Kenilworth Road.

He was always very complimentary whether we had won, lost or drawn. Once, in the boardroom, he told me he had an idea. 'Why don't you have boards in the dugout with numbers on so the team know what move to make next?' I thought he had got the idea from American football set-plays. I told Eric that the players found it hard enough to replicate one pre-planned training-ground move. There would be no way they could cope with half-a-dozen routines communicated to them from the bench during a match. Afterwards, I wondered whether Eric was ahead of his time or just taking the piss.

People are fascinated by fame. Eric would present prizes at half-time, do media interviews and mention Luton Town in his television shows, which at their peak in 1977 drew audiences of 28 million, then half the population of the United Kingdom. He presented an image of the club to the outside world. Eric's son, Gary, would sometimes come with him to Luton, but his charming wife, Joan, was always too busy, often because of charity work. We tried to persuade Eric to bring his stage partner, Ernie Wise, to Kenilworth Road. Eric explained that Ernie was not particularly interested in football and that outside the theatre and the television studio, they were not especially close. They rarely socialised. Theirs was a relationship based on the business of comedy.

There were some on the board who frankly resented Eric Morecambe. Vastly more people knew he was a member of Luton's board than could name the club chairman, Dennis Mortimer. After the club's relegation in 1975, Mortimer asked each director to put £25,000 (around £211,000 in today's terms) into the club. Eric refused. He had too many outside commitments and he felt his PR value to Luton was worth more than the investment. He resigned from the board on 7 November, though he was offered an honorary position of vice president, and continued to come to Kenilworth Road until his death from a heart attack in May 1984.

Domestically, I was very happy. We had bought a bungalow near the Luton and Dunstable Hospital. Our daughter, Joanne, had been born in 1973 and we had what seemed a perfect family of a boy and a girl. Harry Haslam was upbeat when the 1977/78 season opened. Luton had finished sixth the previous season but had won more games than any other club in Division Two, including Nottingham Forest, who twelve months later would be champions of England.

The most pressing problem was attendances. Gates at Kenilworth Road had fallen by a third since Luton's relegation – a loss that would never be recovered – and Harry was persuaded that a column in the local freesheet, the *Luton Herald*, might help at the turnstiles. The paper was owned by Keith Barwell, who would buy Northampton rugby club in December 1995 – previously we had tried to entice him to invest in Luton. By then, he had sold the *Herald* for big bucks.

The only problem with Harry Haslam's column in the *Luton Herald* was that Harry Haslam did not write it. That task was given to me, and I had to present it every Wednesday morning at the paper's offices in the town centre. It was not my first experience of journalism. When I was a player at Peterborough, I had written a comment piece for a national weekly paper called *Inside Football*. I enjoyed writing and expressing my views. It gives me some pride to say that in all my years in management from Nuneaton to becoming Tottenham's director of football, I wrote my own programme notes. I also realised how important it was to have a voice outside the club's own publications.

As a manager, I made it my business to get a column in the local paper, whether it was the *Luton News*, the *Leicester Mercury* or the *Sheffield Star*. The idea was always to project the club beyond its own captive audience. When I was at Tottenham, I had an opportunity to spread the net wider and with the help of Rob Bishop, the chief football writer of the *Birmingham Post*, I wrote a column in the *Sports Argus*, a Saturday night football paper with a huge circulation that covered the West Midlands. I was paid a small sum for my work, but the real benefit was having a copy of the paper delivered to me each week. I would soak in the bath after training and read the Midlands football gossip, which was sometimes a great help when it came to scouting players from the lower leagues.

Despite the optimism at the start of the season, Luton's results remained erratic and Harry told us that his son, Keith, was becoming the victim of bullying at school. It was a hurdle Keith overcame, but it made you realise how a result or an envious child could create turmoil. Harry had two children and each was affected by the attention they received. Keith Haslam later became chairman of Mansfield and was physically attacked after their relegation from the Football League.

The life of a football manager is a life lived in a goldfish bowl. This is especially the case in a small town. Every move is monitored, everyone has a view and in tough times, your children can suffer. You have to be strong willed and isolate your family from the harsh criticism that can come your way.

There was a surprise. Jimmy Hill had launched a new soccer franchise in the United States called Detroit Express, who would be managed by Ken Furphy and whose roster included Trevor Francis, who would shortly become England's first million-pound footballer. Roy McCrohan was offered the job of first-team coach. His wife, Mary, ran a dance school and hoped she could run a similar one in Detroit. Roy resigned and sought a new life across the Atlantic, where he lived until his death in 2015. I was elevated to the position of first-team coach and soon an approach to Harry Haslam from Sheffield United would present me with the biggest opportunity of all.

CHAPTER 5

'I BEGAN THINKING I HADN'T MADE ARRANGEMENTS TO SELL THE CAR'

When Harry Haslam confronted me and Danny Bergara with the news he had been offered the chance to manage Sheffield United, we were stunned. My thoughts immediately turned to self-preservation. What would happen to me?

He calmly explained that Derek Dooley, the managing director of Sheffield United, had approached him and he had permission to bring two coaches with him. Haslam had spent much of his free time fishing in a lake owned by a businessman called Harry Short in the village of Sandy in Bedfordshire. Short was a close friend of Dooley, who was a towering figure in the city of Sheffield.

He had been a brave, goalscoring centre-forward at Sheffield Wednesday, where his tally of forty-six goals in the 1951/52 season remains a club record. However, in February 1953, at the age of twenty-two, he suffered a double fracture of his right leg, which led to it being amputated. Many years later, Wednesday made Dooley their manager, but when he was sacked on Christmas Eve 1973, he vowed never to go to Hillsborough again and eventually went to Bramall Lane as an administrator.

Once Roy McCrohan had left for Detroit, Harry asked me to take over as first-team coach. My first game would be at Selhurst Park on Boxing Day 1977. Terry Venables was manager of Crystal Palace and big things were predicted for his side who were already being dubbed 'The Team of the '80s.'

There were over 20,000 at Selhurst and, with a minute remaining, a solid team performance had put us 3–2 up with goals from Paul Price, Ron Futcher and Phil Boersma. Then, John Faulkner, our centre-half, was forced to the ground after a heavy challenge. From the touchline, we pleaded with John to stay down and attract the referee's attention so the physio would be allowed on. Alas, barely able to walk, Faulkner limped on and Kenny Sansom, later to play for Arsenal and England, equalised at the death. It had been a fine game for any neutral who happened to have spent Boxing Day at Crystal Palace. Despite the late goal, it had been a satisfying result for Luton and a massive lesson that I hoped Faulkner would take on board. We paid for his bravery.

Within weeks, the biggest opportunity of all arrived as Harry informed Luton that he wanted a longer contract and made it clear that, if it was refused, he would take up Sheffield United's offer. The extended contract was not forthcoming and Harry presented me and Danny Bergara with an envelope. In each was an offer from Sheffield United to join their coaching staff that he had agreed with his new board of directors. It was to trigger a chaotic few days.

We both had to speak to our wives and consider the immediate, the long term, the location, the children's education and the salary. Neither knew what the other was offered, although I suspect the amounts were identical. I was reluctant to leave Luton with young children. Maureen had already sacrificed much for my career and was still enjoying working occasionally while being near her friends and family.

Danny was, however, eager to progress and the door opened for him when the Luton chairman, Dennis Mortimer, indicated to me that the board were keen for me to take the reins from Harry. Knowing I had a choice gave a massive boost to my confidence. Clearly this swayed me, and Mortimer, the reasonably wealthy boss of a haulage firm, told me the board had faith in me and would pay me £12,000 a year as manager.

It was a wonderful opportunity. My grounding at Nuneaton had been invaluable and now I had to persuade Danny Bergara to stay with me. Long discussions ensued, with Danny employing every mixed metaphor he had gleaned from Harry Haslam over those long afternoons in the manager's office. Despite this, our relationship never faltered. However, Bergara was pushing for a contract Luton could not afford and he knew the position of first-team coach at Sheffield United was now guaranteed. He joined Harry at Bramall Lane.

There was talk that while at Sheffield United, Harry came close to bringing the teenaged Diego Maradona to Yorkshire. Harry did know Antonio Rattín, the Argentine international who gained notoriety with his dismissal in the 1966 World Cup quarter-final, and he had good contacts in South America. He took Alex Sabella from River Plate to Bramall Lane and was the go-between when Rattín negotiated the sale of Ossie Ardiles and Ricky Villa to Tottenham after the 1978 World Cup in Argentina. They had been initially offered to Arsenal.

Eventually, Harry and Danny fell out. Bergara was a fierce-willed man and had strong principles. Ron Greenwood asked him to coach England youth teams and he worked for Bruce Rioch at Middlesbrough, but his greatest success came with Stockport County. In 1992, when Stockport faced Stoke in the Football League Trophy, he became the first man born outside of the British Isles to lead a team out at Wembley in a domestic final.

At Stockport, he played the long-ball game, tactics that were completely alien to the ones we preached so successfully at Luton. Danny said that the ends justified the means and that at that level of football, he wanted to get the ball among the opposition defence as quickly as possible. He considered that players of limited ability would too easily lose possession if asked to play a passing game.

His explosive nature proved his undoing. Danny was forced out of Edgeley Park after a physical confrontation with his chairman. He did not get on with his chairman, Brendan Elwood, partly because he kept needling Danny, who had kept his house in Sheffield, about not moving closer to the club. That night they turned on each other. His assistant, Dave Jones, who would take Stockport to promotion and the League Cup semi-finals, remarked that watching Danny clear his desk, while trying to decide what to keep and what to leave behind, was unbearably sad. Nevertheless, he won his claim for unfair dismissal and his name is cherished at Stockport County more than any official's. There is now a Danny Bergara Stand at Edgeley Park and a Bergara Close near the ground.

I gave him a role at Sheffield Wednesday, where I was manager, soon after he left Stockport, but afterwards, he drifted from club to club. However, I kept in touch and saw him at the Hallamshire Hospital in Sheffield just before he died in 2007. A coachload of Stockport supporters attended his funeral. It was a moving service full of South American music, and at the end, the Stockport fans, sitting at the back of the church, began chanting: 'There's Only One Danny Bergara.'

Harry Haslam told me he understood my decision to remain at Luton. He had been an invaluable mentor, a man who knew how to keep a happy ship. He had been the tenth manager I had worked for in my career and three of them had employed humour to unite a dressing room and the club's backroom staff. In all the time I knew Harry, I never heard him tell a Jewish joke. The Englishman, the Irishman and the Scotsman appeared frequently in his massive repertoire. The Jew never did. Maybe Harry was aware of my faith and he did not want to offend me. If he was aware, he never told me.

I have heard many Jewish jokes when the company was unaware

of my background. When the punchline was delivered, I always gave the hint of a smile as though I understood the punchline. Subconsciously, I kept my feelings to myself. Perhaps my early experiences at Nottingham Forest had left me feeling suspicious of people's reactions. I was uncertain how they might view me if they knew I was Jewish.

The responsibility of sitting in the manager's chair weighed heavily over those first few days. It produced a tingling sensation, as if you were being frozen. For a few days, I did not eat properly. Despite my experiences at Nuneaton, I was consumed by nerves. Could I cope? I was a Division Two manager and I was no longer under the radar, shielded by a coaching position. My first task was to put together a new staff to shape the immediate months.

I spoke to Ken Gutteridge, whom I knew well through coaching courses at Lilleshall. He had been manager of Burton Albion while I was at Nuneaton. He was now Alan Mullery's assistant at Brighton. Ken was opinionated but not prejudiced. He would not suffer ill-discipline or conceited egos. He had been the instigator of Brighton's signing of Peter Ward from Derbyshire junior football. At the Goldstone Ground, Ward would become Brighton's finest goalscorer. Ken proved to be an outstanding spotter of talent.

He could be blunt and humourless. What I did not know was that in his last days at Brighton, he was taking an evening fitness class. There, he had met a very attractive younger woman called Jenny, with whom he shared an interest in a shop. They would get involved in a disastrous marriage that imploded several weeks after the wedding. The trauma of the break-up was severe and one morning I received a call that his car had been found in a ditch near the village just outside Luton where he was now living. Jenny had stripped the house bare and left him. Through the grapevine, we knew Ken was looking for a job abroad and the chairman, the club doctor and myself sat him down and told him it could not go on like this. After a long talk we decided it would be best if we parted company.

I also invited David Coates, who was part of Jock Wallace's coaching staff at Leicester but found himself sidelined by the tough-talking Scot. David would share the coaching with me while Ken would take on several 'bitsy' roles, juggling office duties, scouting and coaching.

My third appointment was to make John Moore youth-team coach. John was a Luton stalwart who had spent eight years as a wing-half at Kenilworth Road. Honesty, a capacity for hard work and loyalty were just three of John's qualities. When I finally left Luton for Tottenham after eight years, John took over as manager. It was a deserved reward, but despite leading them to a seventh-place finish in the top flight, he was never comfortable as the No. 1.

Deep down, as I prepared for my debut in league management, I felt I had made a series of good choices. I always wondered in sub-sequent years how managers selected their coaching staff. During his incredible reign at Old Trafford, Sir Alex Ferguson employed many different senior coaches. When he first came to Manchester United in 1986, his assistant was Archie Knox, whom he had worked with at Aberdeen – his brother Jimmy was a very good manager at AP Leamington. After Archie left to join Walter Smith at Glasgow Rangers in 1991, Ferguson employed Brian Kidd, Jim Ryan, Steve McClaren, Carlos Queiroz and Mike Phelan as his No. 2s. This con-stant change meant new ideas, a fresh voice in the dressing room and changing philosophies. It kept the players at Manchester United interested and fresh, but the manager was still the manager.

By contrast, when Ferguson's one-time centre-forward Mark Hughes went into management, he kept the same backroom team wherever he went. Loyalty was his watchword. Whether Hughes was in control of Wales, Blackburn, Manchester City or Stoke, the names behind the manager would be the same – Mark Bowen, Kevin Hitchcock and Eddie Niedzwiecki. Did they change their views and ideas as time progressed? Did they adapt to the players? Did they keep their freshness as the training grounds changed? I wonder.

I wanted to be stimulated by individuals whom I respected. I wanted the creative and the competent rather than having close friends around me who would be protective when times became tough. Dressing rooms can be cruel. They are places where many things are said and not all are reported back. Coaches hear things and are then torn between keeping it to themselves or repeating them to the manager. The coach treads a fine line. He must have the trust of the players and the manager.

When Daniel Levy took over from Alan Sugar as Tottenham's chairman, he asked me, as the club's director of football, whether we had the best coaching staff. I replied: 'If you want the best coaching staff in the country, you have to be prepared to offer three-year contracts, get people to relocate – and offer them good money.' At the time, Tottenham employed coaches who were easily accommodated, who lived within a twenty-mile radius of the training ground at Chigwell. They were ex-players or they had played for London clubs; they were friends of friends.

My first game in full charge of Luton was a disaster. Disaster is an overused term in football; it is not a clever word when used to describe a defeat. However, 31 January 1978 felt as disastrous as football can get.

It was the fourth round of the FA Cup, away to Millwall. We had to rely on a rookie goalkeeper, Tony Knight, whom I'd signed from Dover, to replace the injured Milija Aleksic. We were soundly beaten, 4–0. I could already imagine supporters worrying about this 33-year-old novice who had been given the manager's job. When press reports first emerged that Harry Haslam was unsettled, Eddie McCreadie, a Scotland international full-back who had promoted

Chelsea to the top flight and then resigned over the club's refusal to give him a company car, was the name most touted.

Nevertheless, I survived. Luton were seventh when I took over and, when the season drifted to its conclusion, we had finished thirteenth, two points and one place behind Sheffield United.

Financial necessity had forced Steve Buckley's sale to Tommy Docherty at Derby for £350,000, which represented a healthy profit. However, the likes of Ricky Hill, Lil Fuccillo, Brian Stein and Paul Price were emerging. Two players, however, insisted Harry had promised them free transfers to allow them to leave for new careers at Memphis Rogues. I made it clear that I had seen no written agreement that they could leave, that Harry Haslam had never mentioned this proposal to me and that the board would be declining their request. In the end, player power prevailed and Jimmy Husband, an experienced ex-Evertonian, and John Faulkner left for the United States. However, I felt neither of them had really accepted me, the young newcomer. After several discussions, I conceded to their wishes because they were no longer on board. They could go to Memphis in the summer.

In one game at Fulham, in March, we lost 1–0 and John, our centre-half, had been 'sleeping' for the decisive goal. I tore into Faulkner in the dressing room. 'What the hell were you thinking of?' I shouted. His response left me incredulous. 'All of a sudden, I began thinking that I hadn't made arrangements to sell the car.' His departure to America was already on his mind.

I had already made arrangements to replace John with a player who, ironically, was now in America. Chris Turner was playing centre-half in Boston for the New England Tea Men – who quite naturally were sponsored by Lipton's – while on loan from Peterborough. I knew Chris, having played alongside him during my one season at London Road. Then, he had been a raw eighteen-year-old, as brave as a lion. He would head the ball all day long. On 3

July 1978, the Peterborough secretary Arnold Blades and I flew to Boston. My task was to persuade Chris to join Luton and Arnold's was to negotiate the best-possible fee on behalf of Peterborough and smooth the complications of the deal. Turner was Boston's player, but his registration was with Peterborough.

Our timing was slightly out. We would be trying to negotiate a deal on Independence Day. We would be waiting like lemons to see Turner and his manager, Noel Cantwell, who had played full-back for Manchester United under Matt Busby. Our day slipped away in a hotel lobby as it became clear that they were enjoying a party with Noel's Irish friends and they had no intention of joining us. The following day we met but could not reach an agreement with Chris over his personal terms and I flew back feeling slightly wounded.

Later in my career, I may have walked away after receiving this setback. I got the impression that a third party – Norwich City, who were a division above Luton – were also vying for Turner's services. That had strengthened his negotiating position and he was playing a game. I persuaded the board that we should go the extra mile and sign a player who was a strong, big-hearted competitor but a lazy trainer. Chris played a single season at Kenilworth Road before he was sold back to the New England Tea Men for the same £100,000 fee we had paid a year before. His heart had been in Massachusetts.

Chris played for the Tea Men until financial difficulties forced them to relocate from Boston to Florida in 1981. He returned to England to play for and then manage Cambridge before rejoining his home town club, Peterborough. In the 1992 play-off finals at Wembley, he managed Peterborough to victory over Stockport, led by Danny Bergara.

With Peterborough now in the second tier of English football, Chris stepped down as manager to become the club's chairman and owner. This was a man who, when I first played with him, had a greater love for greyhounds than he did for football. As a player, we could never have imagined Chris Turner as a club chairman. I enjoyed his subtle humour. He died in 2015 after suffering from dementia, aged sixty-four, and there is now a statue of him outside the London Road Stadium.

Turner's signing was a lesson well learned. Sometimes, your first instincts on signing a player must be trusted. Many years later, Mauricio Pochettino said he would not sign a player until he had a thorough meeting with them. He needed to look into their eyes when they were talking privately. Pochettino said their facial expression would give away their true feelings. Only then would he go back to the club and do the deal.

CHAPTER 6

'DO YOU HAVE A TOP DRAWER?'

My first full season beckoned. Time for judgement. I would need to get a team together. I had to make a statement.

To finance a summer spend, Luton had to raise money and Paul Futcher had been attracting attention. The previous season I had, for the first time, been caught out by the press. In February, a local journalist, Brian Swain of the *Luton News*, had rung me just as we were setting off for Blackburn on a Friday afternoon. The journalist told me there was an offer on the newswires for Paul Futcher from Manchester City. He asked how I felt about the situation. Manchester City had finished runners-up to Liverpool in 1977 and were then third in Division One.

This was only my second league game as Luton's manager and I was not used to being put on the spot like this. I told him Futcher would not be going anywhere. My response appeared on the Saturday in a national newspaper under the headline: 'Pleat Denies Futcher His Move to Manchester City,' which was embarrassing for me, unsettling for the player and not good for team spirit. I realised after I had been trapped; there had been nothing on the newswires about Paul Futcher.

At the time, I trusted Brian Swain and would speak to him almost every day about the club. What I was not then aware of was that Swain worked as a 'stringer' for national newspapers – providing them with information on Luton for a fee. It put me in a difficult situation as I had a column in the *Luton News*. I had to be diplomatic when talking to Swain.

The Futcher twins, then aged twenty-one, were interesting characters. Ron, a centre-forward, was a leader of the line, brave, with good ball control and physically intimidating. Paul was a class player, a dedicated, talented central defender with an air of superiority compared to other players. He was a bright, confident reader of the game. The other side of Paul Futcher was that he took chances when in possession.

Less than a week after the headline in the Saturday papers, the identical twins walked out of a meeting as Ken Gutteridge was delivering a pre-game tactical talk. The other players looked on in astonishment as the twins got up from their seats and strode out saying: 'That's rubbish.' That afternoon, I had to consider what action to take. They had both been named in the side to play at Notts County the following day. For a couple of hours, I pondered. Should I chase after them, phone them or go round to their digs? Or would it be best to do nothing?

There was pressure on us. We had lost 2–0 at Blackburn and in between the newspaper article and the Friday team talk we had been humbled 4–1 at home by Tottenham. I let the meeting go on and resolved not to contact the twins. I ensured two extra players were added to the squad that travelled to Meadow Lane the following morning.

Just as we were about to leave for Nottingham, the twins turned up as though nothing had happened. I said nothing to them and kept them in a team that was to lose 2–0, although the twins played well and gave everything. On the Monday, I fined both of them heavily and made sure the other players were aware of their punishment.

It was no surprise when I agreed a fee with Manchester City that summer. They paid £350,000 for Paul, which was then a record fee for a defender, and a further £75,000 for Ron. They both lasted only one season at Maine Road. Ron scored a hat-trick at Chelsea on his debut for Manchester City before going to America to play in Minnesota, Portland and Tulsa. Despite the fee and his undoubted ability, Paul failed to displace Tommy Booth in central defence and twelve months later was sold to Oldham for £200,000 less than Manchester City had paid for him.

Having raised £425,000 with the sale of the Futcher twins, Luton could now buy. David Moss, who was to prove a fine winger, was raided from Swindon, upsetting their manager, Danny Williams, in the process. He was signed for £110,000 on Ken Gutteridge's strong recommendation. David would be instrumental in Luton's success. I had asked Dave Gibbons, one of our scouts, to go to a Swindon home game, follow him to his car after the game and tell him he was from Luton. Would he be interested if we made an offer?

Ken also persuaded me to sign the 31-year-old Bob Hatton from Blackpool. I agreed a fee of £50,000 with the Blackpool manager, Bob Stokoe – an outlay that bought Luton two full seasons and twenty-nine league goals from the centre-forward.

The phone lines were buzzing and another deal was to prove a fortunate masterstroke. My Irish connection and scout Bill Smyth, and his friend Eddie Cochrane, had tipped me off about a twenty-year-old central defender from Belfast who was the graduate of one of the city's most celebrated Catholic youth teams, Cromac Albion. A senior Northern Irish club, Larne, had been alerted to Mal Donaghy's talents and he had played about fifteen games for them.

In March 1978, I had flown to Dublin to watch Donaghy play for Northern Ireland under-21s against the Republic at Dalymount Park. There was considerable tension surrounding the match. The flames from the Troubles were flaring high and this was the first ever international between the two nations of Ireland. One of the characteristics that attracted me to Mal Donaghy was that when he suffered a heavy, nasty challenge, he got up and limped on bravely.

There were many scouts at this inaugural game and when I saw Arsenal's chief scout, Gordon Clark, I thought we might have stiff competition for Mal's signature. I moved quickly and persuaded Luton to pay Larne £15,000 for this rookie. With hindsight, it was the snatch of the day. Many seasons later, when I was no longer at Kenilworth Road, after Mal had played more than 500 games for Luton, Alex Ferguson rang me for a character reference.

Ferguson signed Donaghy for £500,000 in 1988. Mal was to be a very useful squad player at Manchester United and was still good enough to play for Chelsea in his thirties. He was thirty-six when he played his final international in 1994. Like so many of his generation in Northern Ireland, the highlight of Donaghy's international career was the 1982 World Cup. He was sent off during Northern Ireland's 1–0 win over the hosts, Spain, but returned for the final match of an extraordinary five-game campaign, the 4–1 defeat by France in Madrid.

Mal was a private man with a constant, soft smile on his face. The game came easily to him. He rarely, if ever, joined the players on a midweek night out. He appeared to have no interest in the pre-match warm-up. He would run on to the field five minutes before kick-off and be away twenty minutes after the final whistle. When, after he had retired, I asked Mal if he would like to take part in a Luton Town reunion, he calmly replied: 'I don't do reunions. I never have.' This rule applied to the Northern Ireland World Cup team of 1982.

While at Nuneaton, I had signed a curly-haired young lad from Massey Ferguson, the works team of the Coventry tractor factory. I gave Kirk Stephens his debut against Chelmsford in the Southern League when he was aged just sixteen. He was a natural right-back. Barely 5ft 8in., he possessed a superb leap, a great mentality, tackled well and passed the ball from full-back rather than blasting it down-field. I had promised Kirk that, if I ever got a league manager's job,

I would come back to Nuneaton and sign him. That summer I kept my word. Kirk was to spend six years at Luton, where he became the life and soul of a happy dressing room. I got all this for £5,000.

My relationship with Colin Addison, who had been a teammate at Nottingham Forest, helped me secure a promising seventeen-year-old from Newport County, where Colin was manager. Mark Aizlewood was a tall and imposing teenager with a lovely left-footed delivery who was already taking the corners, which at Somerton Park were taken on coconut matting. The matting was required because the area between the pitch and the stands was used as a speedway track. Newport, who in 1977 had avoided the need to apply for re-election to the Football League on the final day of the season, were paid £40,000. Aizlewood would win thirty-nine caps for Wales and, though not a native speaker, he learned Welsh and would win a prize at the national Eisteddfod. He would also battle addictions to alcohol and gambling.

One summer; six signings. However, as we prepared for the start of the 1978/79 season, nobody could have envisaged how our opening game would go. We would be playing Oldham at home and at the interval we were a goal down. We stormed the second half with a brace from Hatton and Moss while Lil Fuccillo and Brian Stein also scored. Six second-half goals set tongues wagging, but a lot of the talk was false optimism. Luton lost three of the next four.

Of the summer signings, Moss, Donaghy and Stephens proved excellent long-term successes, while Aizlewood was sold to Charlton in 1982 for £50,000. Hatton, signed at thirty-one, was sold two years later to Harry Haslam at Sheffield United for £30,000 more than we had paid for him. Hatton's value to Luton lay not just in his goals but in the way he helped the emerging talent of Brian Stein.

Throughout his career, Bob Hatton had a reputation as 'a two-year club player'. A five-year stint at Birmingham aside, Bob had spent around a couple of seasons at every one of his six other clubs.

He was also a shrewdie. He was living in the Midlands when he signed for Luton and he gave me the impression he would move house. He never did but requested relocation costs and money for furniture and fittings. It was written into his contract, so it looked like we had no option but to pay. He was doing well and knew his worth. I refused to pay, however, because he had not honoured his side of the bargain. I referred the matter to the chairman, Dennis Mortimer, and it was rumoured that he parted with some cash. In 1980, Hatton joined Sheffield United. Having made a more than useful contribution to Luton, Bob helped them win promotion and then, after two years at Bramall Lane, departed for Cardiff.

Brian Clough once asked me if I 'had a top drawer'. I had no idea what he was talking about, but when I asked Peter Taylor what he meant, he said: 'You should always have some spare cash ready. Sometimes, you need a sweetener.' Throughout my career, I never had a top drawer. If any player suggested he wanted extra outside his contract and I felt he deserved it, I would refer it to the chairman. I did not want to know.

Our final position of eighteenth was an undistinguished one. Our form had been patchy, but the board felt we had the basis of a good side. In December 1978, Tottenham paid £100,000 for our goalkeeper, Milija Aleksic, who three years later would be part of their FA Cup-winning side. For his replacement, I looked to Aston Villa Reserves and Jake Findlay.

Ron Saunders was his manager and the biggest stumbling block to the deal when I met him at Villa's training ground at Bodymoor Heath was not the price. It was Findlay's insistence that he retained his Aston Villa club car. Saunders, a strict, dour disciplinarian, won that argument hands down. We had to loan Findlay a car for the first year of his contract. Findlay, a big-framed Scot from Blairgowrie, filled the goal and gave his defenders confidence with his command of the penalty box. He was as good a goalkeeper in any team

I have ever managed. In one game against Preston, he roared off his goal-line to punch clear a cross and in one movement flattened our centre-back, Chris Turner, and Michael Robinson, the opposing centre-forward.

I had told Dennis Mortimer that the first year would be an assessment with more players out than in. In the second season, the group must show progress. The third year should see Luton knocking on the door for promotion. I was hoping Mortimer had persuaded the board that this time frame represented the best route towards first stabilising and then progressing the club. Luton finished two places and two points off the final relegation position which, sadly for Harry Haslam, was occupied by Sheffield United.

The final Saturday of the 1978/79 season had seen us at Fulham. We won 2–0. Blackburn had already been relegated. Sheffield United lost at Cambridge. Millwall, who had five games in hand but needed to win them all to overtake Luton, drew at Leicester. The final whistle at Craven Cottage brought audible relief. We were safe. It was then that I realised how important David Moss's brilliant late goal the previous Saturday at Preston had been to force a 2–2 draw. Preston had not lost at Deepdale for more than six months. It was the only time I ever met the great Tom Finney and, in the boardroom afterwards, he told me what a fine player he thought our winger was.

The Winter of Discontent, a combination of strikes and bitter weather, meant the season went on for another seventeen days. Our final game was a Monday night at Wrexham, who like Millwall still had five more fixtures to complete. At the Racecourse Ground, we had what seemed a perfectly good goal disallowed and decisions from the referee, Colin Seel, which we thought favoured the home team. The decisions were too much for Dennis Mortimer and his colleague on the board, the elderly, affable Mr Pearson, the managing director of an industrial firm. Perhaps fuelled by one gin and tonic too many, they came down to the referee's room and decided to berate him. Seel shut the door and told the two men he was not prepared to speak to them. Mortimer then kicked the door with a heavy thud. His punishment was an FA charge, which, since Luton were safe, he willingly accepted.

The highlight of my first full season at Luton was a run in the League Cup. After beating Wigan and Crewe, we faced Aston Villa away. Our tactics were to allow the buccaneering Villa right-back, John Gidman, to raid forward. We would then try to exploit the space in the area he vacated with Bob Hatton springing out from a central position into that channel. It worked beautifully. Hatton and Stein, with a last-minute goal, secured a 2–0 win.

In the quarter-final, we were drawn to face Leeds at Elland Road. When I took the team sheet into the referee's room, I felt overawed. Maurice Lindley, who had been Don Revie's gopher and was now Leeds's general manager, was talking to the referee and they seemed to be on first-name terms. 'How are you, Maurice? Big crowd today.' It was clear the referee did not know me from Adam.

I worried about this familiarity. We lost, 4–1, a brave showing against a team that still contained some of the greats of the Revie era such as Trevor Cherry, the Gray brothers, Paul Madeley and David Harvey. However, it was Tony Currie, signed from Sheffield United by Jimmy Armfield, who proved the night's outstanding performer.

Three days later, at the Goldstone Ground, a shockingly timed challenge from Brighton's Paul Clark left Lil Fuccillo, our left half, suffering a terrible leg break. It was so bad that Lil was hospitalised on the south coast for two weeks. Brighton's management were excellent. Their club doctor was Herzl Sless, a jovial Jewish man who had left Dublin many years earlier for Sussex. His care, concern and treatment of our player left an enduring memory. We met several times and when he passed away his wife sent me a lovely letter. It was an acknowledgement of a mutual comradeship, knowing we may have shared similar experiences in the game.

There had been suggestions that Lil, whose parents were Italians living in Bedford, might play for Italy. Sadly, Fuccillo was never able to recover his form. He broke his leg again in his comeback game and faced another long road to recovery. With a heavy heart, I sold him to Southend in 1983. Football can be cruel.

CHAPTER 7

'I ALWAYS SCORE OR MAKE A GOAL. WHY DO I NOT PLAY?'

After one-and-a-half seasons, we needed to better our league position. Alan Birchenall, my teammate from Nottingham Schoolboys, was allowed to leave Luton for Hereford. I had brought him in from Blackburn to lift the spirits of the dressing room. He was a big character who put smiles on people's faces. In one game during a torrential downpour, at Leicester, he went out for the second half holding an umbrella as he took up his position at inside left. He was nothing if not a character.

Unfortunately, at the age of thirty-three, Alan could no longer make me smile with his performances on the field. Despite the fact we had known each other since we were teenagers, it was not a difficult decision to let Alan go. He was travelling to Luton, he was in and out of the team and this was an outcome he would probably have expected. Our friendship endured and from afar I have admired his PR work for Leicester City and his work for cancer charities, which in 2009 saw him awarded the freedom of the city. He was awarded it on the same day as two other citizens of Leicester – the singer Engelbert Humperdinck and the author Sue Townsend.

I decided I needed a tough-tackling midfielder to complement the skills of Hill, Stein and Moss, who were all improving. David Moss, after a difficult, injury-ridden first season, had put in some outstanding performances. In the season ahead, David, operating from wide on the left and able to shoot with both feet, would score twenty-four goals. For a non-specialist striker, this was a remarkable contribution. In the 1979/80 season, Clive Allen, at Queens Park Rangers, would be the Second Division's leading scorer with twenty-eight.

Then, the tribunal system for out-of-contract players was in its embryo stage. I had met Orient's manager, Jimmy Bloomfield, when he was at Leicester and admired his team. John Smith, our chief executive, had worked with Jimmy at Filbert Street. However, despite their friendship, I decided 'business is business' and I wanted to sign his midfielder, Paddy Grealish. My enquiries led me to his home, 71 Kenyon Street off the Fulham Road, a stone's throw from Craven Cottage. I went there furtively to ask if Grealish, an Irish international, would be interested in a move to Luton.

I spent a harmonious hour with Paddy and his charming wife, Pip, and left confident we could pursue the deal. We went to a tribunal, safe in the knowledge the player wanted to sign, and were ordered to pay £150,000. Orient had wanted £350,000. Angry words were exchanged and the friendship with Jimmy Bloomfield lapsed. Days before Jimmy's death in April 1983 at the age of forty-nine, David Coates, who had worked with him at Leicester, went with me to see him at his home in Chingford. His wife carried him downstairs. This fine man had been ravaged by cancer. He looked skeletal and it was hard to hold back the tears.

In those days, the way I had tapped up Paddy Grealish would have seen me in big trouble. I took a chance and had enough chutzpah to furtively seek Grealish out. Many years before, while I was playing for Shrewsbury, Peter Taylor, who had then just joined Derby from Hartlepools, asked me who I thought was the best centre-back outside the First Division. I said I did not know. He, the brilliant spotter of talent, was absolutely sure. Subsequently, he and Brian

Clough went to Roy McFarland's house in the dead of night, spoke to the nineteen-year-old in his pyjamas and did not leave until he had agreed to exchange Tranmere for Derby.

Players have been tapped up since football began, but looking back, I was taking a risk seeing Grealish at such an early stage of my managerial career. If I had been spotted, it would have jeopardised my position, since the practice was against the rules of the Football League. I assumed – correctly perhaps – that nobody would recognise a rookie manager from Bedfordshire in this corner of west London.

As a manager, I was similarly tapped up. In 1981, I met the Sunderland chairman Tom Cowie at the Gosforth Park Hotel. Four years later, I met Alan Woodsford, Southampton's chairman, who smoked a pipe throughout our meeting. There was a meeting at the Farmers Club, an opulent building in Whitehall Court, with John Kerr, a lovely man from an agricultural community who wanted me to take over at Ipswich.

The strangest approach I encountered arrived in February 1984. It came from Maurice Kinn, who had owned pop music's bible the *New Musical Express* and now staged showbusiness and sporting dinners. Through them he had come to know John Gordon, who ran bingo and dance halls in the Midlands. Gordon was a director of West Bromwich Albion and Kinn told me they were about to dismiss their manager, Ron Wylie, and would I be interested in the job? I was not, though I was intrigued, since West Brom's chairman was Bert Millichip, who was also chairman of the FA. His football club was clearly engaged in tapping up a manager while the incumbent was still in post. The job went to John Giles, who returned to The Hawthorns for a second spell.

That summer, I took a phone call from Dave Sexton, who was managing the England under-21 side in the Soviet Union. He rang me on behalf of Jim Gregory, the chairman of Queens Park Rangers.

Having taken the club to fifth in the First Division, Terry Venables had left to become manager of Barcelona.

Dave told me not to be worried by Gregory's tough reputation. 'He's a good man, you'll enjoy working for him and he'll look after you.' I met Gregory at his headquarters, Alton House, on the A3. I went with Maureen, who got on famously with Jim Gregory's wife, the two of them regularly discussing different ways of cooking and, strangely, frying different kinds of fish. Gregory wanted me to take a dual role with Gordon Jago, who had managed Queens Park Rangers and promoted them to the First Division in 1973 before going to Florida to take charge of Tampa Bay Rowdies.

Jim's idea was that I would be the manager at Loftus Road while Gordon would be the general manager. I was dubious about how the relationship between Gordon and I would work in practice, although the system of a head coach working with a sporting director was already widely used in Europe. I asked Jim how he thought the pairing would play out. 'You will have the team,' he said. 'And, if you want something, you can ask Gordon, although he may be on the golf course. He'll give you his advice, but he won't tell you what to do.' Gordon would be purely a sounding board. Neither of us took the offer. Gordon decided to return to America and manage in Dallas while I was too settled in Luton to risk changing jobs.

My second full season at Luton was a strange one. There was a core of consistency in the team – nine players took part in thirty-four games or more in a 42-game season. Luton rose from eighteenth to sixth in Division Two, coming within four points of promotion. Nobody could doubt our improvement.

Luton were top of the table by early November. We had set a marker. Mick Saxby, whom we had signed from Mansfield for £200,000, had settled in at centre-back. Grealish (Ireland), Donaghy (Northern Ireland) and Paul Price (Wales) were maintaining international places. When we signed Saxby, we had no idea that Mansfield's manager, Billy Bingham, was about to be sacked. However, Billy, a wily character, was aware he was soon to be surplus to requirements at Field Mill and was more than happy to push the deal through so that Mansfield would have the money to pay up his own contract. Billy would not remain unemployed for long and was appointed manager of Northern Ireland, taking them to two World Cup tournaments.

Luton were being tipped for big things. On New Year's Day 1980, we faced Chelsea, jointly managed by Geoff Hurst and Bobby Gould. Despite the icy conditions, the biggest crowd of the season – over 19,000 – crammed into Kenilworth Road. They witnessed a ballet on ice on a rock-hard, slippery pitch. The players of both sides gave a fabulous display of fast, exciting football. There were errors, thrills and spills in a 3–3 draw. Ricky Hill scored a sizzler and Clive Walker, a speedy wide winger, was outstanding for Chelsea.

Chelsea would gallingly miss out on promotion on goal difference to Birmingham, who went up with Sunderland and Leicester. Luton were four points behind, but we were moving upwards, something the board recognised.

The following season I received a call from Dennis Roach, one of the first football agents, who had formed a company called PRO with offices in St Albans. He told me that Jim Smith, who was managing Birmingham, had had to pull out of a scouting mission to Zaragoza to see a Yugoslav footballer who might interest us: a defensive midfielder who was comfortable on the ball. His name was Radomir Antić and he would cost only £50,000.

Roach's firm used Bertie Mee, who had managed Arsenal to the Double, and Bob Wilson as consultants – a clever move to give his company some credibility. Roach also had a guy working for him called Sava Popovic, a multi-lingual Yugoslav with a keen interest in football. Sava had married an Englishwoman, lived in St Albans and had many links around the Balkans, which in 1980 were still

Communist-controlled. Apart from his chain-smoking, I enjoyed Sava's company, his knowledge and wide array of contacts, which Roach shrewdly utilised.

I travelled with Sava to Zaragoza for the Sunday game. I was massively impressed with the way Antić came out, never wasting possession and always seeking the return pass to play the killer ball that his acute vision had spotted. I was so taken with Antić, I asked Sava if I could meet Raddy that night and delay our departure by another day. A late-night meeting was hastily set up at Antić's apartment. His charming wife, Vera, made us sandwiches and we talked for one-and-a-half hours. In those ninety minutes, I drew several conclusions: Raddy was both intelligent and keen to come to England. He also made attempts to speak English and seemed a happy, family man with two young children.

Raddy had played football in Yugoslavia, Turkey and Spain and it was clear he fancied a new adventure. His wife was supportive. The following morning at the airport, I spotted a football magazine at the bookstall. On the cover was an action shot of this tall, handsome Yugoslav playing for Zaragoza. If I needed any convincing to do the deal, this was it. Perhaps this was a message from above, delivered via a bookstall.

We agreed the fee with Zaragoza and Raddy asked me if he could drive his family from Belgrade, where he was sorting out family commitments, to Luton – a distance of 1,350 miles. I was a little bit anxious and even more anxious when I received another message that he would be arriving a week late for pre-season training. He had been involved in a collision near Paris and his daughter, Ana, had suffered an injury to her ear that required hospital treatment. I told him not to worry and any fears were allayed when he came in for training. The players embraced him immediately, impressed by his ability and his personality. In the months since we had met in Zaragoza, Raddy had also worked hard on his English.

Sometimes in football, you hit upon a diamond. Raddy Antić glittered. He arranged his own property in Harpenden, he met the schools' welfare officer himself and organised schooling for his children, Ana and Dusan, who at that stage spoke little English. Raddy gave brilliant service. He delighted the fans with his skills, embraced our culture and after three seasons knew all about beer and fish and chips. Above all, he was an absolute gentleman.

On a couple of Fridays, disappointed he had not made the starting XI, Raddy would come to see me in my office to express his discontent. At the time, Luton were on a winning run, the players were high on confidence and there was a structure and balance to the team. Raddy was also coming back from injury. I had to explain the importance of patience, but I hoped he would understand. We would have twenty minutes of discussion in which he would say: 'Whenever I play, I always score or make a goal. Why do I not play?' As he left, he would never slam the door but turn to say: 'Good luck tomorrow, boss. Let's hope we win.'

Raddy would play vital games for us, scoring goals, making chances, culminating in his 86th-minute winner at Manchester City, which kept Luton afloat in the top league. Raddy will always be remembered at Kenilworth Road for that goal, but his overall contribution was much, much more than this.

The young players learned so much from him, in particular studying how he could produce the reverse pass with such control and accuracy. I admired him as a man and a player. By the time he left Luton in 1984, his children could speak fluent English. His son, Dusan, became an outstanding linguist, so much so that he spoke English without a trace of an accent.

After a spell at Partizan Belgrade, Raddy returned to Spain to manage Zaragoza, where he showed a flair for coaching. His managerial career would become a whirlwind. In March 1991, he succeeded Alfredo Di Stéfano as manager of Real Madrid. However, the following January, Raddy was sacked despite the fact that Real Madrid were seven points clear at the top of La Liga and an arrogant Leo Beenhakker, who had been employed as the club's sporting director, slid into the manager's chair. The lead evaporated and the title was lost to Barcelona.

After a spell at Oviedo, Raddy took over at Atlético Madrid, who the previous season had avoided relegation on the final day. In his first season, Raddy took Atlético to a league and cup Double, breaking the twelve-year stranglehold Barcelona and Real Madrid had imposed on La Liga.

He invited Maureen and I to the final of the Copa del Rey, in which Barcelona were beaten 1–0 at La Romareda in Zaragoza, the city and the stadium where I had first seen him play. Diego Simeone, who was to become Atlético's manager, and Milinko Pantic, who scored the winner in extra time, both played superbly. At the post-match banquet, I met Atlético's notorious president, Jesús Gil, who before appointing Raddy had appointed seventeen managers in seven years, including Ron Atkinson and Colin Addison. When Antić won Atlético the title, Gil celebrated by riding through the streets of Madrid on an elephant.

He was a major property developer who had promoted the resort of Marbella with big investments and sponsorship. Jesús was a big, overpowering hulk of a man with many enemies in Spain due to his ruthless approach to business that would see him briefly imprisoned on corruption charges. Six years later, Maureen and I went to his Marbella estate agents' Gilmar, who directed us to buy a small plot of land, where we eventually built a holiday retreat in Elviria, just outside the resort on the road to Fuengirola.

When Barcelona came calling, Raddy Antić became the first man to manage Spain's Big Three and only the second to manage at the Nou Camp and the Bernabéu. At Barcelona, he brought on Carles Puyol by changing his position and encouraged the talents of a young Andrés Iniesta. Throughout his triumphs in Spain, Raddy would always speak warmly about his 'education at Luton'.

Raddy, who managed Serbia in the 2010 World Cup in South Africa, took the break-up of Yugoslavia very badly. He was unforgiving of Croatia's role in the civil war. At our club, it was an unwritten rule that we never discussed politics, religion or money to prevent jealousies and cliques, but Raddy always wanted to tell me how badly his fellow countrymen had been treated.

The last time I saw Raddy and Vera was in December 2019 at a reunion at Luton Hoo, a spectacular country-house hotel that has been the backdrop for every kind of film. His death from pancreatic cancer five months later left me upset beyond words. Among the tributes, Atlético Madrid gave him a permanent seat with his name on it in the technical area of their wonderful new Metropolitano Stadium.

Atlético Madrid was a club where Raddy Antić was adored beyond measure. I was commentating on the 2014 Champions League final in Lisbon between Atlético and Real Madrid and we met for coffee in the lobby of our hotel. Afterwards, we decided to go for a walk to the El Corte Inglés department store. The journey was impossible. The moment we left the hotel, he was confronted by supporters wearing red and white and chanting his name. He was a hero to them and he was a hero at Luton. He epitomised all I ever loved about football.

Raddy's first season at Luton began at West Ham a few months after they had won the 1980 FA Cup. Just to increase the pressure, we arrived late at Upton Park. The team bus had become stranded amid awful traffic on Green Street close to the ground. Cars were parked haphazardly amid the brightly coloured garment stalls and the displays of fruit and vegetables typical of the Asian community who lived in that corner of east London.

I quickly scribbled down the team sheet and one of our staff ran ahead of the bus so we could escape a fine. Breathlessly, the sheet was delivered to the referee right on the button at 2.30 p.m. The players changed on the bus, which arrived minutes later. With no time to prepare, we beat the odds and overcame West Ham 2–1. All three goals were penalties. West Ham's Ray Stewart, who scored seventy-nine penalties in his career, and David Moss were sure shots from twelve yards. Some 28,000 saw our victory over the team that nine months later would be promoted as champions.

Steve White, somewhat uncoordinated but a willing runner, had been signed from Bristol Rovers as our new centre-forward. He had impressed me with his drive, a strong mental attitude and, most importantly, his knack of finding the net. White's physicality helped Brian Stein find spaces and allowed David Moss to isolate full-backs and get into goalscoring positions. Both scored nineteen that season. With three matches remaining of that season, Luton were fifth, one point behind Blackburn in the final promotion place but with a game in hand.

The first of those, at home to Oldham, was lost 2–1. I missed that game with a recurrence of my back trouble, spasms that left me unable to walk, and was in traction at the Luton and Dunstable Hospital. Rather embarrassingly, I had to do an interview with Jim Rosenthal from my hospital bed. Luton were still fifth when I returned to my desk, two points behind Swansea in fourth. On the Monday night we would play each other in south Wales, each knowing that a win at the Vetch Field would propel us into the third and final promotion place with one match remaining.

John Toshack had energised Swansea with some fine, battle-hardened signings, bringing Alan Curtis back from Leeds, signing Leighton James from Burnley and Tommy Craig from Newcastle. John Charles's nephew, Jeremy, led the attack with Curtis. Robbie James ran the midfield as Swansea were promoted from the Fourth to the First Division. All were internationals.

We responded to Swansea's early two-goal lead with strikes from Ricky Hill in front of 21,000 but were distraught when a stunning Antić strike was disallowed by the linesman. Both linesmen were from Wales and the man who had disallowed it was from Merthyr, thirty miles away. He judged that David Moss, while not interfering with play, was offside.

The following day, I took a call from the Arsenal manager, Terry Neill, who had been at the game, scouting. He complimented us on our play, adding: 'It was a crazy decision that robbed you of a win. You deserved it; your performance was outstanding.'

The result had taken Swansea above Blackburn on goal difference. Luton's only path to promotion was to beat Bolton at Burnden Park and hope Swansea and Blackburn lost at Preston and Bristol Rovers. It was an improbable equation.

However, in a performance of great self-belief and determination, we scored three second-half goals through Stein, White and Stephens. On reaching the dressing room, our hopes turned to desolation on hearing the other results and I did my best to console the fallen faces. Swansea and Blackburn had both won. Drinks on the bus quelled the pain a little, though I shed a tear when I got home. I challenged myself to inform the players how proud I was of them and tell them that next season we would win the damn league.

CHAPTER 8

'YOU ROBBED US, YOU CHEATING BASTARDS'

We won the damn league. We were promoted with four matches to spare, won many friends and finished clear champions. It was a golden season.

The platform for promotion was laid on a post-season trip to Florida that might have turned into a wake, given the disappointment we had endured at Bolton. Instead, the squad bonded on Fort Lauderdale's Atlantic beaches and we were invited to watch the local club, whose attack was led by Gerd Müller, in the North American Soccer League.

Ian Greaves, who had managed Bolton and was now in charge at Oxford, provided the half-time television analysis. He was facing the camera with his back to the pitch, when there was a huge explosion. Greaves spun round. 'What the fuck was that?' he exclaimed live on air. He was clearly not used to the half-time entertainment in the NASL, which was rather different from what he was used to at Burnden Park or the Manor Ground. It consisted of 'Dynamite Dick' exploding out of a coffin that had been lain on the centre circle. Other attractions included parading elephants and fire engines emerging from the tunnel and a klaxon sounding whenever the goalkeeper kicked high into the sky. Football was still party time in the United States.

There was plenty of partying on Miami's beaches. At the hotel, we were befriended by a guy who invited us to a nightclub, where we were served by women wearing wigs that changed colour with the lights. Our friend suggested we accompany him to a crowded apartment where we continued drinking until three in the morning. Suddenly, our friend suggested that it might be a good idea if we left immediately. When we encountered him the next day, he introduced himself as a member of the FBI and explained the apartment was about to be busted for drugs.

West Bromwich Albion were with us in Miami, where their manager, Ron Atkinson, was told he was to be the new manager of Manchester United. Ron informed us that Miami was not 'the real America' and if we wanted to experience that we should travel inland. Twenty miles from Miami we discovered 'the real America' in the shape of a bar that was little more than a shack populated by rednecks and Vietnam vets. Outside was a kind of rodeo with a bucking bronco. Inside, the regulars stared at us in silence from the moment we went to the bar to the moment, not long afterwards, when we decided we had seen enough of the real America.

Before we set off for Florida, there was an awkward incident that I was able to turn to Luton's advantage. At an end-of-season drinks party, Paddy Grealish had spoken out of turn to Charlotte, the chairman's wife. The players were aware of the incident but decided to stick together and not tell me. A week later, I received a well-composed letter from Dennis Mortimer, who wished me and the players a good summer and thanked us for an entertaining season. Dennis had a habit of underlining in green ink any message he wanted me to take on board. The part of the neatly typed message he underlined was: 'It may be time to think of moving on one or two marginals; maybe Grealish could be surplus if you get a satisfactory trade.' It was only then I found out what had happened. It was a great shame. Paddy had overstepped the mark after a few drinks that night and had lost control. There could be no excuses.

The consequences of this event were of massive benefit to Luton

Town. We concluded a swap deal with Brighton for Brian Horton, who was to be my skipper for three seasons at Kenilworth Road.

Brighton had already made a tentative enquiry for Paddy Grealish. Peter Taylor had managed Brighton before joining Brian Clough at Nottingham Forest in the summer of 1976. Indeed, he had once invited Maureen and me to his flat on Brighton's promenade and asked if I would be interested in working for him. I was then a coach at Luton, working under Harry Haslam, and I had told Dennis Mortimer that I would be going to Brighton at the weekend to see Peter Taylor who was a lifelong friend. Mortimer's reply was: 'Well, they're a very good club, David, I think you should be quite interested in that.' I was staggered. I turned down the chance to go to Brighton.

Now, I phoned Peter to ask him about Brian Horton, whom he had signed from Port Vale. Brian had come up the hard way; rejected by Walsall as a youngster, he had combined playing non-league football at Hednesford with working on a building site. Brian had spent six years at Port Vale and had captained Brighton from the Third to the First Division. He was very well liked at the Goldstone Ground. Whenever I asked Peter about a player, the reply was always decisive. He could either play or he could not. Peter said Horton could play.

We did the deal and Brian was nothing less than a revelation, cajoling his players, controlling the midfield, leading by example and pinging those precise passes to our outside left, David Moss. With Horton flanked by Ricky Hill and Raddy Antić in midfield, Luton got off to a flyer with three successive wins. The second was the first game played on Queens Park Rangers' artificial pitch.

Under Terry Venables's management, Loftus Road would become the first stadium in England to install an artificial pitch. Three other clubs, including Luton, were to use them before the revolution came to a full stop. I would be on the FA committee that outlawed this kind of surface.

This was the first season of three points for a win, giving clubs a greater incentive not to shut up shop or take a draw. I had a settled team. Only two players had left Luton in the summer. Paul Price went to Tottenham for £250,000, where he would be part of the side that beat Queens Park Rangers to retain the FA Cup. Paul signed his contract in the Tottenham offices, which were in a house on the High Road. The office of Alan Jones, the Spurs secretary, was an untidy shambles with papers everywhere.

The other departure was Alan West, a thoroughly nice guy and a top professional who had been a regular in Luton's midfield. He was sold to Millwall for £45,000. He was a clever passer of a ball. I don't think I ever saw him make a bad tackle. Alan had always been one of the lads in his early years at Luton, but his attitude to life changed when he visited his wife's family in New Zealand when he was twenty-five. He told me he suddenly felt drawn towards Christ. Years later, Alan went into the church. He became a minister at the Luton Christian Fellowship and is now the club's chaplain. Years before, I had been friends with Peter Knowles, whom I had met at England youth trials. He had broken through to the first team at Wolverhampton Wanderers when a teenager. He walked out of the game to become a Jehovah's Witness and stack shelves in the local supermarket.

In October, our centre-half, Mike Saxby, suffered what became a career-ending knee problem in the 1–0 win over Crystal Palace. Twenty-year-old Clive Goodyear pulled on the No. 5 shirt and would go on to win the 1988 FA Cup final with Wimbledon.

We had some tremendous wins. One of the highlights was a 6–0 victory over Grimsby, in which Steve White scored four. The tone was set in September with a 4–1 win over our big rivals, Watford, a scoreline Luton had not bettered against Watford since September 1929, when both clubs were in the Third Division South. In my time at Luton, our shorter game of push and run and making space off the ball was successful against their direct approach. In the ten games we played against Watford, we won seven.

Graham Taylor was gracious in defeat but privately hurting. Graham was in the process of taking Watford from the Fourth to the First Division. He had done wonderfully well at Lincoln before Elton John lured him to Vicarage Road. He was perhaps lucky to get the job since Watford had interviewed Bobby Moore, who was convinced he had been promised the position. Graham became the beneficiary of the funds Elton was prepared to give the club.

We went top after the win over Watford and stayed there. On 5 December, we drew 2–2 at Shrewsbury. We were eight points clear of Oldham and Watford at the top of the Second Division. In the next six weeks we would play one match, a 3–1 win at Norwich. The winter of 1981/82 was so severe that a sports travel agent told me that not only was it warmer in Iceland, but he could also arrange a friendly against the national team. There was so little football to cover and the idea of going to Iceland for warm weather training so absurd that the *Daily Telegraph* sent one of its reporters, Michael Calvin, to cover the trip.

We did get a game against Iceland, on an artificial pitch in Reykjavik, which we won, 2–0. The final quarter of an hour will never be forgotten by anyone who was there. A cold front of frozen Arctic air swept over the open terraces of the stadium. Ricky Hill finished the game with little icicles on his goatee beard. We did not change at the ground but went back to the hotel and on the minibus the language was as blue as some of the players' skin.

The long lay-off ensured a frantic end to the season. Between 3 March and 12 April, Luton played ten league games in forty-one days. Then came the 3–2 win over Newcastle. Shorn of Moss and

Hill, who were both injured, we saw Newcastle, managed by Arthur Cox, take a two-goal lead. We stormed back with referee Alan Seville awarding us two penalties in the eighty-first and eighty-fifth minute, which Brian Stein converted to compete his hat-trick and send the fans at Kenilworth Road wild. On the final whistle, they carried Stein shoulder high off the pitch.

Amid all the excitement of a win that put us six points clear of Watford in second, Arthur Cox appeared at our dressing-room door, shouting: 'You fucking robbed us!' He had not shaken my hand at the final whistle, one of only two managers not to do so in my career. The other was Len Ashurst in the final match of that season, although this was probably more do with the shock that our 3–2 win at Ninian Park had relegated Cardiff to the Third Division. He was a decent man.

We told Arthur to go away and calm down, but he returned fifteen minutes later, accompanied by a steward, still shouting: 'You robbed us, you cheating bastards!' As he was led away, the explanation became clear. During the game, someone had got into the away dressing room and stolen the Newcastle players' money, watches and jewellery. The police were called, but we never found the thief. During the game, Newcastle had had a player taken off because of injury and they unlocked the dressing-room door to let him in. The player went through another door to the communal bath, but the steward did not lock the door after him.

Arthur Cox resigned as Newcastle manager after winning them promotion in 1984 and joined Derby, where he worked for the media baron Robert Maxwell. I had a more mellow conversation with him in his office, which was reached through the narrow corridors of the Baseball Ground. He pointed to a phone on his desk and said: 'That phone is purely for Maxwell. Only he ever rings on that number. Nobody else has it.' He enjoyed working in the reflected charisma that Maxwell then generated. He asked me about the availability of

David Moss. I turned him down. He leaned over and said: 'If this appears in the papers, it won't be from me.' Later, I saw an article in the transfer gossip pages suggesting Derby were looking to sign David Moss. It certainly had not come from me.

The flare-up did not impede our progress to the title, which was sealed by a 3–2 win over the FA Cup finalists Queens Park Rangers. What a season. Donaghy, Stein, Stephens and White were ever-present and Horton was the leader. Stein scored twenty-one goals, White eighteen and Moss fifteen. Luton scored eighty-six in total and finished with eighty-eight points, eight clear of Watford. Unforgettable.

It was not ever thus. However memorable the journey, there had been bumps in the road in my two-and-a-half years. Not long into my tenure, I was sitting in the directors' box during the first half. I was watching a frustrating period of poor play when a well-dressed woman, sitting a few feet away, blurted out purposefully: 'They don't know what they're doing. They don't look fit either.' Depressed at the state of our performance, I told her to shut up. On the Monday, her husband, Richard Larkinson, a well-heeled vice-president of Luton Town and an investor in the club, wrote a pointed letter to the club's chief executive, John Smith, threatening to withdraw his support.

John suggested we offer an immediate apology and insisted I visited his home to say sorry in person. At the time, I thought this an outrageous suggestion, but Luton were not playing well and I did not want to fall foul of John, who had been placed in a powerful position by Dennis Mortimer.

Smith had been recruited from Leicester on my recommendation when the chairman had asked me who I felt were the best administrators to help Luton move forward. The club had provided him with a lovely house in Welwyn, where he paid a peppercorn rent on the understanding from the board he would eventually purchase it. John was a smart operator, well-educated and well thought of in football circles, though he could have a supercilious air. After leaving Leyton Orient for Leicester, he had taken elocution lessons.

However, the principle of keeping the peace was one I had to respect as I travelled with John to meet Mr and Mrs Larkinson at their smart, detached house in Letchworth. Mr Larkinson was a decent man who had made his money from salvage and scrap metal. He was portly, well-dressed and possessed a polished accent. He had the air of a cricket umpire on a village green. After a convivial hour, we shook hands and he continued to be an investor in the club.

CHAPTER 9

'GET US A GOAL'

Having enjoyed the summer accolades, it was time to get ready for the biggest challenge of my managerial career. It had been twenty-three years since Luton Town survived a season in the First Division, the season they met Nottingham Forest in the FA Cup final. It was a summer of clandestine phone calls with the voices on the other end wondering if I could be tempted away from Luton. However, the children were settled at school and Maureen's father had just retired from his greengrocers shop. We lived in Lancaster Avenue for seventeen years while our children grew up. Our son, Jonathon, encouraged by a kind Luton director, Mr Banks, who was from a family of seed merchants, won an open scholarship to Bedford School. What followed was a glittering academic career, a first at Oxford and medical school. He is now a highly respected burns and reconstructive surgeon.

The bungalow was our second in Luton. We had moved from the one near the hospital to one adjoining Lancaster Avenue Recreation Ground. Years later, the young Monty Panesar would come to the park and practise his left-arm spin by bowling to a single stump with his friends looking on. He became a Luton supporter.

My biggest decision centred on our requirements for Division One. In February 1981, I had been to watch an England under-18 team play Northern Ireland at Walsall and I had been excited by the performance of a small forward from Charlton who scored the only goal.

Paul Walsh was a twister and a turner with fine control. Any tall, unathletic centre-half would find him a handful to mark. To get him out of Charlton, I would have to sacrifice our centre-forward, Steve White. He had scored eighteen vital goals in our title win and was a strong, sensitive character. Alan Mullery had resigned as Charlton manager and had been succeeded by his assistant, Ken Craggs. He found himself working for a young, egotistical chairman, Mark Hulyer, who had bought the club aged twenty-eight but, crucially for Charlton's future, did not own the ground. Within two years, Charlton would be in administration; within three, they would have left The Valley for Selhurst Park. Charlton's mismanagement would cost them twenty-one years away from their home before their magnificent supporters took them back to The Valley.

Hulyer was keen on the transfer and insisted on Steve White as a replacement. Our attempts to do a deal had all the hallmarks of a Brian Rix farce, involving as it did two bedrooms at the Ritz Hotel. My chief executive, John Smith, wanted to make a big impression and he booked a suite with two bedrooms leading off from the lounge. In one room was the Luton delegation, including me and Steve White. In the other were the Charlton officials with Paul Walsh. Steve White was, initially, oblivious to what was happening. He was told Charlton wanted to buy him and we had agreed a price. He did not know that, unless he agreed to the move, we could not sign Walsh, who was waiting patiently in the other room.

White, not unnaturally, smelt a rat. Halfway through our talks, he realised he would be going as the replacement for Walsh and that the deal hinged on him. He was very unhappy that I was prepared to let him leave Luton. He was, however, able to drive a hard bargain with his new employers and he deserved a decent deal. We paid Charlton £250,000 plus Steve to get Walsh to Luton in what proved to be a highly successful exchange. Charlton spent the money on buying Allan Simonsen, the former European footballer of the year, from Barcelona. They soon discovered they could not afford his wages.

Walsh, however, flourished and within two years he would be signed by Liverpool. In his first season in the highest grade, he struck two outstanding hat-tricks against Notts County and Swansea. His second goal, in the 5–3 win over Notts County in September, was voted Goal of the Season.

Part of your job as a manager is to protect your players. I was woken up at two o'clock on a Sunday morning by a phone call from Dunstable Police Station to tell me they had one of my players in a cell and that he wished to talk to me. Paul Walsh had been allowed two phone calls and this was one of them. The other had been to his girlfriend, but there had been no response.

My star striker had been arrested for damaging a glass door of a nightclub called Cinderella Rockerfella because one of his party had been refused entry for not wearing a tie. While I was waiting for over an hour at Dunstable Police Station to see Paul, I overheard the desk sergeant saying to his colleague: 'He can wait, that's no inconvenience to him, that's what he's well paid for.' Once more I sensed the jealousy, perhaps mixed in with the antisemitic bias, that I was always able to detect.

Because the police had kept Paul's trousers, shoes and socks as evidence while they examined some shards of glass, I brought him a blanket from my car and drove him back to his digs. Paul Walsh was fined for his indiscretion, but I remember a confident and skilled footballer who delighted thousands.

You should never generalise. I am aware the vast majority of policemen are brave, hard-working and fair but my view of the police has been coloured by my experiences. I found them unconcerned and sometimes insensitive. As I later found out to my cost, some were in the pay of tabloid newspapers in exchange for leaked information.

At the start of the season, I had been invited to Stamford Bridge to speak at the launch of the 1982/83 edition of the *Rothmans Football Yearbook*. I said: 'In previous seasons, the nearest Luton had come to the Liverpools of this world was on page 230 of the yearbook. Now, we'll be playing them.'

Our first three away games took us to White Hart Lane, home of the FA Cup holders, Villa Park, home of the European Cup winners, and Anfield, home of the league champions. We approached these stadia with a mixture of awe and pride.

We drew 2–2 against Tottenham after Gary Mabbutt, playing his first game for Spurs, had scored in the third minute. Months before, I had met Gary and his father, Ray, at the Reading Post House but could not get the deal with Bristol Rovers over the line. I always blamed John Smith for this as he refused to give in to his father's request for help with Gary's accommodation.

Our third game, the 5–3 defeat of Notts County, gave us our first win. Walsh dazzled. The Stein–Walsh partnership, nimble, quick and creative, underpinned by a tough streak, was giving defenders difficulties with their movement. If Stein came short, Walsh would look long. If Walsh came short, Stein would look long. However, they both had an unusual quality: they could both dribble past defenders. I loved a dribbler.

Only once did the partnership threaten to come apart. We were at West Ham when Walsh denied Stein a pass when Brian was better placed. It triggered a terrible, racially charged argument as they came off the field, which developed further in the communal baths. Fortunately, Brian Horton and two others separated them, telling them to calm down and grow up only for it to erupt again.

I addressed the team in the dressing room and said this was not becoming of a First Division football club. 'If this gets out, I will be the most disappointed man in the country,' I told them. 'We must keep this in house.' It never appeared in the press, something I am proud of.

What made it likely to get out was the design of the dressing rooms at Upton Park. Spectators came down from the stands along a walkway and you could hear what was going on in the dressing rooms through glass windows. You might not be able to hear every word, but you would be aware that inside there was a commotion going on. The rift was eventually patched up. Years later, the two men talked it through amicably on the golf course. Paul tells me he deeply regrets what he said on that afternoon in east London.

On 11 September, after an overnight stay at Bollington Manor near Chester, we travelled to Liverpool. Despite a 4–1 defeat at Villa Park three days before, we were not fazed when we saw the 'This is Anfield' sign in the tunnel. However, our goalkeeper, Jake Findlay, was injured in the first half and our full-back, Kirk Stephens, volunteered to put on the gloves. This was an age when only one player was employed as a substitute and it would almost never be the keeper.

However, during the interval, Kirk asked to be relieved of his goalkeeping duties. The Kop had been tormenting him with songs from the pop singer Shakin' Stevens, and the joke was becoming too much. Mal Donaghy volunteered to take the gloves and Raddy Antić came on as substitute. Luton were 2–1 down. We did not stop attacking. David Moss met a long ball on the half-volley to chip past Bruce Grobbelaar then he threaded through Brian Stein, who took the ball past the Liverpool keeper to give Luton a wildly improbable lead.

We held on to it until fourteen minutes from time when Craig Johnston, brought on for Kenny Dalglish, scored the sixth goal of the game to level it at 3–3. Each of our goalkeepers had conceded once. Stein and Walsh had tormented Liverpool's central defensive pairing of Alan Hansen and Mark Lawrenson. The latter, the smoothest of centre-backs, remarked that we had played like Liverpool.

After the game, I was invited into Anfield's inner sanctum. Inside the Boot Room, Bob Paisley, Roy Evans and Ronnie Moran were holding court, joined by Tom Saunders, a former schoolmaster who was highly valued for the work he did with Liverpool's youth teams and for his behind-the-scenes recruitment. The room was tiny. On the walls were pin-ups and photographs of famous footballers. There was a crate of beer on the floor. It was quite an experience to have twenty minutes in such company. When I got on the coach, however, I realised the four of them had gained plenty of information about my players' backgrounds and characters, and I had learned almost nothing from them about Liverpool. They were brilliant at coaxing information from their guests as they patronised them. The next time Luton went to Anfield, we would lose 6–0.

Winning games in Division One would prove increasingly difficult. After beating Birmingham 3–2 at St Andrew's in October, we did not win a match for two months. There was a 3–1 victory over Manchester City in December followed by a 1–0 Christmas win against Watford, who were to finish runners-up to Liverpool. West Ham were beaten, 3–2, at Upton Park in January. Every victory provided a breathing space.

In early April, I had decided to make another signing from Charlton: a 6ft 2in. nineteen-year-old centre-half called Paul Elliott. He possessed the aerial dominance I believed Luton needed and he certainly had a change of pace. Paul made a nervous start in the First Division, but once he settled down, the £100,000 fee proved excellent value.

Elliott's baptism was a rough one; a 5–2 defeat by the 'enemy' – Watford. At half-time, the scores were level at 2–2, but Raddy Antić was sent off by the showy Devonian referee, Les Shapter, who I always thought considered himself more important than the game. It was the first time Watford had beaten us in nine attempts and only goal difference prevented us from going bottom of Division One. I made another signing, Trevor Aylott, a powerful front man who cost £150,000, from Millwall, and we ploughed on. After one game at Luton when I had not picked her husband, his wife approached me in the car park and demanded to know why Trevor was not playing. Wives are a factor in the dressing room. They can be ambitious for their husbands and sensitive to their disappointments.

A Paul Walsh hat-trick on 23 April gave us a 3–1 win over Swansea, the team that two years before had beaten us to promotion and who were now falling deeper into trouble. Our win at Kenilworth Road left the Welsh club bottom of the table and was a major factor in their subsequent relegation. Swansea could not sustain the tough theatre of the top league without continued financial backing. By 1983, they were rumoured to be £2 million in debt. Swansea's relegation cost John Toshack the chance of succeeding Bob Paisley as Liverpool manager.

In 1985, he was approached by the agent Tony Stephens, acting on behalf of Real Sociedad. I received a similar approach and was asked to go to a meeting at the Gatwick Airport Hotel to meet Stephens and a representative of the Basque club. Purely out of curiosity, I accepted the invitation, as did John Hollins, who was then Chelsea's first-team coach. I was still well ensconced at Luton and this lack of enthusiasm must have been obvious in what I would hesitate to call an interview. The prospect of going to Spain and the family turbulence that would have come with it was too much.

John Hollins succeeded John Neal as Chelsea manager that summer. John Toshack, who after a year at Sporting Lisbon already spoke Portuguese and would find Spanish easy, took over at Real Sociedad. Toshack's managerial career became a lesson in geography. A highly intelligent man, he would spend thirteen years managing various clubs in Spain and his journey would take him to Italy, Turkey, Morocco and finally Iran.

With three games remaining, Luton were sixteenth with a game in hand. We were four places and two points off a relegation spot.

The shock was to come on Saturday 7 May at home to Everton. Three points would probably have made us safe. Instead, chasing the game in the second half, we caved in to lose 5–1. David Moss's craft had given us the lead, but we were 2–1 down at the interval. Trying to force an equaliser exposed too many gaps and we were humbled.

Worse was to follow when we reached the dressing room. All the teams around us had won. Sunderland had beaten Arsenal at Highbury. Birmingham had beaten Tottenham and Coventry had beaten Stoke. Manchester City had won at Brighton to relegate them while Swansea had lost at Old Trafford to join them in the Second Division. The table showed that in ninety minutes, Luton had dropped from sixteenth to twentieth and now occupied the final relegation position.

We had two games left, both in Manchester. The first was at Old Trafford on Monday 9 May. Then we finished the season at Maine Road five days later. That Sunday was the most difficult of my career. The players arrived at Kenilworth Road for a warm-down and a bath, but I knew their greatest challenge would be a mental one. Would we have the energy, the belief, the sheer guts to go to United and then City and win? To further complicate matters, I had promised months before to send a team to Vicarage Road on the Tuesday for a testimonial for the Watford striker Ross Jenkins. Luton would not be paid a fee, but I had agreed to the game because I was anxious to tone down the hostility between the two sets of supporters.

I had an hour with my coaching staff and my captain, Brian Horton, on the Sunday morning. We decided to blood two youngsters at Old Trafford – Ray Daniel and Garry Parker. It was a decision Brian fundamentally disagreed with. Nearly 40,000 saw us beaten 3–0 by a Manchester United side that a few weeks later would win the FA Cup. It was a defeat half-expected, the kind of result we had imagined in our private thoughts. We were staking everything on the final-day result.

The Ross Jenkins testimonial was a strange occasion. The team was taunted by a moronic element among the Watford fans who told us we were 'going down, down, going down'. The one important aspect of a game that we lost, 4–0, was that we could give the injured Brian Stein a run-out to assess his fitness before the game at Maine Road. At half-time, Graham Taylor took a microphone to the centre circle and addressed the crowd. He berated the taunters, telling them that no other team, under the circumstances Luton were facing, would have kept their promise to play the game.

The next day, a tired group trudged to Henlow Grange, a Georgian manor house in Bedfordshire that was now a spa and hotel. There, the squad, who had played three games in four days, could relax, have a massage, see a psychologist or do some yoga. We laid down on our backs in a circle while soft music played. We were asked to close our eyes and visualise pebbles falling into a still lake.

My poor wife, Maureen, was suffering, too. On the Friday, as we were about to set off for our hotel, she received a call that her father had died. She had been religiously nursing and feeding him with the help of carers for many months. Jonathon and Joanne, who were thirteen and ten, had to console her while I took the team to Tillington Hall in Staffordshire. The requirement on the Friday night dinner was to stifle nerves and put on the bravest of faces. The rallying call was brief. There was no need for a Churchillian speech. I said: 'We have put ourselves in this position and now we must pull ourselves out of it. It can be done.'

The choice of Tillington Hall was a wise one. It was about an hour from Maine Road – further from Manchester than we would normally have stayed. However, it meant that as we drove steadily up the M6, we could read the telegrams and other messages of goodwill and see the flood of Luton supporters, their orange scarves fluttering from their car windows, their horns blaring, accompanying us north. Among the music on the bus, I can recall 'True' by Spandau Ballet, which was then No. 1 in the charts. We did not feel alone.

When we arrived at Maine Road at 1.45 p.m., the ground was already packed. The result would decide the fate of both clubs, although it was not quite winner takes all. Luton's only route to survival was to win the game. Manchester City, with one point more, could stay up with a draw. My thoughts churned between those of Maureen at home and the realisation that, if we failed to win, all the work that had taken Luton to the top flight would count for nothing. My players; my future.

The game became a blur. Our goalkeeper, Tony Godden, on loan from West Bromwich Albion because Jake Findlay had fractured his thumb, held firm. Elliott, at centre-back, was strong. Aylott took the weight up front. Manchester City, spurred on by the majority of the 43,000 crowd, could not break through.

With time running out and City knowing a draw was good enough, I subbed Wayne Turner, a local Luton boy, for the greater skills of Raddy Antić. He said later that my only words to him as I sent him on to the pitch were: 'Get us a goal.' I cannot recall what I said. By now, I was watching in a semi-stupor, praying that someone, perhaps God himself, would smile upon us. Then it happened. Stein's cross, delivered under pressure from the right, was punched clear by the Manchester City goalkeeper, Alex Williams. The ball fell to Antić on the edge of the area, who drove it into the corner of the net. It was an unforgettable moment.

Arnold Challinor's final whistle provoked pandemonium. I ran on to the field in my suit like a drunken, whirling dervish. I ran straight to my captain and embraced Brian Horton. Manchester City supporters flooded on to the pitch and some attacked our players. City's chairman, Peter Swales, was inconsolable, but I told him that had Luton been relegated we would probably never return to the promised land. A club with the size and resources of Manchester City would recover. It would take them two years to regain the top flight.

I sought out their manager, John Benson, and found him in the treatment room with the comedian Eddie Large, who was a passionate City fan. I wished him well. What else could I say? John was sacked shortly afterwards.

Outside Maine Road, there was an angry crowd, clashing with a few joyous Luton supporters and the police ushered us on to the bus as quickly as possible. Five policemen joined us on the bus and sat on the back seat. Two police vans escorted us out of Moss Side. Whenever the coach was struck by a volley of coins or stones, the police dashed out of the bus and shooed the crowd away.

They accompanied us as far as Manchester's Southern Cemetery. On the short, slow journey, our police escort had consumed more than a few bottles of the beer we carried on board and seemed pretty happy about the result. They were United supporters.

At Tillington Hall, we celebrated our great escape, but my thoughts were already turning to home and Maureen.

CHAPTER 10

'DOES IT WASH ITS FACE?'

After our great escape, Luton desperately needed stability on and off the field. However, there was talk of boardroom changes and of the club leaving its heartland.

Dennis Mortimer, the Luton chairman, had found himself embroiled in a row over relocating the club, not to Stockwood Park, as had been suggested when I signed as a player in 1964, but to Milton Keynes. To our more vociferous supporters, such a move was out of the question. Even before the season began, there were threats of a boycott.

The move appeared constantly in the local press. Luton Town were keenly aware they had to move from the cramped surrounds of Kenilworth Road. However, neither they nor the local authority could come up with an alternative within the town boundaries. When Luton were looking to move to Stockwood Park, Milton Keynes had yet to be built. The first hundred houses of the new town went up in 1971. Over the next decade, more jobs were created in Milton Keynes than anywhere else in England. It was a boom town, though mocked for its concrete cows, sculptured by its 'artist in residence'.

Dennis Mortimer and I met Peter Winkelman, once a music executive with CBS Records and now a developer and evangelist for Milton Keynes. He was long-haired, persuasive and talkative. He was also quite a character. We were shown the MK Bowl, a former clay pit that had been filled in to create an outdoor amphitheatre that, used for rock concerts, could accommodate 65,000 spectators.

Winkelman told us that 40 million people lived within a three-hour drive of Milton Keynes. We would have access to a huge catchment area. In the 1982/83 season, Luton's average gate was 13,400 – the fourth lowest in the First Division, ahead of only Notts County, Swansea and Coventry. The following season, attendances at Kenilworth Road would fall by a further 11 per cent.

To me, it seemed a good time to take the plunge. Milton Keynes was only half an hour up the M1 from Luton and could offer a new stadium with a big potential crowd. The massive downside was that we would have to be renamed, calling ourselves something like Luton MK. It triggered a backlash among the more aggressive Luton supporters. Dennis Mortimer was spat at and the board, somewhat nervously, decided to stick. Winkelman was disappointed. It was an opportunity missed, although it would have meant submerging our real identity.

Peter Winkelman was to attract a football team to Milton Keynes when Wimbledon, who had been tenants of Crystal Palace since leaving their homely little ground at Plough Lane in 1991, moved north. MK Dons were born in 2003 amid the kind of acid acrimony that might have been directed at Luton had we made the move nearly two decades earlier. They played for a couple of seasons beneath the open stands of the Milton Keynes Hockey Stadium before moving to the gleaming Stadium MK with its 30,000 capacity.

When the 1983/84 season began, my hopes were for stability in the First Division, perhaps accompanied by a cup run. Several Luton players were receiving praise nationally. Ricky Hill was a lovely watch, with great energy and delicate touches from his size-nine boots. Although they had occasional differences off the field, Brian Stein and Paul Walsh were in harmony on match day. Paul Elliott was heading ever more powerfully alongside the reliable Mal Donaghy.

On the morning of Saturday 29 October, Luton were fourth, one place below Liverpool, who were intent on revenge after the frenetic and somewhat embarrassing 3–3 draw at Anfield thirteen months before. They hit us for six. Ian Rush, sliding in with clever, blindside runs, led Paul Elliott a merry dance. He finished with five goals. Rush was quicksilver. From a standing start, he could accelerate like a cheetah.

I was now ready to give an opportunity to a local teenager, Mitchell Thomas, at right and then left-back. Mitchell was tall, confident and, importantly, had no fear of failure. He was taken on as part of the youth training scheme from school. His long legs won tackles and his educated right foot passed the ball accurately.

Two more youngsters, Ray Daniel and Garry Parker, were also emerging. The YTS was a joint initiative between football and the government to replace the old concept of the groundstaff boy. In subsequent years, YTS trainees gave way to the apprentice scheme and then the academy system. In essence, the goalposts may have changed, but the aim was the same.

When I joined Nottingham Forest, it was as a groundstaff boy, doing menial jobs in the mornings and training in the afternoons. Education was voluntary. Ian Storey-Moore and I took a course in journalism, which neither of us completed. Our jobs included preparing the training kit, sweeping the dressing room and cleaning boots, as well as hosing down the communal baths after morning training. The YTS included a requirement for compulsory education. This was a sound idea. If a boy did not make it as a professional, he might leave with the odd O-level. Most others might leave with a lesser qualification in leisure management, although since the 1980s saw wholesale closures of sports halls those opportunities began to disappear.

The scheme broke down because the clubs wanted their young players to spend more time on the pitch and less in the classroom.

YTS boys gave way to apprentices who concentrated mainly on football but had educational sessions. The academy system, which was created at the turn of the century, called boys 'scholars'. It seemed a grander title and it has improved the standard of young players. This is not surprising, considering the sheer scale of the money invested in facilities and coaches.

The standard offer is a two-year contract with the academy plus the guarantee of a one-year professional contract. This gives a boy three years to either succeed or fail. Having to commit to a scholar for three years has made the clubs more selective and has made the young footballer feel more secure. There have been some wild incentives to gain a boy's signature, but a massive percentage fall by the wayside and never make it to the professional game. Statistics suggest less than 1 per cent of youngsters joining a professional club make it to first-team football.

As 1983 turned into 1984, Luton were still challenging near the top of the table. A 3–0 win at Notts County on Boxing Day left us third behind Liverpool and Manchester United. However, goals would become harder to come by, especially with David Moss sidelined with pelvic trouble.

We won just one of our next ten games – at Wolverhampton Wanderers, who were beginning their fall from the First to the Fourth Division in successive seasons. In those ten games, Luton scored six goals. From Boxing Day until the end of the season, we won just three times, although when Liverpool came to Kenilworth Road in February, we did force a goalless draw.

Luton finished sixteenth – level with four clubs on fifty-one points – which was an obvious improvement, but we needed to do better and well before the end of the season the bank manager had come calling. Dennis Mortimer had been unable to provide a convincing argument as to why our overdraft should be extended.

As a last resort, I convinced the chairman to allow me to see the bank manager at the National Westminster in Luton town centre. We talked football and I assured him that we had an agreement to sell Paul Walsh to Liverpool and we would soon have £750,000 in our account. As a result, our loan facility was extended for three months. The board members were spared from putting their hands into their pockets.

I negotiated the transfer with the Liverpool secretary, Peter Robinson, the man who ran Anfield for thirty-five years from Bill Shankly's time as manager to Gérard Houllier's. He was as close as any club secretary ever came to his managers and had the trust of them all.

Luton wanted more than £750,000 for Walsh, but Robinson's only concession was to offer us a credit note giving us £100,000 off any Liverpool player Luton might want in the next twelve months. When I tried to use that credit note by enquiring about John McGregor, a Scottish defender whom Liverpool had signed from Queen's Park, I discovered Luton were being offered him for £100,000 more than the fee quoted to the two other clubs who asked about him. He went to Glasgow Rangers. This was a lesson learned. Paul Walsh would have a highly successful career. He would win the Double with Liverpool in 1986 and the FA Cup with Tottenham in 1991 before moving to Portsmouth and Manchester City.

A run in the FA Cup would have brought money into Luton. The third round saw us drawn at home to Watford, who were investing heavily now that Elton John realised Graham Taylor was not a man to waste his cash in the top flight. After twenty-seven minutes, we were two up. The first was from our Nigerian forward, Emeka Nwajiobi, the second from Brian Stein. I had signed Nwajiobi from Dulwich Hamlet after I had persuaded him to reduce his hours as a trainee pharmacist. He had qualified from Cardiff University and was working as a locum in London while playing football part time. He proved a very popular signing, spending four years at Luton until injury ended his career.

Watford, however, equalised before half-time and after a 2–2 draw we went to Vicarage Road three days later for what proved a humdinger of a replay.

Watford, rather fortuitously, went two up through winger Nigel Callaghan and their 6ft 4in. striker George Reilly. Mal Donaghy pulled a goal back for Luton and at the interval we were confident we would turn the tie around. However, John Barnes, who had already made his England debut, extended Watford's lead before Stein and Walsh spun their magic. Walsh scored twice to level the game at 3–3.

Extra time was tough. Brian Horton was limping, Trevor Aylott a passenger. A flick-on from a corner and Mo Johnson, signed from Partick Thistle two months before, headed in under the bar for Watford's winner.

Afterwards, the England manager, Bobby Robson, joined Graham and me, both drained of emotion, in the small, neat boardroom at Vicarage Road. Elton John, who would watch Watford at the 1984 FA Cup final, was also there. Maureen talked to Elton's mother, Sheila, about Spanish holidays.

The conversation Bobby Robson wanted to have centred around Stein and Walsh. The following month England would play France in a friendly in Paris. He had been so excited by their performance that he wanted to play one of them but was unsure which. I convinced him that because they performed so well as a duo, he should play them both. Stein and Walsh started at the Parc des Princes, but England were comfortably beaten 2–0 by a France side that four months later would win the European Championship on the same ground.

I admired the commentator, Barry Davies, but that night he talked down Walsh and Stein, which may have influenced some

DAVID PLEAT

critics. Brian Stein did not play for England again, Paul Walsh made only one more appearance, a 1–0 defeat to Wales in May. When he chose to accept Liverpool's invitation to watch the European Cup final in Rome rather than play in the final of the European under-21 tournament against Spain, Robson decided he would not pick him again.

At the end of the season, we said goodbye to Horton and Antić. Brian became player-manager of Hull City. At the end of season Football Writers' Association dinner at the Royal Lancaster hotel, Jack Charlton came over to my table and asked me to meet Hull's colourful chairman, Don Robinson. Robinson, who had been a professional wrestler and owned hotels and theatres in Scarborough, asked if Horton had it in him to do the job. It was a short conversation.

Raddy returned to Yugoslavia to become assistant manager of Partizan Belgrade. It signalled the end of a dramatic period for the club. We had survived the 'second-season wobble', where promoted clubs, sustained by euphoria in their first season, struggle in the next.

With Antić and Horton gone and Walsh sold to Liverpool, my negotiating skills would be tested. I always recalled the advice of my chairman at Nuneaton, Mr Scattergood, to spend a club's money as if it were your own. I have always been aware of the income and expenditure columns.

Whenever Alan Sugar assessed a proposal during his time as Tottenham chairman, he would ask: 'Does it wash its face?' It was an expression I had never heard before, but I knew what he meant.

I needed a goalkeeper and had heard that Cardiff's Andy Dibble had been travelling to Watford once a week to train there ahead of a possible transfer. I committed myself to a bit of backdoor dealing, persuading Andy that he would have more opportunities at Luton than at Watford, where he would have to displace Steve Sherwood,

109

who had kept goal in the FA Cup final. Watford were most displeased by the outcome.

The signing of Vince Hilaire from Crystal Palace and Steve Elliott from Preston proved less successful. Vince, whom we exchanged for Trevor Aylott, was a lovely, bouncy character and Steve, who cost £95,000, an honest trier, but both flattered to deceive. I also came to terms with the realisation that Kirk Stephens, my link to non-league football, could be replaced by a local boy, Tim Breacker, whose elevation was a reward for his persistence. In his two years at the club amid a very good group of apprentices, our coaches thought he had the least chance of making the grade. However, Tim was the most dedicated of those six apprentices and that dedication paid off. Breacker was proof hard work can breed results. He would play more than 200 league games for Luton and another 200 for West Ham.

Coventry, which was Stephens's home town, had asked about his availability and I was able to exchange Kirk for Ashley Grimes, who had moved to Highfield Road from Manchester United after the 1983 FA Cup final, where he had been a substitute.

The complication in the Grimes deal surrounded (as it seemed to frequently in my career) his club car at Coventry, which was a Peugeot. He thought, mistakenly as it turned out, that he could keep it. One morning, big George Curtis, a fearsome character who was now Coventry's managing director after captaining the club from the Fourth to the First Division, turned up at our car park while we were out training. He had another set of keys to Ashley's car, opened it up, tossed his belongings on to the tarmac and drove the car back to Coventry. Ashley's fury when he returned from training and saw his clothes scattered on the car park, where his Peugeot should have been, was a sight to behold.

Although he was right-footed, I switched Mitchell Thomas to left-back, allowing Tim Breacker to slot in at right-back. A right-footed left-back tends to cover the centre-backs better when the cross comes in from the opposite flank. However, there is an obvious downside when they get forward and do not have the confidence to cross early on their left foot but turn back on to their stronger foot. This can frustrate a striker who feeds on early crosses.

Early in my management career at Nuneaton, I rang Gordon Lee, who was managing Port Vale, and told him I needed a left-back. He said: 'What type of left-back are you looking for? Do you want a strong tackler? A defensive type? One who's good in the air? Someone who's good going forward? A left-footer who's comfortable on the ball? Do you want a young player or someone more experienced?'

I was nonplussed at how analytical Gordon was. I just wanted a left-back. I was learning. When I suggested Mitchell Thomas switching to left-back, I had visions of replicating what Brian Clough had done at Nottingham Forest. In 1975 he signed Frank Clark, a 31-year-old right-footed left-back to cover his centre-backs and pass the ball to his orthodox outside left, John Robertson, who would hug the touchline. It was not Clark's job to overlap but to pass early and allow Robertson to get the better of his opposing right-back. The theory worked well for Luton, as we had the outstanding David Moss to patrol the left flank.

However, a boardroom row had long been brewing and it now came to a head. David Evans was an entrepreneur who had been part of the Luton board since 1977 but was now taking a more prominent role, arguing forcefully for greater investment. Dennis Mortimer, bogged down by the fans' boycott in protest at the proposed move to Milton Keynes and unable to raise the money to drive the club forward, resigned in November 1984. David Evans, pledging a more dynamic leadership, replaced him. He owned a cleaning company called Brengreen which he would sell for £32 million.

Dennis Mortimer had been an honest, low-profile chairman, a

man of integrity. Evans, a man who in my view had a colossal ego, seemed to use the platform that being chairman of Luton Town gave him to propel himself into the media. A working-class Conservative from north London, Evans became MP for Welwyn Hatfield in the 1987 general election. He was always smartly dressed, with beautifully cut, gleaming cufflinks. There was a Rolls-Royce in his driveway and he employed a private secretary.

The Times described him as 'combining the pugnacity of Norman Tebbit with the foul mouth of Alf Garnett, but, in truth, he did not have Tebbit's brains and nor was his language half as decorative as Alf Garnett's.' Evans's regime introduced immediate changes. There would now be board meetings once a month at 8 a.m. sharp so they would not interfere with training. They would last for precisely one-and-a-half hours. I would be asked to go to a weekly lunch with selected supporters and sponsors. This was one of David's better ideas.

At Christmas, he collected Maureen and I and drove us to Southend, where he was bidding for a cleaning contract from the council. He invited dustmen and their wives to a bash in which he promised them better pay and conditions. I was there as his 'celebrity'. There were other celebrities in his circle. Evans had played a few games of minor counties cricket for Hertfordshire and at his imposing house at Mackerye End in Harpenden, he introduced me to Alec and Eric Bedser, whose bowling helped ensure Surrey dominated the County Championship in the 1950s. The Bedser twins were part of his consultancy team.

One story about David Evans is telling. His neighbour in Harpenden was Tony Berry, who became a vice-chairman of Tottenham, where he had been a groundstaff boy. Until 1981, Berry had worked with Evans at Brengreen as chief operating officer. They both grew up in Edmonton, both played good club cricket for Enfield. They were great friends. One day, Berry received a registered letter from Evans informing him of his dismissal from Brengreen for 'abusing his expense allowance'. It left Berry flabbergasted. Tony saw this as a naked attempt by David Evans to oust him from the company.

Tony Berry went on to form the Blue Arrow employment agency, which by 1989, when he was forced out of his own company, was the largest in the world. He became vice-chairman of Tottenham. Their wives, who had been close, never spoke again.

CHAPTER 11

'WELCOME TO LUTON, MACCA'

Once installed in the chairman's seat, David Evans moved fast. He immediately abandoned the planned relocation to Milton Keynes and promised a greater investment in the squad.

The squad desperately needed shoring up defensively. With Brian Horton gone, the midfield lacked an anchor and, after a 3–1 defeat at Arsenal on 1 December 1984, we were second bottom and had conceded more goals than any other club bar Stoke, who would be relegated with seventeen points and were already limping forlornly along at the foot of the table.

Paul Elliott had broken his leg against Leicester in a League Cup tie in October. It was a bad tackle and Paul was never quite the same player again, while Andy Dibble was also injured. The year before, I had signed Les Sealey from Coventry. He was a strong personality who would be good for the dressing room. I watched him and liked him. He was a different type of keeper to Jake Findlay and Andy Dibble, both of whom liked to dominate their area and clear out defenders. Les preferred to stay on his line and let the centre-halves deal with the crosses.

One of those centre-halves would be Steve Foster, who had made a significant impact at Brighton and had been selected for England's squad for the 1982 World Cup. However, a transfer to Aston Villa had gone wrong and he was now rusting in the reserves. Foster's transfer had to be negotiated with Aston Villa's all-powerful chairman, Doug Ellis. After I completed the transfer, I asked Doug:

'Now, tell me the downside of the player.' He said he was 'a strange boy who lives with another man who drives him around'. Despite Doug's innuendo, Steve was not gay.

Foster, who wore a headband after having his head split open by Andy Gray playing for Brighton against Wolves, was a superb header of the ball. He was a strong tackler who would stay on his feet. He lacked pace but knew his limitations and cleverly stayed central, rarely getting caught out of position. Foster was always keen to pull his full-backs close to him to give him additional protection. One of his mannerisms was to stretch his arms out and then flap them down as a signal to his full-backs. This penguin-like gesture was met with amusement in the dressing room. One of Foster's major problems was his weight. He was around fourteen stone and I challenged him on this. He convinced me he knew precisely at what weight he would deliver his highest level of performance. He was a different kind of centre-half from Paul Elliott. Paul liked to hold the line, employing his exceptional pace to cover any balls played behind our defensive line. Foster was more comfortable sitting deep and was ultra-confident when it came to clearing balls around his own penalty box with powerful headers. He complemented Les Sealey, who was far more confident making saves than tearing out of his box to command a crowded penalty area, which would sometimes create confusion. Foster's presence meant it was difficult for Elliott to force his way back in and he went to Aston Villa at the end of the season, having worked hard to regain his fitness. Steve Foster would become a hero at Luton, a relationship that climaxed when he captained them to victory over Arsenal in the 1988 League Cup final.

The hectic signings continued. I had watched a 5ft 6in. midfielder at Walsall called David Preece five times without being able to make up my mind about him. He had a lovely left foot, was always on the move and was a perceptive passer. I worried about his size and lack of physicality. In the end, I took a chance and Preece justified every penny and more of the £150,000 fee. David spent eleven years at Luton and was so highly thought of that after his death from throat cancer in 2007 at the age of forty-four, a stand at Kenilworth Road was named after him. I delivered his eulogy at a packed church by Luton University, where I had received an honorary MA degree a few weeks before for services to football and the media.

I had never watched a player more before signing them. I always relied on a hunch and the feeling that a quick decision was a better decision. However, the great Bill Nicholson is said to have watched John White, the fine Scotland inside-forward, several times playing for Falkirk before deciding to take him to Tottenham in 1959. What clinched the deal was when Nicholson spoke to White's corporal from his National Service days, who assured the Spurs manager that White, who seemed too frail to be a footballer, was their best cross-country runner. He possessed enormous stamina.

I had not satisfactorily replaced our deepest midfielder, Brian Horton, and I still needed a partner for Brian Stein, who, following Paul Walsh's departure for Liverpool, was taking too much weight up front.

I had spoken to Arthur Cox, who had managed Newcastle to promotion the year before, about Mick Harford, a centre-forward whom he had signed from Lincoln in 1980. Harford had lasted only one season at St James' Park before being allowed to leave for Bristol City, who were completing their plunge from the First to the Fourth Division. A season in the top flight with Birmingham had also finished in relegation.

Because of my friendship with Colin Murphy, who had been Harford's manager at Lincoln, I had been long aware of this raw-boned forward, who as a youngster had enjoyed boxing at Gateshead Boys Club. The fact he was twenty-five and had been to four clubs already provoked some discussion with my scout, Ron Howard. Was there a problem? I did know he had been involved with some wild characters at Birmingham.

However, Arthur Cox explained Mick had been unlucky on Tyneside. He may have scored only four times for Newcastle, but he had struck the frame of the goal several times. It was a strange recommendation. In truth, Mick lacked the speed Newcastle supporters associated with their great centre-forwards. I went to watch him playing for Birmingham Reserves in an afternoon game at St Andrew's. Harford did seem to lack acceleration, but his hold-up play was good. He could look after the ball and he could resist a challenge. During the game he delivered a magnificently paced through-ball that cut through the visitors' defence. It was a pass worthy of Johnny Haynes in his pomp at Fulham.

Returning to Luton, I rang the Birmingham manager, Ron Saunders, and was surprised and pleased he was prepared to sell Harford. I agreed a price of £225,000, which was a lot of money for Luton, but I had the club's backing, having convinced them Stein needed a partner to maximise his abilities. When our chief executive, John Smith, rang Birmingham to confirm the payment schedule, he was told the price was £250,000. I told John the agreement over the phone had been £25,000 less. The board agreed the increased price, but I was left embarrassed and unhappy with Saunders.

There was still a gap in the spine of the team – the gap where Brian Horton had been. It was then that Crystal Palace's financial problems played into our hands. I spoke to their manager, Steve Coppell, about signing their tough-tackling midfielder, Peter Nicholas. He had begun his career at Selhurst Park but moved to Arsenal and became captain of Wales. However, he had lost his place at Highbury and returned to Palace.

Coppell was a manager whom I admired tremendously. An intelligent, honest man who I thought should have been seriously considered for the England job, Steve always seemed to be working under massive financial constraints, whether at Crystal Palace or Brighton. I paid Palace £40,000 for Nicholas.

I felt comfortable Luton were now a side that would be much more difficult to beat. It had been a hectic period, but how many times can a manager say that four consecutive signings – Foster, Preece, Harford and Nicholas – were all to prove successful?

In management, recruitment is key. There are hours spent watching the player, checking their character, medical history and family circumstances. Now there is every kind of statistic, including a visual library where you can view every match the player has taken part in. The key is also to get the value of the player right and to make as many checks on their character as you can.

The second half of our season was dominated by the FA Cup. We had done well in the League Cup, beating Orient by seven goals over two legs. Leicester were beaten 3–1, a memory scarred by Paul Elliott's broken leg. We succumbed 4–2 at Sheffield Wednesday in a game where Andy Blair scored a hat-trick of penalties. In one cup game, Blair had equalled the total number of league goals he would score in two years at Hillsborough. On the way home, I almost choked on my fish and chips cursing the referee, Tom Fitzharris.

By the time the FA Cup began for Luton in January 1985, the spine of the team was in place and I was confident we might enjoy a run in it. We began by being drawn at home to Stoke, a game that was saved by a late Steve Foster equaliser and watched by around 7,000. Attendances across the game were collapsing because of mass unemployment that had undermined football's traditional fanbase, mixed in with the fear of hooliganism. Only one club, Manchester United, had average gates above 40,000. Only three more had average gates above 30,000.

I was not at Kenilworth Road either, having put the team in the care of my coaches, David Coates and Trevor Hartley. I was in Paisley, watching Frank McAvennie, a forward who had interested me for twelve months, play for St Mirren. I had been following McAvennie ever since Ron Scott, a journalist with the *Sunday Post*, had tipped me off. Scott was a large, avuncular man who had the ear of many managers in Scotland and travelled with the national team. Much of his instinctive knowledge of football derived from his father, Jimmie, who had been Preston's Scottish scout since the days when Bill Shankly played at Deepdale.

Among the scouts at Love Street that day, I spotted Gordon Milne, the Leicester manager. Gordon, who had won two titles at Liverpool under Shankly, had begun his career at Preston and would have known Jimmie Scott. He, too, had probably been tipped off and Gordon also thought it was a day he could afford to miss a cup tie. In his absence, Leicester beat Burton Albion 6–1.

Frank was a slim, fair-haired, box-to-box, left-sided midfielder with an eye for goal. After tracking McAvennie for a season and a half, during which time St Mirren had endured three changes of manager, I finally obtained permission to do the deal in the summer of 1985. McAvennie flew down from Glasgow with Bill McMurdo, his agent who was a former miner and staunch supporter of the Conservative Party. He was a small guy with a goatee beard. McAvennie, a quiet and slightly naive man, had great faith in him.

Now they were both at the Bedford Arms in Woburn. Luton, however, had brought too many people to the negotiations. I was there, so was John Smith, the chief executive, and the chairman, David Evans, all in one room, trying to persuade him to sign. McAvennie, who was wearing a black shirt, a white tie and red socks, seemed intimidated by so many people talking at him. He wrote in his autobiography that he especially disliked David Evans, who had walked into the room, slapped him on the back of the head and said: 'Welcome to Luton, Macca.'

I knew how important it was, once you got a player in a room, not to let him leave without signing. We explained to him that with his salary and his signing-on fee and bonuses, he would earn more than the £400 a week he was looking for. He could not get his head round these add-ons. All he wanted was a basic wage of £400. The negotiations went on late into the night and during them, McMurdo was asked to take a call. We could not get the deal done that night but arranged for the club secretary, John Wilkinson, to pick up McAvennie in the morning and take him to Kenilworth Road.

However, when John went back to the Bedford Arms, McAvennie had left. The call Bill McMurdo had taken was from the West Ham manager, John Lyall, informing him they would better any offer Luton made. It was a classic sales pitch. After the Luton delegation had left for the night, McMurdo took McAvennie to Toddington Services on the M1, where they met Lyall at two in the morning. I always liked John, whom I found a complete gentleman. If I said: 'Fine,' when he asked how I was, he would reply: 'Mazel tov.' Now, however, he outflanked me. At Upton Park, he successfully converted McAvennie into a second striker and his goals would propel West Ham to third place in the league in 1986. Frank McAvennie was one who, quite literally, got away.

Four days after my journey to Scotland to watch McAvennie, we played Stoke again in the snow at the Victoria Ground. We won the replay, 3–2, with young Garry Parker, a confident, talented passer, beginning to make his mark. A 2–0 win over Huddersfield in the next round with goals from Stein and Donaghy was straightforward enough.

Now there came a stirring of interest as, for the second successive FA Cup campaign, we were drawn against our neighbours, Watford. Some 18,000 crammed into Kenilworth Road to watch a goalless stalemate. On the Monday, at Vicarage Road, we came from two goals down to force a draw after extra time. There would be a second replay, this time back at Luton, where the crowd sensed something special.

Wayne Turner, a local boy with a great attitude, scored for Luton on his twenty-fourth birthday and settled the tie in the fifty-eighth minute. We had held off Watford's dangerous front three of Callaghan, Barnes and Blissett. We would face Millwall in the quarter-final.

Because the third of our matches against Watford had been on the Saturday reserved for the FA Cup, the quarter-final was shifted to the following Wednesday. We were second bottom of the First Division, six points from safety but with three matches in hand over fourth-bottom Coventry. Despite our league position, we were confident.

So, too, were Millwall. They were third in the Third Division with matches in hand. They would be coming to Kenilworth Road on the back of eight straight wins. To reach the quarter-final, they had beaten Crystal Palace, Chelsea and Leicester. They were managed by George Graham and they would end the season promoted.

Millwall had requested the tie be made all-ticket, but their warning was not heeded. Around four o'clock, large numbers of their supporters were congregating on the platforms at St Pancras for the short journey north. An hour later, Millwall fans were in the streets of Luton, breaking pub and shop windows. The Kenilworth Road terrace was reserved for away supporters and by seven o'clock it was clear there were too many in that area. A gate had been forced and, ten minutes before the teams were due to warm up, hundreds of supporters clambered over the fencing and invaded the pitch and taunted the Luton fans in the Oak Road End.

The police were overwhelmed. They were hampered by the fact that Bedfordshire Police had no horses, and by the time they had been brought in from Cambridge, it was too late. Bedfordshire Police did have dogs and they helped restore order. George Graham used the club's loudspeakers to urge Millwall fans to return behind the fences. The players were, naturally, on edge.

Astonishingly, the referee, David Hutchinson, a Cambridgeshire police inspector on secondment in Harrogate, ruled the game should start on time. After fourteen minutes, the fans rioted again and we had to suffer a tense, 25-minute wait. By now, seats were being ripped up and thrown on to the pitch. After thirty-one minutes, Brian Stein scored and everyone in the ground feared the worst.

Incredibly, the tie finished. Hutchinson said he was determined the hooligans would not win. At the final whistle, as the players raced to the dressing rooms, Luton fans who had been forced off their terrace and were now standing three-deep by the touchline were attacked again. Bottles were thrown and the pitch was now scattered with hundreds of ripped up seats.

Looking back on the game from more than thirty-five years' distance, the refereeing still seems magnificent. How did Hutchinson of Harrogate, with the help of the police, get that match finished? The victims, many of them either young or old, were treated by ambulance crews in the players' tunnel. There was blood everywhere. The directors' box did not escape. It became a target as billiard balls were thrown at it during the craziness.

For the first time since 1959, Luton had reached an FA Cup semi-final, but nobody seemed to care. There were eighty-one injured, thirty-one of them police officers and thirty-one arrests. The riot was the lead item on *News at Ten*.

Our emotions were shock and demoralisation run through with a hint of pleasure that we had made it through. In the aftermath, I sat with George Graham, the Millwall chairman Alan Thorne and the Luton directors. The Millwall contingent were apologetic, but the damage had been done. Maureen had been to the game and waited for me for an hour and a half before making her own way home.

In the end, there was just George and I left in the boardroom. He told me that what had happened that night, allied to the fact he had turned Millwall from relegation candidates to a team likely to be promoted to the Second Division, meant he was now looking to leave. Fourteen months later, George got his wish when, having taken Millwall to ninth in the Second Division, he was appointed manager of Arsenal. Their first choice had been Terry Venables, who was then at Barcelona. Venables was a master at knowing when to leave a club to the extent that he became known as 'the Lifeboat Man'. This time, he unwisely decided to stay another season at the Nou Camp, which was to prove his last.

There was little time for sleep. The next day, John Smith, David Evans, club secretary John Wilkinson and I were summoned to meet a government that already seemed to be waging a war against football. When we arrived at the Houses of Parliament, there were questions to answer. Why was the match not all-ticket? What precautions had we taken? Why did we not request extra police? Did we receive any notification there would be trouble? Were the gates forced?

Before the meeting at Westminster, we were invited on to the TV-am station's breakfast programme, which was hosted by Nick Owen, a Luton Town supporter who would become chairman of the club in 2008. The riot was front-page news in every morning paper. I could not stop thinking about those Luton supporters who would not be able to enjoy the fact we had made an FA Cup semi-final.

Subsequently, we found some answers to what lay behind that night's wickedness.

Many of those who travelled from the London area under Millwall's banner were from Chelsea and West Ham. The Metropolitan Police had been far too slow to see the significance of hundreds of organised hooligans gathering at St Pancras at 4 p.m. Had Cambridgeshire Police – the ones with the nearest mounted division to Luton – been mobilised then, the rioting might have been controlled. The riot had been organised as an attack on a group of Luton fans called the MIGs, who were multi-racial, wore designer clothes and had been responsible for incidents in London. I had no knowledge of this.

We were ordered to construct fences around Kenilworth Road. Millwall were fined a measly £7,500, a punishment that was overturned on appeal. To pacify the FA, Luton announced that Kenilworth Road would become an all-seater stadium. There would be a ban on away supporters and home supporters could only come to games via a membership scheme. An artificial pitch would be installed. The seats in the Bobbers Stand were removed and replaced by twenty-five executive boxes. One third of our valued hardcore who sat in the Bobbers never returned. Those decisions made us unpopular within Luton and in the wider football community.

Exactly a month later came the semi-final against the brilliant Everton side constructed by Howard Kendall, which would win the league by thirteen points. They had just forced a draw with Bayern Munich in the Olympic Stadium that would take them a step nearer to the Cup-Winners' Cup final. They were the FA Cup holders.

Luton's form had improved since that traumatic night against Millwall. We were still in the relegation zone but wins against Queens Park Rangers, Ipswich and Stoke had taken us to within a point of safety with a game in hand. I was relaxed when I arrived at Villa Park to take my seat in the stands as I did for the first half of every game. We dominated the opening period. Emeka Nwajiobi had three chances to score – one of which was cleared off the line by Gary Stevens. Seven minutes from the interval, Ricky Hill drove a shot from the edge of the area that curled past Neville Southall's gloves and cannoned in off the post. The 18,000 Luton fans in the Holte End were delirious.

Usually, I would have gone down to the touchline for the second half, but I went back to the directors' box – I cannot recall why. Maybe it was subliminal. We were playing so well, there seemed little need to shout instructions from the edge of the pitch. Steve

Foster and Mal Donaghy were blunting Everton's forward line of Graeme Sharp and Andy Gray. Their formidable midfield of Peter Reid and Paul Bracewell was being kept in check by Wayne Turner, Ricky Hill and Garry Parker – Nicholas and Preece were both cup-tied. We had one more central midfielder than Everton and this overload appeared to have succeeded.

A dream result seemed on the cards. Howard Kendall admitted he had all but given up on the game. Then, disaster struck. Derek Mountfield, who had started the afternoon at centre-half, was pushed up front as Everton threw everything at us. It meant Mick Harford had to withdraw to mark him. The referee, John Martin, then ruled Harford had backed into him and awarded a free-kick. Any neutral who saw the match would not have concurred with that decision. In fact, Harford had climbed over Foster to head the ball clear. Mountfield had ducked to make it look like a foul. Kevin Sheedy's quality left foot sent the ball past the wall and Sealey fumbled. The score was 1–1. Only then, with three minutes remaining, did I go down to the touchline. Extra time followed.

Our boys began to tire as Everton sensed this was their day. With five minutes separating us from a replay, Mountfield, of all people, scored with a header from another free-kick. We were distraught. It was no consolation that Kendall praised our play or that Luton were acclaimed in the press. We had been at the gates of Wembley and had lost. The boys went for a good drink. I went home and shed a few tears.

In the league, Luton had ten games to save themselves and many thought the crushing disappointment of the FA Cup would sink us. Eight days later, we faced Manchester United, who were second in the league and who would beat Everton in the FA Cup final.

Rather than being crushed by the outcome, Luton were stimulated by their performance in the semi-final. Manchester United were beaten, 2–1, with Harford scoring in the last minute. We were clear of the relegation zone. Arsenal and Aston Villa were beaten. So, too, were Everton, who had long been crowned champions of England. Luton finished thirteenth. It was their highest finish since 1958 and they would climb higher.

CHAPTER 12

'WHY ARE OUR STAR PLAYERS NOT WEARING HELMETS?'

It was a grim spring for football. As we came off the field after a 4–0 win over Leicester on 11 May 1985, we were stunned to be greeted with pictures of the Main Stand at Valley Parade engulfed in a fire that killed fifty-six supporters of Bradford City. Television cameras had been sent to cover the Yorkshire club's promotion to the Second Division. They recorded pictures that were beyond their wildest imaginings.

The day after our final match of the season, the 2–0 win over Everton, came the disaster at Heysel, which killed thirty-nine, mostly Italian, fans and would see English clubs banned from European competition for five years. The riots at Luton were a little over two months in the past.

We were preparing for an end-of-season trip to Cyprus, a thank-you to the players who had taken Luton to the semi-finals of the FA Cup and steered them clear of relegation. When we arrived at Larnaca, I had to deal with some form-filling while the players waited impatiently to board the bus in the warm sunshine.

As I walked towards them, one of the players shouted: 'Come on, Jew-boy, we can't wait all day.' I was shocked and upset but decided not to make an issue of it. I felt stunned and hurt that one of my players had made such a racist statement. For some time, I considered the dilemma. Should I speak to the player and attempt to educate him and remind him of the respect he should show? The remark occupied my mind for a couple of days. The players were determined to have a good time, which included a few beers too many. My task was to keep an eye on things without dampening team spirit. They had given everything for eight months.

Trouble flared when the hotel received a call from a man, known to the hotel staff, purporting to be a shipping magnate. He accused two of our players of abusing his daughter after meeting her at a nightclub. I immediately informed the club and David Evans and John Smith told me to hold the fort while they made their way to Larnaca. Within forty-eight hours, they had staved off all sorts of threats and resolved the situation. I never found out how they appeased the magnate. Indirectly, Evans and Smith made comments that I was not making my authority count. The situation was to become worse.

Sitting sipping a cocktail at the beach bar with Evans and Smith, we watched as three of our players sped by on scooters. Neither Brian Stein, Ricky Hill nor Mitchell Thomas was wearing a helmet. I received a further comment about my lack of control. 'Why are our star players not wearing helmets? Did you not advise them of the danger?' Within seconds of that comment, the Luton captain, Steve Foster, crash-landed a hang-glider less than thirty yards away.

I had my mind, however, on other things during those seven chaotic days in Cyprus. Before we left, I had taken a phone call from Harry Harris, a journalist with the *Daily Mirror*, who enjoyed a close relationship with the Tottenham chairman, Irving Scholar. Harris had a question: 'Would you be interested becoming the manager of Tottenham Hotspur?' The position was mine if I wanted it.

After beating Anderlecht to win the UEFA Cup, Keith Burkinshaw had resigned as Tottenham manager in 1984, after a breakdown in his relationship with the board. Scholar had met Alex Ferguson in Paris and offered him the job. Ferguson, who had followed up his triumph of taking Aberdeen to the Cup-Winners' Cup by winning the Scottish title, turned him down. It was partly because his wife, Cathy, had not wanted to move to London, but there was a deeper reason. He discovered Scholar had lied to him in the interview.

Burkinshaw's assistant, Peter Shreeves, was appointed instead. Tottenham began extremely well under Peter. After a 5–1 thrashing of Southampton on 23 March, Tottenham were level on points with Everton at the top of the table. However, Spurs won only one of the next seven games and lost to Arsenal at White Hart Lane. It was then that I had received the call from Harry Harris. He told me Irving would be making a change of manager at the end of the season.

However, Shreeves won four of his final five matches to take Tottenham to third, their highest finish since 1971 – an achievement that then had been rather overshadowed by Arsenal winning the Double. Harry Harris called me to say Scholar would now be keeping faith with Peter Shreeves for another season.

The 1985/86 season was to be a defining one, although a big prize would elude me. Luton would finish ninth in 1986, one place above Spurs. Luton's most pressing staffing problem was that Ricky Hill and Brian Stein were both out of contract. I was able to persuade them that the season ahead would be a good one and would give them the opportunity to project their talents even more. I also told them that, if they were unhappy at the end of the season, I would help them find another club. They trusted me.

Luton were not the most popular team at the start of the season as we had installed an artificial pitch, which many other teams in Division One imagined would give us a considerable advantage. We would be the second club, after Queens Park Rangers, to use this type of surface. A Leicestershire company, En-Tout-Cas, who were specialists in laying tennis courts, was given the contract to lay the pitch.

The board had persuaded me that in our tight financial position, we needed extra commercial revenue. They told me the use of the pitch by the community and our sponsors would bring in £250,000 a year. I had no choice but to accept it. Nylon fibres were woven into a soft carpet and then sand was sprinkled in between the fibres. Among those from the FA who tested the pitch and gave it the go-ahead was England's first football manager, Sir Walter Winterbottom. Certainly, the ball ran true, but it also ran fast. The biggest problem was the strong bounce of the ball. It was, however, a great improvement on the pitch that had been laid at Loftus Road in 1981.

We did not find it that easy to adjust to the artificial pitch, however. Players had to stay on their feet rather than go to ground when making a tackle. Mal Donaghy and Peter Nicholas improved their passing and knew, if they went to ground too often, they would be susceptible to the odd thigh graze. The surface encouraged passing to feet rather than passing beyond players for them to run on to. Any straight or longer pass played into space would run on quickly. We needed to use short, fast, angled passes. One of the advantages, however, was that we could train on it whenever we wanted, night or day.

Our first three games on the new pitch were against Nottingham Forest, Arsenal and Chelsea. All were drawn. Chelsea's equaliser was scored by Kerry Dixon, a Luton boy whom I had allowed to leave as a sixteen-year-old. We were literally finding our feet. The fourth home game, against Queens Park Rangers, who were used to an artificial surface, was won, 2–1.

We were contacted by a Leeds-based agent, Majid Mohammed, who organised Caribbean tours. He had just done one for Manchester United and Southampton and asked if we would be interested in an early-season break on the island of Trinidad, where we would play Norwich and the island's armed forces. We would leave after the 1–1 draw with Oxford and return to play Southampton a week later on 19 October.

David Evans thought it a dangerous ploy, warning me: 'It will be on your head if we lose to Southampton.' However, Luton would be paid a fee of around £5,000 and I thought some football in the sun would relax us and was deserved after a decent start to the season. We spent four whirlwind days in the southern Caribbean. We beat the Trinidad Armed Forces in the national stadium, but the venue for the Norwich game was altogether more ramshackle. The dressing-room toilet was a hole in a mud floor, and some spectators watched the match from the trees that surrounded the ground.

David Evans need not have worried. Southampton were thrashed, 7–0. Peter Shilton was in goal and Mark Wright was part of their defence. Both were England stalwarts. We overwhelmed them to record our biggest win in Division One. Every player was in form. Shilton prevented an even greater avalanche. We skated along the surface. Stein grabbed three and Mick Harford caused havoc up front. Practically Les Sealey's only task was to look on admiringly. Evans came to the dressing room to congratulate the team through gritted teeth.

While Luton made headlines at home, the game that was to have most impact on my career came at White Hart Lane. Tottenham, the team I was to inherit, succumbed to our brilliant, angled-passing football. We won, 3–1, against a team full of international talent from Ray Clemence to Gary Mabbutt, Chris Hughton, Glenn Hoddle and Chris Waddle. According to our directors, Irving Scholar was 'gushing about the style of Luton's play' in the boardroom afterwards.

As I was to discover later, Irving was a bad loser and not at all gracious when being beaten in front of the White Hart Lane faithful. On this November afternoon there were fewer of them than usual. The gate was just 19,163. Attendances were becoming an issue at Tottenham, who that season had slipped to become London's fourth-best supported club.

I felt confident enough to sell Paul Elliott to Aston Villa for £400,000. Paul had recovered slowly from his broken leg but had regained his form well enough to attract an offer from Villa Park before going to Serie A in 1987 to play for Pisa. After retirement, Paul became a major player in the football anti-racism campaign, Kick it Out, and worked on FA and UEFA committees.

With a little money in the bank, I could now start searching for a striker to help ease the workload on Harford and Stein. Just before Christmas, I watched Wigan play Derby at the Baseball Ground in a Third Division fixture and was impressed by the drive of their twenty-year-old front man, Mike Newell. He never seemed to stop running, but he also had the knack of feinting to allow the ball to run across his body. This was a skill Trevor Brooking had perfected at West Ham. He was a master of this particular art, especially when receiving throw-ins.

I met Newell and his chairman, Bill Kenyon, and his manager, Bryan Hamilton, at Watford Station on a cold, snowy day and completed a deal worth £80,000. Mike fitted the bill and enabled me to play three up front on occasions. After I left Luton, Newell would score a hat-trick in a 4–1 demolition of Liverpool, the club that rejected him as a teenager. He would eventually be sold back to Bryan Hamilton, who was now managing Leicester, for a healthy profit.

The final game of the season at Kenilworth Road saw us face familiar opponents. A Harford hat-trick was enough to see off Watford. It completed a double over our neighbours from Hertfordshire to the delight of our most passionate supporters. To some, a double over Watford, whatever our league position, signified a successful season. I always failed to fully comprehend the huge importance attached to a single derby win. A return to Maine Road for the first time since our great escape in 1983 brought us a 1–1 draw and a ninth-place finish.

Having fallen at the semi-final stage the season before, we were geared for a run in the FA Cup. Victories over Crystal Palace and Bristol Rovers brought us a plum fifth-round tie against Arsenal on 15 February. We drew a bruising encounter, 2–2, at Kenilworth Road.

Bitter winter weather meant the replay was delayed until 3 March when we ran out on an icy, barely playable pitch that had surprisingly passed an inspection. The Arsenal manager, Don Howe, seemed less than pleased the game was going ahead. He thought a better surface would have favoured his quality players. His back-four comprised Viv Anderson, Martin Keown, David O'Leary and Kenny Samson. All were or would be international footballers. Up front, they had Charlie Nicholas, whom they had signed from Celtic on terms that would make him Britain's highest-paid footballer. Alongside him was the talented eighteen-year-old David Rocastle, whose life would be tragically cut short by cancer at the age of thirty-three. To Arsenal, the icy, bone-hard surface could only be seen as a leveller of talent. Then, there was no under-soil heating.

As the game ground on into extra time, everyone at Highbury knew that if a second replay were required, it would be played two days' later and the only way of announcing ticketing information was over the Tannoys that night. The venue would have to be decided by a toss of a coin between the chairmen in the boardroom should the scores be level at the interval in extra time. David Evans won. Luton would have home advantage. I was told immediately the game would be at Kenilworth Road while Don Howe claimed nobody had passed this information on to him.

He argued afterwards that our knowledge that Luton would be at home in the second replay meant we spent the final fifteen minutes shutting the game down. In his post-match press conference, Don was both expressive and annoyed, arguing Luton had been given an unfair advantage. I liked Don; he could be charming and was an outstanding coach. He projected an air of superiority, subtly letting you know that he was the manager of Arsenal and he was running a club of the highest standing.

We swept them aside in the third game with goals from Foster and Mark Stein, Brian's twenty-year-old brother, and an own-goal from O'Leary. Luton delivered one of their finest performances of my time at the club. Arsenal could not handle Harford, who pulled away from the back post to climb above Samson to win headers from David Preece's brilliantly directed diagonal deliveries.

Three days later, at Luton, we would face our nemesis, Everton, for a place in the semi-finals. This was our fourth match in seven days.

The games against Arsenal would take their toll. After Luton had taken the lead through Harford and Stein, two late efforts from Graeme Sharp and Adrian Heath forced a replay at Goodison Park four days later. In the press conference, I criticised Gary Lineker for a bad challenge on Mal Donaghy that the referee, Keith Hackett, had ignored. It was one of Lineker's proudest boasts that he was never booked in his playing career and my comment angered him. With a replay pending, perhaps this was not a wise remark and it was one that attracted plenty of coverage in the press. Since Luton had lost a two-goal lead, I was accused of sour grapes. Others commented that Lineker had been very fortunate not to be booked.

Lineker had the last laugh. Speeding between Foster and Donaghy, he settled the replay with a sixteenth-minute goal in front of 44,000 spectators, many of whom ended the night whistling desperately as the minutes ticked away. Everton had done us again. For the third successive year, they would reach the FA Cup final. We were drained, but we could hold our heads high.

However, my eight-year tenure as manager of Luton Town was coming to an end. For the third time, Harry Harris called me about the Tottenham job. This time, there would be a different outcome.

CHAPTER 13

'YOU'LL PAY FOR THIS'

Suddenly, the sports pages were full of my impending appointment as manager of Tottenham Hotspur. I had accepted Irving Scholar's invitation over the phone, but I had not yet signed the contract when David Evans came to the bungalow.

It was a surprise visit. The chairman and his wife, Janice, presented themselves at our front door, carrying a bottle of champagne and a bouquet of flowers, making all sorts of promises if I were to stay. Evans genuinely thought he could persuade me to change my mind. He called me 'maestro', a favourite term of his. There would be a longer contract, a share of transfer sales, a new company car and a salary beyond what Spurs were offering. It was heart-wrenching.

I tried to stay calm, telling myself I had agreed a deal with Tottenham and it was time to go. Janice started crying dramatically as I confirmed I was not going to change my mind. David raised his voice until it became an angry tirade. Once he knew I was going to stand up to him, his mood changed entirely. As he left the bungalow, he turned to me and said: 'You'll pay for this.'

It was a strange thing to say. David Evans was originally a Tottenham supporter and his company, Brengreen, had an executive box at White Hart Lane. He had also met with Irving Scholar and given permission to approach me when the two men had met at Evans's office in Cheapside in the City of London.

I had no agent, just advice from an accountant, and because I wanted a smooth transition, I agreed a salary that was much less than the going rate plus bonuses. I would continue to live in Luton. There would be a change of profile. Luton Town had very rarely been the top story in national newspapers. Luton asked me who I would recommend to replace me. All the names I gave them began with H – Bryan Hamilton, Brian Horton, and Ray Harford. They chose Harford.

Ray Harford was forging a reputation as a good coach who had endured a torrid time at a financially-stricken Fulham. Bryan Hamilton had come within a point of promoting Wigan to the Second Division while Brian Horton had been my captain at Luton and had managed Hull to sixth in the Second Division – their best finish since 1971. Luton would have been in safe hands with Brian.

I agreed to an interview with John Sadler, the chief sportswriter of *The Sun*. He quoted me as saying: 'I have gone from fish and chips to smoked salmon.' It was not a clever quote. The article riled David Evans and there was further animosity between the two clubs when I persuaded Luton's coach, Trevor Hartley, and the physio, John Sheridan, to join me at Spurs. Luton immediately accused me of undermining their club. There was no agreement with Luton that I would not approach their staff. The issue had not even been discussed. There were arguments over compensation. Tottenham agreed to pay Luton £100,000 to settle my contract. If Spurs won a trophy during the initial three years of my contract, they would be due a further £100,000.

In my last year at Luton, I had been approached by Radio 2, which was then the sports arm of the BBC, to be their summariser alongside Peter Jones and Bryon Butler for a few matches. Working alongside them was an education. As a consequence, ITV had asked me to join their commentary team for the 1986 World Cup in Mexico. Irving came out to Mexico himself and, there, we spoke about our plans for the season ahead. We discussed Ossie Ardiles, who would be thirty-four in August. Perhaps it was time to look for someone younger. Wisely, Irving told me to hang on and wait until I had taken a good look at Ardiles before coming to a decision. He was proved right.

Prior to England's final group game against Poland in Monterrey, where Gary Lineker revived our campaign with a fox-in-the-box hat-trick, I phoned Mitchell Thomas from the press box to ask if he would consider a move to Tottenham. Mitchell was enthusiastic, but his decision sparked a row with Luton that was only settled by a tribunal. At the tribunal, Luton accused Spurs of understating what Mitchell would earn at Tottenham to lower the potential transfer fee. They suggested there was a side-agreement. This was not so. They also accused me of reneging on a promise not to take anyone from Kenilworth Road for a period of several months after I joined Spurs. It inflamed the war of words. David Evans, understandably anxious to show his supporters he was protecting his club, was especially aggressive, while John Moore, who had succeeded me as manager, was more controlled in his criticism. The tribunal ruled that Spurs should pay £275,000, which was well below Luton's valuation.

Mexico was fascinating. You came across corrupt policemen demanding money, terrible traffic jams, lively music, excellent food and the smog of Mexico City. I will always remember the jagged four-peaked mountain, the Cerro de la Silla, that dominates the skyline of Monterrey.

ITV asked me to interview my new England player, Glenn Hoddle. I had never conducted a television interview before, but I had already spoken to him privately. He told me Irving had informed him he could leave Tottenham after the World Cup. Glenn had an aura about him. He was the golden boy of his generation and I told him I wanted him on board for my first season at White Hart Lane. I made it clear that I would allow him to leave in the summer of 1987 and I would make sure the transfer fee was a comfortable one for any prospective buyer. Somewhat reluctantly, Glenn accepted this and he was to have a significant role in the fine football Tottenham were to play.

I would cover seven World Cups for the media, finishing in South Africa in 2010. I had been to the 1982 World Cup in Spain with a group of other managers, but this was a first look at the great event from the inside. Our initial base was a sports complex in Saltillo, a city in north-east Mexico that is the centre of the country's car industry. It was where the England team and their press corps were staying.

I managed to snatch a few minutes with Bobby Robson. After the first two games – a 1–0 defeat by Portugal and a goalless draw with Morocco that had seen Ray Wilkins dismissed and Bryan Robson dislocate his shoulder – he was a beleaguered manager. Bobby was being pilloried by the journalists, although I realised on that trip that the press were under pressure for quick copy and interesting stories. They also enjoyed a drink and, in the bar, it would be obvious they desperately wanted England to win, partly because it would extend their stay. However, they could be ruthless in their criticism when it went wrong.

My co-commentator was Martin Tyler, who was very easy to get on with. We were allowed to watch the teams train, which proved an education. Before Italy played South Korea, we saw the Italians, the defending world champions, go through their paces at their training camp. Enzo Bearzot, the Italy manager, tall and elegant, with a coat draped over his shoulders, appeared a giant of authority.

We were surprised to see Irving Scholar at the training session. He had used his position as chairman of Tottenham as a way of gaining access to the tournament. The game between Italy and Korea, in Puebla, was a classic. We were in a very high vantage point in the stadium, which made identifying the players difficult. Puebla is also 7,000ft above sea level and it is subject to violent changes of weather. It was warm and sunny at kick-off and we were in shirt sleeves.

Then a sudden drop in temperature announced a fierce hailstorm. Martin Tyler's notes were blown away and somehow we staggered through the rest of the game, hoping the viewers would not notice any errors. By then, we had grasped the formations and managed to borrow a team-sheet from a fellow commentator. Italy won, 3–2, with Alessandro Altobelli scoring twice.

In the later stages of the tournament, we moved to the Sheraton in Mexico City, where we were joined by the BBC team awaiting the quarter-final between Argentina and England. Jimmy Hill, who was the BBC's main summariser at the tournament, invited me to his room for a drink. Sitting with him was Bob Abrahams, a lovely man who was the BBC's chief sports producer at World Cups and Olympic Games. After a few drinks, they told me the BBC had bigger audiences, more professional presenters and better backroom staff. 'You', they said, 'could be one of us.' I was flattered, but I was just starting in television and had no ambition to be anything other than an occasional pundit. On 22 June, Diego Maradona produced one moment of larceny and one moment of brilliance in the Azteca Stadium to floor England's hopes of reaching the semi-finals. Argentina would win the World Cup, beating West Germany in the final.

When I returned, I discussed Tottenham's youth players with their coach, Keith Blunt, who explained he had two or three in his group who had a chance of senior football. Keith mentioned Vinny Samways, Mark Bowen and Paul Moran. What I remember of our discussion was Keith putting his feet up on my desk while he began talking. Perhaps he was ultra-relaxed, perhaps he had had a hard day on the training field, but I considered it disrespectful. I told him to take his feet off the desk. Years before, I had gone on an FA coaching course, where Keith had been a senior coach and I wondered now whether this was a sign that, deep down, he still considered me to be something of his pupil, that I was still an apprentice.

A more interesting meeting was with Bill Nicholson, the club's greatest manager, who had returned to Spurs in 1976 to work as a consultant and chief scout. He had three assistants in his office: John Moncur Sr, Ted Buxton and Len Cheesewright. All had an opinion, but often I found them arguing with each other to the extent they were often unable to agree a coherent view on a player.

Bill, who had become manager of Tottenham twenty-eight years before and who would run White Hart Lane for another sixteen, was both experienced and shrewd. We discussed the central-defensive pairing of Paul Miller and Graham Roberts. They were two powerful characters; each was a natural leader and they both had a good understanding of how the other played. We watched some films of their games and Bill said: 'Do you think they foul too much?' It was his way of saying Miller and Roberts might be conceding too many free-kicks and putting the team under pressure. It was a good point.

I had already been impressed by Richard Gough, who had irretrievably fallen out with his manager, Jim McLean, at Dundee United and this was an angle I was prepared to pursue. McLean's success, which included winning the Scottish title in 1983 and taking Dundee United to a UEFA Cup final, was founded on securing outstanding young players like Paul Sturrock, David Narey, Paul Hegarty and Gough. They were all on long contracts signed when they were young, which meant their wages were low. This had sparked a dressing-room rebellion. McLean, who ran the club with a rod of iron, responded by blocking all attempts to take his players from Tannadice.

As an insurance policy, I also spoke to the Ipswich manager, Bobby Ferguson, about Terry Butcher. I was surprised Ferguson said he would sell him – but not for anything less than £750,000. That was the same price Dundee United were quoting us for Gough. Butcher, who was then twenty-seven, three years older than Gough, was my first choice. His experience, power and leadership would provide a massive boost to Tottenham Hotspur. When I spoke to him, Terry gave me every indication he would like to come to White Hart Lane. Neither the money nor the length of contract would be a problem. Tottenham appealed to him.

Irving Scholar, however, wanted the younger man. When I asked him to pursue the offer from Ipswich and complete the deal for Butcher, I felt that he kept stalling. Gough was an exciting prospect who had won the league in Scotland and played in the European Cup semi-final against Roma. He would have far more of a resale value than Butcher. In my view, the Tottenham chairman erected barriers to a deal with Ipswich.

Finally, Butcher rang me from Heathrow. Glasgow Rangers had put an offer in writing to Ipswich and it had been accepted. He told me he could not wait any longer as he had been told Tottenham had still not delivered a concrete proposal. Disappointed by several weeks of vain pursuit, I told the club to do the deal with Dundee United for Gough.

I met Richard at the West Park Lodge in Hadley Wood on a Sunday morning. Talks were proceeding smoothly until Ken Bates tried the same trick John Lyall had used when Luton were negotiating with Frank McAvennie. Whatever Tottenham offered Gough, Chelsea would better it. This time I knew I had to keep Richard in the hotel until the deal was done. I need not have worried. Gough told me: 'I gave you my word. I won't talk to Chelsea.' This taught me much about Gough's character. Gough's athleticism, his speed, tackling and sheer, unbridled enthusiasm complemented Gary Mabbutt, whom I placed alongside him at the heart of the Tottenham defence. In that season, only one player troubled him: Cyrille Regis of Coventry City, whom we were to meet in the FA Cup final. Richard was mature, self-willed and opinionated but good company. He was an obsessive trainer.

However, I always believed that had we taken Terry Butcher, Tottenham might have won the league in 1987. His extra knowledge, plus the balance of having a right-footer like Gary Mabbutt along-side a left-footer like Butcher, could have been a dream addition.

Tottenham's training centre was at Cheshunt. We trained hard and I enjoyed working with the quality the club had assembled – Hoddle's cross-field passes, Waddle's trickery, Paul Allen's ferreting, the finishing of his cousin, Clive.

Players were traded. Paul Miller, a loyal Spur, was disappointed to leave for Charlton. He had come up through the ranks at Spurs and had won two FA Cups and the UEFA Cup. Mark Falco, another of the team that had beaten Anderlecht in the 1984 final, went to Watford.

In pre-season Tottenham had gone to Barcelona to contest the Joan Gamper Trophy with PSV Eindhoven and AC Milan joining the hosts at the Nou Camp. Terry Venables was then at the height of his powers as manager of Barcelona. He had won La Liga in his first season in 1985 and taken Barcelona to the European Cup final, which had been lost on penalties to Steaua Bucharest. He joined us in a smart restaurant. Irving seemed in awe of Venables. When he was growing up and supporting Spurs from the stands, Terry Venables had been his hero and now he behaved like a schoolboy, exuding schmalzy hero-worship in his presence. At one stage he said: 'Who would have thought I would be sitting with two of the best football brains in the country?'

Irving was making his presence felt by expanding the club's commercial activities. The club shop was already thriving and he signed up to a service called ClubCall, where fans could use a premium-rate telephone number for news about their team. Over-seas supporters' associations were set up and a book and magazine department established.

Scholar was a hands-on chairman. Every few days he would appear at the ground with a carrier bag with that day's newspapers. He was always keen to be featured in them. Often, his ego would show. One day, Harry Hughes, the shop manager, walked past my office with a sour face. 'What's the problem, Harry?' I shouted over to him. 'You can smile, you know.'

'It's very difficult, David,' he replied. 'I have just had an hour with Irving. Even the flags are blowing the wrong way!'

Another day, I was agreeing a contract with a young winger called Mark Robson when Irving breezed into the room. We had agreed a £45,000 fee with Exeter.

'What do we have here?' he said.

'I told you last week, Irving, that I was meeting the Exeter manager, Colin Appleton, and his chairman. This is Mark Robson, whom we have agreed to sign.'

'What's the problem?'

'Well, he has asked about a club car and I've told him we are phasing out all company vehicles. In that case, he has asked for a percentage increase on his offer.'

'Pay it.'

I felt quite humiliated. I'd been trying to be careful with Tottenham's money by following club policy and had suddenly been made to seem like the bad guy. Mark still smiles at this story. He was a bright jockey of a winger. He did not make it at Spurs but had a good career at West Ham and Charlton before coaching the England under-17 and under-20 teams.

The early months were fascinating. Board meetings were rarely called. Tony Berry of Blue Arrow, Douglas Alexiou, a lawyer, Paul Bobroff, a property developer, and Frank Sinclair, who had first started going to White Hart Lane in the 1930s, were Scholar's directors. All allowed Irving to get on with it. Peter Barnes, the club secretary, made Scholar aware of the rule book. Much of the legal work was allocated to big hitters in the City. It was a cosy group, but I was pleased that my job kept me away from the staff meetings. I enjoyed being on the training pitches.

We had begun with Clive Allen scoring a hat-trick at Aston Villa and five in our first eight games. Clive's father, Les, had played in Tottenham's Double-winning side of 1961 and as early as October Jimmy Greaves was suggesting Clive would break his club record of forty-four goals in a single season. After a 2–0 win over Everton, we had climbed to sixth, five points behind the leaders, Nottingham Forest. Our next game would be at home to Luton. In the days before the game, I had been subjected to some vitriolic comments from David Evans in the national press, building the afternoon into a grudge match.

In my programme notes for the game, I fell victim to this antagonism. I wrote: 'Enjoy the game. May the headlines not be about hooligan chairmen, managers' gossip and slander but entertaining football.' There should have been a comma between 'hooligan' and 'chairmen' and both should have been plural. The sentence should have read: 'May the headlines not be about hooligans, chairmen, managers' gossip and slander...' I was told about the error prior to the programme going to print and expressed a wish to retain it. This was a big mistake. A journalist spotted it and I claimed a printing error. Evans pounced on it and continued his character assassination. The game was a disappointing goalless stalemate that Evans declared a moral victory for Luton.

On leaving Luton, I had been due accumulated bonuses amounting to £25,000. I received a letter from John Smith, the chief executive, informing me the board had decided I was not to be paid. The club claimed I had broken agreements made when I left that I would not take Luton staff members to Tottenham. I was staggered but not surprised. It was a form of revenge. There had been no agreement and neither Trevor Hartley nor John Sheridan was even under contract to Luton when they joined Spurs. However, I reluctantly decided to let it go. I did not want any more aggravation. I was still living in Luton, where I had been heavily criticised in the local press for my 'disloyalty' – I had been at the club for twelve years, eight of them as manager. Eggs were thrown at our bungalow windows. I complained about it to the police, but when I told my friends, they seemed to disregard the seriousness of the situation by making jokes about eggs. I could not laugh it off and to my wife and two young children it was not funny. Indeed, when the police came round, they suggested I should move house. When I asked if they could keep an eye on my property, they seemed completely uninterested.

In October, I signed Nico Claesen from Standard Liège for £600,000. The striker had caught my eye during the World Cup, where Belgium had reached the semi-finals, playing some wonderfully enterprising football. He would make his debut at Anfield, where Tottenham had registered one victory since the sinking of the *Titanic*. Claesen scored the only goal to send us third in the table. He then returned to Belgium to score a hat-trick against Luxembourg. Nico was sharp, made clever movements off the ball and the partnership with Clive Allen looked promising until he suffered hamstring problems in a period in which Spurs, having beaten Liverpool, did not win a game for a month.

We spent one morning looking at a system that would accommodate Ossie Ardiles and would leave Clive operating on his own up front. Glenn Hoddle would play in a freer role behind him. It proved the catalyst for a terrific run. The experiment was launched with a 4–2 win at Oxford. The next two matches brought Tottenham five goals but only one point as we lost to Nottingham Forest, 3–2, and drew 3–3 at Old Trafford, where Alex Ferguson had just taken over as manager of Manchester United.

However, since we were scoring goals and creating chances, the poor return on points did not especially concern me. The next three matches brought eight goals and nine points. The pieces of the jigsaw were fitting. The 2–0 win at Chelsea saw me create another problem for myself. Graham Roberts had made more than 200 league appearances for Tottenham and had been an outstandingly committed performer since joining the club from Weymouth in 1980. He had captained them to the UEFA Cup.

Now, however, he wanted to go and Glasgow Rangers had put together an excellent financial package for him. I agreed a fee of £450,000 with them. In the post-match press conference at Stamford Bridge, I was asked about Roberts by Reg Drury, the respected chief football writer of the *News of the World*. Reg had first started covering Tottenham after the Second World War as a sixteen-year-old and had extensive political as well as football contacts. I would go to his leaving do at the House of Commons. Roberts had not been in the team at Chelsea and Reg wanted to know where he was.

On a high from the win, I replied rather flippantly: 'He's kicked a few in England and now he's gone to kick a few in Scotland.' It was a stupid remark that presented the Sunday tabloids with a ready-made headline. It sparked a derogatory response from Roberts, in which he claimed he rated neither my tactics nor my coaching. He would go into management himself, leading Clyde to victory over Celtic – for whom Roy Keane was making his debut – in a celebrated Scottish FA Cup tie in 2006. Roberts was sacked by Clyde for allegedly making antisemitic remarks on a tour of Canada. They were allegations he strenuously denied.

On more than one occasion, Irving Scholar had told me when dealing with the press: 'Don't make jokes. They don't all understand your humour and they will turn you over.' He was right.

CHAPTER 14

'WHAT DO YOU EXPECT
ME TO DO ABOUT IT?'

Tottenham's football was attracting quite a celebrity following. Although his most famous character, Alf Garnett, was a passionate West Ham fan, Warren Mitchell was a regular attender at White Hart Lane. There were interviews in the club programme with Bernard Bresslaw, who appeared in many *Carry On* films, the singer Frankie Vaughan, the jazz musician Benny Green and Simon Mayo, a Radio 1 disc jockey.

Tony Galvin had joined from Goole Town in 1978 on Bill Nicholson's recommendation. Under Keith Burkinshaw, the club's scouting system was prepared to look at non-league players and had brought both Graham Roberts and Galvin to White Hart Lane. Between them, they would play more than 400 league games for Spurs.

Now, however, Tony was being troubled by a cruciate problem and I needed balance in attack. I went for Steve Hodge at Aston Villa. He was a tireless, workmanlike midfielder who was good enough to have been given a leading role in England's World Cup campaign in Mexico. If Galvin could not regain his fitness, I wanted to play Hodge narrow on the left, while Chris Waddle would be stationed wide on the opposite flank.

Steve was twenty-four, a quiet man and something of a loner who did not find London an easy place to be. In 1988, he would return to Nottingham Forest where he began his career. Although he scored on his debut, a 4–0 rout of West Ham on Boxing Day, and fitted in well, the Tottenham crowd never fully appreciated his contribution.

The game was typical of much of our play. Between the 4–2 win over Oxford on 22 November and the 5–0 defeat of Leicester on 27 February, we scored fifty-two goals and conceded eighteen. We had climbed to fourth in Division One, were into the quarter-finals of the FA Cup and the semi-finals of the League Cup. We were looking good.

The quarter-final of the League Cup had seen us draw 1–1 with West Ham at Upton Park. The replay, on 2 February, would probably count as the finest game Tottenham played under my management. Our neighbours were overwhelmed 5–0 by a truly tremendous team performance. Older supporters still talk of a display marked by a hat-trick from Clive Allen and goals from Glenn Hoddle and Nico Claesen.

The following week, I received a handwritten letter from the West Ham manager, John Lyall. He wrote how proud I must be to look after such a superb group of players who had performed so well on the night. What a gesture by a fellow manager. I also recall John sending me a note of congratulations when Luton won promotion to Division One in 1982. John Lyall was one of the game's special people. He was neither gregarious nor interested in self-promotion. He was decent, hard-working and humble and, I am told, a very fine coach. He was a gentleman.

The semi-final pitched us against Arsenal in a north-London derby with the prize of a place at Wembley. We won the first leg at Highbury, 1–0. I was named manager of a month in which we had won all six fixtures and scored eighteen goals without reply.

Clive Allen extended our lead in the second leg at White Hart Lane. Arsenal hit back twice in the second half through Viv Anderson and Niall Quinn. There was no away-goals rule and no penalty shoot-out. There would be a replay which a toss of a coin determined Tottenham would host. Even outside north London, interest in the game was huge.

For the third successive time in that semi-final, Clive Allen gave us the lead with his twelfth goal in the competition – a record for a single season in the League Cup. We held on to it until ten minutes before the final whistle. These were ten minutes in which everything fell apart. We lost two, preventable, goals to our neighbours. The first came from a long, speculative ball from Paul Davis which Ian Allinson chased, turned Richard Gough and shot past Ray Clemence at the near post. Allinson was only on the pitch because of an injury to Charlie Nicholas.

Then from another long ball, this time from Arsenal's goalkeeper, John Lukic, Allinson, who was a fringe player at Highbury, attempted a shot that struck Danny Thomas's heel and rebounded straight into the path of David Rocastle to score the winner. Within seconds, our supporters began filing out of their seats. When the final whistle blew, White Hart Lane was less than 60 per cent full. Football can be fickle, but I understood the reaction. Ian Allinson, who had done so much to turn the game, did not make the squad for the final with Liverpool. He would be sold to Stoke in the summer.

Tottenham, however, had jumped the gun. During the interval in the first game at White Hart Lane, the Tannoys had given details of the ticketing arrangements for the final. Irving Scholar had, unwisely, already ordered the printing of T-shirts for sale in the club shop which had 'League Cup Final 1987' emblazoned on the front. The press found out and we were held up to ridicule.

Irving was a very confident man. He was handsome, wealthy and chairman of Tottenham Hotspur. He brushed criticism aside. He had an air of effortless superiority. Sometimes, he could annoy me. In September, after we had lost 2–0 at Southampton, I told him about several of our supporters holding up Israeli flags. Perhaps I was being oversensitive, but it gave me an uncomfortable feeling. It was an invitation for anti-Jewish prejudice.

Irving had difficulties understanding the occasional problems a Jewish manager might have in giving instructions to a Gentile dressing room. Tottenham were becoming more strongly identified as a Jewish club and we were never aware of what people, deep down, thought about this. Growing up in a wealthy Jewish environment in north London, Irving had never experienced the occasional antisemitic abuse I had been forced to accept. He laughed off my thoughts with a shrug. 'What do you expect me to do about it?'

In my programme notes for the game against Queens Park Rangers on the Saturday, I wrote:

A few days ago, we suffered a massive disappointment. The feeling has been shared by all those who love Tottenham Hotspur. We wish Arsenal success in the final. To lose 4–3 on aggregate in the last eight minutes of a semi-final could shatter any fainthearted or fair-weather supporter. I promise you that we will continue our resolve to play good, attractive football successfully. This is our first major setback. We will have others but this is the big test.

This was my attempt to keep the Spurs faithful onside while being gracious to our rivals. They were sentiments that were not shared by many of our supporters and indeed certain of our directors. They saw no reason why we should wish Arsenal well in a cup final. They would win it, beating Liverpool 2–1.

A bounce-back after the Arsenal defeat was vital. We beat QPR 1–0 with Clive scoring his ninth goal in eleven games. Some 32,000 were at White Hart Lane to see us continue our league progress with a 1–0 victory over Liverpool secured by a Chris Waddle goal.

Between 1912 and 1985, Tottenham had never done the double over Liverpool. They had now achieved this feat twice in three seasons.

Waddle was a laid-back character but an outstanding winger with a great change of pace and body-swerve. He had the knack of feinting to cross with his right foot and then chopping the ball back on to his left and vice-versa. You had to listen carefully when talking to him because he had a broad Durham accent and spoke softly.

After a 3–0 victory over Aston Villa on 24 January, Chris came to see me, saying he was unhappy out on the wing and would rather play more centrally. I was a little shocked because we had won the game comfortably and I had no intention of changing Tottenham's formation. Glenn Hoddle was revelling in the No. 10 position, where we had removed the need for him to have any defensive responsibilities. It is a role in which he would flourish at Monaco, where he enjoyed the freedom of being a pure creator. Chris, too, would later get his wish of a more central role at Marseilles in an outstanding team that reached the 1991 European Cup final, where he played up front with the brilliant Jean-Pierre Papin.

The second game against Luton, this time at Kenilworth Road, caused more aggravation. We played poorly on the artificial pitch and were beaten, 3–1. Irving Scholar, sitting in the directors' box, was the target of terrible antisemitic abuse, including songs about Auschwitz. The press box at Kenilworth Road was next to the directors' box, ensuring that the vile comments were recorded. I was another target of the vitriol, with continual cries of 'Judas' aimed my way. It was a horrible afternoon and hard for me to reconcile the fact that I had overseen their emergence as a force in Division One. The Luton players who had just beaten Tottenham to send them third in the table were my signings. They were my boys. It was a strange feeling, but I was hurt. David Evans, who would soon win Welwyn and Hatfield for the Conservatives in the 1987 election, made no attempt to apologise for the way his supporters had behaved.

However, we held our nerve and our form. On 25 April, we overcame Oxford, 3–1, which featured Glenn Hoddle's final goal for Tottenham. It was one of his very best. He collected the ball on the halfway line and ran straight through a square defence before dummying the goalkeeper, Peter Hucker, who finished flat on his back. Glenn almost walked the ball into the net. Earlier, Hoddle had sent a chip on to the crossbar from twenty yards. He was a craftsman.

That evening, I sat in a West End restaurant with Irving Scholar and Gérard Houllier, the manager of Paris St-Germain, discussing Hoddle's future. We had promised Glenn he could leave and France was an attractive destination. We agreed a deal in principle with Houllier and shook hands. In retrospect, this was something we should not have done. We acted without any reference to Hoddle's agent, Dennis Roach, who got wind of the discussions and was aware that his player would have to agree the move to Paris.

Hoddle was keen and met Houllier while Irving Scholar oversaw negotiations from the Ritz in Paris. However, the negotiations dragged on, allowing Roach, a strong character, to make an arrangement with Monaco, who had just appointed the 37-year-old Arsène Wenger to be their manager. Glenn had never heard of Wenger and expected to be flown to Paris, but once he met him in the south of France he signed for Monaco, a decision he was never to regret. Gérard Houllier was very unhappy at the news, but as in all transfers, the player had the final call.

After a 4–0 win over Manchester United on 4 May, Tottenham were third, although the same day Everton had won the league with a 1–0 victory at Norwich. We had two matches to go, and at the end of those there was an FA Cup final. Our season finished on a Monday night at Goodison Park. I wanted to rest players for the

final, which would be played against Coventry five days later. I selected Phil Gray, Paul Moran, Mark Stimson, John Moncur, Vinny
Samways, Tony Parks, John Polston and Neil Ruddock – all from
the successful reserve side.

A crowd of 28,287 saw Everton celebrate their ninth league title
with a 1–0 win with a goal from the substitute and my personal
nemesis, Derek Mountfield. After the game, Everton complained to
the Football League that Tottenham had played a weakened team
and devalued the game. The hearing was held at the Great Western
Hotel at Paddington Station and we were accused of depriving the
spectators at Goodison, who had paid full price for their tickets,
of seeing the Tottenham Hotspur first XI. Given that Everton had
already won the title and we were in an FA Cup final a few days later,
I thought this an unnecessary complaint.

I attended the hearing with Douglas Alexiou, a board member
who was also a solicitor. Peter Swales, the chairman of Manchester
City, who had just endured another relegation, was one of those
who sat in judgement. Tottenham were fined £10,000, an amount
that was halved on appeal. Everything about the case was frivolous.

Tottenham would not better that third-place finish for another thirty years. Since adopting the tactics of a lone striker against
Oxford in November, Spurs had won seventeen of their twenty-seven
league matches and risen from tenth to third. The quality of the
football was acclaimed even by those who recalled Tottenham's
glory, glory years. Clive Allen's forty-nine goals in a season won
him the Footballer of the Year award from both the PFA and the
Football Writers' Association.

Helping him achieve those awards was our fabulous five-man
midfield. Waddle, the mesmeric wide man; Paul Allen, a workaholic ferreter of a football; Ardiles, an opinionated but outstanding
link man; Hoddle, the gifted, two-footed craftsman; and Hodge,

an indefatigable, left-sided worker. They were round pegs in round holes. The central-defensive partnership of Richard Gough and Gary Mabbutt made a huge contribution.

Two days after Clive was presented with the Footballer of the Year trophy from the FWA, he would spearhead the attack in an FA Cup final.

CHAPTER 15

'NO. 4 WILL PLAY... NO. 15'

The FA Cup final was, to me, always bathed in a golden glow. My early memories of finals stir the emotions. On those Saturdays, my mates and I would play football in the morning trying to emulate the players we would be watching that afternoon. We would arrive with our boots tied around our necks by long, white laces. We would bring coats for goalposts. A few hours afterwards, we would settle in front of the black-and-white television, watching the build-up. The curtains would be drawn because the sun would always be shining.

My father, like many others, bought a television to watch the 1953 cup final and the Coronation. The final between Blackpool and Bolton was a vivid memory. Stan Mortensen scored three and all the accolades went to Stanley Matthews, the 'Wizard of the Dribble', who tormented Tommy Banks, the burly Bolton left-back. Three years later came the trauma of the Manchester City keeper Bert Trautmann clutching his neck when diving at the feet of the Birmingham forward, Peter Murphy, and playing on with a broken vertebra. In 1959, my team, Nottingham Forest, were at Wembley, holding off Luton, the club that would later define me, with ten men after their goalscorer, Roy Dwight, had broken his leg.

Then, the FA Cup was an institution with its own unique calendar. Schoolboys camped around a transistor radio on a Monday lunchtime to hear the draw for the next round. There would be thousands across the country, in factories and offices, doing the same. Bryon

Butler's deep, mellifluous voice, with its West Country undertones, would introduce the draw from Lancaster Gate. Then you would hear: 'No. 4 will play… No. 15.' The excitement grew.

By time the third-round draw was made in December, the competition would have been running for many months. In August, semi-professional teams would, initially, be divided into regional groups. At Nuneaton, we had to win five games just to make our first-round tie at Torquay.

Nottingham Forest's journey to Wembley in 1959 began on an icy pitch at Tooting and Mitcham, who had already beaten Bournemouth and Northampton after qualifying for the first round. I still have the two-page team sheet from that game at Sandy Lane. Forest escaped to win the replay and then thoughts began to spark that this could be their year. Victories over Grimsby, Birmingham and Bolton followed and then, after a 1–0 win over Aston Villa at Hillsborough, came Wembley and the culmination of a football season.

The hullaballoo around a final would be long and loud. First would come the clamour for tickets. There would never be enough. Wembley could accommodate 100,000, but only 20 per cent of those tickets would go to each club. Touts thrived and players from the two teams that had made the final would probably have the opportunity to purchase at least a dozen or so more on top of their complementary allocation. All clubs would be given an allocation of tickets, although those in the lower divisions would have proportionately less. Usually, a senior player would have the opportunity to buy two tickets. The players would pool the tickets and nominate a teammate to take them to an agency or a tout to get the best price.

I was the Professional Footballers' Association rep at Luton, collecting subs of two shillings and sixpence a week for the players' union. I was asked by the players to go to an address in Barnet and sell their cup final tickets. Then, there were no checks on where the tickets went nor any way of tracing them. With a large envelope in my hand containing thirty tickets, I knocked on the door and was welcomed in by a Scottish woman who invited me in for a cup of tea in the lounge and then ushered me into an office occupied by her husband, Stan Flashman, the self-styled 'King of the Ticket Touts'. Flashman, a small, rather obese man, sat in a chair with a box of various tickets on one side of the desk and a small cash tin on the other. As I left with the money, an Arsenal player, whom I recognised, passed me on the driveway. Mr Flashman had a thriving business.

For the two clubs who had made the final, the day was to be cherished rather than profited from. Tickets were the biggest thorn of contention. The chairman, the directors and the secretary would have full control of the distribution of tickets to the players and staff. At the board meeting before the cup final, tickets would often be the first item on the agenda. The players would invariably be unhappy with their allocation.

They then, however, became the centre of attention, with press interviews galore, television appearances and a new kit for the game. Sometimes, with guidance from the manager, the players would select an agent to deal with the 'extras' that came with a Wembley appearance. One of the agent's tasks was to negotiate the 'cup final song' with a musical entrepreneur, which would make the players money and give the club greater projection. Ten FA Cup final songs made the top ten and none sold more than 'Blue is the Colour', Chelsea's hymn to the 1970 final with Leeds.

A morning would also have to be set aside for the measuring and fitting of the cup final suits. A hotel would be booked for the Friday night, the timing of the coach's departure for Wembley transmitted to the police. En route, there would be certain superstitions. If you saw a black cat or a white wedding, this was supposed to be lucky. You wondered how the luck would be divided if both teams saw the wedding or the cat.

There might be a deal with a television channel for a presenter to travel with the team to talk about the atmosphere on the bus and film the crowds that would surround it as it nosed into Wembley Way. In 1987, ITV's Martin Tyler accompanied my Tottenham team. The toss for use of Wembley's cavernous dressing rooms would already have taken place. There would be more superstition as to whether you were handed the home or away changing room, although the superstition was at its greatest when Wembley's finals were shifted to Cardiff's Millennium Stadium. For the first eleven finals in all competitions, the team that had the north dressing room, the one used by Wales, won.

Then there would be the obligatory walk around the pitch with a wave to family and friends who would invariably have taken their seats early. In the hospitality room, behind the Royal Box, would be the FA councillors and staff, the directors of the two clubs, the county secretaries, the chairmen of other clubs who would have taken their wives to one of the season's great perks.

The dining experience was superb. Speeches would be given between courses and at the top table the FA Cup sat gleaming. The Queen rarely attended; her last FA Cup final was seeing Southampton overcome Manchester United in 1976. Her grandfather, George V, had been much more enthusiastic about football. It became an occasion for politicians and celebrities. When I took Tottenham to the 1987 final, Margaret Thatcher sat in the Royal Box. Irving Scholar recalled: 'She spoke straight through you and seemed totally deaf to anything anyone else was saying.' He found John Major, the guest for the 1991 final between Tottenham and Nottingham Forest, much readier to listen.

The vans relaying the television pictures around the world would have parked up in the media compound by Friday morning at the latest. The camera crews would arrive early on the Saturday before dispersing to their positions. The match was broadcast

simultaneously on BBC and ITV and the audiences reached their peak in 1970 when more than 28 million watched the replay between Chelsea and Leeds from Old Trafford. Half a century later, the audience for the final between Arsenal and Chelsea was 8.2 million. It was still the most watched match of the season.

The commentators, studio guests and summarisers needed to be on site around four hours before kick-off. An old, converted bus would supply hot or cold refreshments to them until what the producers called 'the talent' took up their positions in the commentary box or the studio.

In 1991, the FA decided to allow Arsenal and Tottenham to play their FA Cup semi-final at Wembley. Two years later, the two teams met in another semi-final at Wembley. Sheffield United and Sheffield Wednesday had been due to play their semi-final at Elland Road, but when the Yorkshire clubs protested, their game, too, was moved to enable more of their supporters to watch.

When the new, rebuilt Wembley opened in 2007, it was decreed that all future FA Cup semi-finals should be played there to help offset the £798 million cost of the stadium. No more would th use Old Trafford, Villa Park or Hillsborough – a decision uni sally decried by the football family. Before, semi-final grounds been selected to suit both teams' travelling times. Now there v alternative but north London. The exclusivity of the Wembl was also devalued.

Winning the FA Cup meant qualification first for Winners' Cup and later the Europa League, which was scorned but was nothing like the same money-spinner a pions League. To earn the same prize money for just the Champions League group stages, a club would h Europa League. The rewards for winning the FA Cup to those handed out by the Premier League. When FA Cup in 2020, it was worth £2.6 million to t

sixth in the Premier League earned their neighbours, Tottenham, £32 million.

The first round in November is when the competition properly begins. In 1986, Chris Waddle's old team, Tow Law Town, lost their County Durham derby with Spennymoor. Blyth Spartans, who had made the fifth round of the competition in 1978, would beat Crook Town after a replay. Morecambe thrashed Esh Winning 8–0.

It also featured clubs who had once been at the very heart of the FA Cup but who were now shadows of what they had been. Wolverhampton Wanderers, who had been to eight FA Cup finals, lost to Chorley. Burnley, whose third and last final had seen them lose to Tottenham in 1962, were humiliated by Telford United. Blackpool, the club of Matthews and Mortensen, were brushed aside by Middlesbrough, whose liquidation had been announced three months before. Bolton, who had been to five FA Cup finals, required two replays to see off Halifax.

Tottenham's 1986/87 journey began in the third round, drawn at home to Fourth Division Scunthorpe, who had beaten Southport and Runcorn to reach this far. They were managed by Frank Barlow, who had assembled a team of experienced players, including Richard Money, whom I had signed from Liverpool when I was manager of Luton. We won narrowly, 3–2, although the afternoon was more comfortable than the scoreline suggested. Nico Claesen, Gary Mabbutt and Chris Waddle shared the Spurs goals to earn a home tie with Crystal Palace, who had knocked out Nottingham Forest.

The Scunthorpe game had attracted a shade under 20,000 spectators. Usually, season tickets did not include cup games. There was almost 30,000 at White Hart Lane as we brushed our south London rivals aside, 4–0. We were given another home draw, this time against Newcastle.

Before the tie, I had taken the team away to the Henlow Grange health farm, where I had prepared Luton's players for their decisive

game at Manchester City four years before. However, in the players' view the journey from Bedfordshire to White Hart Lane took too long on the Saturday. We had set off after our pre-match meal of tea and toast and after the game the players said they did not want a repetition. I had just been awarded my second successive manager-of-the month award after a run of seven victories in eight games and a crowd of 38,000 reflected the upswing in Tottenham's fortunes. Newcastle were bottom of Division One, but it required a Clive Allen penalty to send us into the quarter-finals.

For the only time in that season's FA Cup, we would be drawn away, although we would remain in London, facing Wimbledon's rugged, long-ball game at Plough Lane. Unfortunately, we had lost our regular right-back, Danny Thomas, who had been enjoying an outstanding season, to injury. In March, he had been badly tackled by Gavin Maguire while playing Queens Park Rangers and suffered a torn cruciate. He remained philosophical, thanking the fans for their messages of support as he watched the quarter-final from his hospital bed. Gary Stevens, himself recovering from injury, would replace him at Wimbledon. The injury would force Danny's retirement the following year. He would take a degree in physiotherapy in which role he would join West Bromwich Albion. He was an intelligent and perceptive man who wrote me a heartwarming letter when I left Spurs the following season.

I took the squad to Brighton before we faced Wimbledon for some sea air to accompany our normal pre-match preparation. We would then travel to south London for the quarter-final. This time, however, we would set off before the pre-match meal, which we would have closer to Plough Lane. Unfortunately, on the morning of the match we discovered our team bus, which was plastered with logos from our sponsors, Holsten, had suffered smashed windows at the hand of hooligans. A replacement bus drove us to Plough Lane, where 15,000 had crammed into the small ground.

The dressing rooms were tiny, and the showers in the one used by the away team invariably had only cold water. The home dressing room had a boombox that would be playing at maximum volume. It was a ploy and for Wimbledon it was usually a relatively successful one. We were not intimidated and our short, clever passing and craft made the Wimbledon hard men look second best. Two brilliant goals from Hoddle and Waddle propelled us into the semi-final. We would play Watford at Villa Park.

Watford had reached this stage of the competition by beating Arsenal at Highbury. However, between the quarter and the semi-finals, they had suffered a goalkeeping catastrophe. First, Tony Coton broke his thumb saving a shot from Luther Blissett in training and then, in another training-ground accident, Steve Sherwood, who had kept goal against Everton in the 1984 final, dislocated his finger. Graham Taylor's only alternative was the sixteen-year-old David James.

Fearing that James might never recover from a traumatic experience in an FA Cup semi-final and able only to sign free agents because it was past the transfer deadline, Taylor approached Pat Jennings, who was forty-one and had gone to Everton as cover for Neville Southall before the 1986 final. Jennings turned Watford down. So, too, did the 45-year-old Bob Wilson, who had not played professionally in thirteen years.

Then Graham contacted Gary Plumley, the son of Watford's chief executive, Eddie Plumley. He had played for Newport and Cardiff but was running a wine bar in the Welsh village of Caerleon and turning out in a few games for Ebbw Vale. He went to a sports shop in Newport, bought himself some new gloves, and joined up with the Watford squad at Lilleshall. This could not have boosted the confidence of the players. Dave Butler, who was then Watford's physio, told me later the players were astonished Graham Taylor had not taken a chance with Sherwood.

They had seen his fitness test that morning; they all thought he had looked good and was ready for action. The manager, however, had the final say. Graham told Plumley he was impressed with his confidence even though he knew Sherwood was fit. It seemed a strange decision. We were three up inside half an hour. The final score was 4–1.

CHAPTER 16

'THE FINEST FINAL I HAVE HAD THE PLEASURE OF COMMENTATING ON'

Tottenham had reached their third FA Cup final in six years and their eighth in all. The previous seven had all been won. We would play Coventry, who I had seen beat Leeds at Hillsborough the day after our victory over Watford. We were immediately made favourites. It was Coventry's first appearance at Wembley.

The players had chosen First Artist, run by the brothers Jon and Paul Smith, to represent them for the final. The Smith brothers were one of the first wave of football agents and had ingratiated themselves with the England squad. They would look after Tottenham's cup final song.

Even before the semi-final, the song for the 1981 final, 'Ossie's Dream', which had made the top ten after the win over Manchester City, was playing on the radio. Chas and Dave recorded another song with the team for the 1987 final, called 'Hot Shot Tottenham'. This did less well, reaching only No. 18 and was outperformed by 'Diamond Lights' by Glenn Hoddle and Chris Waddle, which reached No. 12. They performed it on *Top of the Pops* the day after a 2–2 draw with Wimbledon on 22 April. They were asked to go to the studio because the video of 'Diamond Lights' was so bad it was considered unusable by the BBC.

Irving Scholar had come up with an idea to place a camera in the dressing room at Wembley that would record the pre-match and half-time team-talks and, hopefully, the post-match celebrations.

The recordings would be used in a video of Tottenham's cup run. The players, rightly in my opinion, refused. The dressing room is sacrosanct. The players formed a committee and asked what extras they would receive if we allowed filming in the dressing room?

I told Irving there was no possibility of the players agreeing to this, regardless of any extra payments. He then came out with the incredible idea of placing a camera in the ceiling of the dressing room and the players 'would be none the wiser'. He had consulted an ITV producer, Derek Sando, who had told him it would be possible to arrange. I did not even consult the players but rejected the suggestion outright. I could be accused of spying on my own team. After the usual discussions about ticket allocations, we were ready. I had decided to play Chris Hughton, now recovered from injury but with very little game time under his belt, in the right-back spot in place of Gary Stevens, who earlier in the season had undergone an operation for a broken collar bone.

We stayed in a hotel in Cheshunt, used extensively by Tesco, whose chief executive, Ian MacLaurin, later to become the chairman of the England and Wales Cricket Board, was a prominent Spurs fan. On a warm spring day, the coach sped south to Wembley, inching the last couple of miles through the crowds. I thought we had too many people on that bus. There were those on board who should not have been there. Scouts and coaches like Ted Buxton and Keith Blunt were on the bus. Martin Tyler was conducting interviews. It seemed claustrophobic. Retrospectively, it was a poor decision, but at the time I wanted as many people as possible to feel part of it.

However, we were heading towards what would be described as one of the great FA Cup finals. A superb cross from Waddle, met by Clive Allen for his forty-ninth goal of the season, gave Tottenham the lead before three minutes were up. Coventry equalised in the eighth minute through Dave Bennett, who had been part of the Manchester City side that had lost to Spurs in the 1981 final.

Slowly, Coventry asserted themselves. Little Micky Gynn ran tirelessly in midfield. Lloyd McGrath marked Hoddle tightly. Cyrille Regis won a couple of vital headers against Richard Gough who looked strangely sluggish. A Regis header, which Coventry thought had given them the lead, was disallowed. Bennett, at outside right, was probably the architect of the win. His trickery baffled Mitchell Thomas on occasions.

Tottenham had our share of the play. Steve Ogrizovic, in the Coventry goal, courted disaster by passing straight to Hoddle and, just before the interval, Gary Mabbutt put Spurs ahead. Then came Bennett's cross, met by Keith Houchen's magnificent diving header and Coventry, once more, were level. Then came extra time.

Tottenham had played thirty-one games since New Year's Day, four more than Coventry and, by now, we were running on empty. When Gary Mabbutt deflected McGrath's cross past Ray Clemence, it finished us off. By then, Mabbutt could barely walk. He was a diabetic and was suffering from circulatory problems and could not feel his toes as we entered the final thirty minutes.

However, it has always been my belief that the terrible studs-up challenge that Brian Kilcline made on Mabbutt around the centre-circle in the fifty-first minute was a crucial turning point. In my mind, Kilcline would have been shown a red card in any league game. Ron Atkinson, who was commentating for ITV, pointed out the challenge was very near the spot where Manchester United's Kevin Moran had been dismissed in the 1985 final. However, Neil Midgley, the referee, whom I rated highly for his ability to communicate with players, decided that the Coventry captain would not even be booked. There is a tendency to do this in big games, but a foul is a foul whether it is in a league game or a cup final, whether it is in the first or the last minute. Kilcline was substituted just before the end of normal time and the man who replaced him,

Graham Rodger, would play a crucial role in Coventry's winner. It was his pass that slipped through Lloyd McGrath to deliver the fatal cross.

After the final whistle, it would be little consolation that John Motson would say that the 1987 final was 'the finest I have had the pleasure of commentating on'. In the press conference, I noted that: 'If your best players don't perform on the day, you cannot expect to win.' It had been Hoddle's last game for Tottenham, ending a relationship that had begun in 1970 when he joined the club as a junior. His had been a glittering career, but I felt he interpreted the remark as a dig at him. It was true that he had been shackled in the final. It was also true that Cyrille Regis had vitally got the better of Richard Gough on several occasions and his flick-ons for Houchen had caused us consistent problems. Dave Bennett's ascendency over Mitchell Thomas also troubled us. I did not shore up our left flank quickly enough.

The biggest post-match dispute had nothing to do with tactics. It had been noted that several prominent Tottenham players were not wearing shirts with the sponsor's name, Holsten, on them. They included Hoddle, whose farewell to Spurs this was, and Mabbutt, who made headlines both with his decisive own goal and by going over to congratulate the Coventry bench on the final whistle. He was a gentleman and I was delighted when he earned himself a winner's medal in the 1991 final.

An investigation began. The press suggested there had been a row over money and that some players had refused to wear the Holsten shirts as a protest. This was nonsense. The cup-final kit had been in the offices of the club secretary, Peter Barnes, for two weeks. On the Friday night before the game, Johnny Wallis, our senior kit man, had gone to Wembley with four sets of shirts. There was a short-sleeved shirt and a long-sleeved shirt, both with Holsten's name on. There were also unbranded shirts, both long and short-sleeved. There were also tracksuit tops.

Johnny knew the team and each player's kit was laid by his peg with the numbers facing outwards. In his autobiography, Clive Allen writes that the mistake Johnny made was not to hang the Holsten shirts on coat-hangers as was the usual practice at White Hart Lane. The tracksuit was on top, then came the Holsten shirt, the plain shirt, a T-shirt, socks, and shorts.

The dressing room was airless. Around quarter to three, with Coventry already in the tunnel, the FA official, Adrian Titcombe, banged on the door urging us to leave the dressing room. Our senior players, some of whom were internationals, motioned to say: 'Let them wait.' Finally, the players hurriedly put their shirts on and put a tracksuit top over it. Just before kick-off the tracksuit top was removed and taken away. It was then that Clive Allen asked Glenn Hoddle why he was not wearing the sponsored shirt. Hoddle replied that it was a bit late to change it.

Up in the Royal Box, Irving Scholar noted the discrepancy about ten minutes before the interval. Mike Rollo, the club's commercial manager who was responsible for the Holsten deal, rushed down to the perimeter fence at the interval, desperate to reach the dressing room and point out the error. Rollo, however, was refused entry to the perimeter around the pitch by a steward. Even when Rollo offered him money, the steward held firm. Inside the dressing room, the players, 2–1 in front, were calm. They washed down and put their shirts back on. Nobody, amid the incredible intensity of an FA Cup final, would have looked at his shirt and noted the absence of a sponsor's logo. Not one of the radio or television commentators on the day noted anything was amiss. Nor, in all probability, did the crowd.

Scholar came down to the dressing room after the match and the inquisition began. On a miserable Sunday with the sunshine of

the Saturday replaced by torrential rain, a board meeting had been called. It must have been the first called by any club the Sunday after a cup final. Scholar said Holsten were going berserk and the press had headlined the error. A sponsorship that had begun in November 1983, when Tottenham knocked Bayern Munich out of the UEFA Cup, was now in jeopardy. It was worth £250,000 a year.

He was not sure who to blame, but I was heavily criticised, as if he suspected that this had been some kind of payback for the refusal to allow cameras into the dressing room. Ironically, had we put a camera in the dressing-room ceiling, Scholar's conspiracy theories would have been put to rest. Had we won the game, the atmosphere would have been considerably less intense.

On the Monday, I went with Irving, Mike Rollo and Peter Barnes to Holsten's offices in Ludgate Circus. Before the meeting, we went to discuss tactics in a cafe, where in the morning papers we could read the adverts taken out by Holsten's main rival, Carling, mocking the situation. After much discussion, Holsten told us they would continue their sponsorship of Tottenham, which would last until 1995 when they were replaced by Hewlett Packard. They had received far more publicity from the affair than had the players all worn sponsored shirts. They certainly had far more attention than the sponsors of the winning team – Granada Bingo.

Heads, however, had to roll. Johnny Wallis had been associated with Tottenham since 1948 when he was appointed the club's A-team manager. He had been reserve-team manager under Bill Nicholson and then from 1968 he was on the bench as trainer and physiotherapist. He had been kit man for a further dozen years. Johnny, who would be awarded the MBE in 1993, was demoted to the reserves.

However, the Holsten affair combined with the fact that this was the first time Tottenham had lost an FA Cup final, changed Irving's attitude towards me. Our relationship became cooler. In contrast to the open-top bus parade through the streets of Coventry, there was a low-key, rain-sodden reception at Tottenham Town Hall. To compound a terrible weekend, when we arrived home, Maureen noted a stone had gone missing from her ring. She was inconsolable. We searched in vain for the diamond.

In the aftermath of the FA Cup final, Richard Gough requested a transfer, telling me that if he did not return to Scotland, he would be facing a divorce. He had needed an operation after the final, but instead of complying with the club's plans, he flew to join family in South Africa. We were disappointed by his attitude.

Bob Harris, a relatively friendly journalist whom I had first met when commentating on an England international against the Soviet Union in Tbilisi in March 1986, phoned me. Bob was friendly with the Rangers manager, Graeme Souness: 'Souey wants to know what you would take for Gough?'

'Tell Souey he should ring me direct. I will tell him the same I will tell you. He is not for sale.'

However, it was clear Souness and Gough had already spoken. David Holmes, the Rangers chairman, rang me, saying he knew Gough was unhappy and wanted to return to Scotland. He would offer the same £750,000 we had bought him from Dundee United twelve months before. I reported this to Irving Scholar who replied: 'They must be joking. We would want double that. We must stay firm.' When I relayed this to Holmes, saying we would want £1.5 million for Gough, he replied in an instant: 'We will pay it.' I was trapped. Gough wanted out, Rangers said they would pay the fee and had already discussed his salary. Such was Glasgow Rangers' financial muscle that they paid the transfer fee in a single lump.

It was a harsh lesson about doing transfer business. When I was working for Alan Sugar at Spurs, he told me if I was asked for a price for a player, I should say: 'Lobster'. When I asked why 'Lobster' – he said it was the price of the day. The price would be revealed when the offer was made.

Richard Gough was a fine athlete; fit, strong in the air, a sound tackler and a leader. He was rarely careless with his passing and very mature for his age. We had doubled our money, which is something Scholar said we would do when he preferred Gough to Terry Butcher. Now, Souness had them both. Richard would win nine straight Scottish League titles at Ibrox, although returning to Scotland did not save his marriage. His warning to me about his wife was not a hoax to force a transfer. I always thought he should have returned to England and really tested himself. It was perhaps too easy for him in Glasgow. Although we had only a single season together, we kept in touch and he would frequently ring me for advice in a career that would take him to California and finish at Everton at the age of thirty-nine. He now lives in San Diego.

As his replacement, I took Chris Fairclough from Nottingham Forest, a strong, upright centre-half, who was also wanted by Howard Wilkinson at Sheffield Wednesday. I sensed some personal animosity between Brian Clough and Wilkinson. Clough respected Wilkinson without liking him. However, the business of transferring Fairclough to White Hart Lane went to a tribunal, which ordered Tottenham to pay £387,000. Howard eventually got his man when Fairclough joined him at Leeds in 1989, after he had endured a difficult second season at Spurs under Terry Venables. He would be part of the side that, three years later, would become league champions.

Glenn Hoddle had left for Monaco and I had paid Nottingham Forest £250,000 for Johnny Metgod, a balding 29-year-old Dutchman, who could play in midfield or central defence. He possessed a fearsome free-kick and was a lovely man who became the butt of some dressing-room jokes because he tended to travel to and from training by bike. However, I soon realised it would be hard for him to fill Hoddle's boots. Metgod would be afflicted by a hernia and would play only a dozen league games for Spurs before he returned to Holland with Feyenoord.

When I was at Leicester, I made the same problem for myself when trying to replace our most creative player, Gary McAllister, who had signed for Leeds. Billy Davies, who had played for Rangers and was now at St Mirren, could not fill the void left by McAllister when I took him to Filbert Street. By giving Davies the No. 10 shirt, supporters associated him with McAllister, a man he could never truly replace. The same thing would happen with Metgod and Hoddle.

In the summer of 1987, we spent many pre-season days amid the beautiful scenery and climate of Sweden, scoring nineteen goals in four games, gaining a rhythm against semi-professional sides. The first game of the new season pitched us against Coventry City, the opponents who had inflicted so much pain on us a few months before. There was more pain. Coventry won, 2–1, at Highfield Road.

However, this was the only defeat in our opening eight league games and following a 1–0 win at West Ham, on 19 September we were second behind the early pace-setters, Queens Park Rangers. Losing a League Cup tie at Torquay was a shock, but the second leg was won, 3–0, at White Hart Lane. Immediately afterwards, we travelled to Carrow Road. We lost the game, 2–1, and Ian Crook, whom I had sold to Norwich, scored a very clever goal. On the Monday, *The Sun* published an exclusive interview with Paul Allen, whose daughter, Sophie, had been born with a serious medical condition.

Irving was very agitated by the interview. He had a very close relationship with Harry Harris, the football correspondent of the *Daily Mirror*. He admonished me for allowing Paul to do the interview. It would not have suited him that the *Mirror*'s great rival had a scoop from Spurs.

Paul had made me aware his agent, Dennis Roach, had organised an interview, but I knew nothing about which paper it was going in. Just as the Holsten row would have carried less of a sting had we

Proudly wearing my England Schoolboys cap, 1960. Author collection

Scoring on my debut, aged seventeen, for Nottingham Forest against Cardiff in 1962. Author collection

I am being presented with a cheque for £500 by Billy Wright for selecting the best post-war XI from Britain and Ireland. The prize should have been a Ford Cortina, but I could not then drive. Author collection

Part of an England under-18 team in the Canary Islands in 1963 that included Tommy Smith and Ron Harris. I am on the far left of the front row. Author collection

Crossing from either flank – for Luton on my debut against Colchester in 1964 and six years later for Peterborough against Hull. Author collection

I took a journalism course in Nottingham when I was a player and have always been interested in the media.

Author collection

Marrying Maureen at Luton Register
Office, 3 June 1969. Author collection

A stable, happy family life is so important in football. Here, Maureen
is with our children, Jonathon and Joanne. Author collection

Two men who mixed laughter
and football: Luton manager Harry
Haslam and Eric Morecambe.
© PA Images / Alamy Stock Photo

Coaching with the brilliant, passionate Danny Bergara at Luton.
Author collection

On the training pitch with Luton's
wonderful winger, David Moss.
Author collection

Running on to the pitch as the final whistle blows on the all-or-nothing encounter at Manchester City, May 1983. Author collection

With the trophy after being awarded the title of 'Canon Sportsman of the Year'.
Author collection

Judging by the lack of a smile on either face, it must have been a draw. Brian Clough and I walk off at full time at Kenilworth Road. Author collection

In football, recruitment is key. These four – Emeka Nwajiobi, Ricky Hill, Mitchell Thomas and Brian Stein – played more than 1,200 games for Luton, their first professional club. Two of them played for England.

Clive Allen opens the scoring for Spurs in the epic 1987 FA Cup final against Coventry.

The artist Paul Trevillion, who was born in Tottenham and illustrated *Roy of the Rovers*, drew this impression of me directing operations at White Hart Lane.

It must have been close. Martin Peters, George Graham, Alan Sugar and I express our emotions from the directors' box at Derby, 1998.

© PA Images / Alamy Stock Photo

Posing with the League Cup after Tottenham's win over Leicester at Wembley in 1999.

Author collection

Watching Nottingham Forest with chairman Nigel Doughty (*left*) and Ian Storey-Moore © PA Images / Alamy Stock Photo

I have enjoyed Barry Fry's company since we were England Schoolboys together. We are in the stands at Milton Keynes. © Matthew Ashton via Getty Images

Chatting with José Mourinho during a Tottenham under-23 game with Liverpool. 2019.
© PRiME Media Images / Alamy Stock Photo

Raddy Antić represented everything I ever loved about football and footballers. Here, we are reminiscing not long before Raddy's death in 2020. Author collection

Taking the applause at a tribute dinner in the glamorous surroundings of Luton Hoo. Author collection

won the FA Cup, so Irving's anger was compounded by the fact that we had lost at Norwich. Paul had not played at Carrow Road and I had been questioned about it by the press.

However, my world was imploding. On a Sunday morning – and it would be a Sunday morning for a reason – I received a knock on the door at my home in Luton. The visit would make Paul Allen's interview seem the stuff of trivia.

CHAPTER 17

'DON'T LET THE BASTARDS GET YOU DOWN'

I opened the front door to be greeted by a man whom I recognised as being from the *Luton News*, a photographer and someone who claimed he was from *The Sun*. He explained they were about to run a story that I had been cautioned by the police for kerb crawling.

I was numb, frozen on my own doorstep, dressed only in my pyjama bottoms. Suddenly, the camera flashed in my eyes. My mind began reeling backwards, to try to imagine what they were talking about. I attempted to keep calm, but in truth, I was gripped by uncertainty. Over endless cups of sweet tea, I talked it through with Maureen. I explained that, maybe three years before, I had been told my car's registration had been taken by police surveillance cameras. I should have told Maureen then.

Given that Kenilworth Road lay in the middle of Luton's red-light district, all this was not as remarkable as it might sound. The ground was in a densely-populated area of the town, with terraced houses cramped together with tight secondary roads leading off them. There were always girls hanging around the area. If you left the ground late, you would have a knock on the car window at the traffic lights. From time to time, the police would make a sweep of the area to drive the sex workers off the streets. My car was easily identifiable because I had a personalised number plate. Later, one of my players would be caught out in this area and fined. When I learned my registration had been taken, I thought little of it. I certainly never imagined it would become a time bomb, ticking beneath my career. However, my name had made it back to Luton Police Station and the information had been stored. Now, someone had made use of it.

I would later learn that when newspapers want to run a sting or a scandalous story, they tend to approach the victim on a Sunday because it is far more difficult to get hold of a solicitor or seek an injunction. It gives the victim very little time to respond. The football industry has become far more sophisticated when dealing with the media. Rio Ferdinand and Ryan Giggs both took out injunctions to stop reports of their private lives being published. Other celebrities have sought injunctions and remained anonymous.

In 1987, I had no idea what an injunction was, let alone how you would get one on a Sunday afternoon. I did not even have a family solicitor. I had only ever used a lawyer to buy a house or for a signature on an insurance policy. It was nerve-wracking being told they had a story without knowing precisely what they would print. I rang Irving Scholar and explained the doorstep accusations. I told him the journalist from *The Sun* who had confronted me was sitting outside in a car with an antenna attached. I assumed he would have the ability to listen in to my phone calls.

Irving seemed quite blasé about the situation. He said if *The Sun* had no pictures or witnesses, the harm they could do would be limited. They had no photographs, but what Scholar did not appreciate was that witnesses could be invented. He suggested I drive down to London and stay in his flat in Mayfair.

Irving seemed to have little appreciation of the acute embarrassment of being confronted by *The Sun* at my own front door. Neither did he appreciate the seriousness of it all. The paper had a story that, without witnesses or alibis, I would have great difficulty in refuting. Despite the reputation of the British press, the majority of tabloid readers believe the stories they read are true.

Very early the next morning, Irving drove to Victoria Station to pick up the early editions of the papers. The story was on the front page of *The Sun*, accusing me of consorting with prostitutes. It was a salacious farrago of inventions. I read the story, which centred around a girl called Wendy Brannigan, if that was her real name. Her story was a complete fabrication. I had never met her and did not recognise the woman photographed in the paper.

When he had read the article, Irving asked me if I had been stopped by the police or had any convictions and if there was a court case pending. My answers were: no, no and no. I told him police had recorded my registration a few years ago in what was known as a book note and it was possible there may be a second note. I did not know. I had never been arrested let alone charged. The accusations, nevertheless, cut into my heart. I felt I was being portrayed as worse than a villain. Meanwhile, Maureen was at home, bravely protecting the front door from newsmen desperate for a quote.

These were reporters quite unlike any we had encountered before. I was used to sports journalists, men with whom you had personal relationships, men who had little interest in printing details of your private life or those of your players. Later, I would be contacted by a rival paper's sports reporter who had been tipped off by a colleague at *The Sun* that their news desk were working on a file on a sports personality with the initials 'DP'. He assumed it might have been the England cricketer, Derek Pringle. Had I been told this information earlier, things might have been different.

Sports journalists referred to the news reporters gathered outside our house as 'rottweilers'. They were fierce and almost uncontrollable. Maureen was at home, dealing with them as they took it in turns to march to our front door before knocking aggressively. Maureen, who showed incredible courage and presence of mind amid a situation she had been completely unprepared for, brushed them away.

We were in the path of a juggernaut. It was the height of the circulation war between Rupert Murdoch's *The Sun* and the *Daily Mirror*, owned by Robert Maxwell. The two papers between them sold 7.5 million copies a day. Under the enthusiastic direction of its editor, Kelvin MacKenzie, *The Sun* had developed a well-deserved reputation for exclusive revelations about the private lives of celebrities and for aggressive price cutting.

The *Mirror* had responded by becoming the first paper to pay out £1 million in a bingo competition. It would run promotions in which readers would be flown to New York on a specially chartered Concorde. Both papers indulged in what Oliver McGregor, the chairman of the Press Complaints Commission, called the art of 'dabbling their fingers into the stuff of other people's souls'.

The headlines were everywhere. Rival newspapers sent reporters to Luton to look for other women who might wish to sell their stories. They found none, but the press now moved to comment pieces, suggesting I was no longer fit to be manager of Tottenham Hotspur. Maureen endured an article asking how 'any wife could stay with such a man'. My parents, living nearby in Borehamwood, were also being subjected to knocks on the door and brusque requests for a comment. They were elderly and distraught. I told Dad he should not worry; the stories were fabricated. I wonder if the reporters who hounded my parents felt any sense of shame when they returned home. My son, Jon, was seventeen but had the advantage of a very supportive headmaster at Bedford School, who threw a protective ring around him to ensure he would be spared the attention. My daughter, Joanne, bravely parried the odd comment. It was not easy.

It was a story that would not go away. When I went out, I felt I was being followed. When I looked around, I thought everyone in the world had read that front page. I could not sleep properly. I was breaking out in cold sweats. I felt nobody, unless they had been at the centre of this kind of media storm, could really understand my feelings. Some victims of newspaper stings had not coped and had taken their own lives.

I wondered how this was playing out in the dressing room at White Hart Lane, which was full of big-name players, intelligent guys with strong opinions. The players would be talking about my private life, wondering if the stories were true. There is an element of showmanship in football management, especially when address-ing your players and, suddenly, I felt uncomfortable standing and talking in front of them. I was retreating into myself and, increas-ingly, I could not carry it off.

I was in a very dark place and as the press continued its attack, I found myself living through a daze, while Irving was by now be-coming increasingly worried that the stories would directly impact Tottenham. I was strongly advised not to respond to the allegations in the belief that it would only perpetuate the story and create more column inches.

I had several calls from other managers. Lawrie McMenemy, whose professional career was in turmoil after a spell at Sunderland that had seen the club relegated to the Third Division, found the time to phone and offer support. Ron Atkinson's advice was to call a press conference and laugh it off. That is something Ron, with his showmanship and rhinoceros-like hide, might have been able to accomplish. However, I was not Ron Atkinson.

Bobby Robson, whose own marriage had been pulled apart in print, told me to ignore it. Our friend Roger Easterby, a well-connected entertainment impresario, who had been chairman of Gravesend, arranged for us to have a lunch with Bobby and the ec-centric racing personality John McCririck and their wives at Henley Royal Regatta. We were on a boat, sailing down the Thames with a jazz band playing and Bobby said: 'You imagine the whole world is watching us, but you look at all these posh people on the riverbank

– do you think they care about football? Only a small percentage of people love football like us.' It was a reality check.

There were still other pillars of support. Spurs fans sent me cards and letters urging me not to give up. Arsenal's David Dein rang me to say the stories were having no impact in the higher echelons of the game and that he still wanted me to serve on FA panels. My stint as an ITV summariser did, however, come to a temporary halt. Watford's chief executive, Eddie Plumley, phoned to say there was no question of my being asked to resign from committees at FLESA (the Football League Secretaries and Managers' Association), the forerunner of the League Managers' Association. He said: 'We've seen these kinds of stories before.' Elton John, the man who had appointed Eddie, sent flowers with the message: 'Don't let the bastards get you down.'

Elton was already at war with *The Sun*. In February, he had been accused on the front page of the paper of consorting with male prostitutes. Elton John's response was to unleash a battery of lawyers. Curiously, when the story broke, Mick Jagger had phoned Elton and strongly advised him not to sue. At the height of The Rolling Stones's fame, Jagger had issued a writ against the *News of the World*, who had responded by tipping the police off about the group's drug use. In February 1967, the police had arrested Jagger and the Stones' guitarist, Keith Richards. The paper was on hand to record their embarrassment.

The Sun did throw enormous and graphic levels of abuse Elton John's way too, but as he reasoned to himself: 'I have the money. I will sue.' The source of the story would admit to it being a complete fabrication. Elton would win damages of £1 million and a front-page apology. When *The Sun* caved in to his lawyers, however, Elton John was the seventy-sixth richest man in Britain with an estimated fortune of £120 million. I was earning £45,000 a year as manager of Tottenham.

Tottenham's vice-chairman, Douglas Alexiou, was a lawyer, but his speciality was divorce rather than media law. At first, he was inclined to follow Scholar and be supportive, although as the story showed no sign of abating, that support would dwindle. In the midst of the storm, Terry Venables had been sacked by Barcelona. He was an obvious, ready-made replacement, a fact the media seized upon. Bob Driscoll of the *Daily Star* reported Scholar had been seen in Barcelona with Terry before the La Liga season began. It rang an alarm bell. I knew that, as a young fan, Irving had hero-worshipped Terry. I began to be convinced Irving was now looking to replace me.

My curtain came down with a flourish. The north-London derby was approaching and I was due for an early-morning television in-terview at the ITV studios at Euston. Driving down to my hotel, I had the strange feeling I was being followed. Then, an unmarked police car turned on its blue lights and I pulled up beside the Victo-ria Sporting Club. I was staggered to hear one of the officers order me to get into their car and justify what I was doing. They already knew who I was and they knew my number plate. The officer said he was making a book note of the incident as I was 'looking suspicious'. He implied I had been attempting to solicit a woman. My head felt like bursting.

The officers were from the nearby Paddington Police Station, fur-ther up the Edgware Road. Corruption in the Metropolitan Police which included feeding stories to the tabloids for money, was then rife. The book note was fed straight to *The Sun*, which printed it the next day. There was another front page and I was in a hole from which I felt I could not climb out.

My final game as Tottenham manager was the north-London derby on Sunday 18 October 1987. The Arsenal fans revelled in my discom-fort. Tottenham lost, 2–1. A month before, we had been second in Division One; this defeat saw us slide to seventh. On prime-time television, presenting his show from the London Palladium, Jimmy

Tarbuck made a joke at my expense. Years later, I met him at the funeral of the former Chelsea manager, Bobby Campbell, who like Jimmy was from Liverpool. By then, Tarbuck himself had been at the centre of a fabricated front-page scandal, having opened his front door in his dressing gown to be greeted by fourteen police officers, arresting him on entirely invented allegations of child sex abuse. He looked at me. There was a lot contained in that look. Perhaps it was because we had shared an experience; perhaps it was because he now recognised that front-page stories about people's private lives do not always make good subjects for comedy.

After the Arsenal game, Irving Scholar rang me saying: 'This cannot go on. A driver will pick you up and take you to Douglas Alexiou's offices in Mayfair.' Scholar and Alexiou seemed to be the only directors involved. Later, both Tony Berry and Paul Bobroff told me they had not been consulted. They felt I had deserved better treatment. At the time, however, they were passive onlookers. I sat there like a lemon, slowly accepting my end while Scholar and Alexiou talked and made some phone calls. Eventually, Irving said: 'David, we have to finish this. If you sign this piece of paper, it is a way out.' I scribbled my signature on a piece of A4 and that was it. I had gone.

In a way, it was a relief. I felt so weak that I could barely stand. I just wanted it to be over. Only later did it occur to me that I had nobody to represent me and Irving and Douglas had exploited my extreme vulnerability. There was no apology and no suggestion of compensation. I did not return to the training ground to say good-bye to the Tottenham players. I could not face up to it.

Weeks later, I saw Scholar in his flat in Chester Terrace with views over Regent's Park and suggested he owed me a settlement on my contract. They had not followed anything like the proper proce-dures when requesting my resignation. He offered me the derisory figure of £8,000.

Had I sued *The Sun* for libel, I might have had to leave Tottenham in any case to pursue the action, much as Terry Venables stepped down as England manager to 'spend more time with his lawyers' after allegations surfaced about his tangled business dealings.

I had been to Soho Square to meet Oscar Beuselinck, perhaps London's most famous entertainment and media lawyer who worked, for among others, Robert Maxwell. There were two hurdles to overcome if I planned to take action against *The Sun*. If I lost, I would pay not just my costs but those of the newspaper. They would be counted in hundreds of thousands of pounds. If I won, the damages would be awarded not by a judge but by the jury, and these sums could vary wildly. He noted that one day in the High Court, a jury had awarded £475,000 damages and another had paid out £5,000. My case could take a year to come to court and if it lasted for a week, it was estimated my bill alone would be £75,000.

I received the following advice from my lawyers: 'I have no doubt that the articles were of the most defamatory nature possible. As far as the Wendy Brannigan stories are concerned, there is not the slightest truth in them. You were never arrested or charged. I believe that, if this matter went to trial, you would succeed in satisfying a jury that you are not as the articles portrayed you.'

However, libel was not a simple matter of winning and losing. In July 1987, the novelist, Jeffrey Archer, had won £500,000 damages from the *Daily Star*, who had alleged he had engaged the services of a prostitute, Monica Coghlan. Although Archer won, Coghlan spent four days in the witness box describing in excruciating detail her relationship with a man who at the time had been deputy chairman of the Conservative Party. If *The Sun* wanted to dig in its heels, what was to prevent Wendy Brannigan doing the same? There was no relationship, of course, but she had already proved she had a colourful imagination.

Not long after the story broke, Dennis Roach, an agent notorious for his lack of shame or sensitivity, brought a journalist from *The Sun* to the bungalow. They wondered if I 'wanted to tell my side of the story'. A five-figure sum was mentioned. I told them there was no way I would co-operate. It would jeopardise my career in football, it would be accepting money for sensationalism. As Alan Sugar was wont to say: 'If you lie down with dogs, don't be surprised if you get fleas.'

Throughout this time, I had been trying to figure out the origins of the story. Although Kenilworth Road was in the middle of Luton's red-light district, I had only met one working girl. One night, after an evening kick-off at Kenilworth Road, a woman and her friend had confronted me outside the club car park and asked me if one of the players had left. She was smartly dressed, seemed well-educated, knew who I was and appeared to know one or two members of the Luton squad. She told me her uncle was a Football League referee. She said she travelled to Luton twice a week from the Midlands with her friend to earn some extra money. I felt it had to have been her friend who had told Wendy Brannigan she had met the man who was now manager of Tottenham Hotspur.

However, Wendy Brannigan would have had to have been aware there was someone who would pay for this information. As Christmas approached, I was told that selling stories to the press was not the exclusive preserve of Paddington Police Station. The corruption infected a minority of officers across the country.

In December, I was contacted by Eric Harris, who had been a detective. He now wrote about football for the *Luton Evening Post*, a daily paper based in Hemel Hempstead which was a rival to the weekly *Luton News*. He told me how he believed the stories had reached *The Sun*'s news desk.

Eric worked closely with two other journalists: Brian Swain of the *Luton News*, with whom I had written a column during my eight years as manager, and Roy Bentley, an assistant sports editor of *The*

Sun and avid Luton fan. Bentley's day-to-day job was at the paper's offices in Bouverie Street, but he had an arrangement with the paper that allowed him to cover all their matches. They travelled to Luton's away games together.

Harris still had contacts with Bedfordshire Police and he knew that my number plate, among others from the club, had been picked up in the sweeps of the red-light district around Kenilworth Road. Harris had heard them discussing it. He was sure that David Evans had been made aware of this. They all knew Evans, now the MP for Welwyn Hatfield, wanted to settle a score with me. Evans was a man, whose hard, right-wing opinions would appear regularly in *The Sun*. He had plenty of contacts in Bouverie Street.

Like a detective, the pieces of this ugly jigsaw now fell into place before me. I could see Evans now, turning towards me on my driveway on the day he had failed to prevent me joining Tottenham, shouting: 'You'll pay for this.' I paid and my family paid a terrible, grievous price.

There were times when I felt unable to leave the house. I felt swallowed up by the shame of the accusations. I was contacted by Roger Easterby. He said: 'You have to get out of the house. You cannot just sit there dwelling on it. There are plenty of people who like and respect you.' Roger told me he would book me to make an after-dinner speech in a hotel in Harrogate. 'It will do you good,' he said.

I had never enjoyed the prospect of speaking in public and sitting on the top table waiting to be called, I was bathed in nerves and sweat. I need not have worried. I was very soon aware how much respect the audience had for me. They wanted my speech to go well.

There came another turning point. I was invited for lunch by the ITV commentator, Brian Moore, and the indefatigable Norman Giller, the former *Daily Express* football correspondent and passionate Tottenham fan, whose proudest boast is that he has written a hundred books. They took me to Simpson's, an old-fashioned steakhouse on The Strand, and persuaded me it would not be in my best interests to sue *The Sun* for libel. They told me a libel action would cost a king's ransom and would put my family, my finances, and my future in football at risk. I was less concerned with the finances, but my family was everything and football was my life.

They said I should hold my head high, remember my record in the game and be what I had always been – a football man. My personality had shrunk, but leaving the restaurant, I felt a little better about myself.

I decided to get on with my life. The telephone did ring. The first offer was from Olympiakos. They were Greek champions and in November I was invited to their headquarters in Piraeus, the port of Athens. In a room reeking with cigarette smoke, they explained their ambitions to me.

Perhaps I should not have gone. I found concentrating difficult, but two days in Piraeus gave Maureen and I a chance to talk and relax in the Mediterranean sunshine. However, I decided to reject Olympiakos's offer. Joe Mallett, my mentor at Nottingham Forest who had spent four years coaching in the Greek capital, and John Barnwell, who had managed AEK Athens, warned me off. As well as detailing rumours of match fixing, they made it clear that, although Olympiakos was a huge club, the job was a risky one. Olympiakos had got through nine managers in seven years. Alketas Panagoulias, the man who had led the team to the championship, had been fired two months into the new season. They joked that I should get my severance payment in the bank before I accepted the contract. Thijs Libregts, the Dutch manager who did take the job, lasted sixty-seven days.

The next offer was from Leicester City. It was December and, sixteenth in the Second Division, they had just sacked Bryan Hamilton, a genuine football man. On Boxing Day, they lost at home to Bournemouth and slid to nineteenth. They were facing relegation to the Third Division for the first time in their history. There was no other offer from a club of substance.

I had been invited to Holborn Circus, the headquarters of Mirror Group Newspapers, to meet Robert Maxwell. I was driven to London by a friend of mine, Harold Cook, a kindly baker who would bring bread and chocolate to the house and always told me I should manage England. He waited in the foyer while I was led upstairs and into Maxwell's palatial, beautifully furnished penthouse office.

I stepped inside to find the fax machines whirring as Maxwell prowled between banks of phones and sheaves of paperwork. In the casino, he would reportedly play three roulette wheels at once and his office was an extension of that. He seemed the ultimate multi-tasker.

Maxwell possessed a famously short attention span allied to a brilliant brain, and during our meeting, he kept glancing away or looking over my head. Then he turned to me and said in his deep baritone voice: 'They have written you've been playing with fire and, if you play with fire, you have to pay.'

In between the faxes and the phone calls, he explained his offer, one that had been suggested to him by Harry Harris, the *Mirror*'s chief football writer. I would work for the *Daily Mirror* and travel extensively, assessing the form and the players of England's opponents in the forthcoming European Championships in West Germany. It was a generous offer and one that very few journalists would have turned down, but I was not a journalist. Leicester were about to make their approach and I wanted to do what I had always done since signing my first contract with Nottingham Forest as a teenager: I wanted to be part of the game. I was a football man.

CHAPTER 18

'MATE, THIS ISN'T TOTTENHAM'

I would have liked to have had more alternatives than a club lying nineteenth in the Second Division. However, the managerial marketplace is always full of people grasping for a job. Turning down offers and waiting in hope can be a high-risk strategy. A bird in the hand…

I had confidence in my ability, but my own feeling of self-worth had taken a heavy knock. Leicester City were a big football club. They were getting bigger gates in the Second Division than Luton were in the First. This was their first season since 1982/83 outside the top flight, but the shock of relegation had lingered and they were now facing a second successive drop.

However, whenever I had gone to Filbert Street on scouting trips, I had always received a warm welcome from the car park attendants and the people behind the scenes like the tea ladies, and the stewards were warm and friendly. Their personnel were knowledgeable and open. They were also just seventy miles from where I lived in Luton and all my enquiries about the board received positive answers.

Leicester's board was led by Terry Shipman, whose father, Len, a police inspector, had also been chairman of the club and become president of the Football League. In 1955, Len Shipman had sacked Norman Bullock, the manager who had won Leicester promotion to the top flight a few months before and taken over the running of the team himself. The experiment had ended in relegation.

His son was a tall, soft-spoken, kindly man. Terry led a very democratic board, but there was not a major money man among them. They emphasised the importance of trading players and making expenditure equal income. At Luton, I had a reputation for trading well. I still believed my greatest strength was as a coach, particularly when it came to attacking football. They had been impressed by the way we had traded players at Luton.

They asked me about my departure from Tottenham and I assured them the accusations were baseless fabrications. I agreed to watch them at Plymouth, on 28 December 1987, where they were beaten, 4–0.

For the sixth successive game, Leicester had failed to score so much as a goal. They were now three points off a relegation place. I tentatively accepted the offer of a two-and-a-half-year contract. My mind was buzzing. In my heart, I still felt I wanted to take revenge for the newspaper stories, but I kept on reminding myself I had to get on with my life and be positive. Although I felt weak, I had to be outwardly strong, although the scars were still livid.

Coincidentally, my first game as Leicester manager was at Millwall, the scene of my first match as manager of Luton. Then, we had lost, 4–0, at the Den. Ten Januarys later, Millwall inflicted another defeat, this time by a single goal to nil. This was Leicester's seventh game without a goal. They were still nineteenth, but the gap to the final relegation place was now a single point. On form, they looked bankers to go down. The supporters were unhappy.

The prospect of a second straight relegation terrified Trevor Bennett, a wealthy, philanthropic Leicester fan who was keen to gain a place on the board. He had made his money from window frames and house improvements. He promised me a 'private bonus' if his beloved club avoided the Third Division. However, although Bennett had money to invest, the older members of the board did not want someone who might threaten their position. I also felt they resented his business success. They felt that should Trevor gain a major foothold at Leicester City, they too would have to put their hands deep into their pockets and he would run the club and re-shape the board. There were meetings, there were letters sent back and forth, but the slightly old-fashioned board resisted Bennett's overtures and he took his passion for football and his money to Newcastle.

Trevor Bennett was a gift to Newcastle. He became president of the club and in 1993 he provided the funds that allowed the club to break their transfer record and pay Bristol City £1.75 million for Andy Cole. The investment in St James' Park was in the form of interest-free loans that he did not want repaid. He also invested heavily in Leicestershire cricket. One end of Grace Road, opposite the pavilion, bears his name. Trevor and his wife, Beryl, were lovely people who genuinely respected what I had done in football.

One of my first meetings after replacing Bryan Hamilton was with the chief scout, Sammy Chapman, whom I knew vaguely from my playing days at Nottingham Forest. Sammy, a genial Irishman, had played for Mansfield. I asked him which players were on his radar and which he would buy. Sammy answered without hesitation that he had good contacts at Crewe and, if he could, he would buy David Platt, their 21-year-old midfielder. 'He would give you three players in one.'

Very quickly, a director, Martin George, asked to accompany Sammy to watch the player in action. On the night, Platt delivered an average performance. George, an opinionated man, killed the possibility of a deal. Sammy still smiled but was acutely disillu-sioned. Shortly afterwards, Platt signed for Graham Taylor at Aston Villa. Within a year, he was an England international.

Several seasons later when he was at Wolves, Sammy rang to tell me about an outstanding teenager they had just brought in from Ireland. His name was Robbie Keane. Ironically, the scout that had initiated Keane's signing for Wolves, Eddie Cochrane, had previously worked for me at Luton and had alerted me to Mal Donaghy.

Leicester's results had been so bad that I felt the club needed some early surgery. Among the players I was keen to get out of Filbert Street was Jari Rantanen. He was a big guy who reminded me more of a hammer thrower and was far from my idea of a striker. Before my arrival, he had also blotted his copybook in a nightclub. In 1989, he was transferred to HJK Helsinki, a club where he would have four separate spells. I allowed Robbie James, a Welsh midfielder, to return to his first club, Swansea, and sold winger Gary Ford to Port Vale for £35,000. However, selling Mark Venus to Wolves was an impetuous decision. He would have a good career, first at Molineux and then at Ipswich. Perhaps I should have given him more time.

Up front, the club needed some thrust to support Mike Newell in attack. Mike had joined Leicester from Luton, a year after I left Kenilworth Road. Luton had made a £265,000 profit on the fee they had paid Wigan in 1986. Sammy Chapman liked the look of a sharp front man he had seen at Walsall, who would end the season promoted to the Second Division. I always felt it important to back your chief scout, otherwise he would start to lose confidence in me and doubt the job he was doing. It was his role to recommend alternatives. We signed Nicky Cross on Sammy's recommendation for £80,000 – a bright, confident forward who made intelligent runs and formed a fine partnership with Newell up front.

Alex Ferguson helped me with my next signing. He had signed Peter Weir both at St Mirren and Aberdeen and the winger had been in the team that overcame Real Madrid to win the Cup-Winners' Cup. Weir was an outside left and I had seen him play for Aberdeen in a friendly at Aldershot in January 1984. Ferguson had taken his team down to Hampshire because the weather in Scotland was so bleak that Aberdeen faced a month without a fixture. Weir's cleverness and ability to cross on the run had caught my eye.

Since Ferguson's departure for Manchester United, Weir had been increasingly afflicted by injury. Ferguson told me he was a quiet player, a loner, who lacked confidence in his own ability. He was, however, a quality player, and a forward threesome of Newell, Cross and Weir very quickly began to gel. In his early days at Manchester United, Ferguson had asked me about two full-backs playing in what is now the Championship. One was a smooth right-back at Sheffield Wednesday called Roland Nilsson. The other was Denis Irwin, playing at Oldham. I told him Irwin was the better defender and more adaptable. There was a greater camaraderie between managers in that era.

The front three were supported by Gary McAllister, who had been used principally as a wide midfielder since he was signed by Gordon Milne as a twenty-year-old. I converted Gary into playing just behind the forwards, a role in which he excelled. I was so impressed by Gary as both a player and a person that I contacted the Scotland manager, Andy Roxburgh, to press his claims. Gary was included in the Scotland squad for the 1990 World Cup in Italy. McAllister had come to Filbert Street in the same deal as his Motherwell teammate, Ally Mauchlen. With Mauchlen and Paul Ramsey, who had been part of the Northern Ireland squad at the 1986 World Cup in Mexico, employed as holding midfielders the team began to take shape.

At centre-half was Russell Osman, who had won the UEFA Cup with Ipswich and had played international rugby and football at schoolboy level. His partnership with Steve Walsh was as good as any in the division. Both Mauchlen and Walsh were combative footballers. On the opening day of the season, Walsh had been given an eleven-game ban and a £25,000 fine, which he revealed he could not pay, for breaking the jaw of the Shrewsbury striker David Geddis.

The revival began on 30 January at Reading, which provided Leicester with their first away win in four months. February was a remarkable month. We played outstandingly to overcome Leeds, 3–2, and followed it up with victories over Ipswich, Manchester City and Sheffield United. We were now seven points clear of the relegation zone. At board meetings, most of the directors' time appeared to be spent exchanging shares. They gave me some, which I held for years until the club changed its constitution, rendering them worthless. I still have the certificate.

We went to Middlesbrough on the final day of the season. Under Bruce Rioch, Middlesbrough were undergoing a remarkable transformation. Two years before, the gates of Ayresome Park had been padlocked and the club faced liquidation. Now, they were one game away from a second successive promotion and a return to top-flight football. Millwall had already been promoted and to join them, Middlesbrough, in second place, had to match Aston Villa's result at Swindon.

In the week of the game, Bruce, whom I knew well from our early days at Luton, called me. It was unusual for an opposition manager to ring in the week of a match. However, he was on the edge of an extraordinary achievement and during our conversation he said, jokingly, that he hoped Leicester would go easy on 'Boro. He knew we would do no such thing. In the teeth of an impassioned full house at Ayresome Park, we played superbly to win 2–1. McAllister, Osman, Newell and Weir were all outstanding. Aston Villa drew without a goal at Swindon to earn Graham Taylor's side the second automatic promotion spot. Rioch, however, was not to be denied. Middlesbrough won promotion through the play-offs, overcoming first Bradford and then beating Chelsea in a two-legged final.

At the end of the game, I got the players together and told them: 'If no one leaves and we all stick together, we will get promotion next season.' Those words were specifically addressed to Russell Osman, who had run his contract down and was looking for a quick return to the First Division. Southampton were bidding for him.

Although I received £360,000 for him, the team never played as well again. Russell was quality. He had played for England and the only consolation was the tribunal ordered Southampton to pay far more than they had anticipated. I enjoyed making Leicester's case at the tribunal. They appealed to the debater in me as I attempted to protect my club's interests while Brian Truscott, Southampton's secretary, argued for a lower fee.

In the final analysis, however, Leicester were the losers. My attempts to replace Osman were poor and the position of centre-half became my Achilles heel. Colin Murphy, who had replaced Bobby Roberts as my first-team coach, recommended Steve Thompson, a muscular, Yorkshire-born centre-half who was playing for Charlton. Colin had managed Thompson at Lincoln. Watching his first game, I blinked as he turned like the *Queen Mary* when the ball was played beyond him. I also took Peter Eccles from Dundalk, who proved out of his depth and was soon loaned out to Stafford Rangers before Dundalk took him back.

We had finished the 1987/88 season with the best record of any Second Division club since Christmas and were made favourites for the new campaign. However, the bookies did not appreciate the massive negative the loss of Osman represented. Neither, really, did I.

After Martin George had forcefully reminded me of my obligation to relocate to Leicester, I found a small, terraced house in the Stoneygate area of the city. It was tiny, but I put in some basic furniture, a television and a toaster. Back at the club, I brought in John Moore from Luton as a youth coach. He had succeeded me as manager at Kenilworth Road and had taken Luton to their highest-ever finish, seventh in the First Division. However, it was an experience he had not enjoyed. He disliked the media attention and the press conferences and returned to youth-team coaching. Brought up in rural Lanarkshire, John was a broad Scot with strong principles. He loved the game but was infuriated by the way footballers were becoming 'personalities'. He was a very good man to have on your side.

James Lawton, the celebrated chief sports writer of the *Daily Express*, had come to Middlesbrough to see them play Leicester on the final day of the season, expecting to see the north-east club promoted. He wrote that my results since coming to Filbert Street after my gruelling experience at Tottenham should make me a candidate for manager of the year.

Nevertheless, without Osman we started the new season hesitantly. I paired Steve Walsh with Grant Brown, a product of our youth team who was only eighteen, when the season began with a 1–1 draw against West Bromwich Albion. However, our position as promotion favourites was belied by only two wins in our opening nine matches.

Peter Weir had become homesick and returned to Scotland to join St Mirren. We missed his outstanding left-footed deliveries. In an attempt to replace him, I gave an opportunity to a young Brummie, Paul Reid, another who had come through the ranks. He was a brave right-winger who tackled like a full-back and was regularly booked for his impetuosity. However, I liked his attitude. He was a '100 per-center'. In two fierce League Cup ties against Nottingham Forest, Paul gave Stuart Pearce, who was then first-choice for England at left-back, a hard time. We drew 0–0 at Filbert Street but went down 2–1 in the replay at the City Ground. Forest would win the trophy, beating Luton in the final.

Another defender I tried alongside Steve Walsh was Simon Morgan, an England under-21 international who was more effective as a full-back. He had joined the club as an apprentice where one of his early jobs had been landscaping the garden of Leicester's then manager, Gordon Milne. He maintained his position in the first team as Leicester meandered in the Second Division. In 1990, I sold Simon to Fulham, where he would enjoy an excellent career and become the Premier League's head of football relations – the link man between the league and the players, managers and referees.

With Cross, Newell and McAllister, Leicester were easy on the eye going forward, but we could not find solutions to our defensive problems. These did not include the goalkeeper, Paul Cooper, who was absolutely reliable. Cooper had been a mainstay of Bobby Robson's Ipswich side and in 1979/80 he saved eight out of ten penalties, which remains a record for an English league season. Saving penalties was almost the least of Paul Cooper's qualities. He was a left-hander and after catching a cross he would thrust the ball out with speed and accuracy to Reid on the right flank to launch a counter-attack. Cooper was not tall by goalkeeping standards, but he was wonderfully agile. With Steve Walsh missing eighteen games through injury, the centre-halves in front of Cooper came and went.

I had known Leicester's PR man, Alan Birchenall, for many years. He told me there had been a lot of drinking and partying among the players. When a manager does not live full time in the place where he is managing and lacks spies in the community, this kind of information can pass him by. One thing Alan neglected to mention was that he knew these parties were going on because he was being invited to them. One of the first things 'Birch', as he was known, had told me when I came to Leicester was: 'Mate, this isn't Tottenham, you know. We've got no Hoddle and Ardiles here to pass the ball.'

I had an issue with Mike Newell. Midway through the season, he had told me he would not be signing a new contract and wanted to leave. On the field, Newell was completely committed, chasing lost causes and running the channels successfully. He could run all day. He was aware not to put his request in writing, because that would nullify the loyalty and signing-on fees he would be due.

Off the field, Mike could be rebellious and very single minded. He had seen Russell Osman leave for top-flight football at Southampton while Leicester had made little progress. He knew we lacked investment and I could not change his mind. I told him not to rock the boat. If he kept his opinions out of the media and did not submit a transfer request, I would help him find a club. He would probably have to forego his loyalty bonuses.

At the end of the season, I contacted the Everton manager, Colin Harvey, and agreed a fee of £1.1 million for Newell. Mike was from Merseyside and had begun his career playing for Liverpool's youth teams. Jim Greenwood, the Everton secretary, did all the paperwork as Mike nodded his agreement. I reminded him of the deal that he would have to waive the money he was owed by Leicester. Everton had already said they would cover those payments.

It was a smooth move, but I had lost my main striker. Shortly afterwards, I was contacted by Mike's father, who was a union official at the Ford plant in Halewood. Over the phone, he suggested Leicester should pay his son the money they owed him. I told him he must be aware of the private agreement I had with Mike and that in any case Everton had agreed to pay the balance. However, Mr Newell persisted, the PFA became involved and eventually Leicester were summoned to a tribunal in Manchester, where Mike and his father presented their case for the non-payment of bonuses. They won the day and I found the decision very hard to take. I could not have been in my best debating form.

At Luton, I had given Mike Newell the chance to play top-flight football and then negotiated a move to his home city of Liverpool. In 1995, he would win the Premier League with Blackburn and become a successful manager at Luton. His time at Kenilworth Road ended shortly after he criticised the financial management of the club and revealed he had been offered bungs by agents.

While I was disappointed about the bonuses, I was glad he stood up for his principles. It is to his credit that Mike and I have repaired the damage done by that tribunal. I like to think I was a big influence on his career and when I would bump into him in later years, he would still call me 'boss'.

CHAPTER 19

'BUT IT'S EVEN WORSE
FOR ME, DAVID'

The sale of Mike Newell may have brought much-needed money into Filbert Street, where the average gate hovered around the 10,000 mark, but we went into the new season with a blunt edge. When we lost 3–1 at Plymouth in mid-October, we were bottom of the Second Division after twelve matches, already five points from safety.

The position of centre-half was a wound that would not heal. We began the season with the pairing of Alan Paris and Allan Evans, who had been part of Aston Villa's triumph over Bayern Munich in the 1982 European Cup final. Allan's best days were behind him, but I felt that his experience might help us in the short term. I always believed an older, savvier centre-half who can organise his defence is better than a younger, less experienced player with perhaps greater talent.

The poor start led me to buy a young, tall, swift centre-back who reminded me of Paul Elliott. However, Tony James, who arrived from Lincoln, was never able to dominate as someone who stood 6ft 3in. should have done. James had all the ability required but lacked mental strength. Towards the end of the season, alongside Simon Morgan, he showed flashes of his true ability but never justified my hopes for him. However, James will be remembered as the man whose goal against Oxford on the final day of the season prevented Leicester's relegation to the Third Division in 1991. I had by then left the club.

We were floundering and I used my contacts to take advantage of the loan system. Two young footballers brought in from north London proved the catalyst for an upswing in our fortunes. Paul Moran was a leggy, 21-year-old winger, slim and swift, on Tottenham's books. Kevin Campbell was nineteen, a forward with Arsenal who had enjoyed a successful loan spell helping Leyton Orient win promotion to the Third Division. Kevin was a strong, forceful gem of a lad. With Gary McAllister's prompting, Campbell and Moran helped galvanise the team. In his eleven games for Leicester, Campbell became a hero, poaching five goals while Moran proved an ideal foil.

The revival began in November with a 4–3 victory over Leeds, who would end the season as Second Division champions. In the post-match press conference, I made a remark about Leeds's use of the offside trap that upset their manager, Howard Wilkinson. He sent me a couple of newspaper cuttings quoting my comments and asked for my observations. Despite this, I had great respect for Howard, the last English manager to win the league and who later had significant roles with the FA and the League Managers' Association. Even the very best can be sensitive to criticism.

This was followed by a 1–0 defeat to Ipswich at Filbert Street, but after winning six of our next seven matches, we climbed to thirteenth in the table on New Year's Day. The crowd responded to the surge. Campbell's penultimate performance for Leicester was an extraordinary 5–4 defeat at Newcastle. Goals from Tommy Wright, Walsh, McAllister and Campbell plus a penalty save from Martin Hodge had put us 4–2 up before Newcastle, their attack led by Mick Quinn and Mark McGhee, scored three late goals. Newcastle, under Jim Smith, would finish third but lose painfully to Sunderland in the play-off semi-finals.

However, George Graham would not extend Kevin's loan period, and after a spell that had electrified the club, Campbell was given a standing ovation after his last game at Filbert Street. He was a model young professional, arriving from London first thing every Monday morning with his suitcase and suit-carrier. Kevin embraced everything about Leicester City. He was one of the game's gentlemen and would have a fine career at Arsenal and Everton. Once, when he was briefly out of favour at Highbury, he wrote me a treasured, handwritten letter suggesting I might be interested in signing him permanently. His son, Tyrese, followed his father into football as a striker and made his Premier League debut for Stoke against Leicester in February 2018.

Paul Moran did well, too, although while Kevin wanted to extend his loan spell, Paul chose to return to London, where his career would continue in relative obscurity. The Tottenham manager, Terry Venables, made it clear that any extension to Moran's contract would involve a further fee that was far more than I was prepared to pay.

I was in London, attending a tribunal, heading back to St Pancras in a taxi, when the driver recognised me. He was a West Ham fan and said we should take 'that useless bugger David Kelly off our hands'. Kelly had lost his place as a striker at Upton Park, although I had seen much of him at Walsall. He was left-footed, lively and with a good spring when he rose to head a ball. He was also an Ireland international, scoring a hat-trick on his debut against Israel in 1987.

I watched him in a reserve game and was impressed by his attitude. The West Ham manager, Billy Bonds, was most considerate during the negotiations. He realised that Kelly was probably not going to make it at West Ham and wanted to give the player the opportunity to return to the Midlands. The fee of £300,000 was half of what West Ham had paid Walsall two years before.

With a first-team place and living closer to where he grew up,

David was transformed. His wife, who was a hairdresser, was also happier in the Midlands than she had been in London. David felt so at home he would sometimes take his dog to training with him. He showed his happiness by scoring seven goals in his opening ten games.

In the final game of the season, we collapsed to lose 5–2 at home to Sheffield United, who needed to win to guarantee their promotion to the First Division. Our goalkeeper, Martin Hodge, made several howlers and Tony Agana scored a hat-trick. It was a bad result to take into the summer. Leicester finished thirteenth in the Second Division. It had been a second, unsuccessful season. Of the three outstanding players I had inherited, Russell Osman and Mike Newell had left. Only Gary McAllister remained, and his contract was about to expire.

In the boardroom we discussed the prospects of losing our jewel. We could not stop Gary from exercising his rights to seek another club and we knew we would probably be at the whim of a tribunal. McAllister would be going to Italy with the Scotland squad for the 1990 World Cup and at the age of twenty-five he would be a great signing for most clubs. Knowing the workings of the tribunal system, we decided to offer McAllister a very lucrative contract, knowing full well he would not accept it. The club was trying to protect its position at a tribunal which would take our proposed wage offer into account. Very honestly, I told Gary the offer was something of a ruse and we knew he would turn it down. Gary understood and was very decent about it; above all, he did not want Leicester to lose out financially.

Brian Clough had shown an interest in taking McAllister to Nottingham Forest and requested a meeting with the player. I suggested to Gary that a move to the City Ground to play Clough's slick, passing football might suit him very well. I told him it might suit Leicester City, too, since we would almost certainly get a better fee from Forest than we would at a tribunal. Gary had no problem with that.

However, I also discovered a local restaurateur with Spanish connections was in talks with Jon Holmes, who was Gary Lineker's agent, about a move to La Liga for McAllister. There was definite interest and a move to Spain would have been catastrophic for the club. There was a formula for foreign clubs to buy from English teams that would mean he would go to Spain for a much-reduced figure. It was based on the player's age and current salary. They would not take into account the length or the financial terms of any new contract offered.

Gary agreed to meet Clough at the Posthouse on the A52 between Nottingham and Derby. The meeting was a disaster and Gary returned to Leicester saying: 'I will never sign for that man.' Evidently, Brian had arrived late and Gary thought he might have been drinking. His manner was offhand and he made remarks Gary found baffling. He told me that many years previously, he had been wanted by Celtic as a youngster. He had gone to Parkhead to meet the club's chief scout, John Kelman, and he and his father had been made to wait hours. Gary decided there and then that they were not being treated with respect by Celtic and he signed for his local club, Motherwell.

Leeds, newly promoted to the First Division, wanted to sign McAllister and instructed their managing director, Bill Fotherby, to secure the deal at a tribunal. Fotherby, a flamboyant showman who had started out in the clothing industry, was representing Leeds because Howard Wilkinson was on holiday. Although we were opposites in many respects, I liked dealing with him. He was charismatic, although sometimes full of bluster. After being forced out of Elland Road by Peter Ridsdale, Bill became chairman of Harrogate Town, although he did not quite live long enough to see them become a Football League club.

The fee was set at £1.5 million, which represented a decent return for Leicester. However, now that McAllister had joined Newell and Osman in the top flight, I had lost the heart and soul of a club that in the summer of 1988 looked destined for promotion. Those three players had made Leicester £2.4 million. It was good money but bad business. In their strange way, the board were more than happy.

By now, Gordon Lee had come back to English football from a spell in Iceland to replace Colin Murphy as my No. 2. As someone who had managed Everton, Newcastle and Blackburn, he was a good sounding board for ideas. He was extremely principled. He lived on the Lancashire coast at Lytham and had a rented house in Leicester. We were playing at Blackburn and I said: 'Why doesn't somebody take your car up to Ewood Park? You can drive it on to Lytham, take Monday off and we'll see you on Tuesday.'

He said: 'I'll be travelling to Blackburn on the bus and, whether we win, lose or draw, I'll be travelling back on the bus to Leicester. We are a team together.' When we reached Filbert Street, Gordon got in his car and drove to Lytham, a destination he would have reached eight hours earlier. Gordon was a football nut; intelligent, principled and straight. He also possessed a good sense of humour. One day on the team bus, one or two players into horse-racing were discussing a possible winner. Gordon, who disliked gambling intensely, walked to the back of the bus and asked which horse they fancied. When he was told, he said: 'That horse can never win on a right-handed track. All his best results have come on left-handers.' They were stunned.

Under Terry Shipman, the Leicester board had been patient. They understood the problems. The board meetings tended to be placid with no shouting. It was a friendly, diplomatic group. Nice people. Only one man – Martin George – provoked controversy. He felt he had a superior knowledge of football to the other directors and, after one disappointing home game as Gordon and I discussed our failings in my office, Martin knocked on the door. His first words were: 'Well, what's the excuse today, then?' His utterances were nearly always coated with a layer of sarcasm.

Once more, a new season began badly. After a 3–2 victory over Bristol Rovers on the opening day, we suffered seven straight league defeats, which left Leicester second bottom, above only Watford. The last of these losses had been a 6–0 rout at Middlesbrough, hastened by Steve Walsh's dismissal – not for the first time. A little over two years before, we had gone to Ayresome Park and outplayed a Middlesbrough side on the brink of promotion to the First Division. This terrible beating was evidence of how a team can regress if it loses its best players.

After the debacle on Teesside, we recovered to win three of our next four. David Kelly and David Oldfield had begun to find their rhythm up front, aided by Tommy Wright, a fiery Scottish winger, who had been signed from Oldham. In December, we played Newcastle at Filbert Street. Astonishingly, the scoreline was 5–4, just as it had been at St James' Park eleven months before. This time it was Leicester who scored the five. David Kelly hit a hat-trick. David would join Newcastle the following year and in May 1993 he would score a hat-trick for Newcastle at Filbert Street as Kevin Keegan's side celebrated their promotion to the Premier League with a 7–1 win.

The first of our goals against Newcastle had been scored by Terry Fenwick, whom I had taken on loan from Tottenham. He had played for England in the 1986 World Cup in Mexico, and he was now thirty-one and no longer quick. His role at Leicester was to organise and direct the defence. He was obsessed with playing a high line and catching teams offside. Fenwick had been a good player and still thought he was. He once remarked after a session: 'Terry wouldn't have done it that way.' Fenwick adored Venables. He lived in London and his heart was not in a loan spell at Filbert Street. Fenwick stayed for nine appearances, as part of another defensive patch-up job.

Any hopes of a run in the FA Cup were extinguished by a 2–1 defeat at Millwall, where we had conceded two late goals. I was livid. Kelvin Morton, the referee, had sent off one of our players and every close decision seemed to go to the home side. I confronted him at the end of the game and was led away by two policemen. Later, the FA issued me with a charge of misconduct. I replied with a polite letter in the allotted time. My explanation was accepted and I was excused a fine. My copybook continued to be clean, but the defeat was another step towards the end. The supporters were angry and on a wall near the ground I caught sight of graffiti demanding: 'Pleat Out.' I had been a manager for more than a decade and I should have been hardened to this kind of thing, but for some reason it upset me. This sensitivity would plague me throughout my career. I never developed the thick skin many managers possessed.

Whoever wrote that would soon have their wish. On 26 January, I shook hands with Don Mackay after he had led Blackburn to a 3–1 win at Filbert Street that left us two points off a relegation place. As I drove home to Luton, I knew the end had come. On the Sunday, I took a call from Terry Shipman. 'We had a meeting after yesterday's game, David,' he said. 'I am afraid we have to say goodbye. I am not happy with this, but the other directors have outvoted me.'

'I understand that, Mr Chairman. That's the game.'

'But it's even worse for me, David. The other directors want me out, too!'

He added: 'You've done well in getting us enough pounds, but you didn't get us enough points.' It was a strange epitaph.

Terry had always said to me: 'If you buy too many players from the lower leagues, you will end up in the lower leagues.' In 1991, Leicester would avoid relegation to the Third Division on the final day of the season. However, if the youth cabinet is bare and there is no money to buy players from the top two divisions, you end up taking risks in the lower leagues. That path always leads to the sack.

CHAPTER 20

'THEY TELL ME YOU'RE
A COWARD, SON'

There seemed little prospect of a quick return to management, at least at any decent level. I had to be realistic. Leicester had been a failure. I was never able to replicate those first eighteen games when we had played so well and raised expectations so high. In truth, I had lost Newell, Cross, McAllister, Weir and Osman – the very heart of my team. Most journalists, surveying my two-and-a-half years at Filbert Street, concluded I had not been given the tools to do the job. However, others wrote that I had lost my mojo. There was truth in both.

I should have been more ambitious and driven. I should have been selfish and demanded finance. I was far too frugal. I was also far too conciliatory. I kept telling the board that I understood their position. However, I left Leicester with no animosity toward the directors. They were nice people, if sluggish in their approach. They were happy to be jogging along in the Second Division.

The day after my dismissal, Michael Calvin, a journalist with the *Daily Telegraph*, came to the bungalow to write a piece about the precarious nature of football management. He described all the managerial flotsam I had taken home from Leicester, all the boxes in the hallway, full of programmes, boardroom notes, scouting reports, player assessments and columns I had written for the *Leicester Mercury*. All history now.

After the debacle of my exit from Tottenham, a solicitor friend had advised me to keep notes of everything I did, to log every phone call. 'When the time comes when they want to get rid of you, you will need to have all bases covered,' he had said. 'Make sure they have no wiggle room when there is a wrangle over compensation.' The boxes went into the loft; another addition to my career.

A few months later, I received a phone call from David Kohler, the managing director and joint owner of Luton Town. He was a property developer who had taken over the club the previous year in partnership with an accountant called Peter Nelkin.

For the third successive season, Luton had avoided relegation on the final day of the season, beating an already-doomed Derby to send Sunderland down. Interestingly, only two clubs were relegated from the top flight in 1991. Had there been the usual three, Luton would not have survived. After the game, they had fired their manager, Jim Ryan, who had twice kept Luton up under very difficult circumstances. The supporters were unhappy at the club's decision to let him go. Kohler asked if I would meet him to discuss the possibility of a return to Kenilworth Road.

I had nothing to lose. Luton were still a top-flight club and, although there had been some offers from teams in lower divisions, none had really appealed. I still felt confident I could manage at the highest level. We talked at Nelkin's house in Hertfordshire. They were jointly in charge of Luton, although I did not realise at the time that Kohler was the driving force in the relationship and would soon want sole control.

The pair had taken over in May 1990. David Evans and his cohorts had left after selling Kenilworth Road to Luton Council for £3.25 million and taking out their loans with a hefty dollop of interest. The move had outraged the fanbase and Kohler and Nelkin had moved in. The club's chief executive, John Smith, had left with a healthy bonus after doing the groundwork for the deal with the council. The supporters never forgave them. Although I was not at the club at the time, I knew the people involved and was distressed by what had happened.

The first thing the new owners did was to overturn the ban on away supporters that had been one of the cornerstones of Evans's chairmanship. Luton's winning of the League Cup in 1988 had given Evans his moment in the sun. Since entering the House of Commons, his speeches calling for the European Union to 'get stuffed' and for the hanging of murderers had brought him to the attention of the hard right of the Conservative Party. There was less time for Luton Town. He was appointed parliamentary private secretary to John Redwood, who in 1995 would unsuccessfully challenge the Prime Minister, John Major, for the leadership of the Conservative Party. Evans would lose his seat two years later during a general election campaign in which he asked sixth-formers at a school in Welwyn how they would feel if a girl was 'raped by some black bastard'.

Kohler offered me the job, despite receiving many calls from other, out-of-work managers. We agreed a contract I thought more than fair and I insisted my £25,000 bonus that the Evans-controlled board had refused to sanction when I moved to Tottenham be paid. He told me the main reason Jim Ryan had gone was that he had not informed the board of offers for a couple of players, including Kingsley Black, and this had caused serious friction. The need for money to keep the club afloat was paramount and Kohler told me he was prepared to pay me a percentage of transfer profits made on players I bought and sold.

It was an attractive carrot, but this kind of incentive carries with it a moral dilemma. I had been offered this clause in my contract when I was last at Luton. John Smith had opposed it. He himself had a clause in his contract that would give him a bonus if the club made a profit. Many managers at smaller clubs, where selling a player is important, have this arrangement. It is regarded as an insurance policy, because every sale reduces your success on the field – a point I had had reiterated to me at Leicester.

Our meeting had come to the attention of the *Luton News*, who speculated I might be coming back to the club. My return did not prove popular with the supporters whose protests against the move dominated the letters page. They felt Ryan had been given a raw deal. Brian Swain, who was still sports editor of the *Luton News*, called me twice. I did not respond. I could not believe what I was seeing when I saw him park his car outside my home, walk down the path and push a note through the letterbox. This was the same man who had gone out of his way to cause me such pain and heartache four years earlier.

Swain wanted to know if the rumours were true and asked me if I would do an exclusive interview with him. Maureen advised me to act normally. I buried my pride and my anger and talked to him. What option did I have if I was going to have to work with him on a regular basis? Since winning the League Cup, Luton had gone backwards, continually teetering on the brink of relegation. We had few diamonds in the squad. Our only saleable assets were Mark Pembridge and Kingsley Black.

Pembridge was just twenty, a midfielder who had come through the youth teams and would become a regular international for Wales. Mark was from Merthyr and like John Hartson, Ceri Hughes and Kurt Nogan had been discovered by our brilliant Welsh scout Cyril Beech, who had played for Swansea and Newport. Cyril assiduously scoured junior football around Swansea and Merthyr and would send me long handwritten letters recommending for trials those he had discovered.

During the school holidays, he would arrange the boys' transport, either taking them in his van or arranging train travel. One of those that Cyril recommended but whom we turned down was Andy Melville, who after leaving Swansea played for Oxford and

Sunderland and earned sixty-five caps for Wales. Hughes, Pembridge and Hartson would all be capped by their country in the next four years. Cyril was one of football's wonderful unsung heroes.

One of my first confrontations was with Lars Elstrup, a bright and brainy centre-forward who had been bought from Odense in Denmark for £850,000 in 1989, which thirty years later was still the record amount Luton had paid for an outfield player. For the past two seasons, Elstrup had been Luton's main striker and had scored one of the precious goals against Derby that had secured Luton's place in the top flight. Now, however, he confronted me and demanded a move back to Denmark.

Subsequently, we discovered that Luton's secretary, Bill Tomlins, had made a private arrangement with Elstrup when he had signed that meant he would be able to move after two years for an agreed fee of £200,000 – less than a quarter of what Luton had paid Odense, who at the time were Danish champions. Legally, we did not have a leg to stand on. Elstrup returned to Odense and the following year he was part of the Denmark squad that won the European Championship in Sweden. He then changed his name to 'Darando' and joined a Buddhist sect. He suffered dreadfully from depression, sold his Euro '92 winner's medal to raise £17,000 for a children's charity and went to live in India.

Bill Tomlins became chairman of Luton in 2004 but was forced to resign three years later when he admitted making £150,000 of illegal payments to agents. For this, Luton were fined £50,000 and given a ten-point penalty, which became thirty points when the club violated the Football League's insolvency rules. I had originally agreed to take Tomlins on the club's commercial side; he was well presented and a good talker. He had been a car salesman at a big local franchise. He made astonishing progress to become club secretary and then acting chairman, a position that his dishonesty made him fundamentally unsuited to.

Mine was not a glittering comeback. We began with a goalless draw at West Ham and held Liverpool to another 0–0 in the opening game at Kenilworth Road, but the first five matches produced one goal and those two points. We were bottom of the table. The bank manager had also come calling. Luton needed to raise money quickly. On the Friday evening before our fifth game – a 4–1 defeat at Chelsea – my assistant, Colin Murphy, and I met Brian Clough at the Posthouse in Crick, just off the M1 in Northamptonshire, to discuss the sale of Kingsley Black.

We had received two phone calls from Nottingham Forest about our outside left, who had been a product of Luton's youth system. I used the press to encourage transfer speculation in an attempt to drive up Black's price, suggesting Wimbledon were prepared to pay £1.25 million. The instruction from the board was that we had to get this transfer over the line for as much money as we could.

Kingsley accompanied us to the hotel. Brian arrived in his trademark green sweater and was in an eccentric mood. He had just signed Teddy Sheringham from Millwall and wanted to strengthen a Forest side that would not have back-to-back league wins until November. Kingsley was a quiet boy, aged twenty-three. He had no agent, there was no member of his family with him and he found it hard to cope with Brian's offhand manner.

'They tell me you're a coward, son; is that true?' was one of Clough's questions. Kingsley, not unnaturally, was stunned by it.

'He's joking, Kingsley,' I quickly interjected. 'It's a way of motivating you.'

Clough's next question was: 'I'm told you have no vices. Is that true?' Then he asked the player to stand back-to-back with him. 'You're not as tall as I thought,' Clough shouted. After all that, he told Kingsley: 'I like you.' He asked him to sign a contract there and then.

Kingsley replied rather nervously: 'I must speak to my parents. I have got a lot to consider.'

It was by now abundantly clear that Brian's chat-up lines were fuelled by drink, and when he conceded that by now it was getting late, he said: 'Go home, son. Talk it over with your mam. I'll see you at the City Ground tomorrow at twelve o'clock.' Then he looked at Kingsley's wrist.

'That's a nice watch,' he said. 'Let me have a look at it.'

Kingsley took the watch off his wrist. Clough calmly put it in his pocket.

'You'll get the watch back tomorrow, laddie, when I see you.'

We calmed Kingsley down on the journey back to Luton and told him to ignore most of what Brian had said. 'He's a top manager,' I told him. 'You could be a big success at the City Ground.' What Black did not know was Luton needed the deal to go through urgently. Morally, I was in a difficult position.

The following day, Kingsley went with his parents to the City Ground to see Nottingham Forest beat Oldham 3–1. He signed for Forest, who paid Luton £1.5 million. With Stuart Pearce aggressively prompting him from the left-back position, Kingsley was a success in Nottingham and played in the 1992 League Cup final against Manchester United, which turned out to be Brian Clough's last Wembley appearance as a manager. Kingsley would also prove very successful with Northern Ireland.

Brian Clough, as everyone knows, was a character. Not long after I became manager, I travelled to see a reserve-team fixture at the City Ground to scout a player. At half-time he invited me into his small manager's office. Maybe he wanted to discuss one of the players at Luton. That was not the case. I listened as he introduced me to a journalist sitting there named Vince Wilson of the *Sunday Mirror*, who ghosted a column for him. When the bell rang for the start of the second half, I got up from the comfortable armchair and walked towards the door. He shouted: 'Where are you going, young man? Stay here – you'll learn more listening to me than watching that crap out there!' I was stunned. I stayed there like an observant apprentice and listened, and I did not see another ball kicked. Driving home, I replayed his thoughts in my head. He certainly made you think; he had a view on everything.

The results continued to be mediocre. I bought Trevor Peake from Coventry to shore up the defence and brought Mick Harford back to Kenilworth Road from Derby for £325,000. Trevor had been part of Coventry's FA Cup final team that had beaten Tottenham and read the game well. Quietly spoken, he was a model profession-al, but he was thirty-four and his best days were gone.

Mick was hailed as the returning hero. We desperately needed some power up front. After eleven games and three months without a win, Luton went into the Christmas programme bottom of the league. No team had conceded more goals and no team had scored fewer. When goal difference was taken into account, we were eight points from safety. These were tough weeks.

There was hope in the progress made by Paul Telfer, a young midfielder from Edinburgh, who had made strong progress in the youth team, and Scott Oakes, whom I had taken from Leicester. Experience came in the shape of Chris Kamara, a worldly box-to-box midfielder who had begun his professional career by leaving the navy to join Portsmouth. He arrived from Leeds in November for £150,000. Chris was full of running and full of enthusiasm but lacked top-flight quality.

The following year, Kamara came to see me, saying he wanted away from this 'losing scenario' and his agent, Hayden Evans, a forceful individual, began pulling strings and manoeuvring for a return to Yorkshire. Evans made all kinds of suggestions designed to wear me down and, in the end, I resolved to let Chris go. On reflection, I was too conciliatory.

I raised a further £400,000 by selling a number of players I thought surplus to requirements. Darron McDonough, who had won the League Cup in 1988, joined Newcastle. Local boy Sean Farrell went to Fulham for £100,000. Graham Rodger, a substitute for Coventry in the 1987 FA Cup final, left for a successful career at Grimsby while Dave Beaumont, a reserve centre-half, was signed by Hibernian.

Earlier in the season, I had introduced a Bedford boy called Matthew Jackson into the side. He was a tall, handsome, intelligent full-back. He had only played a handful of games for Luton. Everton were playing a League Cup tie at Vicarage Road and were staying at the Holiday Inn at Watford.

Their manager, Howard Kendall, and his assistant, John Bailey, had seen Jackson play in our League Cup tie against Birmingham on the Tuesday night. The next morning, I took a phone call inviting me to their hotel. I liked Howard and welcomed the opportunity to talk football. During the afternoon, I realised Howard had a motive. He had liked Jackson's performance and as the conversation wore on and the drinks were ordered, he began talking money.

As more drinks were poured, the size of the offer kept increasing and, after speaking to the chairman, we decided we could not turn down an offer of £600,000 for a full-back who was not yet twenty and played only a handful of games. Matthew spent four years at Goodison Park, culminating in Everton's victory over Manchester United in the 1995 FA Cup final. At the time, I did not realise how good he could become. However, Luton's need for money overrode everything. One bonus was an opportunity to take the Nottingham Forest goalkeeper, Steve Sutton, on loan. He had won two League Cup finals but had lost his place to Mark Crossley.

Steve was excellent, a sound individual who gave the defence some much-needed confidence. He had grown up in a religious family in the Peak District and was a talented musician who spent his Sundays playing in the Salvation Army band.

The Christmas fixtures saw us beat Coventry, Arsenal and Chelsea without conceding a goal. A draw at the City Ground that saw Des Walker score a last-minute equaliser – which turned out to be his only goal in professional football – took Luton out of the relegation zone. Brian Clough had done me a favour by loaning us Steve Sutton, but after he had played a set number of games, Nottingham Forest asked for a fee of £300,000 to make the move permanent, which Luton could not pay. Long afterwards, Kohler told me that Clough wanted a financial sweetener to allow the deal to go through.

Sutton was superior to Alec Chamberlain, our regular goalkeeper whose injury had brought Steve to Kenilworth Road. Steve signed for Derby. On reflection, this was to be a pivotal factor behind our relegation. Chamberlain was later sold to Watford, where he did very well.

At the other end of the table, Leeds and Manchester United were fighting for the title. The pitch at Old Trafford was cutting up badly and Alex Ferguson thought a big striker, to whom they could play long balls, might serve United better than their traditional passing game. He settled on Mick Harford. When he contacted me about Harford, I told him: 'You must be joking. How can we sell our leading striker?' To Alex's credit, he left it there. Had he gone behind my back and approached Mick directly, which he could easily have done, he would have got his man. Mick would have forced the issue. Nobody at Luton Town in 1992 would have turned down Manchester United.

By 20 April, there were two matches remaining and Luton were third bottom. The gap between us and Coventry was two points, but Luton's goal difference was so poor that we were effectively three behind. Our final home game pitted us against Aston Villa. On the Thursday I rang their manager, Ron Atkinson, because Villa had requested some extra complementary tickets, which we had turned down. He had left a message to ring him to see if I could help out.

I had known Ron since he was playing for Oxford as a buccaneering wing-half who played with his shorts rolled up to reveal thighs like tree trunks. As a player he was bang average, but he possessed the confidence of a Maradona, which was to stand him in good stead when he went into management. Our conversation turned to Saturday's game. I asked: 'Have you picked your team yet?' Very confidently, Ron told me about his line-up from Mark Bosnich to Paul McGrath, from Kevin Richardson to Cyrille Regis. He ended up by mentioning his wide-left player Tony Daley.

Jokingly, I pleaded: 'Leave him out, Ron. He'll be far too quick for my right-back, young Darren Salton.'

Completely deadpan, with classic Atkinson timing, Ron replied: 'Pal, Daley plays one good game in three and he's just played it.'

We won the game, 2–0, although that day Coventry also beat and relegated West Ham. Unless we overcame Notts County and Aston Villa beat Coventry, Luton's ten years in the top flight would be coming to an end. For the fourth successive season, they needed something on the final afternoon to stay up.

For the second time, I would be taking Luton to an away ground needing to win to survive. The equation in my home city of Nottingham was different than it had been in Manchester in 1983. Unlike Manchester City, Notts County had nothing to play for – they had already been relegated. However, a win at Meadow Lane on its own would not be enough. We also needed Coventry to lose at Villa Park.

Meadow Lane resembled a building site. There was no stand behind one of the goals and next to where the 5,000 travelling Luton fans had gathered there was a bank of ploughed earth. Everything began well. We took the lead through our full-back, local boy Julian

James, while Coventry conceded an early goal at Aston Villa in a game they would lose, 2–0. However, what followed was a meek surrender. Rob Matthews, a geography student at Loughborough University, scored twice for Notts County on his league debut. Luton finished the season relegated and without a single away win. The television commentary concluded with the observation that the club, unwilling to make the investment the new Premier League demanded, 'had played Russian roulette once too often'.

If we lacked investment, we had also lacked pace. Chris Kamara and Trevor Peake were in their mid-thirties. Brian Stein and Mick Harford, men who had served the club brilliantly in their first spell at Kenilworth Road, could no longer run past defenders. Eleven times that season Luton had taken the lead but failed to hold on to the three points, while the cups had seen us fall at the first hurdle to Birmingham and Sheffield United.

Our one outstanding youngster, Mark Pembridge, had not agreed a new contract and was capable of a higher standard than the freshly renamed Division One could offer. Brian Clough had gone to see Pembridge play at Meadow Lane and, over the phone, queried whether he could pass the ball.

'Of course he can,' I told him. 'And with both feet.'

Clough's reply was instant: 'But can he pass it under pressure?' It was a comment that resonated. Even after fourteen years as a front-line manager, you were always learning.

Pembridge went to Derby, who had lost in the play-offs to Blackburn, for £1.25 million.

At the final whistle, I felt empty and desolate. Luton had voted for the new Premier League, which, backed by television finances, would come into existence the following season. The club would not be part of it. It had been a miserable return.

CHAPTER 21

'IF YOU DON'T SELL HIM, I WILL'

There was no respite in the newly renamed and expanded Division One. Luton won none of our first five games and after a 3–3 draw with Tranmere, we were second bottom, above only Derby.

David Kohler had now assumed sole control of the club as owner and managing director. He was a perky, confident character who could be charming. He would come to work accompanied by his dog, which sat placidly in his office while he checked the finances. Often his wife-to-be, Leoni, a friendly, attractive woman, would also accompany him. He had no previous experience of running a football club.

Kohler was unpopular with supporters and suffered antisemitic abuse, which I found disgraceful. The source of the fans' anger was typical. Luton's last season in the top flight had seen them exist on an average gate of 9,715, which was the lowest in the division. The supporters had no real idea how much it cost to run a successful, professional club. It is an ever-present balancing act.

Once more, I was forced to cut costs. Mick Harford, in the twilight of his career, was sold to Chelsea for £300,000. There was further trouble.

In March, I had signed Steve Claridge from Cambridge United for £120,000 having seen him play one evening at Ipswich. He was shaven-headed, playing with his socks around his ankles and eccentric in his ways. He was also an indefatigable runner who exhausted himself on behalf of his team. The fee was low because his manager, John Beck, wanted him out of the club. I paired Steve with Phil Gray, a forward whom I had signed from Tottenham for £275,000 in the summer of 1991. However, the partnership did not work out and, after Claridge had scored just twice from sixteen games, we were presented with a dilemma.

Luton were faced with a big VAT bill and still had instalments to pay Cambridge for Claridge's transfer. The only way out was to allow Steve to return to the Abbey Stadium. John Beck had left Cambridge by then and the fee was sufficient to get us out of financial trouble. Even during his brief stay at Luton, we knew Steve was troubled. There were reports of him sleeping in his car. He was also addicted to betting. It is to Claridge's immense credit that he became an outstanding striker, an excellent radio analyst and a successful non-league manager. However, Phil Gray's game did develop and he became a Northern Ireland international.

The previous season, Luton had failed to win a single away game. Now, we did not win at home until 29 November, although the 2–0 victory over Watford, with goals from Ian Benjamin, a makeweight signing from Southend, and midfielder John Dreyer gave us bragging rights and took Luton out of the relegation zone. However, before that game, the club had been convulsed by a terrible shock. Two of our outstanding young players, Paul Telfer and Darren Salton, had been involved in a fatal car crash near the United States airbase at Chicksands in Bedfordshire.

Paul had been driving a Mercedes sports car with Darren as a passenger and were returning from a game of golf. They had been involved in a head-on collision in which the passenger in the other car, Eileen Phillimore, had been killed. Visiting Darren at Addenbrooke's Hospital in Cambridge and seeing him battling for life, with his father sat alongside him, made football seem irrelevant.

Darren was in a coma for two-and-a-half weeks and we all prayed for him.

He would never play professional football again, but he held no grudge against Paul, who had been his friend since they were at school in Edinburgh together. Darren, who had been a Scotland under-21 international, pieced his life back together, married his childhood sweetheart and went into football management at Hitchin. Telfer, who was an outstanding golfer, would continue playing until he was forty-two, by which time he was turning out for Sutton United. He signed for Coventry in 1995 and formed a strong bond with their manager, Gordon Strachan, who would take him to Southampton and Celtic.

Needing some punch up front, I asked Southampton about Kerry Dixon, who was now thirty-two and floundering in the twilight of his career. It was somewhat ironic that when he was sixteen, I had decided against taking Kerry, who was a Luton boy, on to the staff. At the time, we had a young prospect of a similar age, Godfrey Ingram, who was an England Schoolboy international. Despite Kerry's father persistently hounding me on his boy's behalf, we decided Godfrey had greater potential.

Ingram left Luton in 1982 and spent most of his career in the United States playing indoor football. Dixon began an electrical apprenticeship and played for Chesham United and Dunstable before Maurice Evans, one of the nicest men ever to manage professionally, took him to Reading. In 1983, Dixon joined Chelsea for £150,000. Only Frank Lampard and Bobby Tambling would score more than his 193 goals for the club.

Bringing Kerry Dixon back to Luton may have been a 'Hobson's choice' signing, but others benefited. Phil Gray finished the season with twenty goals and would be sold to Sunderland for £800,000 in the summer of 1993. Telfer, Scott Oakes, Ceri Hughes and Jason

Rees – another Welsh discovery from Cyril Beech – were all helped by experienced professionals such as Dixon and Trevor Peake.

There was not much else to shout about. Luton finished twentieth with an average gate down 15 per cent to 8,212. A second successive relegation had been avoided by two points.

The supporters were restless and, although the new season opened with a derby at home to Watford, fewer than 10,000 came to Kenilworth Road to watch the 2–1 victory. Phil Gray's departure along with that of Harford and Claridge meant I had lost three quality centre-forwards in the space of a year. This was precisely the situation that had undermined me at Leicester. There was a sense of déjà vu.

Fortunately, there was a ready-made replacement in the form of a tough, raw-boned but skilful striker: John Hartson, aged eighteen. Early on in his time at Luton, John made a mistake, the kind that teenagers do. He was gambling and took the bank card of another youth-team player to withdraw £50, which was double his weekly earnings, to feed the slot machines. I had no choice but to send him home to Swansea. His mother, Diana, who was a nurse, phoned me tearfully to plead his case. I told her not to worry. I believed in John and said he would be back at Luton in a few days. In his autobiography, John wrote about the debt he owes to the club. It was one he was to fully repay.

However, in football, today is always more important than tomorrow, and with the win over Watford followed up by four straight defeats in the league and elimination from the League Cup by Cambridge, I wondered if I would be given time to see the young Welshman flourish. We continued to limp along amid financial worries. It was time to beg, steal and borrow.

Financially, Luton were bailed out by two local men. One was Cliff Bassett, the head of Universal Salvage Auction. He had founded the company in 1969. It would buy wrecked cars from insurance companies for anything up to a quarter of their value. Those that could be repaired would be sold at auction. Those that could not were broken up for spare parts. By 1996, the company would be listed on the Stock Exchange and declare profits of more than £3 million. Bassett joined Luton as a director. He was a warm, quiet character whom I found massively supportive. However, he never warmed to Kohler.

The other investor was Chris Green, a cheerful Charlie of a guy who enjoyed his food and his football. He came to the club after heading a big Ford franchise and his conversation would be peppered with motoring analogies. A forward would be described as having 'plenty of fuel in his tank to help him accelerate away from defenders but just could not get his head into gear'. However, while Kohler was grateful for Bassett's financial support, he was distrustful of his motives. These tensions happen in a boardroom. I had seen it previously at Luton, when some directors found it difficult to accept the man who seemed to be everyone's favourite – Eric Morecambe.

The highlight of the season was the FA Cup. It began with a 1–0 win over Southend in a game that provoked no dreams of Wembley. The reward was to be drawn away to Newcastle, who under Kevin Keegan had emerged as the most exciting team in the country. At St James' Park, in front of a crowd of 32,000, we rose to the occasion. Tony Thorpe, a nineteen-year-old whom I had taken from Leicester, scored a cracker from twenty yards before Peter Beardsley won and converted a penalty.

Some years later, I was in Harrods, which was owned by the Fulham chairman, Mohamed Al-Fayed. By chance I met Kevin Keegan, who was now working for Al-Fayed at the club, and he asked what I thought of Tony Thorpe. He had come from a disadvantaged background – not only were the family poor, but Tony's mother was deaf. He had overcome many obstacles to become a regular goalscorer at Kenilworth Road. Kevin would sign him for Fulham.

The replay would be live on television. Young Hartson, taking the ball calmly past Mike Hooper in the Newcastle goal, and Scott Oakes gave us an outstanding 2–0 victory. In the fifth round at Ninian Park, Oakes scored again in a feisty 2–1 win against Cardiff.

Luton would play West Ham in the quarter-final at Upton Park, where because of an injury to Trevor Peake, I was forced to play a twenty-year-old centre-back, David Greene. He had played only twice before and while he had a strong pivot, he was not the most mobile footballer. West Ham's attack was led by Lee Chapman and Greene coped with him excellently to earn a goalless draw and a replay at Kenilworth Road.

Before the game, I was invited to Sky's studios in Isleworth to discuss our tactics for the replay in a programme called *The Boot Room*, presented by Andy Gray. The recording would not be broadcast until after the game. Andy would also interview the West Ham manager, Billy Bonds, about the tactics he would be taking into the tie. *The Boot Room* was a highly successful show that gave a great insight into management. This was before television punditry became dominated by 'banter' and 'personalities'.

The replay made Scott Oakes a hero at Luton. On a dramatic night, he scored twice after Martin Allen had given West Ham the lead. Once Ian Bishop had levelled the tie, Oakes coolly ran through to complete his hat-trick. Scott had grown up used to fame. His father, Trevor, was a long-standing guitarist and songwriter with the pop group Showaddywaddy. His brother, Stefan, would play for Leicester in the 2000 League Cup final at Wembley, where our semi-final against Chelsea would be staged.

We were the centre of the pre-match attention, but I quickly ran into disputes about ticket allocation. This was a very different board to the one that had watched the League Cup finals of 1988 and 1989. This was their first trip to Wembley and it might be their last opportunity to sit in the Royal Box. The players were unhappy with their allocation and their dissatisfaction sparked a couple of meetings.

Luton's performance against Chelsea was a shadow of those we had delivered against Newcastle and West Ham. Tony Cascarino established a mastery over our centre-halves, Trevor Peake and John Dreyer. Gavin Peacock scored for Chelsea after fourteen minutes and again just after half-time. I always maintained that had the semi-final been played at Hillsborough or Villa Park, our players would have performed better. Many had never been to Wembley and some seemed to treat the game as if Luton had made the final. They set up a players' pool and asked the agent, Eric Hall, to manage it. The occasion was, however, too much for them. In the FA Cup, Wembley should be for finals and I failed to convince the players that this was not a showpiece and there would be another game after this one.

Glenn Hoddle was in charge of Chelsea and was less than gracious in victory. I received a cursory shake of the hand at the final whistle. I was invited to the final as a summariser. Chelsea would face Manchester United, who had powered their way to the Premier League title and would secure the Double with a crushing 4–0 win.

We ended the season with a 2–2 draw at Stoke to finish twentieth, two places off a relegation position. However, seven of the team at the Victoria Ground were under twenty-three. With Hartson, Oakes, Telfer, Hughes, Rees and Des Linton, we had the making of a good young side, one that might take Luton Town far. There was hope.

The merry-go-round of summer transfers began slowly. Kerry Dixon had been a good stopgap, helping Hartson to progress, but his legs had gone and I needed more pace up front. I paid Plymouth £150,000 for their striker, Dwight Marshall, who possessed real speed. With Scott Oakes developing well, I had more attacking options, especially on the counter-attack away from home.

A 4–2 victory at Watford should have given the club a boost, but the reality of life outside the Premier League was underlined by the fact that only 8,890 came to Vicarage Road to watch the game. The boom triggered by the Premier League had not found its way into what would now be the Championship. During the 1994/95 season, only one club, Wolverhampton Wanderers, had average gates of more than 20,000. Eleven clubs had average attendances of less than 10,000. Luton's average crowd of 7,350 was its lowest since 1967, when the club was two divisions lower.

In early November, Tottenham got in touch. Alan Sugar was now chairman and after wresting control of the club from Terry Venables he had appointed Ossie Ardiles as manager. Ardiles's high-octane attacking philosophy had come to grief and after losing 5–2 at Manchester City and enduring elimination from the League Cup at Notts County, he was fired.

I was invited to meet Sugar at his home in Chigwell, but I began to panic when I could not find his house – these were the days before Satnav. Eventually, with the help of a kindly shopkeeper, I managed to meander down a country lane towards his house. His wife, Ann, seemed a lovely woman, producing cake as I talked to a man who had revolutionised the sale of computers in the 1980s. I was not overawed but was quite talkative as he laid out his plans. However, no offer followed.

Harry Harris, the *Daily Mirror*'s football correspondent, was as close to Sugar as he had been to Irving Scholar and told him Gerry Francis was considering leaving Queens Park Rangers and should be a candidate. In 1993, Francis had taken QPR to fifth place in the Premier League's inaugural season, but the club's owner, Richard Thompson, wanted to bring in Rodney Marsh as director of football. This had enraged Francis, who, Harris had learned, was on the point of walking out of Loftus Road. Alan Sugar rang to tell me he was going to appoint Gerry Francis because he seemed 'a mumser' – a Jewish word for the kind of tough, uncompromising character he wanted. Nevertheless, as I put the phone down, I thought these might not be the last dealings I had with Alan Sugar.

In January we lost our main striker, John Hartson, to Arsenal. George Graham had phoned me a few weeks before to discuss the young Welshman, but I had not seriously expected an offer. However, David Kohler, who was aware that Arsenal's interest was genuine, came to see me and my assistant, Colin Murphy, querying whether they had been in touch. I told him George had not yet made an offer and, even if he did, I would not want John to be sold. He was too central to Luton's future.

There were raised voices. Kohler said any fee around £1 million would be very useful. When Arsenal made their offer, David called a meeting. He wanted Hartson sold. Colin and I objected and there were more raised voices. I condemned the sale, which was a further example of Luton's history of offloading its prize assets. The meeting finished with Kohler leaving my office with the words: 'If you don't sell him, I will.'

I accepted the inevitable and spoke to George on several occasions. He eventually revealed he was prepared to pay £2.5 million for Hartson; a record fee for a teenager. That weekend, David Dein, Arsenal's vice-chairman, rang me at home. He wanted assurances that, if they paid that fee, it would not be wasted. He wondered if Hartson would be up to playing for a club like Arsenal. I assured him John would not let him down. Dein seemed unusually worried as George Graham had also agreed another deal for another striker and had offered Ipswich £1.25 million for Chris Kiwomya. David gave me the impression that the relationship with his manager was fraying.

I met George and his chief scout, Steve Burtenshaw, for a breakfast meeting at a hotel by Junction 11 of the M1. We agreed to do the deal. On 12 January, I told John to put on a suit and a tie and drove him to the marble halls of Highbury. John had had to borrow a shirt from his landlord and wore the only tie he possessed – which had a Disney motif on it. He signed a four-year contract worth £3,250 a week – almost ten times what he was being paid by Luton.

I was annoyed by the loss of an exceptional talent but pleased that John had been given a move to the big time. David Kohler was delighted with a fee that was two-and-a-half times more than the one he would have settled for. To this day, I cannot recall whether we paid Cyril Beech, who died in 2001, any bonus for what was then the highest fee Luton had received for a footballer. Sadly, scouts are people who are often taken for granted. The statistics show how much we missed Hartson. Dwight Marshall finished the season with nine goals and Scott Oakes ended up with six. John Hartson's tally was nine goals from eleven games when he was sold.

At this time my assistant, Colin Murphy, was getting itchy feet. He was frustrated by the apparent inability to progress the club while working under these tight financial constraints. Colin was a networker who had a lot of contacts at the FA, and they were regularly being asked to recommend candidates for positions abroad. In the summer of 1995, he left to manage Notts County. He took them to the Division Two play-off final, which was lost to Bradford. Afterwards, Colin coached in Vietnam and Burma.

David Kohler's obsession was now to implement his grand design for a new stadium. He had graduated from university with a degree in surveying and his forte was property. One of Kohler's friends was an architect called David Keirle, whose company would go on to design training centres at Liverpool and Leicester, and together they came up with the plans for a futuristic new stadium, featuring a retractable roof. The plans were fantastic, featuring moveable artificial and grass pitches, underground parking, spacious walkways and a retail park. It was the talk of the town. There are shades in Keirle's vision in the design of Tottenham's new stadium. Many of the ideas came from America.

The mistake was to call it The Kohlerdome, which conveyed to the supporters the idea that this was an egotistical fantasy that would drain even more money from the team. The location was also debatable: just off Junction 10 of the M1, on the Luton Airport flightpath. As if that wasn't enough, it was also close to housing, which triggered a torrent of letters to the local press. There were even talks with the charismatic Peter Winkelman in Milton Keynes that once more raised the spectre of relocation, which would have been the last straw for Luton's supporters.

The Kohlerdome faced too many battles, especially legal and financial ones, and the opposition to the project was fuelled by an inherent dislike of David Kohler among the fanbase. The stadium was rejected by the Department for Environment. In February 1999, three days before an unsuccessful appeal against the decision, Kohler resigned as Luton's managing director after his au pair discovered a petrol bomb pushed through his letterbox at his home in Hertfordshire.

This time, there was no run in the FA Cup to give the season momentum. We overcame Bristol Rovers in the third round and drew 1–1 with Southampton at Kenilworth Road in a game we might have won. The replay saw us torn to shreds by Matt Le Tissier, and at half-time, we trouped into the dressing rooms at The Dell 5–0 down. For Southampton, who had been thrashed 7–0 by Luton in 1985 and 6–1 four years later, this was revenge served cold.

Within a week of the season finishing, the Sheffield Wednesday secretary, Graham Mackrell, rang me. He had worked at Luton as assistant to the chief executive, John Smith, in my first spell at Kenilworth Road and had taken over when John left. I had known Graham well from his early days at Bournemouth; he was a cheery, more than competent man. He had moved to Yorkshire after I had recommended him to the Sheffield Wednesday chairman, Bert McGee, who was to resign the year after the Hillsborough disaster, the year Sheffield Wednesday were relegated.

In subsequent seasons, Sheffield Wednesday had flourished. Under Ron Atkinson, they had won promotion and beaten Manchester United to win the League Cup and under Trevor Francis they had finished third in 1992 and reached two Wembley finals the following year. However, Wednesday had finished the 1994/95 season by winning just three of their final fifteen matches, falling from eighth to thirteenth position. The defeats included a 7–1 thrashing at home by Nottingham Forest and culminated in Francis's sacking.

After four years at Luton, I felt I needed a fresh challenge. Although my relationship with David Kohler seemed good on the surface, tensions were starting to grow. There were aspects of the Sheffield Wednesday job that I knew would be tricky, but the lure of the Premier League was too great to turn down. I would be leaving 'my Luton', a club I had been involved with through four decades, with a heavy heart.

I had first joined them in 1964. It was now 1995 and the financial constraints had become too much. As long as Luton remained in the cramped, outdated surrounds of Kenilworth Road, their route to survival would always involve selling their best players. It was time to break ties. As a manager, I had less control than I did in my first spell at the club. Then, my influence had been such that I had even selected the music for the team to run out to – 'Chariots of Fire' by Vangelis.

As they had been in 1986, the supporters were unhappy that I was leaving. However, I knew in my heart I had given them some memorable times. As I was driving to meet the Sheffield Wednesday board, I almost drove off the M1 when David Kohler came on to a sports bulletin on Radio 5 saying. 'David Pleat has broken his contract and I will be demanding maximum compensation from Sheffield Wednesday. He is probably even now driving up there in his company car, using my petrol.' David Kohler received his full compensation, believed to be £300,000, and did not indulge in the kind of vindictiveness that David Evans had pursued when I first left Luton. I see him occasionally. He told me that, like Alan Sugar, he would look back on his time in football and feel they had been wasted years.

He said that taking over Luton at twenty-nine had been a pure ego trip. When Bradford had won promotion to the Premier League in 1999, Kohler had rung the chairman, Geoffrey Richmond, and implored him that now was the time to sell. Kohler had learned his lesson. Richmond, who would be declared bankrupt after Bradford's relegation, was still to learn his.

My departure marked the end of a long association with Luton Town. Although I received an honorary MA from Luton University for services to football and the media, my years at Kenilworth Road are not physically commemorated. The ground has lounges named after Eric Morecambe, John Moore and Joe Payne, who in 1936 scored ten goals in a single game against Bristol Rovers. There is no David Pleat Lounge and perhaps nor should there be. What I do hope I left behind at Kenilworth Road are plenty of memories.

CHAPTER 22

'STAR PLAYERS WHO HAVE
HAD THEIR DAY'

When I was offered the job, several people told me to ignore the clichéd images of the grimy, smoke-ridden steelworks. Sheffield was a handsome city surrounded by beautiful countryside. Like Rome, it had been built on seven hills, and with Sheffield United in the second tier, Wednesday held tribal superiority.

Around the boardroom table with the chairman, Dave Richards, sat Bob Grierson, an accountant, Keith Addy and Graham Thorpe, who were in property, Geoff Hulley, who had made his money in frozen foods, and Joe Ashton, the Labour MP for Bassetlaw. The board was made up of dyed-in-the-wool Sheffield Wednesday fans. In retrospect, what the club needed was someone who was less attached to Wednesday but was more of an independent-thinking entrepreneur.

One of my first tasks was to bring in a coach I respected. I knew Danny Bergara as an outstanding coach at Luton who in 1978 had left to join Harry Haslam at Sheffield United. Much of his time since had been spent at Stockport. But for defeat in the play-offs, he would have guided them from the Fourth Division to what was now the Championship. However, by 1995 he had left Edgeley Park and was available. I asked him to join Wednesday as first-team coach and retained the thoughtful Frank Barlow and Albert Phelan on the backroom staff. Frank had a degree in sociology and had played for Sheffield United and coached at Wednesday under both Ron

Atkinson and Trevor Francis, while Albert had coached the club to the FA Youth Cup final in 1991.

The board requested I keep the assistant manager, Richie Barker, who like Frank Barlow had worked under both Atkinson and Francis, employing him as a consultant. He would act as a conduit between the training ground and the boardroom. He would 'mark my card'. This arrangement did not work. I never really integrated Richie into my inner sanctum. There was suspicion on both sides. I felt he was Ron's man and I found it difficult to embrace him. He was happy to be on the sidelines, from where he went golfing with Geoff Hulley twice a week.

The stadium looked resplendent. The Spion Kop that could hold 11,000 dominated the skyline, the gleaming Main Stand had been upgraded and the awful memories of the Hillsborough disaster six years before were slowly being pushed into the past. My opening games came early. Sheffield Wednesday had entered the Intertoto Cup, a tournament designed to promote betting on football during the summer months. The prize for winning it was a place in the UEFA Cup – an attraction for some.

The players loathed the competition. Some clubs would simply register fringe or groundstaff players just to make up the numbers. That summer, Tottenham would go to Cologne and lose, 8–0. On their way to the airport, they had picked a couple of lower-league players who were registered purely for this competition. I was unhappy at the decision to play in the Intertoto, which required the players to report for duty two weeks earlier than normal. We played the first fixture in Switzerland on 24 June without any pre-season preparations.

We had to play our home games, against Górnik Zabrze from Poland and the Danish side Aarhus, at Rotherham because the pitch at Hillsborough was not ready. Des Walker, the pacey England centre-half who was Sheffield Wednesday's captain, and other senior players accused the board of entering the competition purely to make money. I had considerable sympathy with them, but the decision had been made before my appointment.

Another decision that had also been taken was the one to sell midfielder Chris Bart-Williams to Frank Clark at Nottingham Forest for £2.5 million. I was unable to persuade him to stay. With the Bart-Williams money, I paid Derby £900,000 to take Mark Pembridge, whom I knew well from my time at Luton. I also took advantage of a tip-off to sign Marc Degryse from Anderlecht, who had played in two World Cups for Belgium, for £1.5 million. I thought two players for one was a fair exchange. Both were to do well.

The next transfer had rather less fairness about it. Dan Petrescu was twenty-seven, a superb right wing-back at his peak. He was a tremendous trainer, who always put in extra work and was one of the cleverest defenders I have ever seen or worked with when it came to making runs inside the opposition full-back. He was to prove my most immediate problem. Petrescu lived in the same complex as I did in Whirlow, where Sheffield begins to merge into the Peak District. I took a phone call from his agent, a Romanian called Ioan Becali, who seemed to have hoovered up all his country's leading players. I agreed to meet him at the training ground at Middlewood.

I thought Becali would be seeking to improve Petrescu's salary, but he told me his client wanted to leave and he knew Chelsea were interested. Of course he knew. He had already spoken to them. It transpired that Chelsea's chief executive, Colin Hutchinson, and their manager, Glenn Hoddle, had already talked to Petrescu and the lure of Heathrow and Harrods was to prove too great. If Dan wanted to return to Bucharest from Sheffield, he would have to drive to Manchester Airport, take a flight to London and then board a plane for Romania. Heathrow offered direct flights. I was also told his wife, Daniela, would enjoy the shopping in Knightsbridge.

Becali made some serious threats. He said Petrescu had no intention of playing for Sheffield Wednesday again and we had no option but to agree to his demands. We agreed a fee of £2.5 million, which Chelsea then attempted to lower. Their chairman, Ken Bates, rang Dave Richards to say the medical had revealed problems with the bones in his pelvic area, a condition called symphysis pubis. Chelsea claimed the problem would cause Dan to miss games and therefore they would not be receiving full value for money.

Richards and Bates were close and Chelsea would later support Richards's bid to become chairman of the Premier League. I had no option but to reluctantly agree to a medical tribunal and £250,000 was knocked off the price. I was unhappy with my chairman but more disappointed we had lost a fine defender. Petrescu spent five years at Stamford Bridge, winning the FA Cup and the Cup-Winners' Cup and barely missed a game. In 2018, Ioan Becali would be jailed in his native Romania for bribing a judge.

I compensated by switching Ian Nolan from left to right-back and introduced a local boy, Lee Briscoe, who would earn a call up for England's under-21 side the following year. Over a post-match drink in my office, after a game in which Briscoe had impressed, Dave Sexton, the under-21s manager, told me he would select him. I told Dave that with all the will in the world I did not think Lee was ready for football at that level. I have always felt that under-21 caps are scattered around like confetti. I was proved right. Lee had ability but lacked self-belief. In the Sheffield Wednesday defence, he appeared intimidated playing alongside the opinionated Des Walker, who had been one of England's stand-out players in the 1990 World Cup.

In the long term, Dave Richards's instructions were clear. He wanted me to remove 'star players who have had their day'. I understood. At its core, Sheffield Wednesday was an ageing side. When I arrived, five players – Chris Woods, Steve Nicol, Chris Waddle,

Mark Bright and John Sheridan – were over thirty. Des Walker would reach that landmark in November. I sensed they felt some trepidation about what my plans were for them.

Richards's strategy was sound, but it would not be popular with the fans. They were usually only interested in short-term results and would have vivid memories of those ageing players, some of whom had taken Sheffield Wednesday to three Wembley finals. I was continually looking to refresh the squad. Marc Degryse proved to be a thoughtful, intelligent forward and excelled when we overwhelmed Leeds 6–2, though he was to become frustrated by the lack of professionalism of some of his teammates outside the game.

When my chief scout, Mick Mills, returned from a trip, he told me he had seen 'the next Kevin Beattie'. I always felt it important to show faith in the chief scout, otherwise what was the point of him? Bobby Robson had described Beattie as 'the quickest defender I ever saw'. Mills, who had played alongside him in the glory years at Ipswich, said he possessed as high a leap to head the ball as any player he had ever seen. Mick had been in what was now Serbia but which had been Yugoslavia. Under Communist rule, the Yugoslav FA had a policy of not allowing players under twenty-eight to leave their club. Now, the system had opened up and Red Star Belgrade needed the money. Dejan Stefanović was a 21-year-old centre-half who was already an international.

Mick had also seen Dejan's teammate, Darko Kovačević, a young striker who would score thirty-seven goals in forty-seven games for Red Star. To bring the pair back to Yorkshire would require a cheque for £4.5 million, which was signed in December. Their debuts were delayed by the need to acquire work permits, although we saw their talent in training and we found them a flat in the complex in Whirlow where Dan Petrescu had lived.

Both had difficulty learning English and they were evidently not following the diet we had prescribed for them. When one of our coaches called round, he found discarded takeaway cartons. Probably because of their youth, they were slow to integrate. Perhaps they were too young. Perhaps they found Sheffield Wednesday to have too many cliques, a problem that was to show itself later when Paolo Di Canio joined Benito Carbone at the club.

Stefanović played only intermittently and was released on a free transfer in 1999. After a couple of whistlestops around Europe, he ended up as captain of Portsmouth, where he led a delegation to the club's owner, his fellow Serb Milan Mandarić. He told Mandarić the players were unhappy with Alain Perrin and suggested he reinstate Harry Redknapp, who had outraged Portsmouth's fanbase by walking out of Fratton Park to join Southampton. Mandarić agreed to sack Perrin and within two years Portsmouth had won the FA Cup.

Kovačević could not impose himself at Hillsborough. He began well, with two goals in a 4–2 victory over Bolton on New Year's Day, which he followed up with the opening goal against Liverpool. There was, however, to be only one more – in a 3–1 defeat by Nottingham Forest. Nevertheless, he had shown enough of his talent to attract the interest of Real Sociedad and he was later sold for a healthy profit in the summer. Kovačević was to become a star in two spells in the Basque Country. In between, he was sold to Juventus for £12 million. He would also shine at Lazio and finish his career with two Greek titles at Olympiakos. His was a great career and perhaps the lesson is that promise needs to be persevered with.

Regi Blinker was an interesting prospect. The agent, Jerome Anderson, told me Feyenoord's outside left was looking for a Premier League club. I told Anderson that if Blinker wanted to come to Sheffield at his own expense, I would look at him and make a quick decision. Regi duly arrived at the training ground but without his boots. Perhaps he was trying to force the issue, but I was not prepared to sign any player without seeing him play in the flesh. I was not prepared to gamble Feyenoord's fee of £275,000.

'We have arranged a practice match especially for you,' I told him. Regi sizzled in borrowed boots. I made a quick, brave decision and for my money got an exciting dribbler in dreadlocks. Blinker had several outstanding games. In March 1996, he made his debut at Aston Villa, scoring both goals in a 3–2 defeat. He followed this mesmerising performance with a brilliant display in a 1–0 win at Southampton. He was speedy, skilful and played very much in the Dutch style, holding a wide position upfield, ready to attack full-backs but not working back too well. So impressed was I with Regi that I went back to Feyenoord to sign another talented Dutchman, the beautifully named midfielder Orlando Trustfull. He was a lovely ball player but appeared to lack the bottle for the English game.

Our first league fixture took us to Anfield where we were beaten by a goal from Liverpool's new £8.5 million signing, Stan Collymore. My first fixture at Hillsborough saw Wednesday beat Blackburn 2–1. The second saw Newcastle win 2–0. It was that kind of season. Not until March did we put together back-to-back victories. We finished with a 1–1 draw at West Ham, which left us fifteenth in the Premier League and some of the travelling support began shouting for Chris Waddle to be made manager. I had great respect for Chris, but the Premier League can be a cruel theatre. When he did become a manager, he did not appear to enjoy the experience.

Neither Chris nor John Sheridan, whose brilliant passing had been part of Sheffield Wednesday's midfield since 1989, was playing regularly. When he was at Tottenham, I had got on well with Chris and allowed him time off to return to the north-east with his wife, Lorna. After talks with the chairman, I suggested to Chris that he might take on a new role as my assistant, an offer he declined. He thought it was a political ploy rather than a real footballing decision. He was partly right. There were politics in the offer because it was a way of helping Waddle while appeasing the supporters. He left Hillsborough in September to join first Falkirk and then Bradford and such was his quiet passion for football, he carried on playing for amateur clubs such as Stocksbridge and Hallam into his forties.

Danny Bergara, my assistant, had difficulty controlling the group and was consistently asking me to discipline certain players, especially Des Walker, who was often disruptive. I told Danny he was dealing with so-called superstars, who I was sure had direct access to the chairman, and he would have to be more cunning, patient and diplomatic. These qualities were, however, not in Danny's armoury and relationships began to founder. Soon, I had to make the difficult decision to relieve him of his duties. I needed a No. 2 who was capable of managing egos. Danny went to manage Rotherham. John Sheridan, who no longer had the athleticism the Premier League required but could still pass a football beautifully, was sold to Bolton in November for £180,000 and would feature in their return to the top flight. John would go on to become a successful manager in lower-league football.

David Hirst, who was a hero at Hillsborough but in the last two seasons of Trevor Francis's management was barely fit to lead the attack, was due to go to Everton. This was his moment. Everton had won the FA Cup in 1995 and appeared to be spending big under Joe Royle. In 1992, Dave Richards had rejected a £4 million offer from Manchester United for Hirst, prompting Alex Ferguson to turn his attention to Eric Cantona. However, as David was driving to Merseyside to conclude the deal, I received a call from Joe Royle. We had sent Everton the medical reports from Hirst's last five seasons. They were not good and Joe told me I should inform David he should return to Sheffield. Hirst was distraught. A year later, in October 1997, Hirst was sold to Southampton for £2 million. He had one good season on the south coast before breaking down again the following year. In his later years, Hirst became an enigma. Some days he was unplayable, while on others he appeared to tread water.

My introduction to the Premier League had been an education. It was an ultra-competitive competition and business was conducted far more thoroughly. The boards were very professional and agents had infiltrated every area of the game. Television had begun its rule and the revenues it generated were often being spent recklessly. Foreign players were attracted to the expanding salaries. Crowds were increasing and football was the new in-game. After four years, the Premier League was well on its way.

I was never one for cashing in on the market for after-dinner speaking. I found the nerves too much. I was once asked to give the toast at the Football Writers' annual dinner at the Royal Lancaster Hotel, which was held two days before the FA Cup final. The guest speaker was Colin Moynihan, who had won a silver medal in rowing at the 1980 Moscow Olympics and was now Minister for Sport in Margaret Thatcher's government. I was horribly nervous. The Thatcher government was considered anti-football and Moynihan's speech went down leadenly. Just before I stood up to make my reply, I went down to the toilets. Gordon Milne, who could sense my nerves, told me on the stairs: 'Don't worry. You have nothing to beat.' I relaxed and coped.

The one delivered when I was at Sheffield Wednesday was less successful. A company called Tailor-Made Sports invited me to give a talk to an amateur club near Manchester. At the time, Wednesday were not doing well and I thought preparing an after-dinner speech would provide a distraction. However, speaking without a lectern in front of a boozed-up audience, I stumbled through the anecdotes. One mistake was talking about how Luton had stayed up by winning the final game at Maine Road. I had not realised many in the audience would be dyed-in-the-wool Manchester City supporters.

The club secretary apologised when handing over the envelope with the £300 fee. I drove back to Sheffield feeling most uncomfortable.

A few weeks later, Dave Richards confronted me. 'Laddie, hast thou been doing after-dinner speeches?' he said in broad Yorkshire.

'I did one and I won't be doing another for a very long time,' I replied.

'I'm not surprised. The club wants the money back. I've had a phone call and a letter.'

I phoned the booking agent who told me to keep the money. The club had done a deal and had to honour it.

Two weeks later, the chairman received a further threatening letter informing him the club dressing rooms had burned down and they needed the money returning immediately. That was the end of my after-dinner career.

CHAPTER 23

'NOW WE HAVE A
PROPER MANAGER'

Behind the scenes, the board of Sheffield Wednesday was enjoying its new Shangri-La. Almost £7 million was spent on a 3,000-capacity top-tier grandstand with thirty gleaming hospitality boxes and office space. A walkway was built over the River Don for supporters. It was finished in time for Hillsborough to host games at Euro '96. Three Star Engineering, owned by the chairman Dave Richards, had been given the contract. A few years later, the company would go into liquidation. One can only assume they delivered the most competitive quote. The training ground at Middlewood was also upgraded at a cost of £2.3 million, although the pitches were still poor by Premier League standards.

As the only socialist on the board, Joe Ashton was more concerned with the towering Spion Kop, which housed the heart of Sheffield Wednesday's support. Ashton was a populist politician who had a national newspaper column and would clash with the other five board members, demanding better toilets and catering facilities for the ordinary fan on the Kop. His arguments would be somewhat smugly dismissed by a board whose politics appeared to be overwhelmingly Conservative.

The club had provided me with a lovely, spacious flat with beautiful views over the village of Whirlow. I paid the bills and the club deducted the rent from my salary. It was there that I met Jimmy Armfield, who was acting as a sounding board for the Football

Association, who were looking for a technical director. I talked to Jimmy on a balcony overlooking sun-drenched fields.

The previous year, in February 1995, Jimmy, as the FA's technical consultant, had accompanied me to southern Italy when I managed a Football League under-21 team against a young Serie B side. Matches between the Italian and English leagues had been a feature of the early 1960s when they were staged at Old Trafford, Highbury and San Siro. By now, they had been scaled back and the Premier League breakaway had denied us top-flight footballers. A crowd of 3,000 gathered at the Stadium of the Olive Trees in the small city of Andria to see the Derby striker Mark Stallard's last-minute, near-post header give the Football League a 3–2 win.

Some of that team, such as Dean Richards, Lee Carsley and Andy Booth, would have fine careers. It was on the strength of that performance that I would sign Booth from Huddersfield for Sheffield Wednesday. The Serie B attack was led by Lorenzo Amoruso, who two years later would sign for Glasgow Rangers.

Jimmy, a kindly, philosophical man, said he was impressed by the way I had handled the team and intimated there would be further opportunities. Becoming the FA's technical director might be that opportunity. Later, he would ring to say he was recommending me for the position, one I did not feel I was fully qualified for. The move was opposed by Dave Richards, who offered me a new contract by way of compensation. The job went to Howard Wilkinson, whose background in education made him a far more suitable candidate.

The rebuilding of Hillsborough had, however, put a strain on Sheffield Wednesday's finances. They were now paying more than £500,000 a year in interest to the Co-operative Bank. Some success on the pitch was now imperative. Pre-season was spent in Holland, where Ritchie Humphreys, a teenage striker, scored a dramatic individual goal against Utrecht. Marco van Basten, who had begun his career at Utrecht, was at the game and comparisons were made.

Did we have a Yorkshire Van Basten in our midst? Ritchie began his first-team career in extraordinary fashion. After four matches, we were top of the Premier League with four wins, having beaten Aston Villa, Leeds, Newcastle and Leicester. Humphreys had scored in three of those games. His debut goal against Aston Villa was timed at 95.9 mph, which was then the hardest shot ever recorded in the English game. It was surpassed a few weeks later at Highbury when David Hirst struck a shot against the frame of David Seaman's goal that was measured at 114 mph.

We possessed a hard-working midfield composed of Wayne Collins, whom I had bought from Crewe for £600,000, Graham Hyde, Peter Atherton and Guy Whittingham. All proved solid citizens. After our 2–0 win at Leeds – a result that ended Howard Wilkinson's reign at Elland Road – the cricket umpire Dickie Bird came to the away dressing room to congratulate the team. He told us he had been a big supporter of Sheffield Wednesday all his life. Dickie was a lovely man, but his celebrity support proved only temporary. The following season, Barnsley would be promoted to the top flight for the only time in their history and Dickie would lend his home town his undying loyalty. Later, he would turn up at Elland Road as Leeds became a powerful force under David O'Leary. Dickie was a true Yorkshireman.

In the wake of Euro '96, the crowds were returning. Those first four matches, at Hillsborough, St James' Park and Elland Road, were watched by 130,000 spectators. However, Sheffield Wednesday's sprint start soon faded. Ritchie Humphreys did not score another league goal that season and we did not win another game for two months, slipping to twelfth until we overcame Nottingham Forest, 2–0, with goals from Orlando Trustfull and Benito Carbone. Six of the next seven matches were drawn. The exception was a 1–0 win over Liverpool at Anfield, the result of an enthusiastic performance and a Guy Whittingham goal.

The last of those draws was at Stamford Bridge. We were two goals down to Chelsea and Gianfranco Zola was controlling the game. I moved Atherton to man mark the brilliant Italian. Atherton, who had stifled Dennis Bergkamp in the previous game against Arsenal, cut off the supply to the Chelsea forwards in an extremely disciplined performance. Mark Pembridge scored and Dejan Stefanović equalised in stoppage time. Pembridge, another utterly reliable performer, scored again in a 2–1 victory over Everton and twice in a 4–2 defeat at Middlesbrough. The reverse at the Riverside Stadium was a rare one. We were a side growing in confidence as the season reached its climax. There was a real honesty to the team.

We beat Tottenham and Wimbledon and drew with Newcastle to go sixth – one point and one place behind Aston Villa with a game in hand. We were on course for a European place, which would mean a lot to the club. Since 1963, Sheffield Wednesday had been involved in just two European ties. Our fate would be decided by three consecutive away games before the season finished at home to Liverpool. Four points would secure Wednesday a place in the UEFA Cup. Instead, we lost all three of our away games, conceding four at Blackburn and five at West Ham. In our desire to chase games, we left ourselves exposed.

After a 1–0 defeat at Leicester, we needed to beat Liverpool at Hillsborough. Manchester United had already won the league, but if Liverpool, under Roy Evans, beat us they would be competing for the European Cup for the first time since the Heysel disaster a dozen years before. A crowd of 38,593 piled into Hillsborough for a defining game. David Elleray, a housemaster at Harrow when not officiating, was in charge. In the seventy-third minute, Kevin Pressman, who had made a couple of fine saves to deny Stan Collymore and Michael Owen, was forced off with injury.

His deputy was Matt Clarke, a local lad who had been signed from Rotherham. With his first kick of the game, Clarke sent up a long ball which O'Neill Donaldson, who had been signed from Mansfield for £50,000 in the last days of Trevor Francis's reign, controlled and drove past David James. There were six minutes remaining when Clarke intercepted a through-ball with his gloves. The linesman flagged that he had done so outside his area, although it would have been a very marginal call. Elleray promptly sent him off and our centre-forward, Andy Booth, went in goal. From the resulting free-kick, Jamie Redknapp equalised with a fine drive. It finished 1–1.

The result suited nobody. We had been denied European football and Liverpool's draw, combined with Newcastle's 5–0 thrashing of Nottingham Forest, meant they failed to qualify for the Champions League on goal difference. I remained convinced a poor decision had cost us and in later years I challenged Elleray about the red card. He explained that once the linesman had flagged, he had been given no alternative but to send Clarke off. Elleray was nearer to the incident, but it would have been a brave decision to overrule the linesman.

Sheffield Wednesday might well have settled for seventh place at the start of the season, but now there was an air of desolation in the boardroom. Europe had been within our grasp and we had blown it. Maureen felt most uncomfortable, sitting with the directors' wives after the game. She did not react to those kinds of comments. She had learned the art of boardroom diplomacy.

The FA Cup had produced similar feelings. We had reached the quarter-final and been given a home draw against Wimbledon, whom we would beat comfortably in the league a month later. We lost, 2–0, in a televised Sunday game, where Robbie Earle, a fine player whom I would later work with on television, scored the opening goal. I always found it difficult losing to Joe Kinnear, Wimbledon's manager. I liked neither his tactics nor his touchline rants, usually directed towards the officials.

The summer of 1997 saw us once more in Holland for pre-season when the news broke that Sheffield Wednesday had had a bid for Paolo Di Canio accepted by Celtic. The rider to the deal was that the new Celtic manager, Wim Jansen, wanted Regi Blinker, whom he had worked with at Feyenoord. I had gone to Glasgow to watch Di Canio and took a taxi to the Albany Hotel. The driver told me I would have a wasted journey since 'our best player is injured and won't be involved'. When I went to Parkhead from the Albany my second taxi driver of the afternoon also told me I was wasting my time since Di Canio would not be playing. Di Canio was not involved and I left Parkhead ten minutes before the end. The taxi driver who took me to the airport said Di Canio was 'far too good for Scottish football'. On the Monday morning, Dave Richards asked what my recommendation was on Di Canio. I told him we should sign him. In my heart, I knew three taxi drivers could not be wrong.

Di Canio had spent one season at Parkhead, which had seen him voted Scottish Footballer of the Year and led him to demand a substantial pay rise. The Celtic chairman, Fergus McCann, had refused and their relationship had disintegrated. Previously, we had thought we could not afford the mercurial Italian. However, we offered Regi Blinker, whom Celtic valued at £1.25 million, in part exchange – which was £1 million more than we had paid for him. The balance on the transfer was £2.5 million.

The deal, which was the biggest in Sheffield Wednesday's history, would be sealed at Schiphol Airport outside Amsterdam. The Celtic officials, Di Canio and his agent would be flying in from Glasgow that afternoon and we agreed to meet. I travelled from our training complex in a hire car with Dave Richards. After half an hour, we took a call from the Celtic chief executive, Jock Brown, the brother of the Scotland manager, Craig Brown.

Jock said: 'Di Canio is not able to come, but his agent has Paolo's authority to agree all aspects of the deal.' I was disappointed, but the chairman was most upset: 'If the player hasn't got enough respect to come and meet us, we ain't going to bloody well sign him.' Three hours later, in a private lounge at Schiphol, we shook hands and signed papers. I was happy with the deal, although slightly concerned Di Canio had not turned up to his own transfer meeting.

Dave Richards was a chairman who did not always do what he said. One of his ex-managers referred to him as 'the Postman' because he never delivered. I had first met him at his modest home in Sheffield, which he shared with his wife, Jan, a prodigious charity worker. They seemed a happy couple. He showed me his treasured scrapbook, full of photographs of his tenure as chairman of Sheffield Wednesday. He also took me to his engineering company, which had some big foreign contracts, but he strangely confided that he would really have liked to have been a surgeon.

A couple of months later, Di Canio would join his fellow Italian Benito Carbone, whom we had signed from Inter Milan the previous year. I had first enquired about the Italian the previous season, when Roy Hodgson was Inter's manager. They were returning on the bus from an away game, a match in which Carbone had been an unused sub, when I called Roy. 'He's a skilful individual and the crowds will enjoy him,' came the reply. 'But he can be a bit surly. He's on the back seat of the bus now, sulking.'

Accompanied by the agent Jerome Anderson, I flew to Monaco to sign the man whom I thought could be the replacement for Dan Petrescu at right-back. The omens around Patrick Blondeau were good. Monaco had just become French champions. Blondeau was playing alongside Fabien Barthez, Thierry Henry and Emmanuel Petit – all of whom would win the World Cup the following summer. I had hoped that, alongside Di Canio and Benito Carbone, Blondeau would restore some of the flair we had lost when Chris Waddle and John Sheridan left Hillsborough. The move was a disaster.

The talks took place in the famed Hotel Metropole opposite the

Casino. Blondeau was an interesting character. He was the son of a Marseilles docker but had been brought up by one of the city's most notorious gangsters: Francois Vanverberghe, who was known simply as 'the Belgian'. Blondeau had been romantically linked with Princess Caroline of Monaco and was to marry the French television presenter Véronika Loubry. Their daughter, Thylane, would start modelling for Jean Paul Gaultier at the age of four. When he retired, Blondeau bought a restaurant in Aix-en-Provence called *Les 2 Garçons*, which had been frequented by artists such as Picasso and Cézanne. In November 2019, it mysteriously burned down.

Strangely, Irving Scholar, now living in Monaco, had heard I was trying to sign Blondeau. He let me know his thoughts: 'Emmanuel Petit is the one'. Petit would prove him right at Arsenal.

For all his outside interests, Patrick Blondeau was not a man who enjoyed heading a football and he never settled in Sheffield or justified the fee of £1.8 million. He was sent off in the 5–2 defeat at home to Derby in September and followed it up with an interview for the French sports paper *L'Équipe* in which he criticised the team's lack of discipline and training routines while describing Sheffield as a 'dark, industrial city'. The Yorkshire press seized on the interview and rumours of unrest circulated. My successor, Ron Atkinson, sold him to Bordeaux for £1.2 million. He would not count as one of my better signings.

The League Cup sent us to Grimsby, a club we had thrashed 7–1 in the FA Cup the previous season. We were a goal down at half-time and Di Canio had gone berserk during the interval, threatening not to reappear for the second half and throwing his boots at the dressing-room door. I had already substituted my lone centre-forward, Nigel Clough, whom I had taken on loan from Manchester City, where his career was petering out. Nigel was a nice guy who understood the situation we were in and did not make a fuss when I told him he would not be reappearing after the interval. Then the physio, Dave Galley, signalled that our centre-half Jon Newsome, who had a reputation of having a low pain threshold, had a muscle problem and he wanted to come off, too. I was suddenly faced with having to make three half-time substitutions. Thankfully, Di Canio recovered his poise and went out for the second half. We lost the game, 2–0.

As the team bus pulled away from Blundell Park, we were being pulled apart in a Radio 5 phone-in hosted by Richard Littlejohn, a journalist with the *Daily Mail* and, incidentally, a prominent Spurs supporter. The Wednesday fans were openly calling for my head. Littlejohn put up a good defence of my record, but the pressure was building. As the coach returned to Hillsborough, my assistant, Peter Shreeves, and I came to terms with the fact that only a marked improvement was likely to save our jobs. Although Grimsby were beaten, 3–2, in the second leg, it was not enough to see us through.

There was no sign of the momentum of the previous season. We had already lost three of our first four games, the last of which was a 7–2 defeat at Blackburn, which had seen us go 5–1 down after twenty-five minutes. Benito Carbone had scored twice and been sent off. A 5–2 defeat by Derby left Wednesday second bottom after eight matches. We were also being weighed down with injuries.

For the next game, at Aston Villa, I paired Di Canio with Carbone. We twice took the lead but were pegged back to a 2–2 draw. On the bus, I remarked to Joe Ashton, who had a close relationship with the players, that the two Italians, working in tandem, might be the solution. The following Saturday, Everton were beaten 3–1 at Hillsborough with Carbone and Di Canio sharing three late goals.

However, on 1 November everything unravelled at Old Trafford. We were 4–0 down to Manchester United at half-time and, having watched their dismal effort, I withdrew both Italians during the interval. We were more competitive after the break but the final score was 6–1. Sheffield Wednesday were now bottom of the Premier League.

Alex Ferguson made some supportive comments towards me in the post-match press conference, but my dismissal had become inevitable. Atherton, Booth and our experienced midfielder Graham Hyde had all been missing through injury for several games and I had been pushing the club doctor, Rav Naik, to pass them fit, but he proved overly cautious. For weeks, I had been concerned about our injury situation and the players' slow recovery times.

Incredibly, the following Saturday all three were involved in the 5–0 demolition of Bolton, but by then I had already left. The day after the defeat at Old Trafford, I was rung at home by Dave Richards. I had already been phoned by Mike Morgan, *The Sun*'s Yorkshire football correspondent. He asked for a comment about my sacking. I told him I had not been contacted by the club and would not be saying anything. When, later, Richards rang to tell me my contract was being terminated, I replied I would see him at Hillsborough the next morning. He told me it was impossible. He would be catching 'the Master Cutler', the fast early express that linked Sheffield with St Pancras, to attend an FA meeting.

'If you want, I can ask the secretary to do the necessary paperwork.'

'Since you appointed me, you should have enough respect to see me face to face when you release me.'

Sheepishly, the chairman said he would see me at Hillsborough first thing and catch a later train to London. Very early, Maureen and I drove up to Sheffield from Luton. We had arranged to take our minimal belongings from the flat in Whirlow later that day. When I met Richards, we exchanged half-hearted good-luck wishes.

As I left Hillsborough, Paolo Di Canio drove up in his car. He shouted: 'Wait! What is happening? You mustn't go; we like you and I will speak with the chairman. We all want you to stay. You are a fine man.'

I told him this was not the way football works. 'Paolo, when it's over, it's over.' I wished him good luck for the future.

It was a touching gesture and not the response I had expected from a man I had substituted at half-time at Old Trafford. However, that was Paolo: an outstandingly brilliant footballer, a showman and a divisive character who would wear a tattoo of Mussolini on his arm.

Three weeks later, I saw a newspaper article by Di Canio referring to my successor, Ron Atkinson. The headline, in bold capitals, was: 'Now We Have a Proper Manager.'

CHAPTER 24

'WHAT KIND OF JOB IS THIS?'

The position of director of football is one of the most misunderstood in the English game. Sometimes, it is seen as a sinecure for a former manager or a conduit between the boardroom and the dugout. It should be one of the three most pivotal roles at a club. Instead, it is dismissed too often as a foreign invention, alien to the game.

It is not new. In 1969, Sir Matt Busby had been effectively appointed Manchester United's director of football, although his title was 'general manager'. On Busby's recommendation, Wilf McGuinness was appointed to succeed him as manager, although he was given the title of 'chief coach'. He was paid considerably less than the likes of Bobby Charlton, George Best and Denis Law.

McGuinness was responsible for picking and training the first team and overseeing the games. Busby sorted contracts, attended board meetings and, much to McGuinness's frustration, he had the final say on transfers. Busby kept his office and continued his rounds of golf with United's senior players on the course at Davyhulme, where McGuinness's management of the first team was frequently criticised. The arrangement proved unworkable and at Christmas 1970, Wilf McGuinness was sacked, again on Busby's recommendation.

The episode became engrained in the folklore of Manchester United as something that should never be repeated. Alex Ferguson always wanted nothing to do with the concept of a director of football. Neither did Arsène Wenger once he became Arsenal manager.

However, these two men had earned their power with their success and their silverware.

When clubs did dabble with the concept of a director of football, it was often to create a position with very little power or responsibility. In 1995, Ron Atkinson was appointed director of football by Coventry immediately after managing the club. When Ron and the new manager, Gordon Strachan, asked the Coventry chairman to define their areas of responsibilities, Bryan Richardson replied: 'You should sort it out among yourselves.'

I recall phoning Harry Redknapp when he was director of football at Portsmouth, a job he accepted after leaving West Ham in the summer of 2001. I asked him what he was doing? The answer was: 'Very little. What type of job is this?' He said he was supposed to be the eyes and ears of the chairman, Milan Mandarić, but added that his principal job seemed to be chauffeuring him. Once, he had driven the wife of the television presenter and Portsmouth director, Fred Dinenage, to Rotherham. 'It's a hopeless position,' he said. 'A waste of time.'

I told him: 'You could make this the most satisfying job in the world. You can arrange the strategy of the club, organise its recruitment, the academy and the training ground. You could influence the whole future of the club.' Harry complained that the coaches at Portsmouth were not good enough and it did not surprise me that, when Graham Rix was sacked, Harry took over as manager, a job he did very successfully.

When Alan Sugar asked me to become Tottenham's director of football, he had very clear ideas of what the role entailed. Very rarely did Alan Sugar's foresight fail him. In January 2002, he would set those ideas down in a letter to the League Managers' Association.

In the past the formation of the board of a football club was made up of an array of people. The chairman may have been a lifelong supporter of the club and had landed on good times to enable him to acquire a major shareholding and hence become the owner or the major shareholder.

Other members of the board were normally a bunch of hangers-on, some of whom hid behind the veil of being solicitors or accountants or of having some commercial expertise. Apart from the finance director, there was no justification for this kind of person being a board member. After seven years as chairman of Spurs with a board of hangers-on who were more interested in directors'-box seats and away tickets rather than the day-to-day running of the club, it was quite clear that the full burden of responsibility actually rested on my shoulders.

Certain issues in respect to the purchase of players and the financial viability of transfer fees were clearly outside my personal knowledge. I was faced with a one-sided view from a manager who had a single, very narrow-minded agenda and a total lack of appreciation of the financial implications of irresponsible transfer and contract awards simply to obtain short-term fixes. I therefore felt I needed a very experienced person from the football world who would sit between the chairman and the manager as director of football. The remit of that candidate was that he would have to take a financial view of the club's affairs as a board member and translate that by balancing the needs of the board with those of the manager.

The director of football would advise the board as to whether a particular transfer or contract negotiation was good business. Just as importantly, he would take responsibility for the youth policy and the club's academy to ensure there was a steady flow of players coming through the system and that there was sufficient support given to that department to ensure its prosperity and survival. The director of football would be a full-time executive employee attending all board meetings and be just as responsible as any other director for the financial well-being of the company.

One has to accept a clash of personalities between the manager and the director of football and it is therefore imperative that the manager, when appointed, is informed of the seniority and importance of the director of football. The manager should not undermine his authority and treat the director of football as one of the previously-described hangers-on.

The traditional opinion of managers about directors has been very low. They consider them to be brainless as far as football is concerned and usually treat them with contempt. In the case of a more polite manager, they are humoured. It is imperative that on the appointment of a new manager one of the first topics discussed is the manager's reporting line to the director of football. This in many cases is like a red rag to a bull. Most Premier League managers have tremendously high egos and tend to want to have their own people around them. In most cases they totally disregard the thinking from anyone outside their own clique.

This has to be knocked on the head once and for all. Whenever a club finds it necessary to appoint a new manager, the appointment should be made by the director of football. If the director of football is not involved in the selection and appointment of a manager, this is a recipe for disaster as the director of football will not be respected by the manager.

Too many times in this industry, the board is padded out with passionate fans and is intimidated into the appointment of high-profile managers to pacify the demands of the fans as well as to seek media approval. This intimidation places the board in a vulnerable position. On many occasions the new manager enters the arena as an Adonis and everything must be his way.

The circumstances surrounding the appointment of a manager normally is that the club is in a panic situation and needs to fill a gap quickly. The pressure of this has tended to create knee-jerk appointments without laying down the ground rules of who is really in charge of the football club. In view of the experience of the director of football, during this panic period he should be quite capable of running the first team for a few weeks, enabling the correct appointment to be made. Next to the chairman, the director of football should be the second most important person in the organisation. The manager is the third.

My only criticism of Alan's letter was his insistence that the manager is only the third most important person at a club. In my view, he must be on an equal footing with the director of football but have sole responsibility on the selection of the team and the final say in the selection of possible transfer targets. The two must have great empathy and respect for each other.

The offer from Tottenham to become director of football was attractive. I wanted to put the disappointments of those last games at Sheffield Wednesday behind me as quickly as I could. However, perhaps I did not consider what it would be like to stop coaching, to no longer have the ultimate responsibility for a football team. Occasionally, I reflect I was only forty matches short of joining the exclusive club of those who have managed a thousand games. This is a milestone I would have loved to have achieved. The total of 960 does not include my non-league apprenticeship at Nuneaton.

However, I would be returning to Tottenham ten years after leaving White Hart Lane. I was most grateful to be warmly accepted back at Spurs. There was a sense of unfinished business and a belief I could make an impact. My appointment was announced at the press conference in November 1997, which saw Christian Gross introduced as Tottenham's new manager with the club sixteenth in the Premier League. A few days before, Alan Sugar had asked me to discover as much information as I could on the man he would choose to be the club's new manager.

I had a fair knowledge of European football but told Alan I had never heard of him. 'Call Alex Ferguson,' he said. 'He's bound to know something about him.' I phoned Alex, but he could not recall meeting him and knew nothing of his pedigree. Gross was appointed from Grasshoppers Zürich, whom he had taken to two Swiss championships using intense fitness programmes, but his name did not resonate outside Switzerland. I sat at home watching what proved a rather disastrous press conference where he produced an Underground ticket as proof he would have little difficulty assimilating into London life.

Alan had suggested I stay away from the press conference because he wanted the focus to be on Christian, which was surely the correct decision. Christian was a big, warm, friendly man. He wanted to overhaul the club's disciplinary and training regimes. He insisted on two training sessions a day, but he was inheriting a strong dressing room that quickly rebelled against his regime and did not enjoy his warm-down sessions, which he held on a Sunday morning. The players thought it an imposition. Crucially, his fitness coach, Fritz Schmid, who had been instrumental in his success in Zürich, was unable to obtain a work permit and did not accompany him to Spurs. There were spates of injuries, with players almost queuing up to see the physiotherapist with muscle strains.

Christian's agent was the unrelated Andy Gross, an eccentric man who sported a giant handlebar moustache. He also represented Jürgen Klinsmann and it was Jürgen's recommendation to Alan Sugar that had been instrumental in the appointment.

A month after Christian's arrival at White Hart Lane, Klinsmann joined him at Tottenham on loan from Sampdoria. The two men may have shared an agent, but they very quickly fell out. Klinsmann was hugely popular at Tottenham, where in 1995 he had won the title of Footballer of the Year. There was a constant flow of press stories about the growing level of discontent at the club. It was difficult to stem the negativity, and on more than one occasion Sugar would come to the training ground at Chigwell to speak to the players in addition to his regular meetings with Gross.

Tottenham finished fourteenth in 1998. Just as significantly for our supporters, Arsenal won the Double. Pre-season was very poor; there was still a significant list of injured players and the opening two league games were lost to Wimbledon and Sheffield Wednesday. On Friday, 28 August, Alan Sugar decided the problems facing Christian Gross were insurmountable. He met Christian before the squad set off for Merseyside to face Everton. It was a knee-jerk decision. I told Alan he should wait a little longer as a change so early in the season was unprecedented and would look bad. I told him: 'What if we win at Everton tomorrow?'

He replied: 'It makes no difference. The players will not accept him and I have already told him he is going.'

Christian, who was a thoroughly decent man, shed a tear when the news was broken to him. A Steffen Iversen goal ensured Tottenham did win at Goodison Park and on the Monday the club announced the termination of his contract. I was asked to look after the team while Alan began the search for a replacement.

I met with several of the senior players – Les Ferdinand, Darren Anderton, Sol Campbell and David Ginola. There were good players in that dressing room, but we did not have a team that gelled. Ginola was the key to that side. I liked him as a man and loved him as a player. I told him to worry less about doubling up on our left-back and carrying out defensive duties and told him to stay forward. David was both talented and charming. His agent, Chantal Stanley, would regularly press for better deals for her man. She would claim that 90 per cent of the Spurs shirts sold in the club shop had Ginola's name on the back and felt he was entitled to some extra recompense for this.

I was in charge of Tottenham for seven games, of which we lost only one, a bad 3–0 home defeat to Middlesbrough where our centre-backs, Ramon Vega and Colin Calderwood, were overrun.

On 15 September, we narrowly overcame Brentford in the first leg of a League Cup tie. As usual, I sat in the directors' box for the first half, but I told the chairman, who like me had taken his wife to Griffin Park, that I might have to leave early if I had a call from my father, who was by my mother's bedside at Barnet Hospital, where she was slipping away. Maureen and I hurried away before the final whistle with Spurs 3–1 up to be with my mother, who died that night. Tottenham conceded a second in my absence and some in the press, not bothering to make any enquiries into my whereabouts, suggested: 'Tottenham were so poor that even the manager left early.'

One journalist who seized on this line with particular glee was Matthew Norman, a clever writer who wrote restaurant and film reviews as well as sport and political journalism. Norman appeared to be pursuing a particularly acidic vendetta against me and my return to Tottenham as director of football. During the 2006 World Cup in Germany, Norman wrote a scathing piece about John Motson's commentary, which had led to thoughts of John issuing a writ. Knowing that my relationship with Norman was poor, he asked if I thought he should sue. 'John,' I told him. 'It is fish and chip paper, and if you make a meal out of it, Norman will never forget it. He is a spiteful journalist.'

Matthew Norman went on to write some complete nonsense about Paolo Tramezzani, the Italian full-back Christian Gross had signed from Piacenza. Norman claimed I was responsible for bringing him to White Hart Lane and had paid £1 million for a player whose value to Spurs, he considered, was next to nothing. Once more, Andy Gross was the agent involved in the deal and it was one in which Alan Sugar broke his own rule that the director of football should be responsible for all incoming transactions.

We had scouted Tramezzani, who had been part of the Inter Milan side that had won the UEFA Cup in 1994, but the reports had quite clearly stated he was not good enough. However, Alan's words when he rang me on a Sunday morning to tell me Tramezzani was at his house were: 'Don't worry, it won't come off your budget.' I still was not happy.

I have to say that Alan, who rarely admits an error, refutes my recollection every time I bring up the subject of Paolo Tramezzani, but the truth was that, while the blond defender enjoyed his time living in Hampstead, our scouting reports were entirely accurate. He was sold to Pistolese, a small club in Tuscany who were then in Serie B, for £400,000.

The day after the win at Brentford, Alan Sugar insisted I come to his house to discuss the imminent appointment of George Graham as manager of Tottenham. My mother had passed away the night before, and mentally, I was all over the place. When Alan said the meeting could not be delayed, I told him the most I could spare him was half an hour. He apologised for having to impose this on me and offered condolences.

It appeared Alan had already spoken to George Graham's agent, Steve Kutner, who had told him George would like to return to London and that it would not be unthinkable for him to join Tottenham. George was in charge of Leeds, whom he had taken to fifth place the previous season, which was their highest league finish since they won the title under Howard Wilkinson in 1992. There would have to be talks with the Leeds chairman, Peter Ridsdale, over compensation that would eventually amount to £3 million.

Sugar asked me to point out the pitfalls if we signed Graham. I started with the obvious fact that George had spent nine highly successful years managing Arsenal and that the north-London rivalry dictated he would be unacceptable to a percentage of Spurs fans. Alan was aware of that. Alan was already aware of the stigma of the Rune Hauge affair, which had seen George sacked by Arsenal after he admitted to receiving a 'gift' of £425,000 from the Norwegian agent after signing two of his players. He was less aware of the argument that George's defensive style of football would not sit easily with Tottenham's cavalier traditions and their belief that the game is about glory. George's safety-first mentality had not just been confined to Arsenal. In 1997, Leeds had finished eleventh in a season in which they had scored only twenty-eight goals.

I put the case for Martin O'Neill, who had transformed Leicester City. In his memoirs, Alan acknowledged this was the right call but wrote that I did not put the case for Martin strongly enough. I had phoned Martin who had told me he was open to offers but did not otherwise commit himself.

This would not be the last time I would try to bring O'Neill to Tottenham. By 2003, the romantic experiment of appointing Glenn Hoddle as manager had failed and, once more, I pushed the case for Martin. By then, Joe Lewis was Tottenham's owner and Daniel Levy was running the club. I was suddenly told to forget the idea. O'Neill was then manager of Celtic and Joe Lewis was a good friend and keen golfing partner of Dermot Desmond, who was the majority shareholder at Parkhead. Joe had been given a message to 'lay off my manager'.

In 1998, the message Alan Sugar wanted answering was whether I could work with George Graham. I told him I had known George since we were schoolboy internationals nearly forty years before. He was a real football man, a student of the game, and I told the chairman I would have no problems working with him.

I was told George would take over after we played Derby on 3 October. Before then, I oversaw a 1–1 draw at Southampton and a

3–3 draw against Leeds at White Hart Lane, where rumours swirled around the stadium that George would shortly be stepping from the away dugout to the home one. When the Leeds fans began chanting that they wanted to know the truth behind the rumours, Peter Ridsdale went over to speak to them during the interval. Sol Campbell salvaged a point with a last-minute equaliser and by the time we went to Derby, George was sitting alongside Alan Sugar, Martin Peters, who had been co-opted on to the board as a PR move, and myself in the stands at Pride Park.

Tottenham won, 1–0, and on the final whistle I experienced a pang of great emotion. It might be the last game I ever took charge of and yet I knew in my heart I was capable of having another successful spell as manager of Tottenham. Those thoughts would have to be sacrificed to my new role as director of football.

George and I got on well. He was easy to talk to, he enjoyed the coaching field and we discussed tactics. He did not always agree with me, but my view was respected. He did not get on with Ginola. The chairman used to joke that the relationship was bound to fail because George and David were such good-looking men – Ginola was the public face of L'Oréal. George wanted David to take more responsibility but the reality was that he was trying to change the role of an exciting forward who was a terrace hero. It was a battle he was bound to lose.

In February, Tim Sherwood was signed from Blackburn for £1 million to add some midfield steel and nous. We met him and his agent, Eric Hall, in George's flat in Hampstead. He had won the title with Blackburn and Sherwood was to prove a good signing, although I would have a dreadful time trying to get him to build bridges with Glenn Hoddle when he took over at White Hart Lane. George showed us around his beautiful patio garden, describing the plants and flowers that grew there. George's great hobby was gardening. It took him away from the passion and stresses of football.

His flat also contained his wonderful display of Arsenal memorabilia, which centred on the two championships he had brought to Highbury.

It was Tottenham's progress in the cups that energised the season. In the League Cup, Liverpool were beaten 3–1 at Anfield and in the next round Manchester United were overcome by the same score. In the final we faced Leicester, who had won the trophy two years before and would win it the following year. This was the game in which Robbie Savage went down very easily after a challenge and, as a consequence, Justin Edinburgh, our left-back, was sent off. Tottenham adjusted their game and settled the contest in the ninety-third minute with a diving header from Allan Nielsen. It had not been a great final, but it was Tottenham's first trophy since the 1991 FA Cup and sparked a happy evening at the team hotel, Sopwell House near St Albans. It also guaranteed a place in the UEFA Cup.

Tottenham finished eleventh in the league with Steffen Iversen and Chris Armstrong scoring twenty-five of the forty-seven goals, which was not a great overall return. The mood might have been higher had Spurs reached the FA Cup final. Ginola had taken us to the semi-final with a superb individual goal in the quarter-final at Barnsley, which had seen him run at five defenders and score. It captured the imagination of fans and media alike and was the sort of goal that would see him voted Footballer of the Year. To many within the game, especially Alex Ferguson, whose Manchester United side would win the Treble, this seemed a bizarre decision. We would face Newcastle in the semi-finals at Old Trafford. The match was a great disappointment, settled by a thunderous drive from Alan Shearer into Ian Walker's goal beneath the Stretford End.

I had taken my son, Jon, to Old Trafford, and as we made our way out, he saw Kelvin MacKenzie standing in a crowded lift with us. He did not know what to do. There was a part of him that wanted to confront MacKenzie, who had left *The Sun* five years before and was now busying himself with the launch of the radio station, talk-SPORT. I had no recollection of his being in the lift. Perhaps I was too dazed and preoccupied by the result or perhaps I had blocked out the man who had affected my career so dramatically.

There was, much later, to be one more chance encounter with the man who had shaped English tabloid journalism. It was at Wycombe Wanderers, where MacKenzie was watching his team, Charlton. I was sat behind him and, as he chatted to his mates, I found myself biting my lip. Hard.

CHAPTER 25

'IT WILL BE LIKE
PRUNE JUICE'

The boardroom table at White Hart Lane was long, oval and beautifully polished. At meetings, it would be circled by Alan Sugar, munching his cheese, celery and grapes, giving his views. It was an arena he dominated. Tottenham had a three-man permanent board composed of the chairman, myself and John Sedgwick, the finance director. John would often busy himself showing Alan's son, Daniel, the everyday workings of the football club.

Alan envisaged that one day, perhaps, Daniel would be able to take a major role in the club. However, Daniel was never that motivated by the intricacies of the game, although he enjoyed watching football.

Other members with expertise would be co-opted on. Igal Yawetz was a brilliant architect who would advise on rebuilding the East Stand. Colin Sandy was Alan Sugar's personal financial adviser and ran his property business. John Ireland was the in-house lawyer, who seemed frustrated that Alan appeared to know as much about the law as himself.

Claude Littner, who had been criticised by the previous management for his parsimony – it was rumoured he queried the milk bill – was the club's chief executive. Often, he was a voice of reason. Sugar described him as a man 'with no time for bullshit or small talk'. When Alan invited Claude to join him on *The Apprentice*, many candidates on the television show discovered exactly how little time Littner had for bullshit.

Howard Shore was an outstanding financial brain whose contributions I found illuminating. He had a strong friendship with Mike Sherwood, the chief executive of Goldman Sachs and a substantial investor in Tottenham. Together, they had shown an interest in buying Watford. Alan also wanted an ex-player on the board to give a different perspective. It was an interesting PR move and, after much discussion, we invited Martin Peters to join. Martin was an absolute gentleman. Nobody watching this smartly dressed man in the boardroom at White Hart Lane would have guessed he was a World Cup winner. However, his shyness meant he made few contributions.

I was questioned most of all. They wanted to know my opinion on the training ground, the likely team for Saturday, who was injured and whom we were looking to recruit and sell. At their core, these powerful men were also Tottenham fans. The worst moments came when the club doctor, Mark Curtin, was called in to deliver the medical report. Mark's father, Brian, had been Tottenham's club doctor from 1962 to 1994. Mark was loyal, polite and hard-working, but his reports were invariably gloomy, which only added to the chairman's frustration. No medical man would have been comfortable with the barrage of questions he was forced to field.

Certain players were almost permanently being treated for injury. John Scales, who had been bought from Liverpool in 1996, played thirty-three league games in four years. Willem Korsten, a winger who was bought from Vitesse Arnhem for £1.5 million in the summer of 1999, did not make his debut until December and played twenty-three matches before a hip injury forced him into retirement at the age of twenty-six. In the 1999/2000 season, Les Ferdinand made just nine appearances and Ruel Fox four.

It was, however, Darren Anderton who was the continual target for the chairman's wrath and tagged by the press with the unfortunate nickname of 'Sicknote'. I, however, considered him a valuable player. However, his agent, Leon Angel, had insisted on a clause in his contract that stipulated that, no matter who came to Tottenham, Darren's earnings would always be on a par with the best-paid player at the club. To Alan Sugar, this was a red rag to a bull.

Tottenham finished tenth in the Premier League and their hold on the League Cup was ended by a 3–1 defeat at Fulham. Later that month, we were thrashed 6–1 by Newcastle in the third round of the FA Cup. Ramon Vega, a Swiss centre-back signed by Gerry Francis, was humiliated in front of 35,000 gloating Geordies as the snow streamed down over St James' Park.

If the scale of the defeat was one trauma, the journey back from Tyneside was another. Our plane was diverted and we arrived at six in the morning. The plane was carrying the club's vice-presidents and other high-profile guests, who had to be pacified by Tottenham's commercial manager, Mike Rollo, a dour individual for such a front-of-house role. On that plane was a promising fourteen-year-old footballer called Chris Eagles and his father. Chris was from Hemel Hempstead, and although he had been part of Watford's academy, he and his father were Spurs season-ticket holders.

He was due to join Manchester United's academy, but his agent wanted us to have a look at him, and we were more than happy with what we saw during a half-term visit. As a sweetener, we invited him to come on the executive flight to Newcastle. The result, the performance and the chaos of the return journey probably strengthened Chris's intention to go to Manchester.

The chairman had invited Sam Chisholm, a New Zealander who had worked for Australia's two biggest media tycoons, first Kerry Packer and then Rupert Murdoch, to join the board. Alan Sugar calculated that, sooner or later, Premier League clubs would be able to sell their own television rights and having someone like Chisholm, who had worked for Sky, would give Tottenham a distinct advantage.

When Chisholm attended one of his few board meetings and heard the medical report of how many of the squad was unavailable, he told the chairman to sack a particular player who was often injured and had a lucrative contract. Sugar spluttered: 'You just can't do that. Sam, you have no idea. The union [the PFA] would never stand for it and the boy has a contract.'

Individual television rights would only be attractive to the Premier League's biggest clubs. For the deal to happen would require a two-thirds majority. One of the reasons Sam Chisholm lasted such a brief time at Tottenham was that he was recruited by the Premier League to negotiate their joint television deal with Sky in 2001. He knew little or nothing about football. The contract Chisholm and his business partner, David Chance, negotiated with the Premier League's chief executive, Peter Leaver, had a clause that could see both men paid up to £50 million if the right deal was negotiated. When Sugar heard the details of this, he was apoplectic. When details of the contract were leaked, the Premier League clubs forced the resignation of Peter Leaver, who had been a former Tottenham director, and the chairman, Sir John Quinton, the former chairman of Barclays Bank. He was replaced by the Sheffield Wednesday chairman, Dave Richards.

I found the Premier League meetings at their headquarters in Gloucester Place fascinating. Tottenham were sat next to West Ham, whose chairman, Terry Brown, rarely spoke. Next to him was the Wimbledon chairman, Sam Hammam, who was rather more engaged. Alan Sugar's train of thought was usually clear, precise and to the point. Along with Sugar, the most powerful and reasoned arguments tended to come from Arsenal's David Dein, Doug Ellis, the chairman of Aston Villa, Martin Edwards from Manchester United and the indefatigable but irritating Ken Bates from Chelsea. Ron Noades, the chairman of Crystal Palace, had great empathy with the rank-and-file players, something lacking from the others around the table. This was in part because he knew the mechanics of the game, something the rest did not. In 1998, he had left Palace to manage Brentford, promoting them from the bottom division in his first season.

The Tottenham chairman was not universally popular at Gloucester Place, but he always stood his ground. When a new television deal was being discussed, Sugar made his feelings clear. 'Gentlemen,' he said. 'It doesn't matter whether we get £3 million, £30 million or £300 million. It will be like prune juice. We must protect the game. If we piss it up the wall again, spending it all on players' wages, we will not recover. We must agree that a certain percentage of the fees we receive go on salaries and the remaining money – say 40 per cent – will go towards stadium development, academies – and for a fighting fund.'

Had football followed Alan Sugar's financial model, that fighting fund would have been in place to protect the game when the Covid pandemic swept into the country in the spring of 2020. Before each meeting, Peter Leaver, who combined his role with that of a deputy High Court judge, said: 'Gentlemen, is it too much to hope for that I will not be reading these discussions in tomorrow's *Daily Telegraph*?' His words were nearly always in vain. The Premier League was sieve-like in its leaking. Every club had its own agenda and many felt it important to have their view prominently displayed in the media.

The 2000/01 season would be a pivotal one for Tottenham Hotspur. It would see the departure of Alan Sugar as chairman, the sacking of George Graham and the return of Glenn Hoddle to White Hart Lane. It would culminate in an FA Cup semi-final against Arsenal and Sol Campbell's bitter departure to Highbury.

It began with a journey to Ukraine to sign Serhiy Rebrov, who alongside Andriy Shevchenko was the spearhead of the brilliant Dynamo Kyiv side that had reached the semi-finals of the

Champions League in 1999, beating Arsenal and Real Madrid before narrowly losing to Bayern Munich. George had been to watch him play, alongside Charlie Woods, the club's respected chief scout who had spent most of his career working with Bobby Robson. Charlie vividly recalled watching Rebrov in a Champions League qualifier in Denmark in which Brøndby had been beaten 4–2.

He and Shevchenko had scored twelve goals between them in the Champions League that season and we were very impressed by Rebrov's movement. He was sharp, bright and moved cleverly to get into shooting positions. If we moved quickly, we were told we could get him for £8.5 million. I travelled to Ukraine with the London-based agent, Jonathan Barnett, who would act for Spurs and deal with Rebrov's agent Sandor Varga, a Hungarian who had excellent linguistic skills and was well connected with FIFA.

Dynamo Kyiv possessed a state-of-the-art training complex, where the players lived, ate and slept. After the weekend game, they would go back to their families and return on Tuesday. They were managed by Valeriy Lobanovskyi, who was on his third stint in charge of Dynamo Kyiv. In his first he had won the Cup-Winners' Cup in 1975, while in the second he had split the job with managing the Soviet Union, whom he had taken to the final of the 1988 European Championship. He had a round, ruddy face and looked older than his sixty-one years.

Lobanovskyi had been one of the first managers to incorporate science into football and the training ground was equipped with thermal chambers and ice rooms to accelerate recovery from injury, while a bank of television screens relayed matches from around the world. I was most impressed. However, it was apparent that Lobanovskyi had problems with alcohol, which would hasten his death from a stroke two years later. Training was taken by Oleksiy Mykhaylychenko, who had played for Glasgow Rangers. In the session we saw, Rebrov looked more than exciting.

However, once we sat around the table to iron out a deal, problems began to surface. Barnett and Varga did not seem comfortable with each other. The Kyiv president, Ihor Surkis, was adamant we had not been given the correct price for the player. Surkis was a man who never convinced me of his honesty. In 1995, he had attempted to bribe a referee before Dynamo played Panathinaikos in a Champions League qualifier. Dynamo Kyiv had been thrown out of the competition and banned for a year. Surkis informed me there was strong interest in Rebrov from several clubs across Europe and that the fee would now be beyond the £8.5 million I had been quoted. There was genuine interest from Spanish clubs and I knew George Graham wanted the player, but I could and should have walked away.

I had a brief conversation with the Tottenham secretary, John Alexander, and agreed a price of £11 million. I rang Alan Sugar to tell him the deal had been done but for £2.5 million more than we had wanted. I added: 'I've done well. I have negotiated staged payments so we won't have to pay too much up front.'

Sugar's reply was terse and to the point: 'You fool! It still has to be paid.'

We found Serhiy and his charming wife, Ludmilla, a house near the training ground at Chigwell and gave him a driver and use of a car for his first three months at the club. We offered help with learning English. Rebrov was something of a radio ham and erected a large mast in his garden to receive transmissions. The mast created havoc with the neighbours' television reception and we had to field a shoal of complaints.

In the dressing room, he was warm and popular, something of a smiler, but he always felt the need to return home early after training to be with Ludmilla and was slow to pick up the language. As a consequence, he never really integrated with the squad. On the field, Rebrov showed flashes of his talent but was not as successful as we had hoped. He scored nine in the Premier League and three in Tottenham's run to the semi-finals of the FA Cup.

George Graham's theory, which I had some sympathy with, was that Tottenham had what some Premier League clubs would consider a third-rate squad and in order to break through, he would have to start buying players who would improve the squad while knowing we could not afford the very best. It was this kind of thinking he used to justify the signing of three footballers who were at Wimbledon or who had played for the club. Chris Perry, an honest centre-half who had grown up within walking distance of Plough Lane, was signed for £4 million. Ben Thatcher, a talented but impetuous Wimbledon left-back, was signed for £5 milion, while Øyvind Leonhardsen, a tireless worker who had been signed by Liverpool from Wimbledon, cost £4 million. Incredibly, the agent acting for Wimbledon under the direction of their chairman, Charles Koppell, was Rune Hauge, the man who had been instrumental in George Graham's downfall at Arsenal. With Hauge's history, we were scrupulous in analysing the finances of the deal. The defence was strengthened at a cost of £13 million and, although the signings were honest, hard-working footballers, none possessed the charisma Spurs supporters yearned for. When the three were sold, they raised a mere £400,000 between them.

One of the tasks I had been given was the recruitment of players from the lower leagues. The chairman believed we would be able to improve them and then either sell them or keep them on as part of the first-team squad. He called it 'the Scattergun Effect'. George Graham gave me his full backing, provided the costs did not come out of his budget. I used my eyes, ears and contacts to scour the country for good young footballers. My friend Barry Fry was manager of Peterborough and always keen to do deals. I went to watch two youngsters who had broken into his first team.

Barry always seemed to give Alex Ferguson first refusal on his players and had allowed Simon Davies and Matthew Etherington to train with Manchester United, the club where he had been an apprentice. However, Ferguson had not made an offer and I was intrigued by the midfield energy of Davies and Etherington's clever wing play.

I went to the Soho branch of Pizza Express to discuss the deal with Peter Boizot, who had founded the restaurant chain and now also owned Peterborough United, his home town club. The branch in Wardour Street where we sat was the first one he opened in 1965. He was a man of many parts with a deep interest in art, jazz and politics – he had stood as a Liberal candidate in Peterborough. His sport of choice was hockey and he knew little of the football business. He did, however, have great faith in Barry Fry, who exploited his kindness with his brand of roguish charm. We paid £700,000 for Davies and £500,000 for Etherington. I suggested immediately loaning them back to clubs in a lower division, but George very shrewdly advised that this would be counter productive. 'We must keep them in the Tottenham fold,' he said. 'We must make them feel that they belong. After all, they've only just arrived.'

I followed this up by signing Gary Doherty from Luton for £1 million. Never technically good enough, Gary was nevertheless a hundred-percenter who was a committed centre-half and scored some vital goals when pushed up in attack. There was another deal for Anthony Gardner who was playing for my old captain, Brian Horton, at Port Vale. A tall, left-sided centre-half with pace and height, he was prone to the occasional error but had a fine career and more than justified the £855,000 fee we paid.

The total cost of these four was just over £3 million. All made their mark on the game, although Etherington only really flourished once he left Spurs for West Ham. Gardner was capped once for England while Davies and Doherty became regulars for Wales and Ireland. All were sold for a profit. If ever a policy justified itself, it was searching for and developing good, young talent in the English lower leagues.

Behind the scenes, however, the chairman was becoming restless. In October, Tottenham had been knocked out of the League Cup at home by Birmingham and Alan Sugar had been the target for some vitriolic abuse from the club's own supporters. His wife, Ann, asked Alan if he really needed this kind of treatment.

This disenchantment was fuelled by a series of stories in the *Daily Mail* highlighting a rift between George Graham and the chairman. George was friendly with Jeff Powell, one of the paper's leading sports writers, and was giving him information, some of which suggested open conflict within the club. Unknown to me, Tottenham had issued George with two warning letters about leaking information. Had I been consulted, I would have strongly advised against issuing these letters. Once you give an employee a warning letter, any relationship is bound to die.

Sugar railed when a feature by Powell alleged the chairman had refused George Graham a proper transfer budget. It was accompanied by a headline which the chairman could not tolerate: 'Why Miserly Sugar Must Come out of His Counting House and Give George the Money.' It had a clear antisemitic undertone. Another headline proclaimed Sugar as being 'The Miser of N17'.

The following few weeks were chaotic. I was requested to attend meetings at Herbert Smith's, one of the country's leading law firms, with Tottenham's in-house lawyer, John Ireland. Alan could not wait to get to court. He blamed George Graham as much as Jeff Powell for the article and was preparing to subpoena his own manager if necessary. It was a crazy situation. I still had to work with Alan and George.

The libel action did not reach the High Court in the Strand until February 2001, fifteen months after the *Daily Mail* article, and it attracted huge media interest. On the first day of the trial, as his own barrister read out the charges Powell had made against him,

Alan broke down in tears in a way he said he had not done since he was a child. Sugar employed an exceptional QC, Richard Rampton, who had successfully defended Penguin Books in an action brought by the right-wing historian and Holocaust denier, David Irving.

The *Daily Mail*'s parent company, Associated Newspapers, pulled out every example they could think of to prove Alan had denied George funds. They made constant comparisons between Tottenham and other clubs, but in football it is almost impossible to compare like for like. I went to the High Court almost every day of the trial, accompanied by John Ireland. Every time I looked across, John appeared to be fiddling with his Rubik's cube. He seemed bored by the whole process.

When I went into the witness box, I was prepared for a grilling. Associated Newspapers saw me as the one person who might perhaps be able to trap Alan Sugar. They produced Graham Hunter, the *Daily Mail*'s football correspondent. He knew that I had been on a scouting trip to Buenos Aires to watch Pablo Aimar and Javier Saviola play in River Plate's forward line. Aimar had gone to Valencia for £13 million and Saviola had been signed by Barcelona for £15 million. We had been particularly interested in Saviola and the QC for Associated Newspapers asked why Tottenham had not signed him. He suggested the deal had been scuppered by the chairman because of the cost. This was untrue.

I told him clubs see a lot of high-quality players, but for varying reasons they do not go ahead with the purchase. Maybe they already have someone in that position. Maybe the manager decides against a player recommended by the chief scout or the director of football. Maybe the selling club rejects the offer. Maybe the player's age or background does not fit the club's philosophy. It was significant that both Aimar and Saviola had gone to Spanish clubs which ensured they would not have to learn a new language.

It was true I loved the way Saviola played, but the discussions never went as far as submitting an offer so George was not denied the money to buy him. I think the judge, David Eady, understood how football works. You do not go out and buy every footballer you see, no matter how good they are.

The jury eventually took only a few minutes to find in Alan Sugar's favour. He was awarded damages of £100,000, which he paid to Great Ormond Street Hospital. Associated Newspapers had to pay Alan's legal costs, which amounted to £400,000. When the verdict was announced, I wondered once more whether, if I had the wherewithal and the gumption, I should have taken legal action against *The Sun*. Alan recalls that I was quite emotional when the verdict came in. Ann was certainly emotional and it may have been my thoughts of 1987 that triggered memories in me.

Interviewed afterwards, Sugar said: 'I hope the case will be used as an example to show the media there are people who will stand up to them. I could afford to finance this long court case, but sadly, there are not too many people who can afford to take them on, so they have to suffer the media abuse. My victory is not just for me, it is for them, too.'

In his autobiography, *What You See Is What You Get*, Alan Sugar wrote that he had asked Sol Campbell and several other players to appear as witnesses but all had refused. He added:

The only person who stood by me was David Pleat. He was prepared to do something unprecedented. The chairman was the enemy and the playing staff would always side against him. It was unacceptable in the football world for an ex-player or manager – someone on that side of the fence – to side with a chairman, let alone stand up in court and support him. Yet David Pleat did. I am sure that, among his contemporaries, he was frowned upon.

I thought it was the honest and honourable thing to do. It was not a problem for me to tell the truth of what was happening at the club.

Alan Sugar was by then ready to give up the chairmanship of Tottenham Hotspur, a post he had held for nearly ten years, in which time they had finished no higher than seventh. The politics of White Hart Lane and the drain on his time and energy had taken their toll. He was thoroughly disillusioned with George Graham, a man he had paid Leeds £3 million to hire. Tottenham had won nine out of twenty-nine games when Tottenham's new owners, ENIC, took the decision to sack him.

As a chairman, Alan Sugar never interfered in team matters. His view was that he paid people well for the job, and if they did not perform, he would hire someone else. He also sent me what can only be described as a kind of warning letter. He had heard I had been summarising on a Champions League tie abroad on a Tuesday night. He wrote: 'In your position, I would expect you to be at the training ground when I ring on the Wednesday morning. You cannot be in two places at once. Remember who is paying you. I pay you decent money and you must get your priorities right. There are many people in the game, like Frank Clark for example, who would love to have a role like yours. Please take this on board.'

As it happened, I was back by one o'clock on the Wednesday afternoon. The letter did disturb me, though. I read it and re-read it and sent a copy to the League Managers' Association, but I decided not to respond in any way. Alan forgot about it. When I rejoined Tottenham in 1997, Alan had said he was more than happy for me to summarise at Champions League fixtures. He thought it would be good for the club's projection.

In his memoirs, Alan wrote that I should have been more forceful with him, especially over my preference for Martin O'Neill to succeed Christian Gross as manager. When dealing with a man with such a strong personality as Alan Sugar, that is easier said than done.

I often found Sugar to be more than fair. Beneath the gruff, intimidating exterior and brusque comments, there was a kindness and a subtle sense of humour. Sometimes, he would make a remark in front of Ann, who would respond with a grimace. It must be hard to be famous. Because of his fame, people found it harder to approach Alan Sugar than the rest of us on the Tottenham board. Once at an airport, a man sidled up to him and asked Alan what charities he supported. Alan was flustered. 'Sorry, son. That's none of your business.' It was a cold, terse reply, which was typical of him, and the casual bystander would have concluded Alan Sugar was both rude and had little interest in charities. In fact, he is exceedingly generous with both his time and his money. Soon after he stepped down as chairman of Tottenham, I had tried to persuade Alan to give some of the money he received from ENIC to the academy, which would be renamed in his honour. He refused. He had had enough of football. Instead, Alan gave £2 million to save and refurbish the Hackney Empire, the theatre and music hall that had captivated him as a teenager.

CHAPTER 26

'VIALLI OR HODDLE?'

Alan Sugar's battle to take over Tottenham alongside Terry Venables had been arduous. A decade on, he wanted his departure to be as smooth as possible. I was asked to go to the offices of Warner Brothers in London and talk to Daniel Levy, who was part-owner of ENIC, the company Alan would be selling to. ENIC's majority owner was Joe Lewis, a Jewish businessman from Bow in east London who had made a fortune from currency trading and lived in the Bahamas. His art collection alone was said to be worth $1 billion.

As well as owning Warner Brothers' stores, ENIC had been acquiring shares in different clubs across Europe. They owned substantial stakes in Glasgow Rangers, AEK Athens, Slavia Prague, Basel and Vicenza.

If the deal went through, Alan thought my role would expand to encompass taking the best talent from these clubs and bringing them to Tottenham. It was an interesting idea but one that was destined to fail.

At that first meeting at Warner Brothers, I found Daniel to be a quiet but obviously intelligent and somewhat deep man. It seemed as though he could learn the football business quickly. He paid Sugar £21.9 million for a 29.9 per cent stake in Tottenham, leaving Alan with 13 per cent. In 2007, ENIC bought out Sugar entirely, as they increased their control of the club to 85 per cent. By then, they had disposed of their interests in their other European teams.

When the original deal went through in 2001, several people left their jobs at White Hart Lane. Claude Littner had undergone three years of chemotherapy to survive a diagnosis of non-Hodgkin lymphoma, the cancer that killed Arsenal's David Rocastle. He was emotional when asked to step down as Tottenham's chief executive. John Sedgwick and John Ireland also left their jobs. George Graham was sacked in March and remained bitter about the manner of a dismissal he was almost certainly expecting when Sugar departed.

Daniel Levy took over as chairman. David Buchler, an accountant who had risen to prominence when asked to salvage some of the wreckage of the collapsed Maxwell empire, was his deputy. He was a fan of the opera and Tottenham Hotspur. His daughter, Sara, would marry David Dein's son, Darren.

One of Alan Sugar's moves had been to appoint John Alexander as Tottenham's club secretary, on my strong recommendation. Alexander had been a professional footballer who in March 1979 had scored all four goals for Reading against Grimsby. He had worked for the BBC before becoming Watford's club's secretary. His nephew, Trent Alexander-Arnold, would win the Champions League with Liverpool. In 2010, John would replace the long-serving Ken Ramsden as Manchester United's club secretary.

Daniel Levy brought in Paul Kemsley, a gregarious bundle of wit and opinion, who had been one of his oldest friends and business partners. Kemsley, who was also close to Mike Ashley, who would buy Newcastle United, had made a fortune in property. His job was to negotiate purchase prices for property on the Tottenham High Road and Paxton Road that would pave the way for the club's new stadium. His bonus depended on his results.

I was given the briefest of spells as caretaker manager. It encompassed two matches – a 3–0 win over Coventry and a 2–0 defeat at Arsenal. The following week, we were due to face Arsenal in an FA Cup semi-final at Old Trafford. With that in mind, I had selected several of the younger players such as Luke Young, Simon Davies and Alton Thelwell for the league game at Highbury. Arsène Wenger's side was at full strength and Thierry Henry scored a beautiful goal.

Buchler met me in my office to discuss the appointment of a new manager. He breezed in with the words: 'Vialli or Hoddle? Any thoughts?' I asked him if anyone had contacted Ken Bates to ask his opinion of Hoddle's time at Chelsea, which had come to an end when he was appointed England manager in 1996. Hoddle's first stint in charge of a club, as player-manager of Swindon, had been exceptional. Operating as a sweeper, he had won Swindon promotion to the Premier League before moving to Stamford Bridge and then England. After his dismissal as England manager amid the storm of his reported comments that disabled people were paying for the sins of a previous life, Hoddle took charge of Southampton, who were then three places above Spurs in ninth position.

Gianluca Vialli was available. He had succeeded Ruud Gullit as manager of Chelsea in February 1998. Within a few months, he had won them the League Cup and the Cup-Winners' Cup. He had followed this up with the FA Cup in 2000. However, he had fallen out badly with Gianfranco Zola, who could claim to be the greatest overseas signing in Chelsea's history, and this had triggered his dismissal. Nevertheless, I had recently met Ray Wilkins, who had worked with him and he told me Vialli was an outstanding coach.

I thought Buchler had already made up his mind and queried why he was bothering to ask me. I said: 'David, you will find that this place leaks and all the media have been saying for days that the new regime only has eyes for one man.' Throughout White Hart Lane, from the boardroom to the stands, Glenn Hoddle was seen as the returning hero. He was massively popular with the fans. To them, he was a Messiah, ready to lead Tottenham to new glories.

His first assignment was to take Tottenham to an FA Cup final by overcoming the old enemy in the semi-final at Old Trafford. Hoddle had been handed a dream script, but the opening lines were fluffed. Although Gary Doherty put Spurs ahead, Sol Campbell was forced off with injury and Arsenal dominated, winning rather more comfortably than the 2–1 scoreline might suggest.

Attempting to exploit ENIC's investments in European football, I paid my first visit to Prague, the terrible beauty of its history encapsulated by the Jewish cemetery, the Charles Bridge and Wenceslas Square. When I met the directors of Slavia Prague, it was clear relations with ENIC were deteriorating. Slavia had been planning to move to a new stadium since the 1970s and wanted more investment to guarantee the project. However, ENIC were withdrawing their foreign investments as they concentrated their financial reserves on Tottenham. While in Prague, Slavia's general manager, Jan Richter, had talked about 'the best young goalkeeper in the world'. He was a teenager playing for a village team near the German border called Chmel Blšany, which had managed to win promotion to the top flight. His name was Petr Čech.

When I returned to London after seeing him play, I recommended very strongly at a board meeting that we sign him. However, my recommendation was not taken seriously, although it was minuted. Arsenal tried to sign him when he moved to Sparta Prague but were unable to secure a work permit. In 2002, Čech was signed by Rennes. Glenn sent Hans Segers, his goalkeeping coach, to France to watch Čech play, but Hans's report was that he had not performed well enough to recommend the signing. It was a season in which Rennes would avoid relegation on the final afternoon. In the summer of 2004, Čech did come to London but to play for Chelsea, where he would perform brilliantly over many seasons. The recommendation was made by Jan Richter, who was now employed by Chelsea as a European scout.

The summer of 2001 was important to Glenn. It was the time he could start casting his influence in pre-season. His talent on the coaching pitches was obvious and he still possessed lovely skills. He could place a ball on a sixpence from forty yards with back-spin. Of the footballers I have coached, only Raddy Antić at Luton was as talented when it came to passing a football with both feet. Gary McAllister at Leicester, John Sheridan at Sheffield Wednesday and Ricky Hill at Luton ran them close but all were essentially right-footed.

The summer was dominated by the departure of Sol Campbell to Arsenal, using the Bosman Ruling to engineer a free transfer. Tottenham had a fine tradition of centre-halves from Maurice Norman, who was part of the Double-winning side of 1961, to Mike England, who anchored the Spurs side that won the UEFA Cup in 1972, to Richard Gough. Sol Campbell was entirely at home in that company.

He was, however, a man of moods and without opening up too much it was clear he was disillusioned with the flow of events at White Hart Lane. Sometimes, he would come to my office at the training ground and ask: 'Who are we signing, David?' He always asked the question without malice or threat. He genuinely wanted better players around him and thought Tottenham were too often inactive in the transfer market.

We met his agent at David Buchler's offices at Conduit Street next to Claridge's. Sol was represented by Sky Andrew, a personable guy who had played table-tennis for Britain at the 1988 Seoul Olympics and had become one of the first black agents involved in professional football. I had first become aware of Sky in 1999. He had forged a relationship with Jermaine Pennant, an England Schoolboy international who had been brought up in a tough and unforgiving part of Nottingham. Sky met with me to arrange the boy's transfer to Tottenham. A little later, I was shocked to discover he had signed for Arsenal. Sky was upset at letting Spurs down but insisted there was nothing he could have done to stop a transfer that had been in-itiated by Pennant's chairman and manager at Notts County, Derek Pavis and Sam Allardyce, with David Dein at Arsenal.

Andrew was personable enough but was late for the meeting to decide Sol Campbell's contract offer, which left Buchler irritated. Sky breezed in, surveyed the pictures on Buchler's office wall and asked: 'Who's that good-looking bird with you on that yacht?'

'That's my wife, Caroline,' said David in a haughty fashion.

There were many pictures on the wall of the office showing Buchler with various celebrities, which revealed something about his ego. However, Andrew's comments about his wife had put him on the back foot and the meeting resulted in a predictable impasse. David Buchler's inexperience in football led him to cobble togeth-er a series of figures he thought Sky might be impressed with. He mentioned bonuses for wins, for position, for European qualifica-tion and a signing-on fee. The only figure Sky Andrew was inter-ested in was the guaranteed bottom line. Arsenal would guarantee Campbell £60,000 a week, which would, until the arrival of Juan Sebastián Verón at Manchester United, briefly make him England's highest-paid footballer. Sol won the Double in his first season at Highbury, played commandingly for England in the 2002 World Cup in Japan and was an integral part of Arsenal's 'Invincibles', who won the Premier League unbeaten in 2004.

Alan Sugar later suggested that when Sol first revealed his disillu-sionment with the club, Tottenham should have dropped him from the first team. He would then have lost his England place and been forced to accept Spurs' offer. This was something George Graham absolutely refused to do at the time and it was an issue I supported him on. He would not deliberately weaken his own team simply to make a point over contracts and in this he was surely right.

Sol Campbell's departure completely undermined our defence, and in the season that followed, Tottenham lacked stability at the back. Colin Calderwood had been sold to Aston Villa at the age of thirty-four and Ramon Vega, a character in the dressing room who could be like a bull in a china shop in his own penalty area, had gone to Watford. Chris Perry was dependable, honest but not outstanding and young Anthony Gardner, while talented, could be erratic.

I was given the awkward task of building bridges with Southampton as Glenn Hoddle wanted their tall centre-back, Dean Richards, to replace Campbell. I met the Southampton chairman, Rupert Lowe, at the Army and Navy Club in Pall Mall. Although he appeared far too posh to be a football club chairman, Rupert was immersed in the game and was very opinionated. He was not popular with Southampton fans after removing the revered Lawrie McMenemy as director of football and was now under more immediate pressure. Lowe had replaced Hoddle with his first-team coach, Stuart Gray, a disastrous appointment that would be terminated after three months. Rupert was friendly enough. He had been hurt by Hoddle's decision to abandon Southampton but understood the harsh realities of football. We settled on a price of £8.1 million for Richards, which was then the highest fee ever paid for someone who had not played international football.

Richards never captured his best form at Tottenham, mainly because he was plagued with injuries. In March 2005, Dean announced his retirement from football. He had been suffering from headaches and dizzy spells, which were the start of a long illness that tragically claimed him at the age of thirty-six.

A 6–0 win over Bolton took Tottenham to the semi-finals of the League Cup, where they would face Chelsea. Two goals from Jimmy-Floyd Hasselbaink gave the home side a 2–1 advantage after the first leg at Stamford Bridge. In the second leg Spurs overwhelmed them, 5–1, to reach the final. It was a significant result not just because Tottenham had reached a final but because of who they had beaten to get there. We would face Blackburn at Cardiff's Millennium Stadium, but in front of 72,000 spectators we were beaten 2–1 by Graeme Souness's men. We played poorly.

The FA Cup was almost a copy of the League Cup campaign. Once more, a big win over Bolton gave us a tie against Chelsea, this time in the quarter-final. There was another humiliation at White Hart Lane, but this time Tottenham were on the receiving end.

The team lacked vitality. Glenn Hoddle preferred experienced professionals such as the opinionated Gus Poyet, who had been signed from Chelsea on a three-year contract at the age of thirty-three. The fee was £2.2 million. Christian Ziege, twenty-nine, was signed from Liverpool while Teddy Sheringham had returned to White Hart Lane at the age of thirty-five. Tim Sherwood and Les Ferdinand's best days were also behind them. It was a policy for today rather than tomorrow, although I understood Hoddle's thinking. He required results quickly.

It was not a policy without merit. Ferdinand enjoyed an injury-free season in 2001/02 and weighed in with fifteen goals. Poyet and Sheringham scored ten each. Attendances rarely dropped below 35,000. However, there were no transfer profits and Tottenham finished twelfth. In another blow to Tottenham's die-hard supporters, Arsenal won their second Double in four years.

One of the players attracting my attention was Diego Ribas, a young, attacking midfielder in a Santos side that was playing some of the most exciting football in Brazil. If I could secure the deal for a fee of around £4.5 million, Tottenham would take him. I flew to São Paulo with an interpreter and then drove to the coast to meet the player at the beachside house he shared with his parents and girlfriend. Within hours of our meeting, the local press was reporting that Diego was wanted by the London club, Tottenham Hotspur.

I was taken to see the club's president. Marcelo Teixeira was in his late thirties and was also the head of the local University of

Santa Cecilia, which his family owned. Since he had taken Santos to their greatest days since Pelé graced the pitch at the Vila Belmira stadium, Teixeira was a powerful figure. We were informed that, seemingly overnight, Diego's father had acquired 50 per cent of his economic rights. The numbers kept increasing and head-to-head meetings became more difficult to tie down.

I was, however, invited to fly with the team to an away game and watch them in action. It was a squad littered with talent. Robinho, Elano and Alex were the stand-out players. Two would play for Manchester City, while Alex would win the Premier League with Chelsea. Renato, an excellent wing-half, would win the UEFA Cup with Sevilla. Crucially, we could not do a deal in Brazil and, after we returned to London, it fizzled out. Diego Ribas joined Porto shortly after they had won the Champions League under José Mourinho and after spells with Werder Bremen and Juventus would win La Liga with Atlético Madrid. His was quite a career.

One of the bright spots was the emergence of Ledley King as Sol Campbell's long-term replacement. Under George Graham's regime the tall, young defender had been playing for the youth team in the Southern Counties East League. I watched all the home games on a Saturday morning before the first team played at White Hart Lane. After consulting the youth-team coaches, I agreed Ledley should be given a chance at first-team level. Patsy Holland and Jimmy Neighbour were convinced that Ledley, from Bow, had the talent. He was two-footed, possessed pace and timed a tackle superbly. By the age of eighteen, he had bypassed the reserves and was playing first-team football.

Being director of football was sometimes a balancing act between responsibilities to the board and the need to back the manager. This came into sharp focus when Glenn Hoddle began having problems with Tim Sherwood. Tim was a strong-willed character, who had captained Blackburn to the Premier League title. Glenn, however, had less regard for him as a player than George Graham. He was slowly frozen out and was asked to train away from the senior players. To make it more awkward, Tim was asked to come back for extra sessions in the afternoons when everyone else had gone home.

Sherwood felt he was being victimised and came to see me to request a meeting with the chairman. I told him I would report his concerns to the board but reiterated that he must realise the manager would have the final say on first-team affairs. It was my job to deal with the matter. However, Daniel Levy said he would allow Sherwood and Bobby Barnes, a representative from the Professional Footballers' Association, to address the board. This had a political subtext to it because the board were beginning to lose faith with Hoddle.

Barnes, who had begun his career as a winger for West Ham, argued for the rights of a player under contract. I made the point that the board had to be seen to be backing the manager. The situation was eventually resolved when Sherwood was transferred to Portsmouth.

However, Tim's comments on Hoddle's weakness as a communicator and his lack of people skills resonated in the boardroom. They were amplified further when Hoddle failed to turn up for a board meeting. One director rang his secretary, Irene Atkins, at the training ground who said the manager had been told about the meeting both verbally and by email. However, she could not get hold of Glenn. As we waited, I thought Glenn would have to be very successful on the pitch that season because he was starting to lose the boardroom and did not realise the importance of maintaining a relationship with the directors.

After games at White Hart Lane, Glenn would never come to the boardroom, which I instinctively recognised as a mistake. Directors were generally pleased to see the manager whatever the result. Harry Haslam had taught me about the importance of respecting your employer. The increase in the number of foreign managers and the heavy post-match media commitments mean this is sometimes less possible. In October, we beat Blackburn at Ewood Park through a late Jamie Redknapp goal. Blackburn were unlucky and Graeme Souness must have been badly deflated, but dressed immaculately, he still made it to the boardroom and spoke to his chairman and directors briefly before coming over to the Tottenham board and saying: 'Goodnight gentlemen,' and wishing them well. He showed some class. The Spurs directors were impressed by this because it was something Glenn Hoddle almost never did.

Robbie Keane scored his first goal for Tottenham in that game. In 2002, Leeds had just failed to qualify for the Champions League, which was to trigger the start of the financial collapse that was to end in relegation and administration. I recommended to the board that they take advantage of this and sign Keane. When he was sixteen, Sammy Chapman, who had been my chief scout at Leicester and was now at Wolverhampton Wanderers, spoke warmly about the boy from Cork. 'Trust me, he is special. He has eyes in the back of his head.'

He was now twenty-two. He had played for Wolves, Coventry, Inter Milan and now Leeds. He had enjoyed an impressive World Cup for Ireland with three goals in four games and was only one of two players to score against Germany – the other was Ronaldo for Brazil in the final. I knew Leeds would sell him for £6 million. However, Glenn was ambivalent about the transfer because he did not feel he had an obvious place for him in the first team. I also had the impression he slightly resented the fact I was the prime mover in the transfer. I argued Keane's sheer talent would increase the level of competition and the value of the squad – and he was a long-term investment. Glenn backed the argument but on the proviso that the fee should not come from his budget.

Robbie signed before the first home game of the season, a 1–0 win over Aston Villa. Once in the side, Glenn immediately embraced his ability, saying White Hart Lane 'would be his spiritual home for many years to come'. He would score eighty league goals for Spurs before being sold to Liverpool for £20.3 million in 2008. He was quite a purchase. Robbie was a quiet, unobtrusive character whose only passion appeared to be playing football. He seemed utterly uninterested in money and I gained the impression he was not even aware what we were paying him. Certainly, I cannot remember ever discussing his salary with him. He was an intelligent player who would drop deep and supply chances with great vision or he would slide behind defenders to score goals that always seemed decisive. He was humble and well-liked, a man without bling or ego.

Tottenham made a deceptively fine start to the 2002/03 season, third in the league behind Arsenal and Liverpool after ten games. However, results became more erratic and we fell away to finish tenth. We were knocked out of the League Cup at Burnley and soundly beaten, 4–0, by Southampton in the third round of the FA Cup. It was at this time that my relationship with Glenn Hoddle grew closer. His assistant, John Gorman, asked if I could have a word with the manager.

In many ways Hoddle, who had worked under Arsène Wenger at Monaco, was ahead of his time. He understood the importance of nutrition and psychology in the modern game and employed a sports scientist called John Syer, who was meeting considerable resistance from the Spurs squad. Tottenham had opened the season at Everton. In the hotel on the Friday night after the evening meal, the four defenders selected for the game were asked to see Syer in his room. Fifteen minutes later, the four midfielders went up, followed by the strikers. It seemed bizarre. Strangely, Syer travelled back to London on the Saturday, not staying to see the game, which finished in a 2–2 draw.

The dressing room at White Hart Lane was full of seasoned professionals, such as Jamie Redknapp, Gus Poyet and Teddy

Sheringham, and they resented Syer's attendance at team meetings. I told Gorman he should not let the players dictate who came to meetings. It was the preserve of the manager. Hoddle had first come across Syer when he worked with the Tottenham team that won the FA Cup in 1982. A decade later he helped Chris Boardman win Olympic gold in Barcelona by persuading the cyclist to accept fear as a natural emotion. However, that Spurs dressing room was full of barrack-room lawyers whose voice seemed to become louder the further the club slipped in the table. It was becoming less easy for Glenn, and Syer was relieved of his duties not long afterwards.

The role of the psychologist in the modern game is crucial. There are many players of similar abilities. It is those with real mental strength who go on to have significant careers and they can be helped massively by interacting with psychologists. Glenn was still using Eileen Drewery, the faith healer who had caused such controversy when he was England manager. Darren Anderton saw her and gained considerable benefits from the treatment. It did not matter whether the faith healing worked; it mattered that Anderton believed it did.

I had gone to Mouscron in Belgium to examine the possibility of it becoming a feeder club for Tottenham. The idea was that we would work in tandem, trade players and develop youth players. Manchester United had used Royal Antwerp as a finishing school for its young footballers and it was hoped we might follow suit. As a consequence, I signed Jonathan Blondel, an eighteen-year-old left-footed playmaker who made his debut in the 2–1 win over Southampton at the end of August. However, he flattered to deceive and possessed an ego out of proportion to his ability. It would take him more than a year to earn another first-team appearance and the sole consolation when he was sold to Bruges in 2004 was that we had lost only £100,000 on the deal. I was never convinced of the value of feeder clubs. They appeared to require a substantial investment for a minimal return.

Earlier, John Sedgwick and I had gone to Nantes, who had won the French league in 2001, to study their academy. The players lived, played and studied in-house and it was made clear to them that they were the club's future. Their ranks were boosted by imports from France's former colonies in north and west Africa. They brought unquestioned talent to French football, but there was a price to be paid. Those that did not make the grade were swiftly returned from whence they came and there was an exploitative feeling to the whole enterprise.

In January 2003, I was negotiating the sale of our midfielder Stephen Clemence to Birmingham City and had my first encounter with Karren Brady. She had grown up near White Hart Lane and become Birmingham City's chief executive at the age of twenty-three. I respected her ability and her personality. As I was to discover later, Brady possessed fine debating skills. In January 2007, Birmingham postponed their game with Leeds because bad weather had made the relaid pitch at St Andrew's unplayable. Furthermore, high winds had caused structural damage to the stands. However, Birmingham acted unilaterally and incorrectly, neither informing the Football League nor involving the match referee in the decision. They employed a local official to make the ruling. The Football League, egged on by Leeds and other clubs, challenged the decision and I was involved in the tribunal. Among the expert witnesses was the BBC weatherman John Kettley. While the Football League arrived with lawyers and presented what seemed an unanswerable argument, Karren defended her club and won the case.

The season finished with a string of defeats. Tottenham lost 2–0 to Manchester United, were thrashed 5–1 at Middlesbrough and badly beaten 4–0 at home by Blackburn. The idea that Glenn Hoddle was a returning Messiah had now disappeared from the terraces and the boardroom.

CHAPTER 27

'DON'T SAY I DIDN'T TELL YOU'

As Tottenham's plane came into land in Johannesburg in the summer of 2003, the sight of the shanty towns below the wheels suggested South Africa had not changed that radically since the overthrow of apartheid. Spurs had arrived on a pre-season tour that would involve playing the country's two biggest teams, Kaizer Chiefs and Orlando Pirates, both based in the sprawling township of Soweto.

Part of my remit was to establish links with Ajax Cape Town. They were a relatively new club that had sold their winger Steven Pienaar to Ajax, where he had won the Dutch Eredivisie the year before. The idea was for Spurs to offer them coaching assistance and the driving force behind it was Donna-Maria Cullen, who was Tottenham's head of communications and a graduate of the University of Cape Town. The theory was good, but in practice it never achieved its aims. I watched their youngsters train at the club's threadbare facilities. However, the players we took on trial were short of the level we required.

After the opening game in Durban, which was lost 2–1 to Orlando Pirates, Glenn Hoddle decided to sign their centre-half Mbulelo Mabizela, who was already captain of South Africa at the age of twenty-two and looked a big prospect. The irony was that Glenn left Spurs before Mabizela could play a game. I would give him his debut in October, when he would score in a 2–1 win at Leicester. One of Mabizela's best qualities was a terrific leap, but he also had problems with alcohol, and a year after joining, his contract was cancelled.

We beat Kaizer Chiefs in Cape Town, a visit made memorable by a meeting with Archbishop Desmond Tutu, who had kept the flame of the anti-apartheid movement burning while Nelson Mandela was imprisoned on Robben Island. I travelled across to the island on choppy seas to see his tiny cell on a morning so grey that the top of Table Mountain was invisible. What particularly moved me was the ravine where the prisoners were gathered to break rocks and the little exercise yard where they played football.

There was also a visit to the vineyards at Stellenbosch, although the case of wine I ordered never did arrive. Unlike several managers of the time, I was not a connoisseur. On a visit to Chateau Margaux, one of the holy of holies of the French wine industry organised by the League Managers' Association, I amused Sir Alex Ferguson, Howard Wilkinson, and Jim Smith, all of whom were wine buffs, by failing to identify any of the wines we were offered in a tasting session.

The summer had seen a strengthening of Tottenham's forward line. Glenn had paid £6.5 million for Hélder Postiga, a nineteen-year-old striker who had been part of the Porto side that had won the UEFA Cup under José Mourinho. A further £3.5 million was spent on Frédéric Kanouté from newly relegated West Ham, while a further £1.5 million saw Bobby Zamora arrive from Brighton. After the disappointments of the previous season, it was a powerful statement of intent. Kanouté was the best of the three but he was an erratic talent that only truly blossomed when he was sold to Sevilla. Zamora, who could not cope with the move to a higher division, did not score a league goal for Spurs, while Postiga's contribution was one. Neither lasted more than a single season.

The campaign got off to the limpest of starts with a 1–0 defeat at Birmingham. There was a recovery with a 2–1 win over Leeds and a goalless draw at Liverpool but Glenn Hoddle's fate was sealed by three straight defeats in London – at home to Fulham and Southampton and a 4–2 reverse at Chelsea.

Before the game at Stamford Bridge, we were invited for the usual lunch in the boardroom. John Alexander and I arrived with our wives, but Daniel Levy and the other Spurs directors were held up in traffic. Ken Bates was on a high, having just seen the sale of the club to Roman Abramovich go through, a move that had made him £17 million. His ebullience extended to making jokes that he would have considered funny, but which I thought were antisemitic. He was at his arrogant worst. When Daniel arrived late, Bates berated him for his timekeeping and told him he would have to forego his meal in the boardroom, which had already begun. Daniel left the room and his discomfort was completed by the scoreline.

There are many dates that you could put forward as being the one 'when football changed', but 13 September 2003, when Ken Bates held such spiteful court on the day he sold out to Abramovich, is as good as any. Abramovich was just thirty-six, a young unknown who had lost his parents before he was four and made a fortune in oil and gas as the Soviet Union fell apart. He had been introduced to Bates by the Israeli journalist-turned-agent Pini Zahavi. Perhaps because both were Jewish, Zahavi had thought Tottenham might be better suited to the young Russian than Chelsea, although the hierarchy at White Hart Lane were always reluctant to confirm they had been approached.

Ever since Glenn Hoddle persuaded Ruud Gullit to exchange Italy for a side that had not won a trophy in nearly a quarter of a century, Chelsea had become a club that had opened itself up to what used to be called 'abroad'. Stamford Bridge soon played host to the elegance of Gianluca Vialli, the brilliant intelligence of Gianfranco Zola and the authority of Roberto Di Matteo. There was still some glamour to be wrung from the King's Road; the proximity of Heathrow and Harrods were attractions and just over three years after Gullit's arrival – on Boxing Day 1999 – Chelsea became the first English club to field a team of foreigners. Their managing director, Colin Hutchinson, described Chelsea as 'a continental club playing its football in England'.

The flip side was that Ken Bates could not afford to run a continental club from London. A foreign owner was a logical step and Abramovich had no limit to his ambition. Chelsea had won the title once, in 1955. Within two years of his takeover going through, Abramovich would celebrate winning the Premier League. By the time Abramovich stepped down, after the club was caught up in the sanctions imposed in the wake of the Russian invasion of Ukraine, Chelsea had won every available trophy in club football.

A succession of world-class managers would be hired and fired, from Mourinho and Ancelotti to Scolari and Hiddink. Two of the more maligned, Di Matteo and Avram Grant, took Chelsea to Champions League finals. Aside from Frank Lampard's seventeen months at Stamford Bridge, all would be foreign. By the time Abramovich left, in March 2022, the club owed him £1.2 billion; a loan he wrote off. By the end, he had been funding Chelsea to the tune of £2 million a week.

However effective his financing of the club was, Roman Abramovich remained a distant figure at Chelsea. He seldom attended meetings and relied heavily on his chairman, Bruce Buck, a New York lawyer who had worked closely with Abramovich's vast oil and gas company Sibneft. The other person he leaned on would be Marina Granovskaia, who had been his PA at Sibneft and would become perhaps the most powerful woman in world football. By the time the sanctions took effect, Chelsea had acquired a stockpile of some of the best young talent in the English game. They had become a football factory.

Between 2012 and 2018, Chelsea appeared in seven successive

FA Youth Cup finals. Players like Mason Mount, Reece James and Ruben Loftus-Cheek would go on to become full internationals. Fikayo Tomori and Tammy Abraham would be sold to AC Milan and Roma for a combined fee of £59 million. In these years, Chelsea would seldom have fewer than fifteen young players out on loan. The club offered salaries to young footballers that other clubs could not compete with. Fuelled by agents, the price tag on a schoolboy footballer would rocket.

It was the same in the first team, as Chelsea's centre-forward Romelu Lukaku was paid £350,000 a week. The trickle-down effect of all this would serve to damage wage structures across the game. The huge television deals meant that for the Premier League, this was largely sustainable, although in 2018/19, three clubs – Bournemouth, Everton and Leicester – spent around 85 per cent of their income on wages. Tottenham, with 39 per cent, was the lowest.

The damage was most evident in the Championship, where clubs strove for the riches of the Premier League without anything like the income of that division. During the 2019/20 season, only four clubs managed not to spend their entire income on players' wages. Reading paid their players £2 for every pound the club earned. At Stamford Bridge, the Abramovich years would seem like a golden age, but with its trends towards foreign ownership, foreign players and managers amid a wage explosion, it triggered something that was sometimes deeply unhealthy.

One consequence of Abramovich's takeover was that, as a Jew, Chelsea's reputation as a home to a minority of antisemitic fans was stamped out. Supporters were taken on trips to Germany and Poland to see for themselves the horrors of the concentration camps.

Glenn Hoddle was sacked after six games of the season, which was a reflection on the disappointments of the last two seasons rather than how he had begun this one. I was asked to become caretaker manager while the board searched for a permanent replacement. Tottenham were in the relegation zone and Paul Kemsley made it clear at a board meeting that if I took the club down there could be no question of my returning to the role of director of football. He asked whether I could guarantee Spurs would stay up.

I was, however, confident in my own abilities and excited by the challenge. I considered it unfinished business. I began with a cup tie at Coventry, with its faint echoes of the 1987 final that had helped define my spell as manager of Tottenham Hotspur. This was in the League Cup and we won, comfortably, 3–0. It was followed by a hard-fought goalless draw at Manchester City, a 3–0 victory over Everton at White Hart Lane and a 2–1 victory at Leicester. As we boarded the bus at Filbert Street, one Spurs supporter shouted to me: 'Take the job, David.'

We were doing well, but my job was to help find Tottenham a new manager. In November, I flew to Rome with John Alexander to meet Roberto Mancini. He was thirty-nine, a superbly gifted forward who had won the Coppa Italia six times. As a manager, he had won it again with Fiorentina and was now at Lazio, whom he would take to another Coppa Italia at the end of the season. Mancini cut an impressive figure. He lived in a beautiful apartment in Rome, complete with its own art collection, and dressed immaculately. He had also prepared well for the meeting. He knew a lot about Tottenham's history and had read several books on the subject.

It was, however, Giovanni Trapattoni who came closer to accepting the job. In contrast to Mancini, he had been managing for nearly three decades – he had taken charge of his first European final in 1974. At club level he had won every available trophy but was faring less well in charge of Italy. In the 2002 World Cup, they had been controversially eliminated by South Korea in the round of sixteen and Trapattoni was examining his options after the upcoming

European Championship in Portugal. Through an interpreter, he explained he was very keen to work in England.

Despite his reputation for defensive football, the Tottenham board preferred the experience of Trapattoni and formulated a plan to offer him the job with Mark Hughes as his No. 2, with a view to eventually succeeding him. Hughes had made an impressive start to his managerial career at Wales, the highlight of which was a 2–1 victory over Italy – managed by Trapattoni – in the Euro 2004 qualifiers. He was an intelligent guy and the long-term choice. On 3 December, Trapattoni came to White Hart Lane to watch Tottenham beat Manchester City 3–1 in the League Cup. The following morning, we met him in the boardroom and he was offered the manager's job.

He told us he had been impressed with our display against City and by the performances of Stéphane Dalmat, the quick, exciting midfielder I had loaned from Inter Milan, and Ledley King, who was growing into a commanding centre-half. Trapattoni said he would give us an answer 'very quickly', although his idea of 'very quickly' turned out to be ten days. Eventually, he told us that his wife, Paola, was in poor health and this would prevent him from accepting our offer. Mark Hughes's agent, Dennis Roach, informed us he would only come to Tottenham as a No. 1. After Euro 2004, which saw Italy eliminated in the group stages, Trapattoni took over as manager of Benfica. Wales had narrowly and unluckily failed to make it to Portugal, but Hughes was quickly rewarded with the No. 1's job at Blackburn.

I was told to continue in charge until the end of the season. A 5–2 win over Wolves, which saw Robbie Keane score a hat-trick, took us to eleventh in the Premier League, seemingly comfortably out of danger. There was a League Cup quarter-final to look forward to. My fine start in the dugout had convinced some supporters that all was now roses and honey at White Hart Lane, but the cracks were still there and in mid-December they opened up again with four straight defeats and elimination from the League Cup at Middlesbrough on penalties. We greeted the new year back in the relegation zone.

It was followed by elimination from the FA Cup in what was one of the most traumatic nights of my career. A Kanouté hat-trick against Crystal Palace had set up a fourth-round tie at Manchester City. Once more the side was starting to find its rhythm. Three straight wins, including a 2–1 victory at Liverpool, had lifted Tottenham back to mid-table safety. Manchester City, in contrast, had not won a league game in more than two months and the pressure was building on their manager, Kevin Keegan, whom I always found a humble, down-to-earth man, given the scale of his achievements as a player. His assistant, Arthur Cox, was rather more abrasive.

Before the game at City, I had problems with Stéphane Dalmat, who when the mood took him could be a superb footballer. However, on the morning of the match, he was evidently not in the mood. We were staying at the Victoria and Albert Hotel on the Manchester quayside and at breakfast I was told that Dalmat could not play. When I asked why, the physio replied: 'He has had a bad night's sleep and doesn't feel well.' I confronted Dalmat in his room and tried to be conciliatory, but it was clear he just did not want to play. I spent some time explaining that we needed him and that he would be fine once he was on the pitch. He did not start the game but came on at half-time and performed very well in a 1–1 draw.

That summed up Dalmat. He could be electric and horribly erratic. He was a nightmare to coach because he lacked concentration and his timekeeping could be as bad as his attitude. His rise until then had been rapid – from Marseilles to Paris St Germain to Inter Milan. Thereafter, however, he became a travelling footballer, never putting down any kind of roots.

We fancied ourselves for the return at White Hart Lane. By the interval, we were three goals up, and as we entered the dressing rooms, I was told Joey Barton had been sent off for arguing with the referee, Rob Styles, as the teams walked off. We were now three up against ten men and my words were simple: 'Stay calm, stretch the game, use the flanks and move the ball quickly.' In the away dressing room, Kevin Keegan turned to his coach, Derek Fazackerley, and said half-jokingly that he expected to be unemployed in the morning.

However, Sylvain Distin pulled one back after the restart. Gus Poyet then had a header saved on the line which surely would have put the game beyond Manchester City's reach, and Shaun Wright-Phillips began hounding Ledley King who was stationed at left-back. On the hour mark a shot that deflected horribly off Anthony Gardner made it 3–2. Our goalkeeper, Kasey Keller, wore contact lenses and was seldom truly comfortable under floodlights. As the goals went in, I could almost hear the commentator's clichéd comment of: 'He'll be disappointed with that.' I, too, must have appeared like a rabbit in the headlights. As the tie turned on its head, I did not make changes quickly enough, partly because we still looked likely to score again. Wright-Phillips equalised for Manchester City with ten minutes remaining and, incredibly, just as the stadium was preparing for extra time, Jon Macken scored their winner. There were no words. There could not have been a greater shock nor a greater comeback in the annals of the FA Cup.

When the teams had walked off at half-time, the commentator, Martin Tyler remarked: 'Spurs have almost rendered the second half academic.' Now in the post-match interview, I was asked to explain the catastrophe. Almost in a stupor, I replied: 'No one died tonight.' In his interview, Keegan called it: 'The cup tie of my lifetime.' The BBC commentator John Motson had somehow worked his way into the boardroom after the match. The directors had disappeared, almost as if they could not bear the shame of the result. However,

I did not want to go home. I sat there talking to John about almost anything.

It was not the first occasion in recent years that Tottenham had collapsed after holding a three-goal lead at half-time. In September 2001, we went into the break leading Manchester United 3–0. Glenn Hoddle was in the dugout and as director of football I was in the boardroom at the interval, watching the directors helping themselves to an extra, congratulatory glass of wine. I did tell one guest, perhaps because my natural defensive instincts were always on display in the boardroom: 'It's far from over yet.'

However, as expected, Manchester United attacked. Andy Cole scored within a minute of the restart and our fragile defence crumbled. At full time, the scoreboard read: Tottenham Hotspur 3, Manchester United 5.

Nearly twenty years later, I met David Beckham at a photo shoot at Tottenham's training ground. I asked him what triggered the dramatic change. He said that as each player entered the dressing room at half-time, Sir Alex Ferguson grabbed them and physically shook them. Beckham said that once Laurent Blanc had scored Manchester United's second with more than half an hour to play, they knew they would overtake us.

Ferguson coined the phrase 'Spursy', suggesting that as a club we possessed a soft underbelly. In both those second halves against the two Manchester clubs, our defending was diabolical, and in truth, Tottenham lacked centre-halves of the highest calibre in those years.

That in flesh and blood represented the disappointment Sol Campbell expressed when he came to see me after training to ask who we were signing. Without him, we were often vulnerable. The FA Cup defeat to City was followed by a 4–3 win over Portsmouth, a 4–2 victory at Charlton and a 4–4 draw with Leicester. We had scored fifteen goals in four games and conceded thirteen. That was 'Spursy'.

After the win at The Valley, Tottenham were five points off fourth place, which guaranteed entry to the Champions League qualifiers. Our elimination from the FA Cup had created a gap in the fixture list and the board sanctioned a trip to Dubai, suggested by Steven Carr and Robbie Keane on behalf of the players, to help them prepare for the final third of the season with some warm-weather training.

I did not go with them, preferring to spend time at home. John Alexander and Chris Hughton led the trip. Evidently, there was a bit of bawdiness on the flight over but nothing too serious. Dean Richards did manage to get himself in the Sunday tabloids after an incident in a nightclub, but there were no major scandals. However, without being able to put my finger on it, there was something not quite right with the squad when they returned to London. There seemed to be a rift in team spirit, which was reflected in the results, which were not good.

Tottenham's PR department had flagged up an article by Martin Samuel, a highly intelligent journalist who had always questioned the role of director of football and was then working for the *News of the World*. There were other articles along the same lines, arguing Tottenham should have appointed a permanent manager by now. Ninety per cent of the press seemed to believe the only way for a club to succeed was through an all-powerful manager in charge of every aspect of the playing side. In time, virtually every major club in the country would have a sporting director, a director of football or a head of football administration.

In March, John Alexander and Daniel Levy asked me which clubs we might approach to see how a relationship between a manager and a director of football could work more efficiently.

Glenn Hoddle had always appeared suspicious of my role and had found it hard to accept I was both his buffer and responsible to the board. He did not seem to appreciate that my empathy was with the dressing room. I suggested PSV Eindhoven was worth examining. Guus Hiddink was manager and Frank Arnesen was director of football and the pair appeared to work well. The irony was that by the time the Spurs delegation went to Holland, the two men had fallen out and Arnesen was looking for another club. That information was relayed to Daniel Levy.

I had met Hiddink before. In 2001, when we were looking to replace George Graham, Alan Sugar and I had met him at a hotel in Brentwood. Then he had made it clear he did not want to work with a director of football in the background. It was nothing personal. Guus was a charming man whom I had instantly liked. However, he turned Spurs down in favour of honouring his contract to lead South Korea into the World Cup they would co-host with Japan. It proved a good choice. South Korea reached the semi-finals, and while I was in the country as a commentator for Radio 5 during a gloriously colourful World Cup, Hiddink was treated almost as a god.

When Alexander and Levy returned from Eindhoven, John told me they had learned a lot. What I did not know was they had been very impressed with what they had heard about Arnesen. So impressed, in fact, that they would make him an offer.

While this was going on, I had arranged a swap deal with West Ham, exchanging Zamora, who had not settled since his move from Brighton, for Jermain Defoe. We now had three outstanding strikers with Kanouté, Keane and Defoe. I became frustrated, struggling to devise a system that could accommodate all three. Individually, they were brilliant. Kanouté could be unplayable on his day; Keane was a cunning, intelligent front man; while Defoe was the ultimate fox in the box. It was difficult to devise a system to accommodate them all. As I kept emphasising to the media, three into two often did not go.

With a couple of games remaining, I took the squad to the Five Lakes hotel and golf complex near Colchester. There we did some serious tactical work and spent time organising the shape of the side. Although we were only there a couple of days, it was a re-freshing change from the training ground environment. When we had finished, Gus Poyet came over and said: 'Why didn't we do this earlier in the season?' Poyet, who had been less than supportive fol-lowing Glenn's dismissal, possessed plenty of chutzpah.

On our return, we won the final two games of the season, beating Blackburn at White Hart Lane and finishing off with a 2–0 win at Wolves. Just before we travelled to Wolverhampton, Paul Kemsley came into my office to tell me I would not be staying on. I sat on the team bus as it pulled away from Molineux knowing it was all over. Ledley King, who knew I would be leaving, signed his shirt and gave it to me, which I thought was a nice touch.

Kemsley was a popular, happy-go-lucky guy who liked to mingle with the players. He was also very thick-skinned. Criticism bounced off him. Kemsley had once rung me at home around midnight to ask why Tottenham had not bid for Atlético Madrid's young centre-forward Fernando Torres. He had just seen Torres, who was then nineteen, on television. I explained that our scouting department was fully aware of Torres, but then so was every other big club in Europe. 'We would love to sign him, Paul. But there is no way At-lético would sell.' It would be three years before they did a deal, selling him to Liverpool for £20 million plus Luis García.

In my first stint at Tottenham, Irving Scholar had made a similar kind of call, asking why we had not scouted the brilliant Uruguayan Enzo Francescoli. I told Irving we could not afford him, and even if we could, we were performing outstandingly well and he might not have fitted into the 4–5–1 system. Irving's cool response was to remark: 'Don't say I didn't tell you.'

Kemsley was the kind of director who would have quite liked to have managed the first team. He was particularly close to Jamie Redknapp. I was a great admirer of Jamie's talent, but a debilitating knee injury was taking its toll and he had not played the number of games that would have triggered an automatic extension to his contract. Paul, almost acting as Jamie's agent, suggested Jamie would hold back some of the bonuses he was due for one year if I extended his contract. I told Paul we should pay Jamie what we owed him and allow him to go on a free transfer.

This was a battle I lost. Paul waved my objections away, saying: 'It's no skin off your nose. I'll take the flak for it.' Jamie did stay but was signed by his father, Harry, on a free transfer in January 2005. They were unable to prevent Southampton's relegation after twenty-seven years in the top flight.

When Kemsley told me Spurs were seeking a new manager and a new director of football and that I was surplus to requirements, I was shattered by the conversation. There had been much speculation I would be replaced. When I took over, Tottenham had four points from a possible eighteen and we had finished a relatively comfortable fourteenth. To be fair to the club, they suggested through Leon Angel of the Base agency a watered-down consultancy agreement for a couple of years. I would do some scouting, be given a company car for a year, medical expenses and a salary of £30,000. I rejected it, feeling a clean break was necessary.

Arsenal were champions after going through the season unbeaten. They completed their triumph in a 2–2 draw at White Hart Lane, where the returning Sol Campbell stood up to a barrage of abuse. Paul Kemsley quit as Tottenham's vice-chairman in October 2007 and his finances took a pounding when he became caught up in the collapse of Lehman Brothers the following year. However, he managed to reinvent himself in the United States and his second wife became a star on the reality show *The Real Housewives of Beverly Hills*.

As a caretaker, even as a caretaker who presided over the vast majority of the season, I was dealing with a squad that deep down knew I would not be the man who decided their futures. Their destiny was not in my hands. Once the season was done, they expected me to either revert to my position as director of football or leave the club.

For the only time I can remember my programme notes were changed for the final home game against Blackburn. Daniel Levy had written a column for the programme, acknowledging this had been a season of deep disappointment and promising radical change in the summer. I had written a similarly optimistic piece, trying to give an analytical commentary of the season, but my words were changed to suit the club's PR.

Generally, a board will not allow a caretaker to make signings lest they conflict with the strategy of the incoming manager. The only significant business I was allowed to do was bringing in Defoe for Zamora, which proved a great success.

I also convinced the board to sign Paul Robinson from Leeds, who had been relegated from the Premier League in complete financial disarray. Alan Hill, an ex-Nottingham Forest goalkeeper who became Brian Clough's chief scout at the City Ground, absolutely convinced me of Robinson's worth.

The fee was £1.5 million which would prove exceptional value for a keeper who would be in goal for England during the 2006 World Cup in Germany. However, when Big Robbo arrived at the training ground with his agent, Jerome Anderson, just before the last game at Wolves, I was not asked to join the photocall or the signing ceremony. I was already yesterday's man.

CHAPTER 28

'WATCH GAMES AND
BE A CONSULTANT'

I was in the Wellington Hospital, having had an operation on my hip. The Wellington backs on to Lord's cricket ground and, as I lay in bed, I recalled my schooldays as a spectator at Trent Bridge. After school, I would sit at midwicket in the George Parr Stand and watch the fine Nottinghamshire side of the era, featuring the elegant batting of their captain Reg Simpson. In the field, the Australian Bruce Dooland, who during the war had been a commando operating behind Japanese lines in Borneo, and the Sri Lankan Gamini Goonesena both bowled leg spin. In county cricket, leg spin would become a dying art. To see two operating together was a privilege, soon to be lost. I may have left Tottenham, but they continued to pay for my private medical insurance and the surgeon did an excellent job. It was my second operation and now I had two false hips.

I had come to him after experiencing difficulty in walking while commentating on the European Championship in Portugal. It was here that I cemented my relationship with 'Mister Bobby'. Bobby Robson was a hero in Portugal, particularly in Porto, where he had won two league titles. Whenever I went with him for a meal, he would never be allowed to pay for it. It was while listening to his stories that I wondered if I should not have pushed myself more to manage abroad.

I had met with Olympiakos and Real Sociedad but pushed for neither post. Graham Hunter, who had left the *Daily Mail* to live and work in Spain, rang to ask if I would be interested in a job in La Liga. He knew I had a holiday home in Spain and wanted to know how much of the language I spoke. My reply was very little, certainly not enough to coach a first-team squad. I would advise any young coach to learn a foreign language, particularly Spanish. Israel did appeal in a strange way and Bobby's great friend Joe Merimovich, who had twice managed the national side, said he could get me any job in the country.

I had been replaced as director of football by Frank Arnesen, although he had not been involved in the choice of Jacques Santini to be Tottenham's next manager. Arnesen had recommended Martin Jol, who had been a tough wing-half for West Bromwich Albion and Coventry and had embarked on a promising managerial career in his native Holland. In 1997, he had won the Dutch Cup with JC Roda and done well at Waalwijk, another small club. However, Santini was a much bigger name who had managed Lyons to the French title and was in charge of France as they defended the European Championship in Portugal.

France lost in the quarter-finals to Greece, the eventual winners, and Santini arrived at White Hart Lane for what proved a short, unsatisfactory spell as Tottenham manager with Jol as his assistant. Their relationship was brief and bad. It ended with Jol taking over.

We had moved to Hertfordshire, nearer to Spurs' training ground at Chigwell. Maureen had spotted a plot of land and began supervising the building of a new house. The children were now grown up and I would be sixty in January. I was still in demand for newspaper columns and commentary. When Ron Atkinson lost his job as ITV's main summariser after his remark about Marcel Desailly, I became his replacement.

However, I still could not bear to be divorced from the main business of football. When I left Tottenham, Alan Sugar contacted me. 'You don't want that rubbish of working full time,' he said.

'With your knowledge of players, you should watch games and be a consultant for someone.' He suggested working for a club in each division and recommending players appropriate to their status. It was an imaginative idea, but the conflicts of interest would have made it unworkable. However, his concept of my becoming a consultant was a sound one, especially since I realised that, if I wanted to go back to coaching, the six years I had spent largely in an office as Tottenham's director of football would count against me.

I was rung by Karren Brady's father, Terry, who was a director at Portsmouth. He asked if I would like to meet his chairman, Milan Mandarić, at the Churchill Hotel in London's Portman Square. Like Alan Sugar, Mandarić had made his money in computers. He had left his native Yugoslavia for California in 1969 and within seven years his company, Lika, had become the biggest supplier of component parts to Silicon Valley. He had also become involved in football, setting up San Jose Earthquakes, where George Best spent a few fitful months playing alongside and rooming with Guus Hiddink, who answered his many telephone calls.

As chairman of Portsmouth, Milan, who had played football to a decent level in Yugoslavia, had enjoyed becoming involved in transfers and, under Harry Redknapp's management, there had been plenty to become involved with. The relationship between chairman and manager went to extremes, and when Harry resigned in November 2004, the media linked it to a row over the employment of his No. 2 Jim Smith, and Mandarić's use of a director of football, the Croatian Velimir Zajec. Harry denied that this was the case.

However, by April 2005, Portsmouth were in a relegation battle along with Southampton, who were now managed by Redknapp, and Zajec, who had taken over the team, resumed his duties as director of football. I was asked to work with Portsmouth until the new manager, Alain Perrin, had bedded in. When I went to the training ground at Eastleigh, I was presented with shambolic facilities. The pitches were poor and there was an old cricket pavilion where the players changed and showered.

The manager's secretary worked in a Portakabin next to the booming music from the adjoining weights room. Joe Jordan also worked in the Portakabin, studying matches on his laptop. The great Scotland striker had been brought in by Redknapp as a coach and had been retained by Perrin. Joe was a warm man, devoid of the arrogance you might expect of someone who had led the attacks of Leeds, Manchester United and AC Milan.

Perrin was a straightforward guy who had managed Marseilles and had previously been sounded out to replace Gordon Strachan at Southampton. My job would involve taking him to games, introducing him to people who might be useful to him and acquainting him with the English game. However, Perrin did not seem that keen to go to matches other than those involving Portsmouth. He was based in a Southsea hotel, where he prepared his sessions and worked on his computer. I spent nearly all my time watching games and maintaining a dialogue with the chairman.

As Portsmouth attempted to stave off relegation, the player that impressed me most was their Dutch centre-half, Arjen de Zeeuw. He was a qualified doctor and a charming man, popular with the Portsmouth fans and staff. The same could not be said of their Nigerian striker, Yakubu, who had been instrumental in winning Portsmouth promotion in 2003 but who had been offered a lucrative move to Middlesbrough and was unwilling to risk injury in his final few weeks at Fratton Park. A couple of years before, I had sat with Daniel Levy as Yakubu's agent, Pini Zahavi, brought him to Tottenham from Maccabi Haifa. Pini pushed him hard but we declined the offer.

Zahavi, who had begun as a football journalist in Israel, became involved in the business of football when he negotiated the transfers of Avi Cohen and Ronny Rosenthal to Liverpool. By the time he took Yakubu to London, Zahavi had become Manchester United's preferred agent. His big moment had come in the summer of 2002, when he negotiated the transfer of Rio Ferdinand from Leeds to Manchester United for £30 million, followed a year later in his role in Roman Abramovich's takeover of Chelsea.

My relationship with Pini was soured by an incident in Ukraine. We were both flying to Kyiv, me in economy and Pini in business. However, there was a spare seat next to him and during the flight I went over to chat. When we arrived in Kyiv, Pini breezed through VIP customs while I queued for half an hour with the rest of the flight. When I eventually got through to the arrivals' hall, I saw a man holding up a sign saying 'Pini Zahavi'. I told him Pini had already gone but we were staying at the same hotel and I wondered if I could have a lift. It is about twenty miles from Boryspil Airport to the centre of Kyiv and as we drove through the wooded countryside, the driver's phone rang more and more incessantly. It was Pini, wondering where on earth he was. The next time I saw Zahavi was in the foyer of the hotel. He knew I had kidnapped his car and he never forgave me for it. Certainly, we did not speak for a long time.

The last day of the season saw Portsmouth safe from the drop. They would finish up at West Bromwich Albion, who were bottom of the Premier League, requiring every result to go in their favour to survive. Their manager, Bryan Robson, carried in his pocket a jade Buddha, given to him by his children for luck. Harry Redknapp, whose Southampton side was also in the relegation zone but were facing Manchester United, had been given a plastic angel. The Buddha proved more successful than the angel. To say that Portsmouth were passive at The Hawthorns would be an understatement. Their display was pathetic. The travelling fans were not in the least concerned, since a defeat would help send Southampton down. West Brom won, 2–0. Crystal Palace, who had begun the morning in nineteenth position, drew 2–2 at Charlton, while Norwich, who were just above the line, were thrashed 6–0 at Fulham. At St Mary's, Southampton took the lead against United but succumbed to goals from Darren Fletcher and Ruud van Nistelrooy. West Brom had pulled off the greatest of great escapes and Bryan Robson found himself drenched in champagne.

My three months at Portsmouth were up. Alain Perrin remained at Fratton Park until November, when he was replaced by the returning figure of Harry Redknapp. Amid the euphoria at The Hawthorns, the West Brom chairman, Jeremy Peace, asked me to join him as a consultant. I would report to him via the scouting staff.

I was diligent and watched plenty of games but had no contact with Bryan Robson. My brief was to speak to the chairman about any player I strongly recommended and the names would be passed on. However, communication was poor and West Brom's results were poorer. This time there was no escape and they were relegated with two games to spare. Bryan left in September 2006 and, while I received a kind letter of thanks from Jeremy Peace, relegation meant there was no longer a role for me. I could completely understand.

Then my boyhood club, Nottingham Forest, came calling. They had first made contact in 2004, when I was told that the manager, Joe Kinnear, was likely to be removed and would I be interested in working with them? I had never been a great fan of Kinnear's style of football and remembered all too vividly the broken cheekbone Gary Mabbutt had suffered when his Wimbledon side had played Tottenham.

I was writing a column for *The Guardian* about promising young footballers. The subject of one of these articles was a pacey young forward at Wycombe called Nathan Tyson. Nigel Doughty, the Nottingham Forest chairman, contacted me about the piece. In January 2005, he spoke to me again. I was in Devon, summarising on an FA Cup tie between Plymouth and Everton. Kinnear had resigned the month before after a 3–0 defeat at Derby had left Forest third bottom of the Championship.

Nigel told me he was going to interview a number of managers and requested my views. The candidates included Dave Jones, who had just left Wolves, and Gary Megson. Joe Kinnear's assistant, Mick Harford, would take Forest to Queens Park Rangers for their cup tie that day. I suggested he should give Harford an extended opportunity. Mick was an imposing figure who had enjoyed a good career as a centre-forward. He had a presence the Forest players would respect.

I asked him what he would do if Forest won at Loftus Road that afternoon. This they did, 3–0, but Doughty said his mind was made up and he would appoint Gary Megson. This turned out to be a big mistake. Megson had played for Nottingham Forest under Brian Clough and his managerial reputation had been forged at West Bromwich Albion, a club he had twice promoted to the Premier League. However, despite these factors, his appointment was not a popular one.

Gary was a confident man with a touch of arrogance. This was in contrast to his father, Don, whom I had played against when he was at Sheffield Wednesday and I was at Exeter. The fans remembered Clough's comments that Megson 'could not trap a bag of cement'. His style of football, the long passes played into the channels, was in contrast to the type of game he had played under Clough, the type of game that everyone at the City Ground still yearned for. Another of Clough's quotes, 'If God had meant football to be played in the clouds, he would have put grass up there,' was dredged up and used against him.

In that January, Nottingham Forest had sold their centre-half Michael Dawson and their winger Andy Reid to Tottenham for a combined fee of £8 million. The chief scout, Ian Storey-Moore, had advised against the sale, but Nigel Doughty was determined to clear the club's debts. I had gone to watch a player at the Forest academy called Craig Westcarr against Crewe. Dawson stood out a mile and was subbed after sixty-five minutes. I immediately rang a friend at Spurs. I thought he was good enough for the top flight. Dawson was an exemplary professional, an ambassador and a leader who was loved by everyone at Tottenham during his nine years at White Hart Lane. He returned to Nottingham Forest in the summer of 2018. He retired three years later and returned to Spurs as a club ambassador.

In April, Forest were relegated to League One after a 2–1 defeat at Queens Park Rangers. They would also become the first winners of the European Cup to be relegated to the third tier of their own domestic league. Megson held on to his job as the board anticipated a quick return. However, after an opening-day win against Huddersfield, they lost five of the next six and on 16 February, following a 3–0 defeat at Oldham, Megson's difficult tenure came to an end, with Forest thirteenth in the old Third Division.

During Gary Megson's time at the helm and still with no specific role at the club, I had paid a visit to Nottingham Forest's limited training facilities on the floodplain of the Trent. I often wondered how Brian Clough had been so successful at such an archaic training ground. The pitches were uneven, poorly maintained and open to the public. The river ran alongside them. Forest's reserves were playing that night and their coach, Ian McParland, was putting the players through their paces. That evening, they carried out their instructions just as their manager had asked. I was impressed.

McParland had come down from the Lothian coalfields to play for Notts County in 1980. He was a fiery striker who always seemed to be in an argument with someone. McParland had been a coach at Forest for nearly a decade and was not in awe of Megson. He was put in charge of the first team and began exceptionally well. Had they not lost 3–2 at Hartlepool, Nottingham Forest would have equalled the club record of seven successive wins that had stood since 1922.

That defeat sent them out of the play-off positions on goal difference; a failure that would cost McParland his job. It was then that Nigel Doughty offered me an official role as a consultant with a salary and a company car. He was anxious to clean up the club. Doughty was a rarity. He was a tall, imposing man who ran a hugely successful private equity firm that restructured companies and had offices across Europe. The company, Doughty Hanson, was headquartered amid gleaming offices in London's Pall Mall. He was also a socialist who was to become assistant treasurer of the Labour Party.

He was born in Newark to a working-class family and his first job was in a bank. He grew up a fan of Nottingham Forest, which he bought in 1999 clearing its debts of £12 million. His friend and fellow Forest fan Ken Clarke said Doughty kept putting limits on how much money he should invest in the club. Those limits would then be continually broken.

Despite his success in nearly taking Forest to the play-offs, Nigel had not appointed Ian McParland. He preferred Colin Calderwood, who at Tottenham had been Gary Mabbutt's partner at centre-half and as manager had just promoted Northampton to League One. McParland left Forest to become manager of Notts County in October 2007, where he found himself working under Sven-Göran Eriksson, who had been appointed as Meadow Lane's unlikeliest director of football.

My role at Nottingham Forest was to give my view on scouting recommendations. Colin's backroom team was headed by David Kerslake, who had played alongside him in Tottenham's defence and had been his assistant at Northampton. John Pemberton, a defender who had played for Crystal Palace in the 1990 FA Cup final, was assistant coach and the team was completed by Keith Burt, who was in charge of recruitment. Together, we would form a democratic committee.

Keith suggested that I watch Nathan Tyson, whom I had previously recommended to Nigel Doughty two years before and who was still at Wycombe. I went to Brighton to watch Luke Chambers, who had captained Northampton under Calderwood. The game was at the Withdean Stadium, the athletics venue the club used as a lifeboat between the loss of the Goldstone Ground and the building of their beautiful new stadium at Falmer.

Nottingham Forest took both players and I also recommended they sign Paul Smith from Southampton. I never felt I was a good judge of a goalkeeper, but watching him, I felt confident he was good enough. When assessing goalkeepers, I asked as many contacts as I could for their opinions. Their reply was that Paul, who was then twenty-six, ticked all the boxes. Forest signed him for £500,000.

Tyson was injured six minutes into the opening game of the season, a 1–0 win over Bradford, and was afflicted by hamstring trouble throughout his time at the City Ground. The highlight was unquestionably a hat-trick against Crewe, completed in eight first-half minutes. Chambers was made club captain by Steve McClaren in 2011 before making a highly successful move to Ipswich. Paul Smith played in forty-six games in his first season at Nottingham Forest and kept clean sheets in more than half of them. It was a fine record, but when Calderwood's regime began to crack Paul would inexplicably lose form.

Colin inherited Wes Morgan at centre-half, a Nottingham boy with power and deceptive pace. Strangely, he was never a good striker of the ball. His greatest achievements would come at Leicester, where he would captain the 5,000–1 outsiders to the Premier League trophy. He was a footballer who improved with age.

On the final afternoon of the season, Nottingham Forest were third, needing to better Bristol City's result to achieve automatic promotion. Bristol City's 3–1 win over Rotherham at Ashton Gate made Forest's goalless draw at home to Crewe academic. Forest would play Yeovil in the play-off semi-finals. The first leg at Huish Park was won 2–0. The second leg at the City Ground ought to have been a formality. With eight minutes remaining, the scoreline was 1–1, but an own-goal from Alan Wright and a header from Marcus Stewart forced extra time. A dreadful back-pass from Wes Morgan allowed Yeovil to extend their lead and by the end they had won, 5–2. As Yeovil turned the game on its head, I was sitting near Colin's young son, Alfie, who could not bear the defeat or the abuse that was being hurled towards his father. He broke down in floods of tears and his mother had to take him home.

Yeovil lost the play-off final to Blackpool. However, we were interested in taking their midfielder Chris Cohen. In pre-season, I drove to Somerset to watch him play, passing Stonehenge in the early morning as I travelled west. I arrived at Huish Park in plenty of time and, as I sat in my car reading the papers, I noticed Cohen arrive. He got out of his car, carrying his washbag in one arm and holding his girlfriend's hand. He was smartly dressed, and his polished shoes sparkled. It was a good first impression, even if he was not aware he had made one. I also enjoyed the way he played.

I rang Alan Pardew, who had managed Chris at West Ham. I wanted to know if Cohen had a downside. Alan's reply was: 'Cohen is a top-class person and an honest worker, but the pitch might be just too big for him.' Pardew doubted whether Cohen had the legs, the motor, to cover the ground. He could not have been more wrong. We took the chance and for £1.2 million signed him along with Arron Davies, who had scored twice for Yeovil in that extraordinary night at the City Ground. Cohen made a huge contribution to Forest anywhere down the left side. There was no lack of energy in his play.

It may have been coincidence, but when Cohen made his debut

for Forest in September, they were fourth bottom, having won none of their opening four fixtures. The fifth, at Port Vale, was won 2–0, and Nottingham Forest began a revival that finally justified their position as favourites to win League One.

However, they went out of the FA Cup with a whimper at Luton and Colin Calderwood confided in me that he had received an email from the chairman questioning the team's formation. Nigel was big on stats, but it would have been wiser for him to have kept his enthusiasm in check. Colin was a gentleman, a genuine, approachable figure, and he asked for my advice. I told him to ignore the message and not be dragged into any argument. Kris Commons was also asking for an improved salary. I told Colin that giving into him would create a queue outside his door of players looking for similar increases. I urged him not to buckle. Commons would leave for Derby in the summer and subsequently have some successful seasons at Celtic.

As the final morning of the season dawned, Forest were third, one point behind Doncaster in second. Swansea, under Roberto Martínez, had already been promoted. Doncaster were at Cheltenham. Forest were at home to Yeovil, the club that had dashed so many hopes the season before. Cheltenham won and so did Forest. They were 3–1 up before the half-hour mark and this time they did not let go. Colin Calderwood had found a reward for his two years of hard work. He was also to find that celebrations can very quickly turn sour.

CHAPTER 29

'THIS SHOULD HAVE BEEN ME'

As the new season approached, there was plenty of optimism and a good atmosphere at Nottingham Forest. There was also, perhaps, a sense of complacency. The manager of a promoted side faces a dilemma. Does he keep faith with the men who have taken him this far or does he refashion the squad and risk alienating the players who have been loyal to him?

Maybe it reflected his character, but Colin Calderwood chose to stay loyal to the footballers who had taken Forest up. He was a good man, quiet, calm and well respected, and he had made few enemies in the fierce theatre of the game. Colin should, however, have been more ruthless, because Nottingham Forest floundered badly in the Championship. The one significant signing he did make was Robert Earnshaw, who had endured Derby's disastrous return to the Premier League when under first Billy Davies and then Paul Jewell they had scraped together eleven points in a season.

Earnshaw was a small, swift forward who had been born in the Zambian copper belt to an English father and a mother who played football for Zambia. He was nine when his father died and the family moved to south Wales. He had been part of Bryan Robson's West Bromwich Albion squad that had survived dramatically on the last day of the season and was a Wales international. It was the chairman, Nigel Doughty, who was the main driving force behind the transfer, which saw Forest pay Derby £2.65 million. Earnshaw scored seventeen goals in thirty-six games, but the cost of the transfer prevented Colin strengthening the squad elsewhere. There would be consequences.

On Boxing Day, Forest, third last in the Championship, faced the bottom club, Doncaster, at the City Ground. At half-time, Doncaster were 4–0 up and Doughty took the painful decision to dispense with Calderwood, a man he admired immensely. He asked if I had a phone number for Billy Davies. Although his season in the Premier League had ended in ignominy, there was much to recommend Davies. In 2007 he had promoted Derby to the top flight, beating West Bromwich Albion in the play-off final. He was a small guy, with strong principles and was a student of modern football analysis. He had a reputation as being a very fine coach.

As I player, I had signed him when I was manager of Leicester as a replacement for Gary McAllister. Perhaps because McAllister's boots were big ones to fill, the transfer did not work out and when his wife suffered a miscarriage he understandably wanted to return to Scotland and signed for Dunfermline. Later, when I was at Tottenham, he was doing his coaching badges and rang to ask if I had any contacts abroad. I arranged for him to go to Atlético Madrid, where Raddy Antić was manager, to complete his thesis.

I met Billy at Nigel Doughty's imposing country house in the Lincolnshire village of Skillington near Newark. We sat together and I put specific football questions to him while Nigel listened. How much did he know about Forest's playing staff? If he brought in new players, would he be buying for today or tomorrow? Who would he be bringing in as his backroom staff? Would he be prepared to live in Nottingham?

The chairman then spoke to Billy alone to discuss his contract and salary. It was then that Davies told him that he already had an offer to take over at Charlton, who had replaced Doncaster at the foot of the Championship. This was an old managerial ploy, designed to up the offer, and had I been in the room, I would have alerted the chairman to it. Despite Billy's politicking, Nigel was convinced he was the man he wanted. Billy took three days to accept the deal. He told us he would take up his position on 4 January 2009.

That left two games to be filled – a Championship fixture at Norwich and an FA Cup tie at Manchester City. The Forest chief executive, Mark Arthur, who had joined the club from Nottinghamshire County Cricket Club, asked me to travel to Norfolk and look after the team with John Pemberton, the reserve-team coach. Mark was an affable guy, controlled by the chairman, and eventually returned to cricket, his first love, as Yorkshire's chief executive. His tenure would come to an end following the racism crisis that engulfed the county in 2021.

He asked me to speak to the players at the hotel and then assist John during the game. The team did not know me that well, but I told them they were playing for their futures and their families. They should stick out their chests. In the dressing room at Carrow Road, Wes Morgan and the goalkeeper, Lee Camp, who had joined on loan from Queens Park Rangers, looked especially motivated. Camp was particularly boisterous. The result was a thrilling 3–2 victory in a game in which Forest scored all five goals – two were in their own net. Earnshaw sealed the win in the final minute. As I stood in the dressing room in the afterglow of victory, I was seized by a thought: 'This should have been me.' I was still only sixty-three and knew I could still motivate. A few days later, Earnshaw scored again as we knocked Manchester City out of the FA Cup, 3–0. The tide appeared to be turning.

Billy took over for the next fixture, a 2–0 win at Charlton, and brought in David Kelly as his assistant. When he was at Nottingham Forest, Peter Taylor used the phrase: 'In football, two's company, three's a crowd.' What he meant was that too large a backroom staff is a hive of gossip and that he preferred to speak to just one other person. Over the bridge at Notts County, Jimmy Sirrel was even more paranoid. He would never have more than one person in his office at a time and would lock the door. Later, there were rumours that some clubs would have their manager's office bugged.

Davies and Kelly appeared to cut me out of any discussions. It seemed an age since I had managed them both at Leicester, but now the relationship was very different. Maybe, deep down, they had a suspicion I might still want to manage the club. As he was commuting from Scotland, Billy left much to David. Sometimes, he would not be seen at the training ground until Wednesday or even Thursday. They were openly dismissive of my role, even though they had been informed from the outset that Forest would have a transfer committee. It was composed of Keith Burt, Billy Davies, Nigel Doughty, Mark Arthur and me. It was not that dissimilar to a board. Make no mistake, the manager would always have the final say on any incoming player. Billy would regularly leak details of the meetings to the *Nottingham Post* and suggest the committee was a burden to his making quick decisions. He dubbed it 'the acquisition committee' and ridiculed it in the media.

We secured our survival at Blackpool with a game to spare. Some 29,000 came to the City Ground to celebrate with a 3–1 win over an already-relegated Southampton. It is strange how the final game of a season can define a full year's work, but the crowd went home happy. It is so important that the last game of the season is a success.

In the summer, we signed Chris Gunter, a highly intelligent Welsh defender from Tottenham, for £1.75 million. By 2018, he would have won a record number of international caps for Wales and played in the semi-finals of the European Championship. Lee Camp was brought in on a full-time basis from Queens Park Rangers for £150,000. Another QPR player, the striker Dexter Blackstock, was brought in for more than £1 million while Dele Adebola, a forward who had played for Birmingham in the League

Cup final against Liverpool in 2001, joined on a free transfer from Bristol City. David McGoldrick, a Nottingham boy who had begun his career at Meadow Lane, was signed from Southampton for £1 million, although he would score only three goals in his first season at the City Ground. Paul Anderson, a twenty-year-old winger who had yet to break into Liverpool's first team, was signed for £250,000. The board had backed Billy to the hilt.

It had been a summer of considerable investment and Forest responded. After a 1–0 defeat to Blackpool at the City Ground on 19 September, they did not lose a home league game for the rest of the season and finished third behind a rampant Newcastle and West Brom. In the play-offs, Nottingham Forest would face sixth-placed Blackpool in the semi-final. Although Chris Cohen put Forest ahead in the first leg at Bloomfield Road, Blackpool won 2–1. However, we were not dismayed and with our home record we were confident of overturning the result at the City Ground.

Before the match, I was in the Forest boardroom when Ian Holloway, the Blackpool manager, marched in. He was wearing a Blackpool tangerine tie with a matching buttonhole. Among the Blackpool contingent was their wealthy and eccentrically dressed owner Owen Oyston who had been a substantial donor to the Labour Party before his conviction for rape. They looked at Holloway adoringly as he strangely and suddenly addressed the room: 'Ladies and gentlemen, whatever the result, may we see a good game and may the best team win, get to Wembley and win promotion.'

After seven minutes, Robert Earnshaw had scored to level the scoreline on aggregate. He scored another equaliser with twenty-four minutes remaining but with a clear advantage, Forest shrivelled in front of a crowd of 28,000. DJ Campbell struck a hat-trick to give Blackpool a 4–3 victory. Blackpool had played Forest four times that season and won the lot. Ian Holloway was to get his wish.

It had been a good game, the best team did win it and when Black-pool reached Wembley, they would beat Cardiff 3–2 to make the top flight for the first time since 1971.

The next time I encountered Holloway was in August 2014. He was now manager of Millwall, preparing for the opening game of the season against Leeds. I had been asked to summarise at the New Den alongside Alistair Bruce-Ball, who was making his debut for Radio 5. Ali was asked to do a pre-match interview with Holloway and, as he had never met him before and was slightly nervous, I agreed to make an introduction. Ian was a man I had long admired, not least because he had raised two daughters, both of whom had been born deaf. England had just endured a disastrous World Cup in Brazil, which had been won by Germany. Raising his voice, Ian praised the Germans' meticulous preparations for the tournament and lambasted England's substandard efforts. It was quite a rant. His solution, delivered in his West Country burr, was that the Queen should take over the running of the English game. Ali sent the tape straight down the line to Salford, where BBC Sport was based. In their wisdom, the BBC decided not to broadcast it.

Ian Holloway was a man who often made outrageous comments, but he always spoke from the heart. With Billy Davies, you never knew. By the time Billy's third season at the City Ground began, I was coming up to Nottingham only twice a month, but I was in almost daily touch with the club, particularly the head of recruit-ment, Keith Burt.

Keith was a diligent worker who would follow the motorways of Britain looking at players, often returning home in the small hours of the morning. He operated in the true traditions of an English scout. Nowadays, the scouting fraternity has receded dramatically as young people from universities can analyse every kick and shot from every player in Europe's major leagues from their computer screens. A modern manager receives more information from his analysts than from the scout who sets off to sniff out a player on a dark winter's evening.

Burt did not have deep connections to his manager, who tended to rule with an element of fear. Davies's staff were nervous around him. John Pemberton had found the atmosphere intimidating, and in the summer of 2009, his contract as reserve-team coach had been terminated. He joined the former Nottingham Forest manager, Paul Hart, at Crystal Palace. A run of five wins in their final six games ensured that once more Nottingham Forest would finish in the play-offs. They would face Swansea, who were now managed by Brendan Rodgers, at the City Ground in the first leg. Despite the fact that Swansea had their defender Neil Taylor dismissed after two minutes of the match, the Welsh side forced a comfortable goalless draw.

The second leg at the Liberty Stadium was not much of a contest. Swansea were two up before half-time. Earnshaw pulled one back with ten minutes remaining and Forest hit the frame of the goal, but when our goalkeeper, Lee Camp, was pushed up for a corner, Swansea won possession and Darren Pratley passed into an empty net. At Wembley, Swansea overcame Reading to win promotion to the top flight for the first time since the glory days under John Toshack.

I returned to my hotel in Cardiff, where in the bar and unable to sleep, I was phoned by Nigel Doughty who informed me he was sacking Billy Davies and wondered if I could ring Steve McClaren. He said he was ready to give Nottingham Forest one more go. I called Steve who said the chairman should contact his agent, Ian Gordon. I had mixed feelings about the fall of Billy Davies. He had prevented Nottingham Forest's relegation and twice taken them to the play-offs, but given Nigel's financial backing he had fallen short. He was still a good coach, but his man-management was nothing short of disastrous.

This arguably contributed more to his dismissal than the defeats in two play-off semi-finals. In football, you have to trust colleagues and communicate. His relationship with the chairman had broken down too frequently and, were it not for the hopes that Billy could get Forest to the play-offs, he would have been sacked long before he was.

Davies's press conferences were frequently counter-productive, as he accused the transfer committee of blocking his targets. Once, he suggested I had prevented a loan deal with Tottenham for Gareth Bale. Nothing could be further from the truth. In the early months of the 2009/10 season, Bale had struggled to win his place back in Harry Redknapp's side after returning from injury and Tottenham had explored the possibility of sending the young Welshman out on loan. However, Bale was an £8 million player and there were Premier League clubs across the country who were willing to take him on loan. We asked, but realistically, Nottingham Forest had no chance of getting him. In the event, Bale stayed at White Hart Lane, won his place back and helped Spurs qualify for the Champions League. Nevertheless, Billy remained popular among the supporters and his claims were believed by some.

Ian Storey-Moore had conceded that Nigel Doughty could be intransigent in his dealings with his managers. When Doughty informed the *Nottingham Post* he had given Davies a £10 million transfer budget, it was counter-productive. It served only to drive up the price of every player the club enquired about and, in Ian's eyes, demonstrated Nigel's naivety.

I once went to Billy's office after a game. It was full of his friends from Scotland who included his agent Jim Price, a Glasgow lawyer who was also his cousin. Only David Kelly showed any warmth. I felt unwelcome. David was a decent man, but he had hung his career on Billy's coat-tails, and as Davies's behaviour became ever more erratic, this was to become a dangerous ploy.

One of the people Steve McClaren brought to Forest was Bill Beswick, a sports psychologist he had worked with since the days when he was assistant manager to Sir Alex Ferguson at Manchester United. At Old Trafford, Beswick was credited with improving the mindsets of Roy Keane, David Beckham and Gary Neville. Nigel Doughty had massively improved Nottingham Forest's training facilities and had built a state-of-the-art academy at West Bridgford, which now bears his name. I arranged to meet Steve there. He was very engaging.

McClaren's time in management had been nothing if not eventful. He had followed up his success at Manchester United by taking Middlesbrough to the first trophy in their history and then to a UEFA Cup final against Sevilla. He steered Twente Enschede to their first-ever Dutch title. Mixed in with this was the debacle of his time as England manager and a short, unsuccessful spell in the Bundesliga with Wolfsburg. He was relaxed, smiled often and did not appear under undue pressure. He invited me to watch the team talk he would give the day before Forest opened their season at home to Barnsley.

I sat in the audio theatre with the other players as Steve handed over to Bill Beswick. A film began screening. It showed hyenas being attacked by a lion at the side of an African watering hole. One hyena was left stranded and badly wounded. However, the rest of the pack regrouped and ran towards the lion to chase it off as it closed in on the wounded hyena. The animal was rescued from certain death. Bill Beswick explained the moral of the story. 'You fight back; you never leave your teammates in the shit,' he said. 'You must never know when you are beaten.' I thought this was good stuff, but as the players glanced at each other, they seemed utterly bemused, as if wondering how watching hyenas was going to help them beat Barnsley. The result was a toothless, goalless draw.

In football, there are no messiahs. Under McClaren, Nottingham

Forest won two of their opening ten fixtures. On 2 October, after a 5–1 thrashing at Burnley had been followed up by a 3–1 home defeat to Birmingham, Forest had fallen to fourth bottom of the Championship. After 111 days at the City Ground, McClaren and his staff resigned. After twelve years as chairman of the club he had supported all his life, Nigel Doughty quit with him, realising his dream would never be fulfilled. Frank Clark, who had won the European Cup under Brian Clough and managed Forest to third place in the Premier League in 1995, took over as temporary chairman.

Mark Arthur, the chief executive, asked to meet me at the Post House at Crick. It was a hotel I was familiar with. It was here, in Northamptonshire, that I had witnessed Brian Clough's bizarre attempt to sign Kingsley Black when I was Luton manager. In 1986, when I had taken charge of Tottenham, I had met Glenn Hoddle's agent Dennis Roach there. Clough had suggested that Hoddle would be better off at Nottingham Forest and, provided there was a good financial package involved, Roach could not see any objections. Brian had asked Roach to investigate whether Tottenham would do a deal. I told him it was a complete non-starter.

Mark Arthur's suggestion was less outrageous. He simply explained that Forest were restructuring the club and could no longer afford to keep me on as a consultant. They had to rebuild. I admired his honesty. Calderwood, Davies and McClaren had all fallen short. With Nigel gone, subsequent appointments fared no better. Steve Cotterill, a bright, bouncy individual who had promoted Notts County to League One, took over. Forest avoided relegation in 2012 but, following the club's takeover by the Kuwaiti Al-Hasawi family, he left the City Ground in the summer. Sean O'Driscoll lasted five months; Alex McLeish, forty days.

The door was revolving fast and in February 2013, Billy Davies returned to the City Ground as manager of Nottingham Forest, where he still had many admirers among the supporters. His mantra was that Forest's failings had been down to Nigel Doughty. Once more, David Kelly was his assistant and Jim Price, who was to be struck off as a solicitor for financial mismanagement, was employed as chief executive. The finance director, the operations manager and the head of media were all sacked. The *Nottingham Post*, BBC Radio Nottingham and *The Guardian* were banned. Journalists were filmed during press conferences. One rival chief executive compared Forest to 'the Midlands version of North Korea'. I was pleased not to have been involved in Billy's second term.

Once more the chaos off the field outweighed progress on it, and in March 2014 Billy was sacked a second time. He has not worked in football since. By then Nigel Doughty had been dead for more than two years. One Saturday afternoon in February 2012, he collapsed and died in the gymnasium of his home. He was fifty-four. The irony that it was a Saturday afternoon struck me hard. He would far rather have been cheering on Nottingham Forest at the City Ground. At his memorial service in Westminster Abbey, I sat with the hierarchy of the Labour Party, led by Tony Blair. Later, there was a function in his memory near Grosvenor Square where Stevie Wonder flew over from America to entertain the guests. It was a lavish affair. Maureen and I sat on a table with Ed Balls, who was then shadow Chancellor, and his wife, Yvette Cooper, who was shadow Home Secretary. Ed had attended Nottingham High School and enjoyed football. They were warm and engaging company.

When I first met him, Nigel had asked me to look at the footballing ability of his son, Michael. He would have been in his early teens, schooled at Harrow and was playing for Chelsea under-14s. Nigel was a close friend of the Chelsea chairman, Bruce Buck, and wondered if his boy had the makings of a professional. I saw him play at left-back on an uneven pitch against Tottenham at Enfield, which would shortly be turned into Spurs' magnificent training facility. Michael Doughty was bang average and I told his father, as politely as I could, that his son needed greater mobility. I suggested agility exercises, hop-scotch, anything to improve the speed of his feet and his speed on the turn. He had a very good left-foot range.

Michael worked hard on his weaknesses and months later Nigel, perched on his shooting stick, and I watched him play for Queens Park Rangers under-16s against Brentford. The pitches at QPR's facilities at Harlington were poor, the noise of planes coming into land at Heathrow was incessant while the wind whipped across the ground. Michael had improved immeasurably. He took all the set-plays and drove balls long and wide with admirable accuracy. He was the captain, a natural leader. Alongside him was a small, mobile, sharp young forward called Raheem Sterling, who showed very little on the day. Nigel assured me he was an outstanding young player. Queens Park Rangers knew what they had, but Sterling was seduced away to Liverpool for £500,000. Without banning transfers of boys under eighteen, the smaller clubs can never be properly recompensed for the work they put in.

Michael left Harrow with ten GCSEs and four A-levels in Latin, French, Spanish and geography. All were A or A*. At the age of sixteen, he was considered good enough to sign with Queens Park Rangers, where he became a professional. He went on to play for Peterborough and Swindon. Against the odds, he had achieved a dream, one he would have longed to have shared with his father.

CHAPTER 30

'NO CHANCE, TRUST ME'

You meet many decent people on the scouting circuit. They are usually men who have played professionally and have kept their hand in the game. Some have had major positions in management while the majority are part of the dedicated flat-cap brigade, forever looking for that elusive gem.

Ian Broomfield had been a very promising youth-team player at Bristol City who had never quite made the grade. He had been George Graham's right-hand man at Leeds and was now working at Tottenham as their chief scout under Harry Redknapp. At the Football Writers' annual dinner, Ian suggested I should come and work for him as a scout.

I had known Harry for many years. When I was managing Luton, I went over to Watford to see them play West Ham in a reserve game. The seventeen-year-old Frank Lampard was playing for West Ham. He looked heavy and certainly did not seem quick. I would have worried about his shape, but Lampard possessed energy and had good technical skills. Frank Burrows was manager of Swansea and his assistant, Bobby Smith, phoned to say the club was on the lookout for a midfielder and did I know of anyone suitable? I told him that, although Lampard might look dumpy, he could cover a lot of ground, and in October 1995, Frank drove his blue Ford Fiesta from his home in Romford to south Wales. It was at the Vetch Field that Frank Lampard began his journey to become one of England's great midfielders.

Harry Redknapp was a man who never forgot. In 1997, when he was in charge of West Ham, he had asked my opinion of John Hartson, who was floundering at Arsenal after his transfer from Luton. He was also interested in Paul Kitson, who when I was at Filbert Street had been an outstanding talent in the Leicester youth teams. I told him both were young men who played without fear and could at times be over-physical, but they were good players. West Ham were third bottom when Hartson arrived from Arsenal and Kitson was signed from Newcastle in February. They did not lose another game at Upton Park and finished fourteenth.

I was working for Nottingham Forest when Ian Broomfield got in touch. I had been to Bramall Lane to watch Lee Johnson, a midfielder with Bristol City who had played in the 2008 play-off final against Hull and would be available for around £150,000. I did not think Lee was worth that to Forest, but Ian asked me what I thought of Sheffield United's full-backs, Kyle Naughton and Kyle Walker. Spurs signed them both. Walker became England's first-choice right-back.

In 2011, shortly after Steve McClaren and Nigel Doughty resigned at Nottingham Forest, I returned to Tottenham as a scout. The club had been on a rapid upswing under Harry's management.

Redknapp had taken over at White Hart Lane in October 2008 after Spurs had made a disastrous start under Juande Ramos, taking two points from their opening eight matches to leave them bottom of the Premier League. Gary Mabbutt and I spoke with Daniel Levy before he appointed Harry. Daniel would, of course, have consulted others. He was convinced that Redknapp, who had just taken Portsmouth to the FA Cup, was his man. Harry steered Tottenham away from relegation and took them to a League Cup final that was lost on penalties to Manchester United. By 2010, he had qualified them for the Champions League, which triggered heavy investment. He had a loyal backroom team ready to go, led by Kevin Bond, Joe Jordan and Tim Sherwood. Of those, Sherwood was forceful and unafraid to voice his opinions, which made him a good foil for Harry. Joe was affable but quiet while Kevin would agree with whatever was said.

Kevin's father, John Bond, had a reputation as a superb coach, particularly at Norwich. Kevin lived in Southampton while Harry lived nearby in Sandbanks. The two would share the driving. Harry rarely stayed overnight in London but would leave Dorset very early and have a half-hour nap at the training ground before starting work. Under his management Tottenham had abandoned the concept of a director of football.

Frank Arnesen had lasted only a year at White Hart Lane before joining Chelsea in 2005. When he left, after some chaotic recruitment, Daniel received considerable compensation from Stamford Bridge. Daniel asked for my opinion on a replacement. The shortlist included Guiliano Terraneo, a former goalkeeper who had worked with Lazio and Inter Milan. I recommended he sign Mark Wotte, who was Feyenoord's technical director. Daniel said immediately: 'No chance. Trust me.' I know now he did not want anyone who was too close to the manager, who was then Martin Jol. Wotte and Jol were great friends and had grown up in The Hague. Wotte would join Southampton and would briefly manage the club, though he was unable to prevent their relegation to League One. He became technical director of the Scottish FA.

Levy settled on Damien Comolli, who had been Arsenal's European scout and was now technical director of St Étienne. He would take plenty of credit for the signing of Gareth Bale, although Eddie Presland, who played cricket for Essex and football for Crystal Palace before becoming Tottenham's chief scout, was the most forceful mover in that transfer. Comolli also took the credit for the signing of Luka Modrić from Dinamo Zagreb. Comolli was well read, smartly turned out and spoke several languages. He relied heavily on statistics and was adept at cultivating friends in the boardroom. I met him several times at White Hart Lane, where Daniel Levy's wife, Tracy, would invariably sit us together. He was a gentleman.

Conversationally, we sparked off each other, but it was always my mindset that a director of football should not be watching his own team play too often. He should be away, looking at potential signings. Comolli, perhaps, did not think this was part of the job description. He did not survive Harry Redknapp's arrival at White Hart Lane. Harry was not the kind of manager who enjoyed the presence of a director of football. He wanted full control.

White Hart Lane had long been in thrall to its entertainers. It was Danny Blanchflower, the man who had captained the club to the Double in 1961, who had said:

> The great fallacy is that the game is about winning. It is about nothing of the kind. The game is about glory. It is about doing things in style and with a flourish. It is about going out and beating the lot, not waiting for them to die of boredom.

No words epitomised Spurs more than those. There had been occasional trophies, but the memory of the men who played with dreams of glory lingered longer – Ronnie Burgess, Eddie Baily, Blanchflower himself, Alan Gilzean, Ossie Ardiles, Glenn Hoddle, Chris Waddle, Paul Gascoigne, and David Ginola. Gareth Bale and Luka Modrić belonged in that company.

Small with wonderful balance, Modrić displayed great bravery on the ball and, like Hoddle, would accept a pass even when tightly marked. His great strength was his ability to resist the strongest of challenges. He could play short combination passes or deliver a longer ball with stunning accuracy. However, in January 2012 with Tottenham challenging the two Manchester clubs for the title, Harry and his chairman at Portsmouth, Milan Mandarić, were put on trial on charges of tax evasion. Tottenham, the former chairman Alan Sugar and the League Managers' Association lent their support, and both men were acquitted at Southwark Crown Court.

It was not the trial that undermined Redknapp's position with Daniel Levy, however, but his complete openness with the media. Fabio Capello had resigned as England manager and as soon as the not-guilty verdict was returned Harry became the clear favourite to take over. His agent, Phil Smith, was seeking an improved contract from Tottenham, helped by the speculation from the England press corps. Tottenham became irked by the fact that Harry refused to deny he was interested in the job. Although Spurs had finished fourth in 2012, Redknapp was sacked in the summer. Despite his interests in horse-racing and property and the fame he found as the winner of *I'm a Celebrity*, Harry was first and foremost a football man. In my time in the game, only Ron Atkinson could match Harry when it came to recalling events and players.

His replacement was André Villas-Boas, who had been a protégé of Bobby Robson's during his time at Porto and as manager at the Dragão Stadium had won four trophies in a single season. He had been appointed as Chelsea manager but lasted only eight months at Stamford Bridge. The team he left behind would beat Bayern Munich in their own stadium to win the European Cup a couple of months later.

Modrić was sold to Real Madrid for £33 million, the kind of money Tottenham could not turn down. Half the fee was spent on Mousa Dembélé from Fulham. The Belgian's ability to twist and turn and shield the ball in midfield was to become a major asset in Tottenham's play. He was never encouraged enough to surge forward and take shots at goal. However, as he won his midfield battles with his waspish left foot, songs about him began to be sung from the stands. The crowd loved him, but I considered there should have been a greater end product to his play – he rarely scored.

Villas-Boas's first season saw Spurs finish fifth, with Bale producing a dominant twenty-six goals from his fierce wing-play. He was a very quiet individual who had made no splash during his early days at White Hart Lane. I talked to him in the training-ground car park just as he was beginning to hit the big time. I told Gareth I had enjoyed watching him as an attacking full-back at Southampton and asked what his preferred position was. His response was almost inaudible. 'I don't mind.' He was completely unaffected by celebrity.

By now, I was becoming very familiar with Terminal Five at Heathrow, scuttling over to France, Holland and Germany to watch games. When he was in charge at Tottenham, George Graham would always use the short-term car park so he did not have to get on the shuttle bus to the terminal. I would have to deal with the receipts for the car park, which were usually around the £100 mark. I took the bus.

Tottenham had always enjoyed a close relationship with Ajax, a club that also had Jewish roots. Their old stadium, the De Meer, had been in Amsterdam's Jewish quarter and the Israeli flag was often flown or displayed there. That identity was diluted and arguably lost when they moved to the south-east of the city to the Amsterdam Arena, which was renamed after their greatest player, Johan Cruyff. Their academy, De Toekomst, had long been one of the finest in Europe and they had become specialists at recruiting talent from Asia and South America. They were also a selling club, epitomised by the young team that had won the European Cup in 1995 and then dazzled in Italy, Spain and England – Van der Sar, the De Boers, Rijkaard, Davids, Seedorf, Overmars and Kluivert.

I went to Amsterdam to watch a 21-year-old attacking midfielder named Christian Eriksen, who as a teenager growing up in Denmark had turned down offers from Barcelona, Real Madrid and Manchester United to learn his trade in Holland. Ajax were playing PSV Eindhoven, which was a match that decided titles in the

Eredivisie. The size of the crowd, plus a late request for a ticket, was probably the reason I was given such an awful seat, low down by the corner flag. Eriksen had talent but went missing for long periods of the contest. His skills were obvious, but his lack of involvement concerned me. On that evidence, I could not recommend him. In other games, I would watch him put a ball on the proverbial sixpence. When the time came to take the decision, I was not 100 per cent for Eriksen but, after much discussion, we resolved to spend £11 million on him. He matured well at White Hart Lane and was to become a major influence at the club.

Another trip to Amsterdam saw me join a bevy of scouts, nearly all of whose eyes were turned towards the left centre-back Jan Vertonghen. My report on Vertonghen said: 'He has an easy style, nice left foot. He is tall and not over-physical. He looks a leader.' We signed him in the Olympic summer of 2012. Arsenal had been strongly in contention and we had invited Jan to London to give him a tour of White Hart Lane and to meet the board. He brought his girlfriend, Sophia, who was to become his wife.

Arsenal had finished one place and one point ahead of Spurs, but I tactfully explained that in terms of the structure of the clubs, Arsenal were well ahead of us. 'Quite frankly, we are not yet up to Arsenal's standards,' I said. 'That does mean you will probably get less game time there. Here, barring injuries, you will be a regular.' I like to think that this twenty-minute chat helped influence his decision to sign for Tottenham.

Jan was one of the best professionals Tottenham ever had. He was polite, thoughtful and always willing to contribute to discussions, especially when it came to talking about young players who were making their mark in Holland and Belgium. He became the first Belgian international to win 100 caps, and in the summer of 2020, he left London for Lisbon to join Benfica.

In that same year, 2012, I was sent to Hamburg to watch a young

Korean forward called Son Heung-min. I made my way to the Volk-sparkstadion by train and tram and was soon in the midst of the Hamburg fans who were singing songs and swigging beer without seeming in the least bit drunk or threatening. It was hard to see what they were so excited about, since Hamburg were dreadful.

Frank Arnesen was now Hamburg's sporting director, a job he would leave at the end of the season. He was a man who always seemed to know how to land a big job. He was easy to talk to and had ingratiated himself with many leading agents, particularly his fellow Dane, Soren Lerby, whom he had known since he was a teenager. When he had taken over from me at Tottenham, he told me this would be his last job, since he was looking to retire to the villa he owned in Marbella. Then he was forty-eight. Arnesen, who had been a top player, particularly at Ajax, was a man who could never free himself from football. After leaving Hamburg, he went to Ukraine to work for Metalist Kharkiv, where he lasted a month before the civil war forced him out. Undeterred, Frank accepted jobs at PAOK Salonika, Anderlecht and Feyenoord.

The Sunderland chief scout Pop Robson, a fine forward for New-castle and West Ham, was also at the game looking at Paul Schar-ner, the Austrian defensive midfielder who had spent four years at Wigan. Sunderland passed on the opportunity to sign him and Scharner returned to Wigan, where he would win the FA Cup. If Hamburg were poor, Son was average, although I was told he was recovering from injury. My report was not positive, but Tottenham maintained their interest.

I was in the boardroom at White Hart Lane when the agent Leon Angel arrived with Son's representatives to meet Daniel Levy. They agreed a fee of £12 million. Donna Cullen, a Tottenham director, understood marketing opportunities and explained that the financial spin-offs in Asia from signing Son would be immense. The discussions fell through, however, and Son remained in Germany, signing for Bayer Leverkusen for £8.9 million. Leverkusen got value for their money. Son helped them qualify for the Champions League and when they sold him to Tottenham in the summer of 2015, the fee was £22 million, making him Asian football's most expensive player.

His start in London was tough, chiefly because Tottenham's new manager, Mauricio Pochettino, had difficulty finding him a place. There was also the question of his having to do national service in South Korea. It takes time for a player coming to the Premier League from outside Europe to assimilate. A quiet, intelligent man, Son broke through in the 2016/17 season, becoming a fabulous addition to Tottenham's forward line. In April 2020, he returned to Korea for national service, which he undertook on the beautiful southern island of Jeju. Of the 157 cadets, Son came top. Donna Cullen was correct in her original assessment of Son's commercial impact. Spurs have a sizeable Korean following and at matchdays outside the Tottenham Hotspur Stadium you can see big groups of them waiting just to catch a glimpse of their hero.

As they had done the season before, Arsenal pipped Tottenham to the fourth and final Champions League place in 2013. The rivalry meant that feelings of envy persisted among the supporters. The two sets of players, however, were often close friends. When I managed Tottenham in the 1986/87 season, the club was contacted by a horrified supporter saying he had seen Hoddle, Roberts and Miller having Sunday lunch in an Islington restaurant with Rix and Sansom. Years later, Serhiy Rebrov would invite me over to the house belonging to his great friend Oleg Luzhny, who was playing full-back for Arsenal. When I arrived at his home in Barnet, the conversation was dominated by talk of Arsène Wenger's training methods and those of the great Ukrainian coach Valeriy Lobanovskyi, a man with such authority that he made a point of never raising his voice to his players. I enjoyed these off-piste discussions.

There were, however, consequences of Tottenham's failure to make the Champions League. The rumours that Gareth Bale would be sold were becoming a crescendo. As the headlines quickened, I met the chairman at the training ground. I was aware Daniel had received what he called 'a staggering bid of £65 million' from Real Madrid. However, he insisted the club was determined not to buckle. A few weeks later, the bid had grown to £85m. Levy was still inclined to say no, but by then he was under great pressure from Bale's agents, Jonathan Barnett and David Manasseh. When Bale presented himself to the chairman and pleaded to be allowed to go to the Bernabéu, Daniel knew he could no longer hold the line. The fee was ten times what Spurs had paid for the Welshman. Southampton would have been entitled to a share of Real Madrid's money had they not sold their buy-out clause to us a couple of years before, after a shrewd intervention by Tottenham's finance director Matthew Collecott.

In September 2020, Bale would briefly return to Tottenham on loan after a fall-out with the management at Madrid. José Mourinho, who was then in charge at Spurs, did not immediately make a place for Bale in his team. However, when he did, the Welshman justified his selection. There was no chance of the loan being made permanent. Real Madrid had paid the vast bulk of Bale's wages during his brief return to north London and we could not have afforded them had we bought him back. His long-term fitness was also open to question. Collecott would manage the club's finances with considerable skill. When I asked how we managed to show such good financial figures at the end of a season, Matthew would reply: 'With great difficulty.'

From his base in the Bahamas, ENIC's owner, Joe Lewis, gave Daniel the signal to use this windfall to open the coffers at White Hart Lane. Three times in the summer of 2013, Tottenham broke their own transfer record. The money was not spent well. We finally took the decision to sign Eriksen for £11 million. His fee and the £30 million paid to Roma for Érik Lamela could be justified in retrospect. However, the £67.5 million spent on Paulinho, Nacer Chadli, Roberto Soldado, Étienne Capoué and Vlad Chiriches proved disastrous investments by the suave Italian Franco Baldini, the new director of football.

He had been Fabio Capello's No. 2 with England but had stayed in this country after Capello's resignation. When he was Capello's right-hand man, Baldini had proved himself a charming guest in the boardroom at White Hart Lane, never intimidated when guests and directors gave their forthright views on England's performances. He would spend hours on the phone with a stream of Italian coming from his office, where he often spent the rest of the day studying his computer. One thing Baldini rarely did as director of football was watch football matches away from Tottenham. Once when I asked how he was getting on with Daniel, he replied, not knowing my background: 'He's always with his agents and some of his Jewish friends.'

Selling Steven Caulker, a centre-half who had wasted his ability, to Cardiff and allowing Clint Dempsey, Jermain Defoe, Scott Parker and Tom Huddlestone to leave raised a further £29.5 million and ensured Tottenham made a profit in the summer. However, it demonstrated the folly of spending a windfall in a scattergun manner on half-a-dozen footballers to spread the risk to the senior team. I would always have spent that kind of money on two high-class players.

Tottenham would miss Bale badly and after a 5–0 defeat at home to Liverpool, for whom Raheem Sterling shone, Villas-Boas was sacked on 16 December. In football, there is a saying: 'The result is the only thing that matters; all the rest is gossip,' but relationships between the manager and some players had become strained to breaking point and beyond.

Tim Sherwood took over until the end of the season. He was a straightforward kind of man who did not like to overcomplicate matters. He won thirteen, drew three and lost six. Spurs were seventh when Tim took over and they finished sixth, ten points off a Champions League place. It was an improvement, but Tim never appeared to graduate from being a coach to having the stature and presence a manager requires. He did, however, have some success at Aston Villa, guiding them to an FA Cup final that was badly lost to Arsenal. He had hoped for a permanent deal at Spurs, but Tottenham already had their eye on the latest in a line of interesting, left-field managerial appointments made by Southampton: Mauricio Pochettino.

CHAPTER 31

'HE HAS A WONDERFUL CHANCE OF A TOP CAREER'

I was now spending some time at Milton Keynes watching a young midfielder I was increasingly convinced had the tools to play first-team football for Tottenham Hotspur. His name was Dele Alli. There is no better feeling among the cloth-capped scouting brigade when a footballer you have identified is transferred to your club. The delight when Ricky Hill and Brian Stein, men I had discovered in college and non-league football at Luton, won England caps is hard to describe. It is possibly only matched by seeing players you have worked with go on to become coaches and managers. Nowadays, attempting to persuade a Premier League club to take a prospect from the lower leagues is daunting. It is too often seen as a gamble. They tend to prefer talent from another Premier League academy. The golden signing is one who is spotted early in the lower leagues and is then transferred to a big club.

From my years at Luton, I had developed good relations with MK Dons. It was Christmas, a time when scouts never travel far from their homes. Milton Keynes was a relatively short drive up the M1 from my home in Hertfordshire. On the last Saturday of 2012, I went to Stadium MK to see them play Coventry. Ray Lewington's son Dean, who was to play 800 times for the Dons, was in his usual station at left-back. Coventry won, 3–2. Alli, who was making his first start for MK Dons, lasted seventy-one minutes before he was subbed. I wrote: 'He is seventeen, possibly sixteen [he was]. He looked nervous, is tall with a nice build with good energy. We must look again.'

I did not look at him again until August when he played in a 1–0 win over Crewe. I wrote:

He needs to come from deeper. He doesn't know the game yet but has a wonderful chance of a top career. He is 6ft 2in., an easy mover, not electric but covers the ground easily. He has good passing skills and is not selfish. He made the correct selections. He was played here linking to the front man, a boy called Bamford, on loan from Chelsea.

Patrick Bamford was to break through in the Premier League with Leeds. Patrick was a very intelligent boy and an outstanding young talent who had been best friends with Nigel Doughty's son Michael.

I continued: 'I know the Milton Keynes chairman, Peter Winkelman, very well. The player will not be sold this season. There were fifteen clubs scouting. Newcastle, Arsenal, Manchester City and Everton were all represented. Liverpool have already suggested £2 million. The chairman thinks he will get a better price. We must monitor this and make sure we offer the right price if and when we get the green light for availability.'

The report went to Tim Sherwood, Darren Eales, the club secretary, and Franco Baldini. Eales had joined Tottenham from West Bromwich Albion to replace John Alexander when he was recruited by Manchester United. I had met him at a tribunal when he was defending West Brom's troubled striker Lee Hughes on a disciplinary issue. Eales was a trained solicitor and his presentation was highly impressive. However, I always thought he lacked ruthlessness at key moments. Whenever we had a meeting about a transfer, I sometimes looked at Darren and thought of the phrase: 'My indecision is final.' His wife was American and in 2014 he joined Atlanta, a club he helped transform in the MLS. This gave him the platform to become Newcastle's chief executive in the wake of the Saudi Arabian takeover.

Whenever I sat with him, I always pushed the young midfielder from Milton Keynes, but I received little reaction. In September, I watched Alli at Ashton Gate against a strong Bristol City side, who would be promoted from League One with MK Dons. Alli played in a five-man midfield and Milton Keynes were two down within minutes. They lost 3–2. My report said:

> Alli is an easy mover who covers the ground. Is right-footed but will use his left. Competes in the air. Unselfish. Feel he could do more but restrains himself. A quiet game but will tackle back when necessary. Maybe we go for him in the January transfer window but competition will be intense and we must be careful not to get involved in an auction. Maybe an early take-it-or-leave-it figure with a loan-back agreement for the rest of the season might be the answer. Two years ago, I would have gambled £1.5 million. Now I genuinely believe it will take £3.5 million plus. Discussion urgently required.

In January the rumours swirled around Dele Alli. On the last Saturday of the transfer window, I was driving to Luton when Daniel Levy came on the phone. Alli's agent had told him they would be speaking to Aston Villa and Newcastle the next day. Milton Keynes had agreed a £5 million fee.

'What do you think?'

I gulped: 'Daniel, don't let this guy go. Pay the fee.'

'It's a lot of money for a League One player.'

'Don't worry. Pay it. Please.'

He told me Baldini had left me to make the call, as he had not seen enough of Dele Alli to make the judgement himself. I had actually taken Franco to watch Alli and he had spent most of the game on his phone.

Daniel got busy. The agent told him the boy would prefer Tottenham if it were a straight choice between the three clubs. The medical at Aston Villa was cancelled and Dele Alli signed for Spurs for £5 million, which would be paid in a single instalment. It also suited MK Dons that we agreed with their demand that Dele would be loaned back for the remainder of the season.

It later transpired that Karl Robinson, the Milton Keynes manager and a proud Scouser who had worked at the Liverpool academy, had taken Alli to meet the Liverpool management at a London hotel. Dele's hero as a boy had been Steven Gerrard. Peter Winkelman had found out about this clandestine meeting and had reminded his manager that Alli was under contract to Milton Keynes and no fee had been agreed with any club. He warned Robinson against any more freelance deals.

Scouting has changed. There are fewer former players scouring the motorway networks to watch games and more young analysts studying computer screens. The rage for statistics came from the United States. When in 1981 I loaned the Luton winger David Moss to Tampa Bay Rowdies, I was shocked before kick-off to be given a sheet of statistical information that included a list of which goalkeepers kicked the longest. Stats are vital to reinforcing your view of a player, but they should never be the main thrust of the deal. You need to watch a footballer live to get the full picture. His attitude in the warm-up might tell you something. How does he act when a teammate is on the ball? How does he react when possession is lost? Is he unselfish?

I am proud of the role I played in bringing Dele Alli to Tottenham. However, for every successful signing, there were several I missed. Everyone does. While I was in charge of Luton, the manager of Wealdstone, Ken Payne, suggested we had a good look at his left-back. His name was Stuart Pearce. I invited him up to train with our reserves for a week and afterwards I asked John Moore, who looked after the reserves, what his thoughts were. 'He did okay, but he was nothing special.' We never involved Pearce in a full eleven-a-side match so we could see his true qualities. That was my mistake. You will not find out about a player in five-a-sides or any amounts of drills. Had we played him in a full-sized game, we would have found out about Pearce's tackling, fierce left foot and ability to drive forward, not to mention his passion for the game. It was not a mistake the Coventry manager, Bobby Gould, was to make.

Some scouts can also watch a player too much. If your first impression is very good, I would see the target quickly afterwards, preferably away from home, for one further look. That should be enough to make a decision. If you watch a player too much, doubts can begin to intrude.

During my second spell in charge of Luton, I was watching a young striker from Baldock Town trialling for Watford in their reserve side. My immediate reaction was that Kevin Phillips was too small. One question I always asked myself when scouting was: 'Has this player got an outstanding quality?' Or is he, as one scout put it to me, 'an overround medium.' By that he meant a footballer who was okay at everything but not outstanding at anything. I thought Phillips fell into that category. However, he did enough for Glenn Roeder to sign him for Watford and in 2000, while at Sunderland, he won the Golden Shoe as the best goalscorer in Europe.

The temptation as a scout is often to slip away five minutes before the end to beat the traffic and because after eighty-five minutes you have usually seen enough to have made up your mind. When Jimmy Sirrel was managing Notts County, he told his coach, Colin Murphy, to go home and put on a suit because after training they would be driving to Scotland to watch a second-division player. After only fifteen minutes, Jimmy told Colin: 'Come on, we're going. I've seen enough. He's not for us.' They returned to Nottingham after a ten-hour round trip.

I was at Hayes, watching a young striker who had a good turn of speed but did not get overly involved. Then in the last minute, Cyrille Regis rose imperiously to rocket a header against the bar. I made a note that we must see him again, but I was already too late. West Bromwich Albion had come to Church Road in force, led by their manager, Ronnie Allen, and their chief scout, Roy Horobin, and they moved quickly. Regis was to become a legend at The Haw-thorns and an inspiration to young black footballers.

In 2004, when I was Tottenham's director of football, I trav-elled to Rotterdam to check out a young forward named Robin van Persie. Steve Stammers, a journalist with the London *Evening Standard*, had tipped me off about him and I decided to take a look for myself. Steve was a staunch Arsenal supporter, but his son was a Tottenham man. Steve told me that Arsenal had taken a look at Van Persie, who was leading Feyenoord's attack under the management of Ruud Gullit, but were not pursuing their interest because of his 'bad boy reputation'. His father was a sculptor and his mother was an artist. His upbringing had been Bohemian.

As I stood in the trophy room of Feyenoord's stadium, the De Kuip, I noticed Arrigo Sacchi, the man who had transformed AC Milan and was now also scouting. I knew who he would be looking at. Van Persie came on as a substitute, his socks rolled down, his shirt pulled out of his shorts, appearing dishevelled. He seemed un-interested. I could not recommend him to Tottenham. Weeks later, Steve Rowley, Arsenal's chief scout, made a big decision. Despite his reservations, Arsenal took a chance, signing him for £2.75 million, which was almost half the fee Feyenoord had been demanding. It was a gamble that was justified many times over.

Sometimes, you turn down a talent because you cannot see where they will fit in. In 1986, I was in my office at Tottenham when I was contacted by John Barnes's agent, Athole Still, who had been an international swimmer, an operatic tenor and was now doing deals in football. Barnes was at Watford, but Still suggested we could do a deal to take him to White Hart Lane. The fee would be £750,000. However, we already had Chris Waddle and I felt I might need the money for another signing. I let the deal pass. What an addition John Barnes would have made to the Tottenham team of that era.

CHAPTER 32

'I LIKE YOUR NO. 10'

It was a wild and windy Saturday morning at Tottenham's training ground in early 2013. The under-21s were playing Manchester United. As they trudged off the pitch at half-time, I spotted a man wrapped in a jacket and wearing a bobble hat emerging from the United dugout. I thought it might be the kit man or the bus driver. On closer inspection, it turned out to be Sir Alex Ferguson.

As we walked off for our half-time tea, I said to him: 'It's a difficult game in these conditions, but the truth is, Alex, there's no pathway for these boys.' He turned and replied with a hint of sarcasm: 'Aye, but there's always a pathway at Manchester United.' He was forever proud of how many products of the United academy ended up playing first-team football at Old Trafford. The side that was playing Spurs included Jesse Lingard, who three years later would score the winning goal in an FA Cup final.

That February day, Spurs won 3–1. Despite Ferguson's comment at the interval, more of that Tottenham side made it in the Premier League than the one Manchester United fielded. Of their side only the goalkeeper Sam Johnstone, who went on to play for Crystal Palace, would join Lingard in the big time. Jake Livermore, Tom Carroll and Kyle Naughton would all play first-team football at White Hart Lane. Jonathan Obika, who scored a hat-trick that day, did not make it in the Premier League but found success in Scottish football. It was none of those who caught Alex Ferguson's eye, however. He came over to me and said: 'I like your No. 10.' Our No. 10 was Harry Kane.

Although Alex would stand down as Manchester United manager three months later, he prompted his staff to delve into Kane's background. Had he remained, there might have been a serious attempt to take Harry, who was then nineteen, to Old Trafford. It would take United another ten years to put a deal together for Kane, who was sufficiently interested to ask agents to look for properties near Wilmslow, where many of Manchester's leading footballers live. That the deal broke down over £2 million worth of wages would leave Ferguson, now watching from the sidelines, furious.

I have been fortunate enough to see astute deep-lying centre-forwards, such as the Hungarian Nándor Hidegkuti, who helped destroy England at Wembley in 1953, and Alfredo Di Stéfano, who was part of the Real Madrid side that overcame Eintracht Frankfurt 7–3 in the 1960 European Cup final at Hampden Park. I also saw more orthodox centre-forwards who possessed goalscoring brilliance. Tommy Taylor's death in the Munich disaster meant the Manchester United forward never got the chance to fulfil his potential. However, Bolton's Nat Lofthouse – 'the Lion of Vienna' – Bobby Smith, who was Tottenham's leading scorer in their Double-winning season in 1960/61 and my own hero, John Charles, epitomised the powerful English centre-forward of the time. Later, Alan Shearer would come to symbolise what most people thought of as a centre-forward in the modern game. However, in my sixty years' obsession with football I have never seen anyone who has combined the gifts of playing as a deep-linking front man so intelligently with being a pure goalscorer as Harry Kane. His is a story of utter determination and dedication to his career.

It was while watching the academy that I first saw this big-boned boy, who seemed to have an almost telepathic understanding with Ryan Mason, a player who was to become a senior coach at the club but who was then Kane's strike partner. They were both local boys. Kane grew up in Chingford, while Mason, who was two years older, was from Enfield. They gelled wonderfully well. Mason would dummy over the ball and then spin while Kane would slip a perfectly weighted pass into his path. Harry's weight of pass and his accuracy was already catching people's attention.

Mason did not quite fulfil his promise at Spurs. He was perhaps too impatient, though he did play for England in a friendly in Turin in 2015, laying on the equaliser for Andros Townsend against Italy before leaving for Hull for £13 million in the summer of 2016. His career on Humberside would last only five months before it was ended by a dreadful clash of heads with the Chelsea defender Gary Cahill, which forced Mason's retirement. Mason then returned to Tottenham as a coach. He is now often consulted in the enquiries to determine the impact of heading a football on dementia. He would show real promise as a coach and managed the club in the League Cup final against Manchester City, following the dismissal of José Mourinho. Mason was in charge of Tottenham for four games, of which they won three. In the frenzied aftermath of Antonio Conte's dismissal in 2023, he was again asked to step up.

Kane worked closely with his coaches Alex Inglethorpe and Bradley Allen, who took numerous sessions encouraging Kane to shoot early. His right foot was then considerably better than his left, but it was his readiness to practise constantly that made him a genuinely two-footed forward. One afternoon, I asked our goalkeeper Brad Friedel who he thought was the best finisher at the club. Without hesitation, he replied: 'The young man Kane.'

By the time Alex and I watched him against Manchester United, Kane had already made his first-team debut for Tottenham in the Europa League, scoring his first goal for the club in Dublin in a 4–0 win over Shamrock Rovers. Given that his father was from Galway, this seemed appropriate. That goal came in December 2011 and the following month Harry Redknapp sent him on loan to Millwall alongside Ryan Mason and I was sent to monitor Kane's progress in south London. I wrote in my report:

> He has a good frame. Six foot and strong, he is difficult to knock off the ball. He played as a lead man with his back to goal to receive balls rather than run down channels. He showed good control and brought other players into the game. His movement in the penalty box was intelligent. The downside is that it looks as though he lacks agility and speed and I did not see any acceleration, although he is a strong runner. Overall, his performance was good.

This was Kane's second loan spell; the first had been at Leyton Orient. At both Brisbane Road and now at the New Den, he was facing hardened professionals. This was a useful apprenticeship after stepping up from academy football, where he had trained with some excellent young players such as Andros Townsend and Steve Caulker, who would be capped by England. Tim Sherwood, who was then Redknapp's first-team coach, was adamant that playing lower-league football was twice as beneficial as academy and friendly fixtures. At Orient, Kane had scored once in every three games.

He seemed less impressive in subsequent loan spells at Norwich and Leicester, where he spent some afternoons warming the bench. He picked up a metatarsal injury while at Carrow Road, but in a strange twist his rehabilitation and recovery, supervised by the Tottenham medical staff, had a notable effect. His running seemed less sluggish, while the gym work he had put in during his rehabilitation toughened him up. His main attribute had always been his ability to size up a situation quickly. He instinctively understood when and where to move. His eyes and brain worked simultaneously to make a move particularly in the box. He was generally able to react more quickly than his opponent who would know what to do but could not cope. It was a gift.

By April 2014, Tim Sherwood was in charge at White Hart Lane and gave Kane his first Premier League start against Sunderland. He scored in a 5–1 win and in the next two matches after that. However, Tim had a decision to make. Emmanuel Adebayor was nearing the end of his time as Tottenham's leading striker. Shortly after he became manager, Sherwood was presented with a proposal that Spurs should attempt to take Álvaro Morata, who was expressing dissatisfaction with the amount of game time Carlo Ancelotti was giving him at Real Madrid. Sherwood, however, thought that in Kane he already possessed exactly the kind of striker Tottenham required.

Harry blended perfectly into first-team football. He would learn when to overload in central areas of the pitch – to make a 3v2 or a 4v3 – and find space to score. He perfected the ability of shooting one touch without hesitation, giving the goalkeeper little chance to balance himself. He had by now improved his heading ability; he was able to jump early and almost hang in the air to reach a driven cross. Most of his goals would come from cutting in from either flank and assessing the angles between the goalkeeper and back post to perfection. His work on becoming completely two-footed meant he did not have to take that extra touch.

The forward triangle of Kane, Christian Eriksen and Dele Alli thrived as the fulcrum of the team that would finish third in 2018 and reach the Champions League final the following year. However, once Eriksen left for Inter Milan in 2020, Dele became less effective. By then, Son Heung-min had developed into a remarkable foil for a man who was now captain of Tottenham and England.

Lucrative endorsement deals started rolling in for Kane, from Coca-Cola to BT Sports. An articulate family man who did not touch alcohol during a football season, he was an advertiser's dream. When talking to Harry Kane, you meet a polite, unassuming person who always seems interested in what you have to say. As well as his enormous ability, it was this approachability, the fact that he was a local boy – he went to the same school in Chingford as another England captain, David Beckham – that made Kane adored by Spurs fans.

This relationship was to come under severe strain in the summer of 2021, when Kane made a botched attempt to leave. He had finished the season not only as the Premier League's leading scorer but as the player with the greatest number of assists. He had captained England to the final of the European Championship. Tottenham had not only finished seventh, but they were also managerless following the sacking of José Mourinho. He suggested that Daniel Levy had given him the green light to find another club. This was disputed and Harry was ill-advised to stay away from training, although he argued he had permission to delay his return to Tottenham. Kane was in a different situation than Sol Campbell had been two decades before. Both Alan Sugar and I had been desperately disappointed when Sol went to Arsenal, but the player was out of contract. It was entirely up to him where he went and we could not persuade him to stay. Kane had three years remaining on the most lucrative deal Tottenham had ever offered a footballer.

Harry's problem was that his brother Charlie, who was now his agent, had no experience of negotiating a transfer deal. Rather recklessly, he mentioned at a gathering that his brother was interested in a move to Manchester City. It followed an increasing pattern in the game: that of leading players being represented by a family member. Neymar, Lionel Messi, Eden Hazard, Juan Mata and Jesse Lingard employ their fathers as their agent. A parental relationship ensures the agent will always have the player's best interests at heart, but some professional agents feel that a relative is often naive in their dealings with the club or the media. Tottenham felt Charlie Kane was reckless in his approach to the transfer. As soon as Harry remarked in an unnecessary and suspiciously timed Sky interview with Gary Neville that Kevin De Bruyne would make a good team-mate, the respect between player and club began to unravel.

In past seasons, Teddy Sheringham, Michael Carrick, Dimitar Berbatov and Kyle Walker had all thought Manchester would give them a greater stage than could be found at Tottenham. However, when Walker demanded to leave, he was certain it would be backed by an offer from Manchester City. The difference with Kane was that Manchester City never made a written or verbal offer to Daniel Levy. City presumably encouraged Kane to attempt to leave Spurs but gave him no support when the story broke. In Daniel's view, City had 'hung Harry out to dry'. Their focus was soon elsewhere.

That same summer, Aston Villa were faced with a bid for Jack Grealish. Like Harry Kane, Grealish was an academy product who was now club captain and who had enjoyed a successful European Championship. When Manchester City met the £100 million release clause in Grealish's contract, Villa had no option but to do a deal. Daniel Levy knew that every footballer has his price. The £150 million that was quoted as the sum Manchester City were prepared to pay for Harry Kane was the press price. Tottenham were never given the opportunity to negotiate over it.

When media speculation over Kane's transfer reached its peak, I suggested we should take two graduates of the Manchester City academy as part of the deal. One was Liam Delap, a striker and the son of Rory Delap, who had enjoyed considerable success with Southampton and Stoke in the Premier League. The other was Cole Palmer, an attacking midfielder who was to make his England under-21 debut that summer and would be sold to Chelsea. There was never an opportunity to discuss those two moves because Kane's transfer to the Etihad Stadium never reached that stage.

When Kane issued a statement saying he was staying at Spurs, it was depicted as a victory for Levy, who was portrayed in the press as a master negotiator. Daniel is a wise and cautious chairman who has proved himself an exceptional custodian of Tottenham's interests, but he is no tougher than many chairmen I have worked with. The fact that Daniel very rarely gives interviews and never uses the media to deny speculative pieces makes him appear harder than he is. Levy has always understood that top clubs do not tout in the press for business. They keep their counsel.

There was a statement of reconciliation from Kane and he was swiftly forgiven. Goalscoring records continued to tumble, but the fall of Antonio Conte emphasised that the gap between the management, the board, the senior players and the academy had become unbridgeable. Kane was approaching his thirtieth birthday and playing for a side that had finished eighth. A friendly against Shakhtar Donetsk on 6 August 2023 was to be his last appearance for Tottenham. He scored four times in a 5–1 win. The £86 million deal to take him to Bayern Munich, who had pursued him all summer, had not been announced. However, the way in which he walked around the pitch on the final whistle, accompanied by his wife and three children, was a sign he was saying goodbye. The way he took his leave befitted a man whose desire to move to new fields was understood by nearly all who applauded him.

CHAPTER 33

'HAVE YOU THOUGHT ABOUT THIS?'

The more time I spent at Tottenham's magnificent new training ground assessing young players, the more I sensed the language of football had changed. Phrases like 'circulate the ball', 'get the block on', 'break the lines', 'find the pockets of space', 'lock on', 'corridor of uncertainty' were all bellowed out across the pitches at Enfield.

I never quite understood why so many coaches felt the need to re-invent the game. Ron Greenwood once said of football that simplicity is genius. Brian Clough rarely took a training session, but his message in the dressing room was always that football is a simple game.

When I became a Football League manager in 1978, Charlie Hughes had been a successful coach of the England Amateur team, which led to his appointment as the FA's director of coaching. Hughes believed in direct play. His analysis had shown that the majority of goals came from moves involving three passes or fewer. The more quickly the ball could be moved up the pitch, the more successful a team would be. Long passes delivered quickly to forwards running into channels would force defenders to turn and face their own goal. This became known as POMO – the position of maximum opportunity – the area at the back post, where you would receive an early cross. His work had been based on that of Charles Reep, an RAF wing commander who had heavily influenced the Wolverhampton Wanderers' manager Stan Cullis. When in December 1954 Wolves beat Honvéd, the great Hungarian passing team captained by Ferenc Puskás, Reep's ideas appeared to be vindicated. The fact that before kick-off, the Wolves groundstaff boys, including a young Ron Atkinson, had turned hosepipes on to the Molineux pitch to make it as hard as possible to pass a football went unacknowledged.

The rise of the great passing teams, first at Tottenham in 1961 and then at Manchester United and Liverpool under Matt Busby and Bill Shankly, sent Reep's ideas into the wilderness. Nevertheless, a generation later, they were back in favour, with Charles Hughes demanding the ball be delivered quickly. I found it a slightly alien philosophy. Terry Venables accused Graham Taylor of putting back football ten years with these tactics. However, it remains a fact that Watford enjoyed their greatest days under Graham and that Ireland qualified for the first two World Cups in their history with Jack Charlton insisting the ball be thrust forward.

Howard Wilkinson briefly enjoyed success with it, although by the time Howard won the title with Leeds in 1992 he had adapted his tactics considerably, using Gordon Strachan and Gary McAllister to link the team together. Neil Warnock promoted eight clubs, more than any other English manager, with aggressive forward tactics, a philosophy Hughes would have applauded. However, Warnock's stats rarely refer to his relegations – he failed to keep any of his promoted teams in the top flight, mainly because amid the euphoria of promotion, he would overspend, with his club suffering the consequences.

When I worked with him at Luton, Danny Bergara was a man who loved intricate football. He could demonstrate any football skill with aplomb and I learned plenty from him. However, by the time he was manager of Stockport in the early 1990s, Danny had gone the other way. His attack was led by the 6ft 7in. striker Kevin Francis, and he explained to me that his squad was simply not good enough to pass their way up the pitch. I understood. The ball had to be hit long to Francis. My argument was that, if everyone played similarly, the public would simply abandon the game. Spectators like to see clever football, passing movements, patterns and dribbling rather than athletic running and balls pumped high into the sky. Great players adjust, knowing when to play short and when to go long.

At Luton, I played 'shadow football' in training. Starting with the goalkeeper, we would move the ball forward until there was a shot at goal. There would be no opposition. The important factor was the choice of pass and of positioning. Brian Horton, who joined Luton in 1981, said he had never before experienced shadow-play and he had made his league debut eleven years previously. The players would be asked to do their warm-ups in the positions they would take on the field. An onlooker would see forwards running towards an imaginary ball, then sprinting away and changing direction, passing, shooting and heading without the ball. It sounds crazy, but it worked.

Teaching is an art. I learned most from men like Joe Mallett and Gordon Lee, who were not great footballers. It was no coincidence that the best goalkeeping coach I employed, Bob Wilson, who spent time with me at Luton, had a strong educational background.

Much which seems new has been done before. During England's campaign at Euro '96, Terry Venables was praised for his inventive 'Christmas tree formation', which employed the 4–5–1 formation I had used at Tottenham a decade before. When Malcolm Allison became manager of Plymouth in 1978, he occasionally played without a recognised striker. The centre-backs were suddenly uncertain of who and where to mark. It was a very short step from this to the false nine employed by Pep Guardiola when he managed Barcelona. Malcolm, one of the most innovative coaches England has produced, was himself borrowing from the Hungarian teams of the 1950s. They had not even been the first to attempt the tactic – that was the Austrian *Wunderteam* that had been favourites to win the 1938 World Cup until Austria was swallowed up by the Third Reich.

One of the yearly delights was the managers' get-together for senior coaches at Lilleshall, where ideas would be exchanged and lectures and demonstrations given. Whether speaking or running a course, Malcolm Allison was always an impressive speaker. He stood 6ft 3in., a handsome, charismatic man who could hold an audience spellbound. He could talk, he could teach, and he could make you believe. When Allison turned up for one session at Lilleshall, there was much speculation in the press he was about to accept a highly lucrative position in Saudi Arabia. On a hot June day, Malcolm was taking a session on how to play a second half when you are two goals down, having had a man sent off. It was based on a scenario he had encountered while playing for Charlton.

As we worked, a long black limousine parked up alongside the pavilion about eighty yards from the pitch. Out got a man in flowing robes. Alan Wade, the director of coaching, decided to halt the session for a tea-break while Malcolm strode over towards the limousine, chest out, arms pumping. He shook hands with the sheikh, who tore off his robes to reveal himself as Graham Williams, the former West Bromwich Albion full-back.

Williams was one of the many experienced coaches on that annual summer refresher course. I was one of the youngest, if not the youngest, and had qualified for my full coaching certificate in 1977. I was the only Jewish coach on the course. One evening after a lecture, my ears pricked when I overheard Ian Greaves, who was then manager of Bolton, say to Howard Kendall: 'I am certain he is a four by two, you know.' I pretended not to hear. Overall, I was accepted within the group and I have to say no coach in my career showed outward signs of antisemitism.

One of the jobs of a coach is to allow the players to take responsibility and be involved in the tactical decisions. The Arsenal manager Don Howe was a thoughtful, studious man who, if challenged on a tactical point, might say: 'Have you thought about this?' It was a phrase that resonated with me and was one I employed.

During the European Championships in Portugal in 2004, I found myself sharing a table with my fellow ITV pundits, Ruud Gullit and Terry Venables. Over a lunch of sardines, steak and sangria, Ruud told Terry it was the Dutch players themselves who had come up with the idea of Total Football, where players would rotate positions during a match. He suggested Rinus Michels, who managed Holland to the 1974 World Cup final, where the words 'total football' entered the dictionary, had little to do with it. Terry argued that something as radical as this could only have been imposed by the coach. However, Ruud, who was part of the Holland side that Michels managed to the European Championship title in 1988, was adamant it had been a bottom-up movement.

In May 2014, Mauricio Pochettino became Tottenham's tenth manager in a dozen years. The chairman, Daniel Levy, had told him I knew a lot about the club's young players and he should ask me about them. Mauricio invited me into his office where he had clips of various players on a computer screen. He was charming, easy to talk to and was interested in my own career. I broke the ice by telling him I had a long-time friend, a Spanish travel agent in Maida Vale, who was a Luton supporter and had been a passionate fan of Espanyol, the club where Pochettino had made his managerial reputation.

Pochettino asked me which young players I liked. I mentioned Miloš Veljković, a smooth centre-half whom we had signed from Basel but who lacked real pace. Another was Tom Carroll, an England under-21 midfielder. Mauricio asked what I made of Josh Onomah, a seventeen-year-old forward whom he liked very much. I replied I had not seen enough to make a definitive judgement.

Veljković did not make the grade and was sold to Werder Bremen for £260,000. Carroll was sent on a season-long loan to Swansea and was eventually sold to the Welsh club for £4.5 million. Onomah would go to Fulham as part of the deal that took Ryan Sessegnon to

Spurs, which valued Josh at £8 million. Veljković would represent Serbia in two World Cups; Carroll and Onomah played for England at under-21 level. Retrospectively, it proves just how high the standards had risen in the Premier League.

Pochettino brought a tight group with him from Southampton. Jesús Pérez was his assistant and right-hand man, who attended press conferences with him. Pérez had worked with John Toshack as a fitness instructor at Murcia before joining Pochettino at Espanyol and Southampton. Michel D'Agostino, a fellow Argentinian who had played with Pochettino under Marcelo Bielsa at Newell's Old Boys, was first-team coach whose powerful frame disguised a friendly conversationalist. Toni Jiménez, who had played with Pochettino at Espanyol and worked with him throughout his managerial career, was the goalkeeping coach. They were men who had been with Pochettino over several years and would join him when he took over at Paris St Germain in January 2021 and return to England with him when Pochettino became manager of Chelsea two years later. They were a closed group who would have their meals together in a small round table in the canteen.

One person allowed into their circle was Ossie Ardiles, a man whose football had lit up White Hart Lane and who had stayed on in England after he was dismissed as manager in 1994. Whether living in Hertfordshire or in his magnificent white three-storey villa in Marbella, his great passion had become golf and his popularity meant he was employed by the club to meet and greet box-holders during home matches.

The highlight of Pochettino's first season was the 5–3 win over Chelsea on New Year's Day. Marked by John Terry, Harry Kane, who was emerging as a golden talent, scored twice. However, when Eden Hazard found the net to make it 4–2 with half an hour remaining, a tremor went round White Hart Lane. Would Tottenham throw away another big advantage? Would they once more be 'Spursy'?

This, however, was a far tougher team and Nacer Chadli put away the fifth.

This was a satisfying victory because by now Chelsea were rivalling Arsenal as our most disliked opponent. The rivalry with Arsenal was built on history and geography. Chelsea represented something different. There were the results that saw Tottenham win one game in thirty-eight attempts against them between 1988 and 2006. There were the barbed comments made by the chairman, Ken Bates. Stamford Bridge was also home to a section of right-wing support whose views were sometimes openly antisemitic.

Over the years, I have been on the rough end of antisemitism, but I kept it low key. Once, over a period of three years, I received some horrible telephone messages and was suspicious my phone was bugged. Several years later, during the phone-hacking scandal, I was told by the Metropolitan Police that a journalist from the *Sunday Mirror* had a list of various numbers that had been hacked and mine was among them. I was not surprised.

In March, we met Chelsea in the League Cup final, but once more the run that had seen the club win a single piece of silverware since the turn of the century continued. One goal from John Terry and another, put through his own net by Kyle Walker, settled matters. Chelsea, under José Mourinho, would win the Premier League in 2015. Pochettino's first season saw him finish fifth, but there was plenty to build on. Walker, Rose, Vertonghen and Dier had provided solidity; Chadli and Eriksen, the midfield flair. Kane had scored thirty-one goals.

One of the players who might have been part of that side was the Brazilian forward Willian. We had tried to buy him in the summer of 2013. He had joined Anzhi Makhachkala, a club based in a remote, war-torn area of southern Russia called Dagestan. Its chief attractions were the enormous salaries paid by its owner,

Suleiman Kerimov, and the bonus that the squad lived and trained in Moscow and was only flown down to Makhachkala, on the shores of the Caspian Sea, on match days. However, in 2013 after a high-powered team managed by Guus Hiddink had failed to win the Russian League, Kerimov imposed savage cuts in the Anzhi budget. The stars, including Samuel Eto'o, who was sold to Chelsea, were disposed of. Willian was also transfer listed.

Anzhi accepted Tottenham's fee and he was brought to London for a medical. It was then that Chelsea intervened. They contacted the player's agent and at the last minute made him a more attractive offer. However, they still needed a work permit and, although I worked for Tottenham, I was part of the permit panel that heard the case. Usually, these panels would have a representative from the Home Office, the Professional Footballers' Association and the League Managers' Association and would have an FA chairman.

They would be shown details of the proposed contract, a film of the player's abilities and a statement from the manager or the club secretary. The decision from the panel had to be unanimous. The Home Office representative often had little knowledge of the game and would sometimes be very impressed if the manager presented the club's case, especially if he were a big name. José Mourinho, who had just rejoined Chelsea from Real Madrid, was certainly that.

The permits were for players who did not hold a European Union passport. To qualify for a permit, the player would have needed to have played 80 per cent of their country's competitive internationals over the past two years. The panel was for players who did not meet this criterion. I asked José why Willian had only played two games for Brazil. 'You obviously don't know the Brazilian scene,' said Mourinho, smooth and smiling. 'They seldom consider footballers who play in eastern Europe. They are focused on those who play in the big European leagues.' This was Mourinho on duty, bright as a button and charming. To speak five languages as he does, you need to be able to learn and process knowledge quickly and José is often at his best in situations such as these.

Willian was given his permit, partly because Chelsea agreed to pay him £150,000 a week, which would put him among the top earners at Stamford Bridge. It was a condition that, if he were given a permit, Willian's wages had to be commensurate with his presumed status as an outstanding international.

The year before, I had been part of another permit panel that investigated an application from Nottingham Forest, whose owner Fawaz Al Hasawi had been refused permission to sign a goalkeeper from his home city of Kuwait. Forest sent their acting chairman, Frank Clark, their chief executive, Mark Arthur, and their manager, Sean O'Driscoll, to plead the case for Khaled Al Rashidi. Only Mark Arthur made the case for Al Rashidi while Frank and Sean, who did not really want the keeper because he was not good enough, kept shtum. Nottingham Forest lost the case but won on an appeal. By then O'Driscoll had left, sacked by Al Hawasi hours after a 4–2 win over Leeds. Al Rashidi spent a year at the City Ground, where he did not play a single league game.

Graham Taylor had advised me not to become involved with disciplinary panels, saying I would quickly turn friends into enemies. I was not too concerned about this. However, one of my most high-profile cases would bring me into direct conflict with Sir Alex Ferguson. In April 2008, Manchester United had been beaten 2–1 at Chelsea. After the game, Patrice Evra, who was doing warm-down exercises on the pitch, became involved in an altercation with Sam Bethell, the groundsman at Stamford Bridge. The pair had to be separated and both were charged by the FA with improper conduct. Evra accused Bethell of using racist language against him.

I was part of the panel assembled at the FA headquarters at Soho Square to judge the case. Manchester United were represented by

Maurice Watkins, a lawyer who had been a member of the board at Old Trafford since 1984 and who had organised Eric Cantona's defence when he leapt into the crowd at Selhurst Park. Chelsea employed Jim Sturman, a leading sports lawyer and Tottenham fan, who regularly appeared on their behalf. Sturman was well paid and earned his money. He was a brilliant cross-examiner, something Manchester United's assistant manager, Mike Phelan, and their fitness coach, Tony Strudwick, were to discover to their cost. To my astonishment, Chelsea employed as many as fifteen groundsmen, some of whom came to give evidence in defence of Bethell, who had been angered when Evra and other Manchester United players warmed down on an area of the pitch they had been working on. Dressed smartly, they made a strong impression.

Evra was given a four-match ban and a fine of £15,000. When Ferguson discovered I had been on the panel, he contacted me. Initially, he was quite aggressive. His wrath was focused on the chairman of the panel, Nicholas Stewart, a barrister specialising in human rights. Ferguson had found out Stewart was an Arsenal supporter and felt his judgement was biased. At the time of the tribunal, Alex was still locked in a bitter rivalry with Arsène Wenger.

It was to develop into a friendship, but in 2008 the dislike of Wenger was still there. Ferguson was a man who had been slow to appreciate the rise of the foreign manager. He believed they stifled British talent in the Premier League. That the chairman of the panel was a fan of a rival club was a far-fetched argument but one that was typical of Alex. He always knew which clubs people supported. Once, in his office after a game, I mentioned I had been told that the referee, Dermot Gallagher, was a Manchester United fan and had also been informed he had a United tattoo. Immediately, Alex replied: 'You're wrong; that's his brother.'

CHAPTER 34

'GLORY, GLORY, HALLELUJAH'

The Tottenham High Road swarmed with construction workers as a new White Hart Lane emerged beneath the cranes that filled the skyline. Daniel Levy had worked prodigiously hard to give Spurs what they wanted – a stadium that would allow them to compete financially while keeping the club rooted in N17. The stadium would stand alongside the new training ground in Enfield as his legacy.

The academy system was changing, and like all changes from the abolition of the maximum wage in 1961 and the decision to stop sharing gate receipts to the Bosman Ruling and the setting up of the Premier League itself, it benefited the bigger clubs. The best academies employed increasing numbers of staff, boasted superlative facilities and offered high standards of coaching. The top category-A academies had to have an indoor centre, and those in the Champions League also played regular fixtures against the youth teams of their opponents.

The increasing costs of running an academy was offset by selling the graduates on. Between 2014 and 2017, the Big Six clubs – Manchester United, Manchester City, Liverpool, Arsenal, Spurs and Chelsea – sold a combined sixty-five academy products who had not played a first-team fixture, raising £65 million. Among them was Jadon Sancho, sold by Manchester City to Borussia Dortmund for £8 million. Dortmund would sell him to Manchester United for £73 million.

Tottenham had no choice but to build a new stadium. Although media income was worth around 60 per cent of the club's revenues, match receipts on gates of 35,000 were way short of what Manchester United and Arsenal could command. The club had formed strong links with the NFL and were hopeful of staging American football at the new ground. It was a strange feeling, peering down from the fourth-floor boardroom at White Hart Lane to the new arena taking shape alongside the stadium that had been Tottenham's home since 1899.

By the summer of 2015, Mauricio Pochettino appeared to have made up his mind about a swathe of players. Aaron Lennon, Lewis Holtby, Roberto Soldado, Étienne Capoué, Younes Kaboul, Vladimir Chiriches all left for a combined fee of £33 million. Andros Townsend, an academy product, was frozen out and left for Newcastle in January for £12 million. Mauricio's philosophy often left little room for wingers. The money was spent on players Tottenham had been interested in before – Toby Alderweireld and Son Heung-min.

Tottenham finished third, their best league performance for more than a quarter of a century, although all the headlines were taken by Leicester City, quoted as 5,000–1 outsiders at the start of the season, breaking the monopoly of the Big Six and winning the Premier League. They did so on 2 May when Tottenham, the one club that could have gate-crashed the fairy tale, failed to beat Chelsea at White Hart Lane. Chelsea had played on their rivalry with Spurs and the fact that their former manager, Claudio Ranieri, was at the helm at Leicester City. They publicly promised Ranieri they would do their utmost to stop us and second-half goals from Gary Cahill and Eden Hazard forced the 2–2 draw that made it mathematically impossible we could catch the unlikely lads from the Midlands. It was a spiteful game in which referee Mark Clattenburg showed twelve yellow cards, which equalled the record for the most bookings in a Premier League game.

Pochettino had, nevertheless, firmly established himself at the club. His elder son worked in the sports science department while his younger son, a forceful outside-right, played in the academy. Only Manchester City had scored more goals; only Manchester United had conceded as few. The team was an exciting one. The future beckoned.

The task I had set myself was to find a new Dele Alli, although this was becoming more difficult. Lower-league managers, whose jobs were becoming increasingly insecure, were reluctant to put their faith in young players. Each pre-season there seemed to be a host of 'old sweats' seeking employment and being swapped around by managers in Leagues One and Two, who with an average lifespan of two years needed success today rather than tomorrow. There was no time to build a team or leave a legacy.

Peter Taylor once told me: 'You cannot succeed without chimney pots.' What he meant was you need a substantial fanbase to survive and attendances in the lower leagues were being eroded. You need fans, the lifeblood of the game, and Tottenham's new stadium, with all its attractions, will keep bringing supporters in.

It was now the academies of the Premier League and Championship clubs where young talent was nurtured. One evening I was watching an under-18 game at Loftus Road. Steven Pressley, Coventry's manager, sat in a deserted directors' box berating the referee and his players. The Queens Park Rangers manager, Harry Redknapp, with his assistants, Joe Jordan and Kevin Bond, were watching from a sponsor's box.

One player took the eye. Coventry's No. 10, James Maddison, stood out from all around him. He was so good that Tottenham could have done a deal there and then. Maddison had no agent. Coventry had been relegated to League One. It was an open goal. I rang Kirk Stephens, my old full-back at Luton who now lived in Nuneaton and was a matchday host at Coventry's new ground, the Ricoh Arena (it has since been renamed the Coventry Building Society Arena). He knew everyone there and gave me a glowing reference. I contacted Paul Mitchell, Tottenham's head of recruitment, and urged him to do the deal.

Mitchell moved so slowly that he might have been outmanoeuvred by a tortoise. Maddison signed up with the Base Agency and very quickly a number of clubs began to take notice of his potential. In February 2016, Maddison was signed by Norwich for £3 million. In the summer of 2018, aged twenty-one, Leicester paid Norwich eight times what they had paid Coventry and he became a mainstay of the exciting side built by Brendan Rodgers. After Leicester's relegation in 2023, Tottenham finally bought James Maddison. The cost was £40 million.

As a Grecian old boy, I had always followed Exeter's progress and was friendly with their manager Paul Tisdale and their director of football Steve Perryman. There, I had watched Ollie Watkins, a nineteen-year-old box-to-box midfielder who scored goals. All my contacts in the lower leagues concurred that Watkins was the most promising player in League Two. I began scouting Watkins and Steve Perryman confided he had fantastic statistics in terms of stamina and high-intensity runs and was a good guy off the field. The fee, Steve told me, would be about £750,000.

I knew Steve well enough to ask what the downside to Ollie Watkins might be. He told me that Ollie, who had grown up in Newton Abbot on the south Devon coast, was very much a West Country boy. Would he be able to cope with a big London club? I was unable to get Tottenham to green light the deal. Other scouts employed by Spurs had seen weaknesses in his game. I argued in vain that Watkins could be signed and then loaned back to Exeter. Mauricio Pochettino studied videos of him but decided to leave alone. I accepted his judgement. He was the manager.

In July 2017, Dean Smith paid £1.8 million to take Watkins to Brentford. At Griffin Park, he had occasional quality games from wide left and midfield. However, it was not until he was converted into a striker by Smith's successor, Thomas Frank, that Watkins truly blossomed, scoring twenty-six goals in the 2019/20 season that saw Brentford beaten in the play-off final by Fulham. It was quite a tactical hunch by Frank, because in the 2017 League Two play-off final, Exeter had experimented with Watkins as a striker. He had played poorly and Blackpool had won.

Shortly afterwards, Smith, now managing Aston Villa, paid £28 million for Watkins. I had mixed feelings about the deal. I would have liked Watkins to come to Tottenham, but I had recommended him as a midfielder and it was not until he made the switch to centre-forward at Brentford that the case for him became irresistible. When José Mourinho succeeded Pochettino, he rang to ask my thoughts on Watkins. I strongly suggested he would be excellent cover for Harry Kane and, if he was not up to the standard required, he could be sold for a small loss. However, the price deterred Mourinho and he decided to take Carlos Vinícius from Benfica for a small loan fee. I understood. He was the manager. Watkins proved to be an excellent signing – for Aston Villa. That is the frustration of scouting.

Tottenham's final season at White Hart Lane would see them play their European fixtures at Wembley, ensuring that an average of 77,500 saw their three group games in the Champions League. They said farewell to White Hart Lane by not losing a home game in the league for the first time since 1964/65. Although both seasons climaxed with Spurs putting six goals past Leicester, they are hardly comparable. In 1965, Bill Nicholson's side finished sixth, having lost sixteen of their twenty-one away games. Now Mauricio Pochettino steered Spurs to second – their best finish for fifty-four years.

The achievement was in spite of the fact that the summer signings – Vincent Janssen, Georges-Kevin Nkoudou and Moussa Sissoko – did not prove successful. Sissoko, who arrived from Newcastle, failed miserably to justify his £30 million fee in his first season in

London, making just four appearances in the league between October and May. To his immense credit, the Frenchman rallied and had an excellent second season, forceful in the tackle and showing immense energy on the ball. Sissoko is proof that, if you accept the bad times, you can work to change people's perceptions.

It was remarkable that, having seen each one of his summer signings falter, Pochettino should have taken Tottenham to second in the league for the first time since 1963. Dele Alli had his finest season at Tottenham, scoring twenty-two goals, Son Heung-min hit twenty while Harry Kane, now captain of England, struck thirty-five in thirty-eight matches. By the end of the season, no team had scored more goals and no team had conceded fewer. The season finished with Kane scoring four in a 6–1 rout of Leicester and three in a 7–1 demolition of Hull. The title, however, went to Chelsea, who also knocked us out of the FA Cup at Wembley in the semi-finals.

There are any number of adjectives that could be used to describe a game that for emotion alone would eclipse all others that season – the farewell to White Hart Lane. Tottenham Hotspur would play Manchester United. Invitations were sent to ex-players and managers. The programme was turned into a glossy history of the club. The High Road was crammed long before kick-off.

I took my eleven-year-old grandson, Ben, to witness this piece of history. We walked past the mural of Harry Kane that helped screen off the building works of the new stadium and into White Hart Lane for the last time. It triggered a strange feeling in me. The previous occasion I had taken Ben to Tottenham had been in May 2014 to watch a 3–0 win over Aston Villa. His father had stayed behind with Maureen.

When we came back, neither Maureen nor Jonathon was at home. Then the phone rang. Jonathon explained he was at Watford Hospital with Maureen, who had tripped in the stone hallway and gashed her head. They returned with her head heavily bandaged. The fall was to exacerbate Maureen's declining health. The injury to her head accelerated the development of motor neurone disease, which was to haunt the rest of our lives together. I would occasionally be struck by the thought that, if I had taken Maureen to the game, this would not have happened. Life is so often a random process.

When we arrived in the Bill Nicholson Suite, it was to be greeted by a mass of memorabilia laid out on tables to sign. Balls, shirts, wallcharts, programmes. The room was full of everyone who had ever been anyone at Tottenham Hotspur. I met people I had lost touch with. Martin Jol, having discovered that winning the Egyptian Premier League was not enough to keep him his job at Al Ahly, told me he was living in west London 'adrift from football'. Keith Burkinshaw, having lost his beloved wife, Joyce, had left his home in Welwyn and was now remarried and living in Dorset.

Peter Shreeves, who had been my predecessor as manager and whom I had worked with at Sheffield Wednesday, was also there. I had a brief but friendly conversation with Glenn Hoddle, the legend of White Hart Lane, which pleased me, because our relationship had often been a strained one. Poignantly, Clive Allen was with his father, Les, who was badly afflicted by arthritis. Both had been fabulous players for Spurs but had fallen out. Happily, they were together to say goodbye to the arena they had both graced.

Wayne Rooney scored White Hart Lane's last goal, although it was not enough to prevent a Tottenham victory. Fittingly, Harry Kane struck the last goal by a Spurs player at the old place. Spurs won, 2–1, and throughout the game the demand for autographs and selfies was constant. Concentrating on the game was difficult. Jonathan Moss's final whistle triggered a pitch invasion with supporters grabbing a handful of the precious turf. The fireworks went off, the flags waved and the big screen began showing footage of the glory, glory years. As a rainbow covered the ground, the North London

Community Choir began singing 'Glory, Glory Hallelujah' and by now quite a few were in tears.

The former players came on to the pitch to wild applause but timings meant it was impossible for the former managers to have a similar introduction. I made my way up to the boardroom to hear Daniel Levy, who was rarely comfortable speaking in public, deliver a speech. He singled me out as someone who had supported Tottenham in a number of different roles and thanked me for my contribution, particularly the signing of Dele Alli. I felt deeply touched. He also thanked Damien Comolli for the signing of Gareth Bale, whose transfer to Real Madrid had earned £85 million. He pointed out that, when the deal to build the new stadium was signed, it was important we had high-value players to use as collateral. All but one was English. Kane, Alli, Trippier, Dier, Walker and Son were the names that guaranteed Tottenham's ability to pay for their new home.

No more would any director sit around that beautifully polished oval table where so many big decisions had been made. Photographs were manoeuvred off the walls. The honours board had already been taken down and stored. Time was already moving on.

CHAPTER 35

'JUST ONE MORE GOAL'

Tottenham now shifted lock stock and barrel to Wembley. Supporters would complain of parking problems and traffic congestion while the trains to Wembley Park were jammed.

They came in their droves. Tottenham's average attendance of 67,953 was the second highest in the Premier League behind Manchester United while the north-London derby drew a crowd of 83,222. This was the second highest attendance ever recorded for a league game in England. The top three all featured Arsenal. It fell thirty-eight short of the 83,260 who had watched Manchester United play Arsenal in 1948 – the game was played at Maine Road because of wartime bomb damage to Old Trafford. It did, however, eclipse the 82,905 who had come to Stamford Bridge to watch Chelsea face Arsenal in October 1935.

Meanwhile in N17, the great shell of the new stadium was taking shape. I was taken on a tour of the works. As I approached the ground, I saw row upon row of construction workers, all in their hard hats, sitting on the pavement on Tottenham High Road eating with their flasks of drink beside them. I assumed work had stopped for lunch when I arrived, but no, it was a rota break. Inside were hundreds of yellow-vested, hard-hatted workers. I was told that at any one time, there were 4,000 on site, many of them from eastern Europe, working through the night. The steel was transported from the north of England. The glass for the stadium roof was from Ireland and Dubai. The lifting jacks were from Switzerland, the cabling was imported from Italy. The site was overseen by German engineers from the company that had built the Olympic Stadium in Munich for the 1972 Games.

Lilywhite House, the gleaming building attached to the stadium, was where the club was now administered from. You walked into the foyer where a massive flat-screen television broadcast Sky Sports News around the clock, past the commercial department who were busy finding clients for the corporate hospitality boxes. Past accounts, who paid salaries for more than 500 full-time employees, and through to the IT department. Daniel Levy's office was right at the back of the building. The architects and the project managers were also based there. Beyond them was merchandising and the press office. Football had long been big business and Tottenham were now at the forefront of it.

Inside the stadium, a prayer room and a television studio were being built. The club shop would be the biggest in Europe. The stadium would have its own microbrewery operated by Beavertown, brewers based in Tottenham. The bars, with equipment designed to pour a pint in three seconds, the street food stalls, the restaurants and fine-dining experiences were designed to bring in £800,000 at every home game, more than four times what the Etihad Stadium generated. The dressing rooms covered the widest area I have ever seen. There would be similar locker rooms for the NFL on the other side of the stadium. The pitch could be split lengthways into three sections, each in its own tray that weighed 3,000 tons. The total cost would be more than £1 billion.

The summer of 2017 saw increased investment in the squad. I had summarised on the Europa League final in Stockholm for UEFA, which had seen a punchless Ajax easily beaten by Manchester United, managed by José Mourinho. I had, however, been impressed with their central defender, the Colombian Davinson Sánchez, although I doubted how comfortable he was on the ball.

Afterwards, Mourinho told me that one of Manchester United's tactics was to allow Davinson possession because he was so prone to surrendering it.

Mauricio Pochettino had fewer doubts and once more the special relationship between Ajax and Tottenham produced another deal, this time worth £42 million. Another £45 million was paid to Paris St Germain for the winger Lucas Moura and the full-back Serge Aurier, who was to provide competition for Kieran Trippier, whose career I had followed at Burnley. He was a full-back, on loan from Manchester City, whose crossing from the middle third onwards had been exemplary. In one game at Watford, I appreciated his accuracy in consistently finding the tall Jay Rodriguez at the back post.

Kyle Walker, who had been displaced by Trippier as the club's first-choice right-back, was sold to Manchester City for £50 million. Walker had upset the manager by making his dissatisfaction with Pochettino's selection policy public. He flourished in Manchester, but Walker irritated Spurs by stressing how much he had learned about defending under Pep Guardiola. He seemed to suggest Pochettino, who had played as a defender for Argentina, had taught him little. It reminded me of Paolo Di Canio, who quickly forgot the platform for his successes at West Ham had been built at Sheffield Wednesday.

Kevin Wimmer, who had been bought from Cologne for £4.3 million in 2015, had seldom impressed and was offloaded to Stoke for £18 million after turning up to pre-season overweight. In the Potteries, his career as a centre-half began to fizzle out. During the lockdown of 2020, I did some research and calculated that over the previous thirty seasons, Tottenham had made a profit on only three foreign signings – Luka Modrić and Dimitar Berbatov were two, and Wimmer was the third.

For all the efforts Tottenham poured into overseas scouting, the profits were provided by academy players or British buys. My argument has always been that we know far more about the qualities, personalities, lifestyle and habits of British players and, although they might cost more than footballers brought in from abroad, they were far less of a risk. Tottenham's then manager, José Mourinho, was unhappy about my conclusions, which I had shown to the club's chief accountant Matthew Collecott. There must be a crucial balance. Scouting is a complex issue and I am always reminded of Althea Gibson's statement after she became the first black woman to win Wimbledon. 'No one achieves anything without the help of others.'

Having not lost a single home fixture in our final season at White Hart Lane, we lost the opening league game at Wembley to Chelsea. Tottenham recovered their balance in the autumn, beating Liverpool 4–1 and Real Madrid 3–1 in the Champions League. Both matches represented considerable statements of intent against the two clubs who would contest the Champions League final in Kyiv. However, Manchester City cruised to their first title under Pep Guardiola, with 100 points and 106 goals. Tottenham slipped one place to third, which was a creditable performance given the predictions that Wembley would be a destabilising factor in our season.

However, once more the stadium was the setting for two savage disappointments in cup competitions. Again, Tottenham were beaten in the semi-finals of the FA Cup, this time by Manchester United. In the Champions League, a fine 2–2 draw in Turin against Juventus was overturned by late goals at Wembley from Gonzalo Higuain and Paulo Dybala. There was, however, an increasing steeliness about Spurs in Europe. They were no longer just along for the ride.

Visiting the training ground, I would often sit with Steve Hitchen, the softly spoken Mancunian who was now the club's head of recruitment. Steve had been an average player whose career had begun at Blackburn and finished at Macclesfield. However, he excelled at identifying talent in others. Working first from his base in France, he did so for Tottenham before joining Damien Comolli at Liverpool, where they had brought Luis Suárez to Anfield. However, when Daniel's relationship with Paul Mitchell faltered, Steve returned to Tottenham in February 2017.

Mitchell had been very good at self-publicity, claiming the credit for bringing Sadio Mané and Toby Alderweireld to Southampton and doing the deals for Dele Alli, Eriksen and Son at Spurs. I was never sure about Mitchell's competence and, after various in-house disagreements with Daniel Levy, a parting of the ways became inevitable. After a year on gardening leave, Mitchell turned up at first Leipzig and then Monaco before becoming Newcastle's sporting director in the summer of 2024. He was always a good networker who had excellent presentational skills.

Steve would increasingly act as a buffer between Daniel and Mauricio as Tottenham prepared for their first campaign in their new home which would end in the first European Cup final in the club's history. Although Daniel was happy to release funds, Mauricio did not push hard for more signings. He was relaxed about the quality of footballers he had assembled and convinced he could be successful with them. The chairman was becoming increasingly frustrated by problems besetting the new stadium. There were electrical failures and difficulties in obtaining a safety certificate from Haringey Council.

The opening three games were won, but a casual last twenty minutes at Vicarage Road saw Watford beat us 2–1. There, I met Rita Taylor, the first time I had seen her since her husband Graham's funeral. They had been partners since their schooldays in Scunthorpe. She had backed him fiercely, especially during his turbulent time as England manager. Rita seemed to be coping, but when you lose the person who has been with you for almost your entire life, you wonder.

Elton John was also there, preparing to take his leave of the stage as he embarked on the farewell tour that, because of the pandemic, would not finish until the summer of 2023. He introduced his two sons, Zachary and Elijah, both dressed in their Watford shirts. I had first come across Elton around 1978. He had come to watch Watford in a midweek reserve game at Kenilworth Road with his great friend Dennis Bond, a midfielder who had begun and ended his career at Vicarage Road with a spell at Tottenham in between. He was probably Elton's favourite player and before the game, because there was no food in the boardroom, Elton asked where they could get some fish and chips. I directed them over the railway bridge attached to the ground. They returned to eat their food in the directors' box. Since the crowd comprised the two men and a dog that came to Luton Reserves, hardly anyone noticed him, not even in a brightly coloured hat and platform shoes.

Once more we reached a domestic cup semi-final, this time facing our great nemesis Chelsea over two legs in the League Cup. Tottenham had won the first leg 1–0 through a Harry Kane penalty, but the return at Stamford Bridge was lost 2–1 and with no away-goals rule the tie was decided in Chelsea's favour on penalties.

Everything at Tottenham was, however, eclipsed by the Champions League. We reached the final, despite spending most of the season careering on the edge of elimination. The first two group games, against Inter Milan at San Siro and Barcelona at Wembley, were both lost and, after a 2–2 draw at PSV Eindhoven, we had one point from three matches.

When Luuk de Jong gave PSV the lead after two minutes at Wembley, Spurs were staring at elimination, not just from the Champions League but from all European football. The fact that there were just 46,000 at Wembley, compared to the 82,000 who had come to see Lionel Messi dazzle for Barcelona, was a demonstration that faith in Tottenham's European adventure was seeping away. However, in the final few minutes, Harry Kane once more rode to his club's rescue, scoring twice to set a pattern for the remainder of the Champions League campaign.

An eightieth-minute goal from Christian Eriksen overcame Inter and meant that with one game to go we needed to equal Inter Milan's result to go through. The problem was that our game was away to Barcelona. Inter were at home to PSV Eindhoven, whose previous five matches had brought them a single point. Ousmane Dembélé gave Barcelona the lead after just seven minutes at the Nou Camp but with 21-year-old Kyle Walker-Peters performing creditably at right-back despite being booked after a quarter of an hour, we held out. Lucas Moura equalised with five minutes remaining. At San Siro, Inter had drawn with PSV. We were through because away goals meant we had a better head-to-head record in our two games with the Italians.

Walker-Peters was an academy product and one who unusually had not been sent out on loan. I was disappointed when he was sold to Southampton for £12 million. Although small, he possessed lovely tight control at close quarters and was excellent when going forward. He was one of many academy products to be developed and sold – Pritchard to Norwich, Townsend to Newcastle, Mason to Hull, Bentaleb to Schalke and Smith to Bournemouth.

The round of sixteen against Borussia Dortmund was the only time in the entire Champions League campaign in which Tottenham were comfortable, winning 3–0 in London and 1–0 in the Ruhr.

On 3 April, Tottenham played their first Premier League fixture in the new stadium. Son Heung-min scored the opening goal in a 2–0 win over Crystal Palace. Much as Spurs fans were dazzled by the new structure, there were complaints that with 60,000 rather than the 35,000 who travelled to White Hart Lane, the traffic congestion was sometimes unbearable.

Son scored again as Manchester City were beaten 1–0 in the first leg of the Champions League quarter-finals to clear the stage for a remarkable encounter in the second leg. I thought that, for drama and emotion, the game at the Etihad eclipsed even the contest between Liverpool and Arsenal in 1989, when George Graham's side had to go to Anfield and win by two clear goals on the final evening of the season.

City did not have the protection of an away goal and, although Raheem Sterling scored as early as the second minute, two goals from Son meant Manchester City needed three more to go through. Such was their firepower that they were 4–2 up before the hour mark. Then Poch threw on Fernando Llorente, who had been bought from Swansea as cover for Harry Kane. With seventeen minutes left, the tall striker scored from a ball that struck his thigh, although many in the Etihad believed it had come off the Spaniard's arm.

Manchester City needed to score again, and in the ninety-third minute, it appeared Sterling had sent them through. After a delay, however, it was ruled out for offside by VAR. The change of emotions was astonishing. Pep Guardiola had been running down the touchline punching both arms above his head. Poch had been staring up at the night sky. Then everything was reversed.

A semi-final with Ajax beckoned. In many ways, it was even more heart-stopping than what had happened in Manchester. Having lost the first leg 1–0 at home to a side that had knocked out first Real Madrid and then Juventus, Tottenham went into the interval at the Johan Cruyff Arena 2–0 down. We needed three goals in forty-five minutes.

Were Ajax complacent? Did they sit too far back? Did Spurs, realising they had nothing to lose, toss away their inhibitions? In my view, it was a combination of all three, and Lucas Moura, having already scored twice, snatched the third in stoppage time. The Ajax defence fell to the pitch. They had been disturbed by Pochettino once more introducing the tall figure of Llorente into the attack. The arena stood in shocked silence.

For the first time in their history, Tottenham Hotspur had reached the final of the European Cup. They had come through a daunting group that included Barcelona and Inter Milan on the away-goals rule. They had won the quarter-final and the semi-final on away goals. They had repeatedly snatched victory from defeat. Now in Amsterdam their players danced on the pitch in a daze.

In the final they would face Liverpool, who had completed their own remarkable journey to Madrid by incredibly overturning a 3–0 first leg defeat in Barcelona. The final would be between two teams of escapologists, both of whom would have echoed Joe Merimovich's plea for 'just one more goal'.

CHAPTER 36

'DID YOU EVER THINK WE WOULD SEE THE DAY?'

I had been involved in television and radio commentary for most of my managerial career and carried on when I moved into football consultancy. I had done my first radio commentary in the early 1980s and to commentate on Tottenham in their first European Cup final would fulfil a personal ambition. However, at the age of seventy-four, I realised this would probably be my farewell.

I would be summarising for the UEFA feed, which would be broadcast to countries who could not afford the enormous fees charged for the rights to screen the Champions League final. The feed would go mainly to Africa, Asia, the Middle East and Australia.

I had been the lead summariser for ITV from 2004 when Ron Atkinson had been stood down after making a racist comment after Chelsea's Champions League quarter-final in Monaco. However, my own relationship with ITV also ended acrimoniously after the 2009 Champions League final in Rome, where Barcelona comfortably overcame Manchester United. It was a game where Wayne Rooney was stationed ineffectually wide on the left to quell the threat from Lionel Messi, who was played on the Barcelona right. After the final whistle, I saw Sir Alex Ferguson on the stairs in the Stadio Olimpico. His features were ashen; he seemed in a daze. I could only imagine how he must have felt. Barcelona had been by far the better team.

Towards the end of the commentary, Clive Tyldesley remarked that he felt Messi had been the stand-out performer. I considered

Andrés Iniesta the most creative influence in Barcelona's victory. Curiously, UEFA voted Xavi Hernández man of the match. Clive was an exceptional commentator who did his research thoroughly but sometimes gave the impression he knew more than the expert alongside him. Clive's progress through local radio had seen him befriend many famous personalities, particularly from his early days in Liverpool. We had a good relationship, but I felt he would have been happier with a more 'famous' personality alongside him.

On the flight home, I sat next to Niall Sloane, the new head of ITV Sport. When we exchanged goodbyes at Gatwick, Niall said: 'I'll be in touch shortly to discuss arrangements for next season.' A couple of months later, Niall phoned to say: 'We have decided to stand you down.' I have often wondered whether Clive had any influence on that decision. Nick Randall, a QC who became chairman of Nottingham Forest, told me I had a case against ITV, who had not followed the proper procedures when terminating my contract. He would win me financial compensation.

Niall Sloane had earlier been in charge of BBC Sport when I decided to leave for ITV, who then had more games to broadcast. Niall had told Jeff Weston, an agent who looked after a number of pundits for the Jerome Anderson organisation, that he was most unhappy at my defection. I am sure this influenced Niall's decision. He himself had switched allegiances and he sent me a letter apologising for the way the ending of my association with ITV had been handled.

When at the BBC, Niall sometimes had a strained relationship with John Motson, although he would not have been the only one. This was nothing compared to the furore when Sloane terminated Clive Tyldesley's status as ITV's lead commentator in July 2020, which led to Clive unwisely broadcasting an emotional video in which he said he was 'upset, annoyed and baffled' by the decision.

I enjoyed my time as a summariser for UEFA commentating alongside Tony Jones, a Welshman with a strong voice and a keen eye. He was neither brash nor thought he was more important than the game. He described the action and let the pundit interpret it. Three days before the Champions League final, I was in Baku, the capital of Azerbaijan, for the final of the Europa League. Like the Champions League final, it was an all-English affair with Chelsea comfortably beating Arsenal, 4–1. Despite the fact Baku was nearly 3,000 miles from London, UEFA's arrangements were already in place and there was no possibility of changing the venue. The Olympic Stadium was, predictably, far from full. Indeed, the authorities opened the gates in one corner to allow people in for free. All the UEFA technicians, cameramen and commentators flew directly from Baku to Madrid.

The night before the Champions League final, we drove from our hotel, near Barajas Airport, into the centre of Madrid, which was awash with colour and noise. The cafes and bars were crammed with Liverpool and Tottenham supporters, all mingling well. It was the first all-English final since 2008, when Manchester United had beaten Chelsea in Moscow amid torrential rain and John Terry slipped as he took the penalty that would have won Chelsea the European Cup. I will always remember the sight of Avram Grant consoling his players in his sodden suit – he did not wear a raincoat – as Manchester United celebrated their victory around him. The game had kicked off at 10 p.m. Moscow time, and in the small hours of the morning, Clive and I walked to three different locations in pouring rain where we had been told a car would take us back to the hotel. Long afterwards, we sat in the hotel nursing a whisky and cursing ITV's arrangements.

Now, the weather in Madrid was hot and sultry. Raddy Antić came to the hotel to see me. His days were now consumed by his grandchildren. Over olives and a beer, we discussed everything from football to politics before I had to get changed to travel to the Metropolitano Stadium. Outside the ground, I met Tottenham supporters who had flown in from South Africa without tickets just to be in the same city as their team. Liverpool had attracted a swathe of fans from Asia. I met Glenn Hoddle, who was also commentating on the game: 'Can you believe this?' he said, enchanted by the thought that his Tottenham had made a European Cup final. 'Did you ever think we would see the day?'

In the Metropolitano's media room, I began revising my notes to include anecdotes I might bring up. I reminded myself of the principles of summarising a match without baffling those watching at home. 'Why is one team gaining ascendancy? Where is the penetration? Who is using the width better? Why does one team look more organised? Which players are combining well?'

When I was commentating with the BBC during the 1998 World Cup in France, Barry Davies told me the art of punditry was being able to predict what might happen and why – and explain it when it did. Barry thought Don Revie had been excellent when it came to explaining why something was happening. Barry added that pundits on the radio were never debriefed or mentored. 'Provided they keep asking you back, you must be doing something right.'

There were several principles of summarising. You learn never to talk over your colleague. Always fade away quickly when the ball nears the eighteen-yard box. Most importantly, keep it brief. If there was a doubt about the identity of the goalscorer, look to where the cameraman was panning.

In Madrid, the start was explosive enough to catch out many commentators, who were delivering their opening preamble. I thought Liverpool's penalty, awarded when the ball struck Moussa Sissoko's arm, was harsh. Referees do not change their minds and Mohamed Salah converted from the spot.

Mauricio Pochettino's game plan had been to exploit the space behind Liverpool's full-backs, Trent Alexander-Arnold and Andy Robertson, as they pushed high up the pitch. Alexander-Arnold, in particular, was seen as a defensive weak point. However, once they had taken the lead, Liverpool played cautiously. There was little space to exploit and there was a lack of intensity from both sides. Before the game the big question had been whether Pochettino would start with Harry Kane, who because of injury had not played for two months.

Lucas Moura had scored the hat-trick in Amsterdam, but Kane was Tottenham's captain and icon. I had watched Spurs train on the day before the final and he looked fit and confident. However, I was told afterwards Kane was not fully fit and had been selected on reputation. Kane, perhaps understandably given his lay-off, did not seem himself and his usual movement towards the play and out wide was lacking. He allowed himself to be tightly marked by Virgil van Dijk, who dominated him. However, none of Tottenham's big players sparked. When Moura was brought on for Harry Winks on the hour mark, it seemed a positive move. It was, however, a Liverpool substitute, Divock Origi, who settled an unenterprising final late on. There was a two-hour wait for transport back to the hotel, and amid all the fierce Liverpool celebrations, I bit my lip hard.

Commentary was more relaxing than football management, which I found all-consuming. Often before matches you would be allowed to watch training or speak to the respective managers. You would often be given information in confidence, which commentators like Mike Ingham and John Murray, who succeeded him as BBC Radio's football correspondent, would not betray. They were accepted as part of the football family. Mike became the BBC's football correspondent in 1991. He was eloquent and never lost for a phrase. John, who was brought up on a farm near Hadrian's Wall, possessed a beautiful Northumberland accent with which to paint his pictures. Dreadful weather was invariably described as '*pooor*'.

Commentary is an art. On the radio, you need to paint the picture, you have a greater need to explain and communicate. On television the commentator must be sure of facts and identification. The viewers can see the pictures and make up their own minds. Identifying a goalscorer in a packed penalty area has to be spot on.

Sometimes, as a summariser, you make predictions. Sometimes they come to pass. In March 1995, I was on the gantry at The Dell, watching an FA Cup tie between Southampton and Tottenham for BBC radio. Southampton went into the break 2–0 up, mainly because the Spurs manager, Gerry Francis, had attempted to man-mark Matt Le Tissier, a tactic that had gone badly wrong. I suggested Spurs should take off the man-marker, Stuart Nethercott, and bring on Ronny Rosenthal, a striker they had signed from Liverpool. Gerry did just that, Rosenthal scored a hat-trick and Tottenham won, 6–2.

Sometimes, things go less well. In the 1994 FA Cup final when Manchester United crushed Chelsea 4–0, I continually mispronounced Eric Cantona's name. I called him CanTOna. The producer, the loyal, experienced Charlotte Nichol, prodded me four times, passing me notes to alert me to the fact that it was pronounced CantoNA. I carried on regardless. We were given phonetic pronunciation sheets before a game for the foreign players, but I could seldom get my head round them. I would freeze whenever Bixente Lizarazu appeared on any team sheet. Jack Charlton would get round difficulties in pronunciation by referring to the 'big lad' or the 'No. 10'.

I was summarising at White Hart Lane in March 2012, when in an FA Cup tie between Tottenham and Bolton, Fabrice Muamba collapsed with nobody around him, having suffered heart failure. He survived because of the attentions of the medical staff of both clubs, led by Tottenham's doctor, Shabaaz Mughal, and the fact that a cardiologist, Andrew Deaner, was in the crowd and came on to the pitch to help after a public appeal. In a silent stadium, Dr Deaner persuaded the medical team to take Muamba not to the North Middlesex Hospital, which is less than a mile away from White Hart Lane, but the specialist London Chest Hospital in Bow. That decision saved Muamba's life. I was summarising with Ian Dennis, and we had little information, although we knew we were witnessing what seemed like a tragedy. We simply had to keep the broadcast going and when we handed over to the studio, I felt drained and exhausted, hoping we had not said anything out of keeping with the occasion. The BBC sent us a message congratulating us on holding the programme together.

Ian's great attribute was being able to describe the game while absorbing and delivering scores from matches that were going on elsewhere.

Six years before, I had accompanied Ian to commentate on the latter stages of the Africa Cup of Nations, which was being held in Egypt. We were shocked by the poverty, the hundreds of people sleeping under railway bridges not far from our hotel in Cairo. When we checked in, we were given a questionnaire in which you had to state your religion. Since the Egyptian president, Hosni Mubarak, was then taking an aggressive stance towards Israel, I left the answer blank. One afternoon, armed men marched into the hotel and ordered the foyer cleared. The head of Hezbollah was hosting a conference and his arrival was imminent.

The quarter-final between Cameroon and Ivory Coast was played at the Cairo Military Academy. There was a crowd of only 4,000 in a stadium that held six times that number and most of those were soldiers who had been given shirts of the two quarter-finalists and been told to put them over their uniforms and stand behind each goal to provide colour for the television pictures. The game finished in a penalty shoot-out, in which all twenty-two players scored before Samuel Eto'o missed his second penalty for Cameroon. Ivory Coast made the final against Egypt which attracted 70,000. Egypt won after an altogether shorter shoot-out.

In 2018, the BBC's head of sport Barbara Slater, whose father Bill had won three championships with Wolverhampton Wanderers, invited me to a drinks reception at Portland Place to mark John Motson's retirement, after a career with the corporation that began half a century before in 1968. John gave a passionate speech, the focus of which was how the BBC set the standard in sports broadcasting and how those standards should never be lowered. talkSPORT, he claimed, would allow on anyone who picked up the phone. A few weeks later, he joined talkSPORT.

John lived not far from me in Hertfordshire and his great strength was the sheer intensity of his research. Despite his unassailable position at the BBC, he was nervous before games and could be most irritable before kick-off. He disliked any disturbance to his concentration and would have people fluttering around him attending to his needs. Once, meticulously preparing for a commentary in broiling heat during the 1998 World Cup, he looked up, turned to his producer, and said: 'Could you move the sun, please.'

Another time, I was summarising with John for radio at Alan Curbishley's first game as West Ham manager in December 2006. John had wagered that Tottenham would beat Manchester City and West Ham, who were in the relegation zone, would beat United, the league leaders, in the late kick-off. Tottenham had won 2–1 in Manchester and, with a quarter of an hour remaining at Upton Park, Nigel Reo-Coker put West Ham ahead. It provoked wave after wave of Manchester United attacks and with each one John's commentary grew more excitable. I did not get a word in edgeways and was not asked for my opinion on anything. John won his bet.

Jon Champion, who left Britain to work in the United States, was less famous than Motty but was someone whose commentary contained plenty of pauses, allowing the game to breathe. He would never use three words when two would do. He did not, as a rule, state the obvious. Jon had the appearance of a rugby lock-forward but one from a public school. He was a devoted fan of York City as was another up-and-coming commentator: Guy Mowbray, who became the BBC's lead commentator.

When Ron Atkinson was ITV's lead summariser, I often worked with Peter Drury, a skilful wordsmith. He was a great enthusiast for the game who had a season ticket at Watford, where he would take his family at every opportunity. He ran a boys' team in his village in Hertfordshire. He lived the game he commentated on. I am sure when he finishes commentating, he will continue to be a season-ticket holder at Vicarage Road.

In my opinion, nothing irritates a viewer more than being told exactly what he can see in front of him. If the ball strikes the post, he does not need to be told that 'he's hit the post'. He needs to be told why the ball did not go in. I cringe when I hear pundits say: 'To be honest with you,' as if they have lied their way through the previous half-hour of commentary. Another irritating phrase is: 'If you know what I mean.' If we did not, the pundit would be taken off air. Jimmy Armfield, a fine footballer for Blackpool and England and an astute observer of the game in his broad Lancashire accent, would say: 'I was right behind that and I can tell you exactly what happened.'

On Radio 5, Jimmy often worked alongside Alan Green, an Ulsterman who sharply divided opinion. Some thought him a courageous and brilliant commentator, others thought him an egotist who was not a team player. What he did have were strong opinions he was unafraid to broadcast. I was sitting next to him before the 1995 FA Cup final between Everton and Manchester United. Alan had been given advance news of the United team but said live on air that he doubted this was the real team. He had learned 'not to believe the propaganda that comes out of the Manchester United manager's office.'

Alex Ferguson did not speak to him again. Sam Allardyce banned him from the Reebok Stadium after Alan said he would not pay to watch Bolton. My own moment with him came in December 2005, when we were commentating on the Club World Cup final between Liverpool and São Paulo in Tokyo. Liverpool were trailing 1–0 and Rafa Benítez looked about to make a double substitution, bringing on John Arne Riise and Florent Sinama Pongollé, both of whom were warming up.

Alan had not noticed the second player and said on air they would only be bringing on one substitute. I replied that Liverpool would probably be bringing on both players, a scenario Alan rejected. I replied, somewhat testily: 'I will bow to your better judgement, Alan. After all, Liverpool is your team.' This was a red rag to a bull. I immediately regretted the remark. I should not have associated a commentator with the club he supports and tried to cover my tracks by saying: 'What I meant was, you admire their style of football.'

It was easy to fall out with Alan Green. During the 1994 World Cup, I was with him and Ron Jones, his lyrical Welsh co-commentator, in a Chinese restaurant in San Francisco. They had such a ferocious argument over the bill that when we returned to our base at Stanford University, Alan refused to speak to anyone for two days. Alan was in many ways a solitary person. He preferred not to mingle with other journalists in the media room before a game. He had little time for football's gossip but would go up to the broadcasting positions early to prepare for the match. He was his own man.

I liked Ron Jones, a man who understood football, who had a deep knowledge of the Welsh teams and whose son became a professional golfer. The observations he made were regularly followed by the expression: 'I can tell you.' Darren Fletcher was one of the more interesting commentators I worked alongside. He was an ebullient, self-confident man who, like me, was from Nottingham. Unlike most of his contemporaries, Darren did not have a university education and advanced through local radio.

In the summer of 2013, we commentated on the European Under-21 Championships in Israel. The surroundings, in Netanya by the rippling Mediterranean, were delightful. England's performances, under Stuart Pearce, were dreadful. Well-paid Premier League stars like Jonjo Shelvey and Andre Wisdom from Liverpool, Danny Rose from Tottenham and Wilfried Zaha, whom Manchester United had agreed to sign from Crystal Palace for £15 million, were woefully disappointing. England were eliminated after losing every one of their group games and failing to score a goal from open play.

We visited the Western or Wailing Wall in Jerusalem. For me, it held a special significance as I pushed a message of hope into the crevices before walking with other journalists through the old city to the Garden of Gethsemane. On the same day the German team, led by the great Günter Netzer, made the same journey to the foot of the wall on which Herod's temple once stood. It was in Jerusalem that Shlomo Scharf, one of Israel's most successful managers who was now a television pundit, told me Joe Merimovich, whose phrase 'just one more goal' had stayed with me for so long, had died at the age of eighty-six.

Sometimes, you hear a phrase that lingers. Kenneth Wolstenholme's 'they think it's all over' remains the most famous. However, Brian Moore's 'it's up for grabs now', as Michael Thomas ran through for the second goal at Anfield that would give Arsenal the title in 1989, also resonates. I liked Barry Davies's 'just look at his face', when Francis Lee wheeled away after scoring for Derby against Manchester City, the club that had controversially let him go.

There are so many words spoken in a commentary that some are bound to go wrong, although I always wondered whether the majority of entries that appeared in Private Eye's 'Colemanballs' column were doctored or even made up. Many were too stupid to be true. However, my comment made during the 1986 World Cup, as Diego Maradona delivered a cross, that 'Maradona gets amazing elevation on his balls from the tightest of angles' is entirely accurate.

After Maradona slalomed through the England defence to score his astonishing second goal in the Azteca Stadium, I remarked: 'I believe we have now seen the great Pelé dethroned.' When Maradona died at the age of sixty in November 2020, it was his first goal, 'the Hand of God', that was hotly debated once more. I maintained that at 5ft 5in., he thought he was going to be clattered by Peter Shilton, who had been a shade late coming off his line to challenge. As he put his arm up for protection, he guided the ball past the England keeper. He knew he was in the wrong and glanced sheepishly at the referee and looked over to the linesman. He had cheated but was never going to admit it.

Pelé, Garrincha and Alfredo Di Stéfano were only glimpsed on television, but I saw other greats in the flesh; men like John Charles, Duncan Edwards, Tom Finney, Eusébio, George Best, Johan Cruyff, Franz Beckenbauer, Paolo Maldini, Kenny Dalglish and Bobby Charlton. You cannot compare them. When asked who was the best footballer I ever saw, my reply is always: 'The best at what?' My mind, however, goes back to the first game I ever watched, Nottingham Forest v. Leeds, the Christmas afternoon in 1953 when John Charles became my hero.

I can, however, answer the question of who was the complete commentator I worked with. Brian Moore would always make you feel relaxed and appreciated. He would arrive early, having been briefed by the managers, who always trusted him. He told me he had learned from the horse-racing commentator Peter O'Sullevan never to have a big meal in the hours before going on air because it made you feel tired. That encapsulates Brian's attention to detail. Small margins. If I ever asked Brian a question prior to the game about whether to mention a topic, he would invariably reply: 'It's up to you, maestro.' It made you feel important and valued.

We worked together for ITV on the May night in 1989 when Arsenal won 2–0 at Anfield to take the title in the final game of the season. The rendition of 'You'll Never Walk Alone' a month after the Hillsborough disaster was unforgettable. Everyone was on edge. With the score at 1–0 and Arsenal pressing for the vital second with time draining away, I said, rather bizarrely, that it would be poetic justice if Arsenal lost the league by one goal despite beating Liverpool home and away. Brian said, very calmly: 'I don't think Arsenal would see it that way, David.'

CHAPTER 37

'WATCH THE PLAYERS; THEY WILL TAKE THE MILK OUT OF YOUR TEA'

Despite taking Tottenham to their first European Cup final, Mauricio Pochettino found himself under a strange type of pressure. He could only improve on that display by winning the Champions League, as Liverpool had done after losing the final to Real Madrid in 2018. Or he could win the title, something Spurs had not done since the far distant glory, glory days.

The major summer signing was Tanguy Ndombele, a tall, box-to-box midfielder with a surge, who was signed from Lyons for £55 million. He had thrust himself into the spotlight with a superb performance for Lyons against Manchester City in the Champions League.

Jack Clarke, a highly promising young winger who had worked under Pochettino's mentor Marcelo Bielsa at Leeds, was brought in for £8 million. I had seen him turn in a brilliant display for Leeds in a thrilling 3–2 victory at Aston Villa just before Christmas 2018. I saw him again at Queens Park Rangers and prior to the game I spoke to Eddie Gray, who commentated on every Leeds game. He predicted a big future for the boy.

Clarke had only just turned eighteen when he delivered these performances and this was a signing that carried some risk because he had lived all his life in Yorkshire. We were also aware that when at Leeds Clarke had suffered an asthmatic attack while sitting on the subs' bench but we were happy with his medical. The question marks over him were whether he would cope in London away from his family? Would the management embrace him early on – or wait to be impressed?

The solution was to loan him back to Leeds to complete his development under Bielsa. However, when Pochettino was replaced by José Mourinho, that agreement was terminated and he was recalled to London and loaned out to Queens Park Rangers and then to Stoke. He then signed for Sunderland. I was quietly pleased by his performances in the north-east. He had taken longer to develop and come to terms with league football than I had hoped, but at Sunderland he appreciated encouragement from the management.

Although the applause at the opening game of the season, against Aston Villa, signalled the crowd regarded the defeat in the Champions League final as a glorious failure, Pochettino's regime never recovered from an indifferent start. They won just three of their opening twelve fixtures, which included defeat in the League Cup to Colchester and a humiliation by Bayern Munich in the Champions League.

The club had invested £25 million in the young Fulham winger Ryan Sessegnon, who arrived with a considerable reputation. It was a move I supported, advising the club not to make it a double deal with his twin brother, Steven. Ryan's greatest asset was his speed. He had already played over 100 league games and possessed an enviable scoring record. However, he was only nineteen and found the change in dressing-room mentality hard. He had gone from playing Championship football at Craven Cottage to mixing with millionaires and internationals. He made little impression on the Premier League and Mourinho would loan him out to Hoffenheim in the Bundesliga.

The departure of Kieran Trippier to Atlético Madrid weakened the team. He had replaced Kyle Walker as Tottenham's first-choice full-back and was used as a right wing-back by Gareth Southgate during England's World Cup campaign in Russia. Walker possessed greater pace, but Trippier was a smooth defender, starting off moves with sensible passing. In the final third of the field, nobody crossed the ball better. He was a quiet lad, easy to get on with; a down-to-earth northern boy. However, his form had declined towards the end of the previous season and Mauricio had lost faith in him. It was, however, little surprise he should become a success in Diego Simeone's powerful Atlético side. At Newcastle, he proved the best passer from full-back in the Premier League with more than twenty assists in the 2022/23 season.

There seemed to be a casualness in Tottenham's play, as if the team had thought they had done enough in reaching the Champions League final. You could see and sense it on the pitch and on the training ground. In the north-London derby, Tottenham were two up at the Emirates Stadium but conceded just before the half-time whistle. Afterwards, Arsenal tore into us. We were physically second best, outfought by their midfielders, Matteo Guendouzi and Lucas Torreira. Pierre-Emerick Aubameyang equalised in the seventy-first minute. I was watching from a hospitality box. Among the guests was Piers Morgan, a flamboyant Arsenal fan, and his stepfather. His stepfather was a lifelong Tottenham supporter, who told me: 'I have no control over my son.'

In October 2017, Mauricio had released an autobiography that centred on his time at Tottenham. Entitled *Brave New World*, it was written in collaboration with the Spanish journalist Guillem Balagué, who had first met Pochettino when he signed for Espanyol as a player in 1994. Tottenham were unhappy at the timing of the book. They thought it should have waited until he had left the club. *Brave New World* revealed private conversations between the manager and players, some of whom were still at Spurs. Walker had been particularly offended. Although it was not a major issue, the board felt it was ill advised.

The players had enjoyed Pochettino's coaching. His sessions were inventive and conducted with humour but now he was less hands on. More of the training was now left to his assistant, Jesús Pérez, whom he relied on a lot. Pérez was a regular at Pochettino's press conferences. He had a better command of English than Poch and could interpret the occasional tricky question. I was sitting in the club restaurant at Enfield and answered a phone call. Jesús came over and politely reminded me that 'mobiles are banned here'. I promptly turned it off. Ten minutes later, three players walked in and two of them put their phones on the table and took calls as they ate lunch.

Their manager was becoming more frustrated and stories began to appear in the press that Pochettino had lost his edge. Perhaps he was tired. There were constant links in the media to other clubs, especially to Real Madrid and Atlético, where Simeone earned £15 million a year, making him the highest-paid manager in the world. The press suggested he would be a more effective manager of Manchester United than Ole Gunnar Solskjær. The rumours would not go away and Poch would not deny the stories. There were shades of Harry Redknapp refusing to commit to Spurs after his court case and appearing to use every interview as an audition for the England job.

Steve Hitchen, the club's head of recruitment, appeared to be engaging in eggshell diplomacy between the manager and the chairman. For someone who had cost £55 million, Ndombele appeared to be making precious little impact. The Champions League was another source of pressure. In September, we had lost a two-goal lead against Olympiakos in Athens and faced Bayern Munich at home the following month.

Bayern were irresistible, finding and exploiting space brilliantly, particularly on the flanks. Son had given Spurs the lead, but goals from Joshua Kimmich, Robert Lewandowski and a brace from Serge Gnabry had taken Bayern into a 4–1 lead until a penalty from Harry Kane gave Tottenham hope of staging another unlikely Champions League comeback. In attempting to repeat their heroics of the previous season, Spurs went gung-ho, leaving space that Bayern exploited ruthlessly. Gnabry, who embarrassingly had once played for Arsenal, scored four of Bayern's seven. It was Tottenham's worst European defeat. On my journey home, I thought I had just seen a side that would win the competition. However, few could have predicted Bayern Munich would lift their sixth European Cup in an empty stadium in Lisbon after the coronavirus pandemic had driven crowds from the game.

Headlines began appearing that Poch had 'lost the dressing room'. This is more than a journalistic phrase. Players can suddenly lose faith in the man in charge and their salaries now give them considerable power.

When the civil war between Terry Venables and Alan Sugar reached its peak at White Hart Lane, several players went to Sugar's house and stood outside the gates with banners supporting the manager. Several years later, they would show their hand once more when senior players went to Sugar's house and informed him they were unhappy with Christian Gross.

Poch was sending out mixed messages in terms of his enthusiasm for the job and his ability to turn the results around. Players can smell the loss of control. Tottenham were now eleven points off a Champions League place. Agents who had football managers as clients were becoming busy. It seemed that Mauricio himself was no longer sure he was the right man to manage Tottenham. He bore a troubled look and, with the season slipping away, Daniel Levy felt he had to be decisive.

José Mourinho was a world-class manager who lived in London and had not worked since leaving Manchester United in December 2018. He had won nineteen major trophies since leading Porto to the Primeira Liga in 2003. In that time, Tottenham Hotspur, the glory, glory club, had won a League Cup. Spurs needed a trophy and Mourinho seemed the ultimate deliverer of silverware. He could start immediately and there would be no compensation to pay. The goal gaped. On 19 November 2019, Mauricio Pochettino was sacked and the following day José Mourinho walked in. There was a sadness in the air, but that was football, in all its brutal logic.

When Mourinho walked through Tottenham's door, there was a sense of surprise mixed in with the excitement. His background was well known. He had won trophies. However, there were plenty of stories of alleged dressing-room arguments at Old Trafford, particularly with Paul Pogba and Luke Shaw. Towards the end of his time in Manchester – a city he refused to move to – there was talk of a toxic atmosphere at the club. By November, Mourinho had been out of work for nearly a year and had been busying himself with punditry. It was lucrative work. For one trip to Qatar to give his views on that weekend's Premier League games for BeIn Sport, I was told he was paid a six-figure sum. His charisma, allied to his massive trophy haul, meant that these were the fees he could demand.

In his appearances in Doha and on Sky Television, Mourinho was charming and perceptive, but he did not have to man-manage anybody. Mourinho possesses an aura, a feeling that his fame and his achievements have made him untouchable. It was this feeling, that he was still hot property, that saw Mourinho rushed in after the decision had been taken to remove Pochettino. As Mauricio's star had started to wane, we had informally discussed possible replacements with our scouts, but Mourinho's rapid appointment raised eyebrows. It was a surprise. He had not been among the front runners.

Aside from the tales of discontent at Manchester United, there was his disciplinary record to consider. The row with Anders Frisk that had led to the Swedish referee's retirement; the £200,000 fine for tapping up Ashley Cole while he was still at Arsenal. Those incidents had come in 2005, when he could claim to be a young manager. However, in 2011, while at Real Madrid, he had poked Barcelona's assistant coach, Tito Vilanova in the eye. Then there was the bitter falling-out with Chelsea's club doctor, Eva Carneiro, that led to the club paying her damages and issuing an unreserved apology. Nevertheless, we had landed 'the Special One', a man whose success appeared to excuse his erratic behaviour.

By 16 February, Tottenham had climbed from fourteenth to fifth. Then came elimination from the Champions League by Leipzig, followed by the coronavirus pandemic that shut down all football for three months.

The game resumed in June but in empty stadiums. Tottenham, who had built the most advanced spectator facilities in the country and who needed the matchday income of around £4 million that every Premier League game provided to finance the new stadium, would be especially badly hit.

Three straight wins over Arsenal, Newcastle and Leicester meant the final game of the season, at Crystal Palace, gave us the chance of salvaging something from the season with qualification for the Europa League.

We drew 1–1 at Selhurst Park, scoring early through Harry Kane and then retreating deep to protect the advantage. Palace had been second best and another goal was there for us if Spurs continued to press. However, a pattern that was to emerge the following season was already being set – Tottenham attempted to cling on to what they held – and we succumbed to an equaliser from Jeffrey Schlupp. Mourinho's backroom staff celebrated qualification for the Europa League, but for many fans, the jury was very much out. They would give their verdict the following season.

It was a season that began well. Mourinho marked his return to Old Trafford by thrashing Manchester United 6–1. Manchester City were beaten 2–0, and after victory in the north-London derby in

December, Tottenham were top of the Premier League. Spurs had built a platform only to slide down the other side. Two months later, after defeats to Liverpool, Brighton and Chelsea, they had fallen to eighth, fourteen points adrift of Manchester City. Three England internationals – Dele Alli, Harry Winks and Eric Dier – had been sidelined.

You did not have to look too far to see the signs of discontent. The central defensive pairings and the full-backs were being continually interchanged. Gareth Bale, whose return on loan from Real Madrid might have become a catalyst, discovered his role was to be that of a permanent substitute. His time at the Bernabéu had ended un-happily amid newspaper reports that Bale spent too much time on the golf course and had a poor command of Spanish. Nevertheless, Tottenham were acquiring a man who had won three European Cups since he was last at the club while Daniel Levy had negotiated an outstanding financial package that ensured Real would still pay the bulk of his wages. He would return to Madrid at the end of the season. In his all-too-brief appearances, he had excelled.

Nevertheless, under Mourinho, Bale would barely start a game while Giovani Lo Celso, who had been brought to Spurs on loan under Pochettino but whose deal had been made permanent by Mourinho, was dogged by injury. Just as everything was coming to a head at Tottenham, Paul Pogba gave a television interview in which he accused Mourinho of 'casting players aside like they don't exist' while at Manchester United. There were some at Tottenham who knew exactly what he meant.

A couple of days after that interview screened, José Mourinho was dismissed. The end came after a poor performance at Everton, where two goals from Kane managed to spare the club's blushes and earn Spurs a point they had barely deserved. Flying back to London, the plane was gripped by an icy silence. Nobody spoke. Something inside of the club had snapped. He was fired a few days before

Tottenham played a League Cup final against Manchester City. Not since his time managing União de Leiria, where he outperformed big teams like Porto, had José Mourinho left a club without winning them a trophy.

It might seem extraordinary timing that Mourinho, the arch-winner of silverware, should have been sacked days before a Wembley final. Nobody knows how Spurs would have performed, but his recent touchline demeanour had been poor. He rarely consulted his coaches and would sit morosely in the dugout, seemingly at odds with the world. Perhaps he should have taken Tottenham to Wembley and then been sacked whatever the result. The decision echoed one of the first Daniel had taken when he succeeded Alan Sugar – to fire George Graham just before an FA Cup semi-final with Arsenal and replace him with Glenn Hoddle.

It was a big call to allow Ryan Mason, who was then in charge of Tottenham's under-18s, to take over with two other coaches and I wondered if the players themselves could not have formed a collective to run the team until the end of the season. Hugo Lloris, the captain, had won the World Cup. However, there was no great leader within the dressing room and Ryan was given the task of overseeing the final. The players had enjoyed his training sessions and went into the final in far better spirits than had been the case in Mourinho's last games. However, it was not enough to counter Manchester City. The loss was only by a single goal, but the defeat was comprehensive.

Seventeen months was not long enough for Mourinho to have made an impact, but perhaps Daniel Levy had no choice but to remove him. Corroding relationships with directors and staff sometimes force a chairman's hand. At Tottenham, it was personal relationships or the lack of them that did for Glenn Hoddle. At Nottingham Forest, Billy Davies seemed to have no kind of relationship with anyone but survived longer than he might have done because his results were above expectations. When the results dipped, he fell.

However, ordinarily, three years should be a manager's time-frame. After the initial bounce of the appointment, it is too much to expect very much from the first season. Players need to leave and others need to be brought in. Progress has to be seen in the second season and success should come in the third. Tottenham, who had won a single League Cup in the previous twenty-two years, badly required silverware.

The foundation of a sound club is the appointment of a manager. It is the biggest decision a club can make. Too often the men who make that decision take advice from the wrong people – agents out to make a profit, friends eager to make a recommendation, famous players with no relevant managerial experience. Clubs now even employ firms of head-hunters to recommend people they should already be aware of. The idea of 'promoting from within' often seems an easy option, mainly because it is almost invariably the cheapest one.

The key quality for a manager is man-management. In the Premier League, he will walk into a dressing room where virtually everyone he casts his eye over is a millionaire. He has to bring unity and a sense of purpose to a group of young men who too often are motivated by selfishness. When I first went into management, with Nuneaton, Peter Taylor advised me: 'Watch the players; they will take the milk out of your tea.'

For all his silverware, it is in this area that José Mourinho, who chopped and changed without giving his players sympathetic explanations, failed to move with the times.

Tottenham replaced a man who had won twenty major trophies with someone who had never won significant silverware. Nuno Espirito Santo and José Mourinho were both Portuguese and both employed Jorge Mendes as their agent. There the similarities ended.

Nuno was not Tottenham's first choice. In fact, he was not even on their original list of candidates.

As soon as the decision was taken to fire Mourinho, Daniel Levy called daily meetings with Steve Hitchen, whose job title was now head of performance, and Fabio Paratici, the newly appointed managing director, who had been recruited from Juventus. The role of director of football was back at Spurs. With Daniel wanting more of a back-seat role and with his time consumed by the business of keeping Harry Kane at Tottenham, Fabio had in effect been given the keys to the club.

Paratici had made his name in a similar role at Juventus, who during his time in Turin had won nineteen trophies in eleven years. He came with a big reputation for astute recruitment. However, his involvement in a financial cover-up at Juventus would prove a time bomb that would one day explode. Antonio Conte was top of his wish list. Paratici had worked with him at Juventus, he had won the Premier League with Chelsea and he was suddenly and unexpectedly available. After leading Inter Milan to their first league title in eleven years, Conte had quit after the board informed him they would have to sell €80 million worth of players to address the club's debts. However, he was expensive – his salary at the San Siro had been €13 million – and Conte wanted a break from football. It would prove rather shorter than he anticipated.

There was a meeting with Erik ten Hag, whose Ajax side had been dramatically beaten by Spurs in the Champions League semi-finals. I would have preferred a British coach, but although a tentative approach was made to Graham Potter at Brighton, it never went beyond a phone call. Tottenham had a good relationship with Brighton where Paul Barber – who had previously worked for Spurs – was proving an outstanding chief executive. However, Potter was firmly ensconced at the Amex Stadium and his appointment would have triggered a huge compensation clause. When Potter did leave for Chelsea, Brighton were paid £21 million for the manager and his staff. Roberto Martínez was approached. He knew the Premier League from his time at Wigan and Everton and had taken Belgium to third place in the World Cup in Russia. He was also a good communicator but made it clear he would prefer to remain in the international game.

Nuno was appointed on 30 June. He seemed a strange choice. His CV was solid rather than spectacular and he had a reputation for playing counter-attacking football, which seemed far removed from Tottenham's traditions. He seemed rather aloof, somewhat shy and a little introverted. He did not give the impression of a confident leader. His relationship with Mendes had been one of the keys to his success at Wolves, where he had promoted them to the Premier League and kept them there. Mendes was able to manoeuvre a succession of high-class Portuguese footballers to Molineux.

At Tottenham, Nuno proved pleasant and friendly, but he was not a good communicator. There were rarely deep discussions and few of the players took to him. He seldom consulted his coaching staff during the ninety minutes. During the October international break, the club arranged a private friendly with Millwall. Nuno instructed senior players such as Eric Dier, Harry Winks, Dele Alli, Lucas Moura and Tanguy Ndombele to play alongside the academy players. The effect on those five was utterly demotivating. Winks and Alli played in a 1–0 defeat at Vitesse Arnhem in the Europa League, a game in which both seemed demoralised.

Nine days later came the 3–0 defeat to Manchester United, which triggered Nuno's dismissal. The irony was that in the wake of a 5–0 home defeat to Liverpool, the United manager, Ole Gunnar Solskjær, was under far greater pressure. It was in this fixture that Nuno's tactical inflexibility was his undoing. In September, against

Chelsea, the score was goalless at half-time, but it was clear Thomas Tuchel's side was in the ascendancy. On the left, Marcos Alonso had been making regular forays forward. It seemed obvious we needed to mirror Tuchel's system of three centre-halves supported by two wing-backs. At Wolves, Nuno had enjoyed considerable success with three centre-halves, but throughout his brief reign in north London, he employed a flat back-four. It was suggested that the tactics had been laid down by Paratici in his role as managing director of football. If so, it gave his manager no room for manoeuvre and stripped him of his tactical authority. Tottenham did not change their formation and twelve minutes into the second half were two goals down.

Solskjær, who had seemed wedded to the idea of a back-four, changed to three centre-halves against Spurs and employed Aaron Wan-Bissaka and Luke Shaw as wing-backs. Tottenham were both slow to react and slow to move the ball. Once more, Nuno did not change his formation and the result was the same – a 3–0 home defeat. He was sacked two days later.

As a manager, you have to anticipate what your opponent will do. I had great contests with Watford, who would have Pat Rice at right-back facing David Moss, a fine player on our left wing. If Moss was on top form, skittling Rice in the first half, I always anticipated Graham Taylor would adjust his formation at half-time to cope with the threat. Anticipating this, I would alter tactics and change Moss's position. It invariably worked.

Nuno's dismissal cleared the way for Antonio Conte, whose break from football had lasted three months. It was enough. Tottenham were prepared to pay the salary he demanded. Conte took charge of twenty-eight Premier League games, of which seventeen were won. Tottenham, who were ninth when he took over, finished in the top four to reclaim Champions League football. Son Heung-min shared the Golden Boot with Liverpool's Sadio Mané.

Conte began by reorganising the defence into a back three of Cristian Romero, Eric Dier and Ben Davies. Four of his first six league games saw Tottenham keep a clean sheet. They won four of their final five games, including the north-London derby, to secure Champions League football. The other match was a 1–1 draw at Liverpool. As a climax to the season, the finish was anything but 'Spursy'.

Paratici continued to impose his authority at the club, easing out Steve Hitchen and the chief scout, Brian Carey. My role continued during this exciting upheaval. At the end of that season, I strongly recommended we should sign two young players: Sonny Perkins, at West Ham, and Cameron Humphreys, a left-sided midfielder at Ipswich. We got neither. I was very frustrated. Perkins went to Leeds while Humphreys signed a three-year contract at Portman Road.

For me, the saddest aspect was the departure of Dele Alli in January 2022. His box-to-box energies, unorthodox skills, and his ability to run off the ball to create space had been quelled by a succession of Tottenham managers. When at his best in a triangle with Harry Kane and Christian Eriksen, he was a constant threat to the opposition. Crucially, in 2020 Eriksen had left to join Conte at Inter Milan.

I could not believe that at twenty-five his race was run, but I am told Dele's initial love for football receded with his lack of opportunities. The London scene had also provided too many distractions. His demise in a Tottenham shirt left me bewildered. In 2018, he was valued at £100 million and playing in a World Cup semi-final. He left on a free transfer to Everton, who then loaned him out to Besiktas. In Istanbul, Dele found himself sometimes unable to command a place on the bench and returned to Merseyside with his reputation in shreds and concerns about his mental health.

His rise and fall encompasses the precarious nature of football. It holds a wonderful fascination and unpredictability. I fell in love with the beauty of the game that gave me some memorable moments, but I did my best to cope with the disappointments. Winning is fleeting and superficial, but the scars of losing last longer. As Brian Clough once said, the best you can hope to achieve in this game is to survive.

CHAPTER 38

'THE WIND BENEATH MY WINGS'

As I sat beside the hospice bed as my dear wife prepared for her next life, I recalled all the sacrifices she had made on our behalf. Within hours, on 25 July 2020, I lost my loyal, brave Maureen.

In my lifetime, football has been an all-encompassing focus. I have enjoyed some highs and several lows and all would have been impossible to negotiate without her. She was supportive at every twist and turn. My family all know God will look after her for her kindness, her generosity and loyalty. She was totally unselfish.

Successful football managers invariably have stable relationships. It is vital. Football consumes your life. Football is an addiction. When I was about nine, the owner of a chip shop on our housing estate said to me that he could not understand all the fuss about the game and why so many people would want to watch twenty-two men kicking a pig's bladder around a field. I was too young to explain the alternative point of view. We all knew Bill Shankly's ill-advised quip: 'Football is not a matter of life or death; it's far more important than that.' Certainly, the excitement, the movement, the athleticism, the skill, the conflict, the speed – it attacks your senses, you cannot shake it off and eventually it becomes a drug.

The moment Maureen married me at Luton Register Office in the summer of 1969, she became a football wife. Then, I was playing for Exeter in the Fourth Division. She had no idea I would become a coach and then a manager. Once I was done with management, football would not leave me. I would become a director of football, a board member, a football consultant and then a scout. It would become an unbreakable attachment.

As the years went by, I cannot recall going to more than two parents' evenings to discuss my children's progress. I only went to one Christmas play at their junior schools. Whenever Jon or Joanne had a medical problem, it was Maureen who took them to the doctor's surgery. When I was managing Nuneaton, it was Maureen who took Jon to hospital when he had been scarred by some boiling water. Perhaps it was that incident that had a small influence in my son becoming a burns surgeon.

Until my retirement, I rarely went shopping. Most managers I know could change neither a fuse nor a lightbulb and seemed quite proud of the fact. It would be up to the wife to book a builder or a repairman. Maureen would do all the cooking, the washing, the ironing and be up at the crack of dawn to take Jon to catch the bus to Bedford School, sixteen miles away. When the children were young and I was involved in Saturday football, Maureen would take them to weekend activities, swimming, parties, or the cinema.

In the same summer of 1986 that I joined Tottenham, I was asked to join the ITV team in Mexico to commentate on the World Cup. I was excited by this. I would be looking at leading players and gaining valuable experience. I told the Tottenham chairman, Irving Scholar, that when I returned, I would be taking my wife and children on a two-week family holiday. He replied that would be impossible as I would not be back when the players reported for pre-season training, the date for which had already been set. 'First impressions count. It's important you are there,' he barked.

'When I arrive, they will get their first impressions,' I replied. 'Meanwhile, the coaches will have the responsibility of proving they are capable.' Irving climbed down. Having just been appointed, I was in a stronger position than I realised. I would not let him brow-beat me. I would soon find out plenty about our relationship.

Something similar occurred when I became manager of Sheffield Wednesday in 1995. The club had been allocated a place in that summer's Intertoto Cup and were due to play at Karlsruhe on 15 July. The players were not happy playing in a qualifying group, at late notice and without any pre-season fitness preparation.

The game in Karlsruhe coincided with Jonathon's graduation cer-emony at Oxford University. The Sheffield Wednesday chairman, Dave Richards, was most unhappy when I told him I would not be going to Germany and would be accompanying Maureen to the Sheldonian Theatre for the ceremony. I was proud to be there. The game with Karlsruhe was drawn 1–1.

Time with family is precious and yet it is very hard to request a break from your club once you are appointed to a senior coaching or management role. In a usual week, Saturday is match day. Sunday is reflective, often a day spent on the phone or attending youth games at the training ground. It is no use asking why a manager does not delegate. Once you are in that chair, you have to feel fully responsible, because you know if anything goes wrong, it is down to you. To be there and to be aware of everything is so important.

At the start of David Moyes's first full season as Everton manag-er, Tottenham travelled to Goodison Park. After the match, David asked what advice I would give him. I replied: 'Take Wednesdays off'. Many 'travelling managers', whose family home was not near their club, attempted to break the week up. However, instead of giving that day to their family, to help a possibly beleaguered spouse, they would spend it on the golf course or maybe at the races. However David arranged his week at Everton, it worked. He would run the club for eleven years.

One of the reasons why Brian Clough stayed so long at Derby

and Nottingham Forest was that he always went home to his wife, Barbara. In his less successful forays into management, at Brighton and Leeds, he generally stayed in hotels – the Courtlands in Hove and the Dragonara in Leeds. Clough used his pay-off from Leeds to buy a beautiful house in the Derbyshire village of Quarndon that became his base. One of his great pals at Forest was a director called Mike Keeling, who would drive Brian home after long evenings watching games or attending functions.

Most managers who have signed a three-year contract would find a clause requiring them to relocate to the area within six to twelve months. Often, rather than disrupt the children's education, the manager will find a bolthole that will allow him to mix in with the local community and identify with the team's supporters.

After a few months of commuting to manage Leicester City, I received a letter from the acting chairman Martin George, reminding me of the relocation clause in my contract. Within four weeks I had found myself a small, terraced house in a cul-de-sac called Francis Street where there were several boutique clothing shops. It served a purpose during my two-and-a-half seasons at Leicester; a bedroom to put my head down in and a kitchen of limited size. The menu was mainly tea and toast. I was always back at Luton for Sundays and would come home in midweek if I was watching a night game in the south of England and leave early the following morning.

If a manager shows no respect for his employer and does not make himself available for meetings or functions such as prize-givings or supporters' club nights, his days would be numbered, unless he were an instant success and maintained that success. Only then can you call the tune and, even then, there is always a bad result or a fallow period lurking. The manager's wife will be in the family home, hoping her husband is eating and sleeping well and taking the strain that comes with having to win football matches. The divorce rate among football managers is high.

Although Maureen was massively supportive, she did not read match reports or listen to football on the radio. She would occasionally watch it on television. She had her own friends and interests and spent much time nursing her parents. When she did come to games, she was able to assess the mood and the politics of the boardroom. It is a tricky area. You hear the gossip, see the interaction between people and where the power lies. When games are lost and there is a sour mood in the room, she could be affected by a bitter comment.

When Maureen came to the football, I always told her to listen carefully and be as diplomatic as possible. Often, people try to find out something about the manager by asking his wife some personal questions. They usually sit the wives on a table with guests in the boardroom and only very occasionally are they allowed on the directors' table for the pre-match lunch.

Some boardrooms are small, only coping with about thirty people. At White Hart Lane, there would be ten tables of eight. There would always be a flurry of discussion when the team sheets were handed round the tables before kick-off:

'I am surprised he has picked him.'

'He's playing him again. I can't understand the reasoning behind it.'

'This looks a very strange formation.'

'Why doesn't he play the youngsters?'

When I was Tottenham's director of football, Maureen and I had to be careful when I was asked, either at half-time or after the game, the loaded question: 'What would you have done?' This was particularly true when the game had gone badly. Wives can detect the supportive directors, the suspicious directors and those just enjoying the ride. I knew my views would be shared. One vice-president would always sidle up to me and ask what I thought of the team's performance. My stock answer: 'I will have to analyse it over the weekend.'

During my time at Luton, we won a lot of games at Kenilworth Road and the mood in the boardroom was often good. We would usually be hospitable and gracious to our opponents, but once they had left, the chairman, Dennis Mortimer, fuelled by drink, would march around the boardroom playing an imaginary trombone. It became an expected cabaret routine, but we all found it amusing. One of the many pieces of advice Harry Haslam gave me was:

> Make sure that when you go to the boardroom after a game, you drink nothing stronger than tea and stand in the corner of the room so you can see everyone. Later, when someone suggests you have made a particular comment, you can recall soberly what you said and exactly what was said to you.

Up to the late 1980s, boardrooms were almost a no-go area for women. We travelled to Middlesbrough's Riverside Stadium early in Daniel Levy's reign as Tottenham chairman. We had been politely informed the women would have to use an adjoining room. They would not be allowed into the boardroom for the pre-match lunch. Steve Gibson, the Middlesbrough chairman, was a warm host, but the club had a long-standing tradition and he felt he should stick to it.

After a League Cup semi-final between Arsenal and Tottenham in 1987, I offered the Arsenal manager, George Graham, a lift back to his home in Cockfosters. I had known George since the England–Scotland Schoolboys international more than a quarter of a century before. Because of antagonism from the Spurs supporters, the police had advised that the Arsenal bus should leave as soon as possible. George decided to stay on for a drink. His wife, Marie, was at home, oblivious to the excitement of a north-London derby only ten miles down the road. George said Marie did not like football. She did not understand the passion, the kick, that millions derive from the game. Maureen had a partial interest in everything I did, though she never did come to grips with the offside rule. By the time George Graham became manager of Tottenham in 1998, he and Marie had long been divorced, but he seemed to have gained little idea of how to run a house. While he was at White Hart Lane, all his household bills were dealt with by his secretary.

There are now many women involved in football's administration. Many have degrees in sports science and finance. Some have been co-opted into the boardroom. The pioneers in the 1980s were Christine Matthews at Chelsea and Brentford and Sheila Marsden at Queens Park Rangers who were both outstanding club secretaries. At Birmingham and West Ham, Karren Brady has proved a solid partner for David Sullivan and David Gold. She was twenty-three when she became managing director of Birmingham City and when Sullivan told her she would 'have to be twice as good as a man to do that job', Karren replied that that wouldn't be difficult. She tells the story about a player who came to see her and suggested as he sat opposite that he could see her cleavage. She told him not to worry because the following season he would not be there to see it.

Marina Granovskaia went from being Roman Abramovich's personal assistant to Chelsea's chief executive. She became responsible for negotiating Chelsea's sponsorship and transfer deals and had a difficult relationship with Frank Lampard when he became manager. Tottenham's director of football operations, Rebecca Caplehorn, studied sports science, physical education and mathematics at Loughborough University. She spent five years at Queens Park Rangers before coming to White Hart Lane in 2015. Now, when a manager's wife goes to a game or a club function, it can be reassuring for them to know they will not be alone in an all-male gathering.

Footballers' wives, managers' wives are so important but so rarely praised. They need to be a rock through thick and thin. I considered Maureen to be the wind beneath my wings.

CHAPTER 39

'YES, BUT HE CANNOT SHOOT'

While Tottenham's pre-season in the summer of 2022 took them to South Korea, Scotland and Israel, where they lost to Roma, now managed by José Mourinho, I began at Ruislip, watching Watford play out a goalless draw with Southampton.

The game was supposed to have been staged at Vicarage Road but, after an Elton John concert, the pitch had been declared unfit. Wealdstone's ground had been pressed into service instead. Both clubs played their best teams. I wrote of Southampton: 'No pattern. They are weak at the back post when defending and have no runner from midfield. They lack a presence up front.' Two weeks later, Tottenham began their Premier League season by dismissing Southampton, who would be relegated at the end of the season, 4–1.

I listened from an NHS bed, having been taken to hospital suffering with kidney stones. My health was becoming a concern. I had long been under surveillance for prostate cancer. My surgeon indicated surgery was imminent without telling me directly, and he floated the idea of radiotherapy.

'How long have I got if I don't have the proposed treatment?' I asked.

'Three years, maybe,' he replied.

As a consequence, I decided immediately to undergo the treatment. I was told the radiotherapy would not be overly intrusive and that I would still be able to work. Others were not so fortunate.

Of Antonio Conte's extensive backroom staff, none was more

respected than the fitness coach, Gian Piero Ventrone. He had coached Conte when they were both at Juventus and he was famous for his brutally intense sessions and his saying: 'Winning belongs to the strong.' His players called him 'the Marine'. In October 2022, Ventrone died of leukaemia, aged sixty-one. Tottenham's entire backroom staff attended his funeral in Naples. His influence was in evidence at the start of the season, when Spurs's fitness levels were often the difference.

Conte also looked to Italy to recruit players, bringing in the Swedish winger Dejan Kulusevski on loan from Juventus in January 2022. The £30 million paid to Brighton for the Mali midfielder Yves Bissouma raised eyebrows. Tottenham took advantage of Everton's financial struggles by paying £50 million for their Brazilian forward Richarlison. We were surprised to get him. Certainly, Richarlison had not been on our list of targets, although we had monitored his progress during his time at Watford, where he had seemed overly erratic. He would provide support for Harry Kane, who seemed far more relaxed than he had been after his flirtation with Manchester City. However, although the Brazilian had excelled at Goodison Park, he would not have the same opportunities to shine at Spurs, and as Tottenham's season began to sour, so did Richarlison's.

Conte proved himself ruthless in dispensing with people. Tanguy Ndombele, who had never quite justified his club-record transfer fee of £55.4 million, was loaned back to Lyons. Giovani Lo Celso was loaned out to Villarreal. Harry Winks, who had displayed such promise in midfield alongside Dele Alli, was a reluctant leaver when joining Sampdoria. He would later be part of the Leicester side that won promotion to the Premier League in 2024.

José Mourinho once asked what I thought of Winks. I replied: 'I think he should play higher up the field. He plays too deep. He just borrows the ball.' Mourinho replied: 'Yes, but he cannot shoot.' I thought this was very strange. Surely Winks could shoot? However, when I looked at his record, his shooting and goal stats were poor. Apart from one fluky goal against Fulham, I could not remember him scoring. He was good at looking after the ball and playing it out wide, but he did not ping it with the in-step as Christian Eriksen could.

Gareth Bale also left, going back to Madrid before choosing to end his career on the Sunset Strip of Los Angeles. His return to Tottenham had shown displays of intermittent brilliance, often from the bench, but he was seldom the game's hardest worker and his pace was starting to falter.

As a tactician, Conte was conservative and a pragmatist, content to surrender possession, drop deep and strike the opposition on the counter-attack. His tactics were never better illustrated than when they faced Leicester in September. Leicester were bottom of the table with one point from six games. Their manager, Brendan Rodgers, was under growing pressure.

Led by James Maddison, Leicester dominated. Away from home, they were ahead on possession and goal attempts, although the sides were level at 2–2 at the interval. Two minutes after the break, Tottenham's Uruguayan midfielder Rodrigo Bentancur seized on one of the defensive errors that had bedevilled Leicester's start to the season. Son Heung-min, whose own start to the season had been so subdued he had begun on the bench, scored a hat-trick in the space of seventeen minutes. Spurs had won, 6–2, but had fewer attempts on goal.

The reckoning came in the north-London derby at the Emirates Stadium. Arsenal's wide players, Bukayo Saka and Gabriel Martinelli, claimed an early ascendancy over the Spurs full-backs they rarely looked likely to lose. Although the front three of Kane, Son and Richarlison worked hard, the result was still a tepid defeat that gave much food for thought. Once more, Tottenham had sat off and conceded the ball; this time it was a tactic that did not work.

Although Spurs were expected to go through a Champions

League group that included Marseilles, Sporting Lisbon and Ein-tracht Frankfurt, by the time they faced Sporting on 26 October, a win was required. I desperately wanted to see this match, not least to watch Marcus Edwards, whom I had watched develop in Totten-ham's academy. I had met his agent, who had rented an office from my accountant on the Finchley Road. His agent complained of a lack of communication with the club when trying to renegotiate his contract. I thought Edwards had a fine left foot and could be a mesmeric dribbler, but Tottenham had doubts about his character.

Mauricio Pochettino had compared Edwards to Lionel Messi after an appearance in a League Cup tie against Gillingham in 2016. It was a statement Mauricio quickly regretted. Edwards was sev-enteen – at that age Messi had been playing for Barcelona along-side Ronaldinho. Pochettino would later state that Edwards had to become 'more committed'. He was loaned out to Norwich. Edwards was of Greek–Cypriot descent and his mother was a big influence on him. The family bravely encouraged him to go to Portugal, first with Vitória Guimarães then with Sporting Lisbon. In September, he had shone as Sporting overcame Tottenham in the José Alvalade Stadium.

Perhaps inevitably, Marcus Edwards scored for Sporting Lisbon in the return game in London. Eric Dier gave Spurs hope and then what seemed to be Kane's winner was ruled out by a very belated intervention from VAR. In the furore that followed, Conte was sent off. To qualify for the knockout phase, Spurs needed at least a draw in Marseilles – and the result of the Sporting Lisbon–Frankfurt game to go their way. They got both, despite another lifeless open-ing forty-five minutes that pushed even the most fervent Tottenham fan to the edge of despair.

I had made so many friends in the media during my seven World Cups in the commentary box that it was somewhat strange to be watching a winter World Cup from my armchair. When I went to

Mexico in 1986, it was unheard of that women would be employed as commentators and pundits. It would be unthinkable a woman footballer would become BBC Sports Personality of the Year, as Beth Mead did in December 2022 and Mary Earps a year later.

The World Cup also showed how African teams, especially Morocco, had closed the gap on Europe through great athleticism, speedy counter-attacking and deep defending. England's new generation was unlucky to lose to France in the quarter-finals. When they returned home and speculation swirled around Gareth Southgate's future as manager, I sent him a text: 'Remember – family first.' He replied: 'Absolutely.' That he decided to take England to the European Championship in Germany was an indication that his family was behind him.

Usually, if there are doubts, the opinion of a manager's wife or children can be crucial. Harry Haslam loved being manager of Luton and Sheffield United, but his family was less keen on his role. When he left Bramall Lane in 1981, he did not seek another job.

The day before the 2024 European Championship final in Berlin, I texted Gareth to wish him luck and told him I had just been watching the Channel 4 film of the 1966 World Cup final. He texted back to thank me and mentioned he had also watched the film a few months back, adding: 'I can't believe how much space there was in that game.'

Tottenham had two players – Hugo Lloris with France and Cristian Romero with Argentina – in Doha's emotional and extraordinary World Cup final, which culminated with Messi lifting the trophy that had always eluded him. Nobody really knew how a mid-season World Cup would affect the Premier League on its restart. In terms of minutes played in Qatar, Tottenham's players ranked fourth behind the two Manchester clubs and Chelsea. Harry Kane had missed a crucial penalty against France in the quarter-final. How would he carry that weight back into the Premier League?

Tottenham's results continued to be erratic, emphasised by a reverse at Manchester City after we had been two goals to the good at half-time. It followed defeat at home to a resurgent Arsenal. Supporters were increasingly restless. Criticism was mounting in the media. The pressure was once more mounting on Daniel Levy's shoulders. A 1–0 defeat to AC Milan at the San Siro should not have been fatal, but Tottenham slid out of the Champions League with a limp, goalless draw. What added to the frustration was that the week before Spurs had been knocked out of the FA Cup at Sheffield United. Suddenly, there was a storm of discontent.

The fact that Conte had a year's option on his contract and the season had reached March without talks with the Tottenham hierarchy showed which way the wind was blowing. Kane had passed the twenty-goal mark for the fifth consecutive season but Richarlison, with limited opportunities, had yet to score in the Premier League and was now clashing openly with his manager.

Every time I went to the training ground there seemed to be more suits, worn by more people with more titles. I came across Lorenzo Giani, the club's new Italian scout. Grétar Steinsson, who had played for Bolton and had just been released by Everton as head of player recruitment, became our performance director. Simon Davies, who had been Vincent Kompany's assistant at Anderlecht, was recruited to become head of coaching methodology. Leonardo Gabbanini was brought in from Watford as chief scout and was credited with signing Guglielmo Vicario, the goalkeeper who was to replace Hugo Lloris. Andrew Scoulding, a quiet man who had worked for Steven Gerrard at Glasgow Rangers and Gary Neville at Valencia, also joined as assistant director of performance. Gianni Vio had been appointed as Tottenham's first set piece coach. I suggested that everyone wore lanyards with name tags because you were not always sure who you were shaking hands with. There were so many scouts, most of them data scouts who never left the office, that if you wanted to bring a boy in for a trial, you had to go through three different people.

In the midst of all these appointments, Paratici was banned from football in Italy for thirty months for his part in the financial scandal that had seen Juventus docked fifteen points in Serie A. It was hard to see how he might survive, but the club allowed him leave to appeal – and when that was lost, resignation was the only option. By then, Antonio Conte had already signed his own death warrant.

By the time of Tottenham's elimination from the Champions League by AC Milan, Conte was clearly unwell. His usual animation on the touchline had disappeared. He seemed isolated. There were fewer talks with his staff. At times he could be seen eating alone in the restaurant at the training ground. He never now showed his face at the club's academy, where his absences were resented.

I had felt for a long time that successive chief scouts had been driven by foreign agents. Tottenham seemed to be abandoning their quest for the best British talent such as Bristol City's brilliant young midfielder Alex Scott, who was signed by Bournemouth. At Sheffield United, Iliman Ndiaye, born in France, had proved himself the kind of footballer the Premier League would welcome. At Tottenham, only Oliver Skipp of the academy products seemed ready to make a major contribution, filling in manfully for the injured Rodrigo Bentancur.

There had been little investment in securing talent for the academy. This was partly because agents were demanding fees that Tottenham were not prepared to pay. A seventeen-year-old from a Category-A club would cost around a million pounds and expect a wage of £10,000 a week. Paying this kind of money would destabilise the structure of a youth system that at Spurs was performing well at under-18 level and below. Tottenham's under-17s won the Premier League Cup with a 5–1 win at Nottingham Forest. Tottenham, however, needed to be more proactive in their recruitment.

At first-team level, Spurs were by the spring of 2023 weighed down by injuries and lacking a creative midfield. Only Kane could be relied on to score. Son, after displaying so much brilliance in a Tottenham shirt, was misfiring, cast out to play on the wide left in a team playing with wing-backs who were not good enough for the top division. On 20 March, everything came to a head at Southampton, where a 3–1 lead was thrown away against the Premier League's bottom club.

Asked about the performance, Conte launched into a rant:

> We are not a team; we are eleven players who go onto the pitch and I see a lot of selfish players. I see players who don't want to help each other and don't put their heart [in] … They don't want to play under pressure, they don't want to play under stress. It's easy this way. Tottenham's story is this.

Conte had blamed everyone except himself. Five of the regular players had been his signings. There was no alternative to the dismissal of another manager.

CHAPTER 40

'I KNOW WHO YOU ARE, MATE'

As I passed him in the corridor, I introduced myself and he responded in his Australian drawl: 'I know who you are, mate.' We did not speak for more than five minutes, but from the start, I sensed Ange Postecoglou would be easier to talk to than either of his predecessors as Tottenham manager.

His appointment as Antonio Conte's permanent replacement highlighted two organisations that had become increasingly important at the club. Before coming to Celtic, where he won two Scottish League titles, Postecoglou had managed Yokohama Marinos in Japan, one of a number of clubs across the world owned and run by the City Football Group, who were ultimately controlled by the government of Abu Dhabi. Manchester City was its centrepiece. Postecoglou was also a client of the Base Sports Agency, who would supply a significant number of executives and players to Tottenham.

Postecoglou's agent, Frank Trimboli, an Australian based in London, also represented Son Heung-min and already had a good working relationship with Daniel Levy. Before Postecoglou's appointment, the media suggested Daniel might turn to Mauricio Pochettino, but there was never to be a conversation between the two men and he joined Chelsea. One of Postecoglou's attractions was he was prepared to travel light and work with the coaches already at Tottenham like Ryan Mason. Pochettino would have brought all of 'Team Poch' back to Spurs.

Because Postecoglou was on a one-year rolling contract at Parkhead, the amount of compensation Celtic could claim was limited. Because of the compensation the club had paid to settle the contracts of José Mourinho, Nuno Espirito Santo and Conte, the funds available to Tottenham were limited. Celtic were paid around £5 million for their manager, almost half the sum they received when Brendan Rodgers, who was in the middle of a four-year contract, joined Leicester in 2019.

The club's HR department was busy in the summer of 2023. Although Fabio Paratici had been forced to resign as director of football after his role in the financial scandals at Juventus, he had not entirely gone away. He was a man whose phone was never far from his ear and he was still using it to give Daniel Levy the benefit of his advice.

Spurs, however, required a permanent replacement, although when he arrived at the club, Scott Munn was so untidily dressed I thought he was a worker who had come to install a piece of equipment, rather than be the second most important man at Tottenham Hotspur. He did not look like a chief executive. Scott had been working for City Football Group in China and was now head of Tottenham's football operations. Munn, a confident Australian, would be the man who would take some of the pressure off the chairman, who at every home match faced protests from those agitating for ENIC to get out of the club. He would be in charge of all the club's football departments, from the first team to the academy and the women's team.

Scott quickly made his mark. There were two outstanding youngsters within our schoolboy group who were being tracked by other clubs. In previous seasons, they may well have been offered financial inducements, fuelled by avaricious agents, to go elsewhere. I advised him to keep them both on. Scott was also determined we would not lose these two and in signing contracts with Tottenham, it showed he wanted Spurs to shed our frugal image. Far too many youngsters had been spirited away. Dean Rastrick, who had headed up the academy since 2017, was released. He was succeeded by Simon Davies, who had been a lesser-known member of Manchester United's 'Class of '92' but who had not followed David Beckham and Paul Scholes to the stars.

There were other exits. Leonardo Gabbanini, who expected a promotion from chief scout, was instead dismissed. The performance director, Grétar Steinsson, left and joined Leeds. He would be replaced by Johan Lange, who at Aston Villa had gained a reputation for data-driven analysis of players. By March 2024, five senior scouts had been released, the most senior of whom was Ian Broomfield, who had been chief scout under Harry Redknapp. My feeling has always been that there is no need to fix something that wasn't broken. It seemed a revolution for revolution's sake.

The saddest departure was that of Hugo Lloris, one of Tottenham's great goalkeepers and, like Harry Kane, a World Cup captain. He had been a massive influence in the dressing room and a wonderful ambassador for the club. His departure for Los Angeles in December 2023 was marked by a low-key presentation on the pitch, when in truth he almost deserved a statue.

You could hear the change of tone on the training pitches. The dictatorial, sergeant-major approach of Mourinho and Conte was gone. Rather than barking orders, Ange was prepared to oversee training in a quiet, observant way. He allowed his coaches to coach. You could see it on the touchline. While Antonio Conte stalked the technical area, Postecoglou simply stood, impassive. In this, he reminded me of Carlo Ancelotti, or Marcello Lippi, who when managing Italy stood, seemingly emotionless, as his players took penalties to win the World Cup in Berlin. The modern way, epitomised by Jürgen Klopp and Mikel Arteta, is to stand aggressively close to the touchline becoming involved with the action. Sir Alex Ferguson would only approach the touchline at Old Trafford if there was a crisis that needed addressing. I would start many games watching high up in the directors' box.

The great question of how Spurs would cope now that Harry Kane had left to join Bayern Munich was initially answered in style. Postecoglou's strategy was one of risk and reward. He wanted his team to play a high line, pressing the opposition defence and using the two full-backs, Pedro Porro and Destiny Udogie, to play advanced and infield. This put great responsibility on the two centre-halves, who had to cover the width of the pitch, using the halfway line almost as a marker. This often left dangerous space for opposition forwards to run into. The two centre-halves Cristian Romero, who had won the World Cup with Argentina, and the young Micky van de Ven, signed from Wolfsburg, proved a fine combination. Romero was a strong, rugged tackler, prone to occasional displays of recklessness. Van de Van possessed exceptional pace and a fine left foot.

With James Maddison, bought for £40 million years after I had pleaded with the club to take him from Coventry, there was plenty of creativity in midfield. There was a proliferation of right-sided players to support Son, who showed no signs of slackening off in the absence of Kane. I would joke with Son that, if he ever left, Spurs would lose 10 per cent of their support. His Korean fan club was wildly vociferous.

Brennan Johnson joined from Nottingham Forest for a fee of £47.5 million. Brennan's great attribute was timing his run into the six-yard box to convert low crosses. However, his game required more guile. It was a bold move to bring Timo Werner on loan. He had failed at Chelsea and had not scored many goals when he returned to the Bundesliga with Leipzig. Nevertheless, Werner possessed great speed.

Briefly Tottenham led the Premier League. Their style of play and

Postecoglou's refusal to criticise referees in post-match press conferences won him plaudits from neutrals. Playing with such a high line going forward carried its own risks in transition. Spurs were vulnerable to counter-attacks. Three successive home games were lost to Chelsea, Aston Villa and West Ham when we had failed to press home a significant early advantage. The fact that Tottenham kept a high line after being reduced to nine men against Chelsea with the dismissals of Romero and Udogie seemed suicidal management. A low block was required with the nine remaining men defending deep, but Postecoglou insisted his tactics were non-negotiable.

In December while taking a break with my daughter Joanne, I was in the Puskás Bar in Budapest, watching Tottenham play Manchester City and receiving a reminder of the spirit the new regime had created. Although Spurs were second best, I jumped up when Giovani Lo Celso equalised. In the closing minutes, City then scored again to make it 3–2. That seemed to be that. I paid the bill and we returned to our hotel. To my delight, an hour later, I opened my laptop and saw that Dejan Kulusevski had equalised in the closing seconds and the final score was 3–3.

Without European football and because of early exits from the League and FA Cups, the team's only focus came to be the Premier League, and but for an abnormal injury list and disastrous spring that saw heavy defeats at Newcastle, Chelsea and Liverpool, they might well have finished ahead of Aston Villa to claim the final Champions League spot. The gap between the sides was two points.

It seemed strange that across the Premier League there should be such a constant stream of injured players at a time when seemingly every club employed a larger number of medical, fitness and rehabilitation staff than ever before. Ange took the setbacks with equanimity. Players had come on during the season such as Pape Sarr, the Senegal midfielder signed from Metz, Udogie, Van de Ven and Maddison. There had, as ever, been a lot of reliance on Son, who passed the milestone of 300 appearances for Spurs. Collectively, there had been too much inconsistency.

The women's team reached the FA Cup final, losing 4–0 to Manchester United. Wembley was sold out for the occasion, reflecting the dramatic upswing in the women's game that had seen England win the Euros and reach a World Cup final.

The failure to qualify for the Champions League cost the club around £15 million. Some of that would be offset by an exhausting journey to Australia to face Newcastle in an exhibition game just a few days after the end of the league season. The match would be staged in Melbourne, where Postecoglou had grown up and where his popularity was still clear. South Korea was a natural venue for a pre-season tour where Son would captain Spurs in Seoul. There would also be games in Japan.

I found the season more of a struggle. Driving to matches, I realised I was becoming more irritated more easily. Traffic, speed restrictions, motorway hold-ups and potholes all played their part, as did new technology. Match tickets had to be transferred to phones, scouting reports inputted on computers. There was less interaction with the staff at the grounds we visited, the viewing positions tended to be poorer, the hospitality less in evidence. Seats for corporate clients were now the main driver of matchday operations. Clubs in the lower leagues displayed a more homely and welcoming atmosphere.

Simon Jordan, the one-time chairman of Crystal Palace and now a successful media pundit, argued that you could not expect the bigger clubs to support the smaller ones, using the analogy that supermarkets did not feel obliged to support corner shops. With English football about to be overseen by an independent regulator, I would argue that protection for the underdog should be paramount in an era when the playing field has become ever less level.

Nothing, however, annoyed me more than VAR, the technical innovation that was supposed to help referees with their on-field decision-making. Former referees now sat in a television booth analysing every remotely debatable decision. Instead of correcting 'clear and obvious errors', which was supposed to have been its brief, VAR now actively looked for mistakes, however small. Decisions to confirm or deny a goal took an age, leaving the paying public in the grounds who had no access to screens unaware of why the match had been stopped. The instantaneous delight that comes with scoring a goal or seeing one scored was removed from the game and the referees' authority was further undermined.

Vital matches were won or lost by decisions that were not 'clear and obvious', reaching a climax in the FA Cup semi-final when Coventry, having come from three goals down to level against Manchester United, were denied what would have been one of the most remarkable victories in the history of the competition by an offside ruling that appeared impossible to call.

However, I did enjoy my visits to the training ground to sit and talk football and exchange stories. It was good therapy and the company and camaraderie of the coaches was stimulating. The Tottenham under-21 side won its league with five of the playing squad representing England at under-19 level during the season. Tottenham were helped by the fact that other Premier League clubs were selling their academy players to cover themselves against the Premier League's financial sustainability rules. As Everton and Nottingham Forest discovered, breaching them would lead to points deductions. Manchester City sold several of their academy graduates including Cole Palmer, for whom Chelsea paid £40 million. Arsenal and Brighton loaned out several players.

When supporters asked if our under-21s could become the heart of a future Tottenham team in the Premier League, I replied that the standard at the top is now so very high that it must be unlikely, but I hope one or two will defy the statistics and my pessimism.

In the European leagues, Paris St Germain and Real Madrid

continued their ascendancy while in Holland and Germany, PSV Eindhoven and Bayer Leverkusen disturbed the monopoly of Ajax and Bayern Munich. Here, Manchester City gained a fourth consecutive Premier League. It had been a fascinating season and despite the frustrations I had maintained my love for the game.

On their return to top-flight football for the first time since 1992, I watched Luton five times. They budgeted well and competed hard but narrowly lost several games to the big boys and were relegated. Luton did, however, win countless friends with their attitude and philosophy. The money the club made from their return to the big time will help finance a new stadium.

When I first came to Luton as a player in 1964, I was shown some land where they planned a new stadium. Better late than never!

During the season, I went to Stevenage, who were playing Peterborough, where my lifelong friend from England Schoolboys days, Barry Fry, was director of football. Sir Alex Ferguson was there to watch his son, Darren, who was on his fourth spell as Peterborough's manager. We discussed the League Managers' Association. Under Richard Bevan, the LMA's committee had become increasingly sidelined. Sir Alex was now in his eighties, I was seventy-eight and other members such as Frank Clark and Dave Bassett were well past retirement age. We needed to make way for a new generation. I had served on the committee since 1982, a fact I was proud of.

At an LMA awards evening in London I received a present for my forty-two years as a committee member. As the pictures of colleagues who had passed away rolled across the big screen at the Grosvenor House, I reflected how fortunate I was to still be on my journey.

CHAPTER 41

'NO CAREER FOR
A JEWISH BOY'

Football, my parents gently told me, 'was no career for a Jewish boy'. They knew how hard their journey had been.

I did not realise the significance of their thoughts. I had no specific ambitions when I went to junior school, but football seduced me. I was captured. They, however, were wary. Their experiences made one thing clear: 'You will not have to be as good as the next person, you will have to be better.'

I understood. I assimilated and merged into the mix, rarely, if ever, discussing politics, money or faith. A journalist once described me as 'the Invisible Jew'. I coped and married Maureen, who was a Protestant. Ours was, until her passing in July 2020, a wonderful marriage. She was a beautiful, selfless woman who insisted her organs be used for medical research after her death. She was generous, caring and had no prejudice.

I played for five clubs and managed five more. I listened to mentors, spotted youngsters, developed players, bought and sold hundreds more, wrote numerous columns for national newspapers and was proud that from my first game at Nuneaton to my last at Tottenham, I penned my own programme notes. I sat in commentary boxes, summarised seven World Cups, chaired commissions and met politicians, pop stars and millionaires. I was awarded an honorary MA for my contribution to football and the media. It made me proud, as did my induction into the LMA Hall of Fame.

I challenged the chancers, heard the abuse, tolerated the agents, was criticised and praised. I observed and commented on the changes that swept over the beautiful game. I smiled in victory and coped with defeat, almost always needing 'one more goal'. I accepted many outside commitments from radio, television, newspapers, the League Managers' Association and the FA. A friend suggested I should have been more ruthlessly focused, but I was consumed by whichever club I worked for. Professionally, I always put their interests first, particularly at Leicester and Luton, where I had to sell players to keep the accountants happy and by doing so made my job more precarious. Football, in all its forms, was my life.

Another great satisfaction was seeing so many of the players I worked with, men like Brian Horton, Raddy Antić, Mike Newell, Chris Houghton, John Sheridan, Glenn Hoddle and Mick Harford, become successful managers and coaches in their turn.

I'm still in love with the beautiful game, but it is a game that has sadly lost some of its charm. I cannot look back and regret. Once, when walking up the stairs at White Hart Lane to the boardroom in my first stint as Tottenham manager, I passed the boxing promoter, Mickey Duff. He had been born Monek Prager in southern Poland. His father was a rabbi who had fled with his family to London to escape the Nazis. Spurs had lost and Mickey turned to me and said: 'Good luck, I have just been listening to the "would haves", "could haves" and "should haves".

Everyone, when it comes to football, is an expert. I have been lucky and grateful to have survived the trials and tribulations. I have cherished the journey in management that began at Nuneaton and led to Luton, Tottenham, Leicester, Luton once more, Sheffield Wednesday and then back to Spurs as a director of football, caretaker manager, scout and consultant.

Mum and Dad would have smiled.

ACKNOWLEDGEMENTS

Without the advice and assistance of so many people, I would never have penned 'my story'. Thanks go to my sisters, Susan and Marion, and my children, Jonathon and Joanne, who have provided constant encouragement.

Bob Harris, a much-travelled journalist, for years insisted I should record my experiences in football. However, it was not until Brian Horton, my captain at Luton, introduced me to Tim Rich four years ago that the work began in earnest. Tim's thoughtfulness, patience and excellent writing style shine through in the pages of this book. I would like to thank Ryan Norman, Olivia Beattie, Suzanne Sangster and all at Biteback for their help in producing the finished work.

I would like to thank all the football club chairmen who gave me an opportunity to manage. The first was Alf Scattergood, who when appointing me at Nuneaton in 1971 said he wanted me to become the 'new Frank O'Farrell', whose managerial journey had taken him from Weymouth to Manchester United. Dennis Mortimer at Luton gave me my first taste of league management. I particularly enjoyed my time with Alan Sugar at Tottenham and with Nigel Doughty at Nottingham Forest.

I would not have been offered these positions without my mentors: men like Peter Taylor, Joe Mallett, Gordon Lee and Alan Wade at the FA instigated my interest in coaching, while Harry Haslam gave me my first job coaching top-flight footballers. I would like to thank the League Managers' Association, on whose committees I served. I found the company, camaraderie and advice of their members invaluable.

Managers need players, and some wonderful footballers and characters have graced my teams. Sports editors at national and regional newspapers provided me with a platform to express my views on the game I have always loved. Television and radio producers gave me the chance to work on World Cups and major domestic and European fixtures.

I would also like to thank the many people, especially at the University College Hospital, London, who cared for my wife, Maureen. Money raised from the sales of this book will go towards research into motor neurone disease. I have not emerged unscathed in recent years and thanks must go to my cancer surgeon, Dr Alonzi.

Finally, I would like to express my admiration of the loyal fans of all teams, large or small, without whom there would be no game.

David Pleat
July 2024

INDEX

TO TEDDY

GOOD LUCK IN
YOUR FOOTBALL
CAREER

MEL JOHNSON